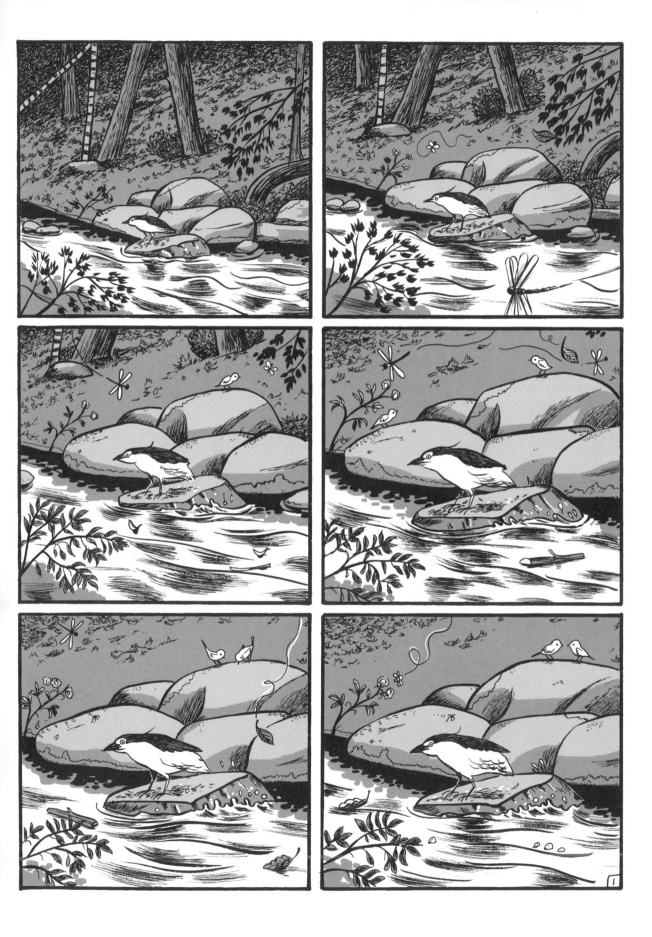

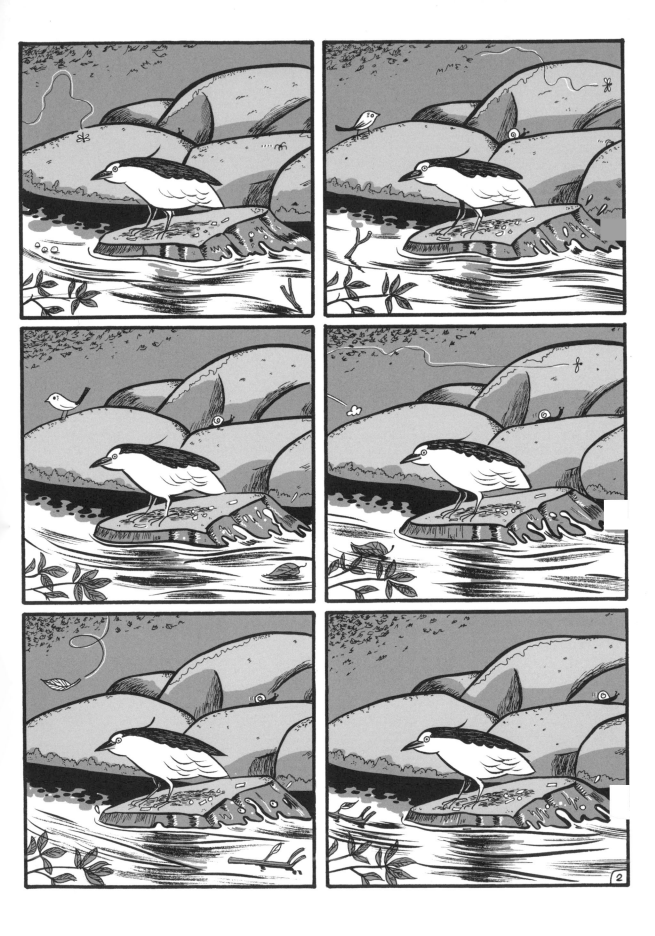

drawnandquarterly.com
michelrabagliati.com

ISBN 978-1-77046-414-8
Printed in Canada
10 9 8 7 6 5 4 3 2 1

Originally published in French by La Pastèque 2019

Cataloguing data avilable from Library and Archives Canada

Published in the USA by Drawn & Quarterly, a client publisher of Farrar, Straus and Giroux. Published in Canada by Drawn & Quarterly, a client publisher of Raincoast Books. Published in the United Kingdom by Drawn & Quarterly, a client publisher of Publishers Group UK.

Drawn & Quarterly acknowledges the support of the Government of Canada and the Canada Council for the Arts for our publishing program, and the National Translation Program for Book Publishing, an initiative of the Roadmap for Canada's Official Languages 2013–2019: Education, Immigration, Communities, for our translation activities.

Drawn & Quarterly reconnaît l'aide financière du gouvernement du Québec par l'entremise de la Société de développement des entreprises culturelles (SODEC) pour nos activités d'édition. Gouvernement du Québec—Programme de crédit d'impôt pour l'édition de livres—Gestion SODEC.

Michel Rabagliati

Paul at Home

Translated by
Helge Dascher and Rob Aspinall

Drawn & Quarterly

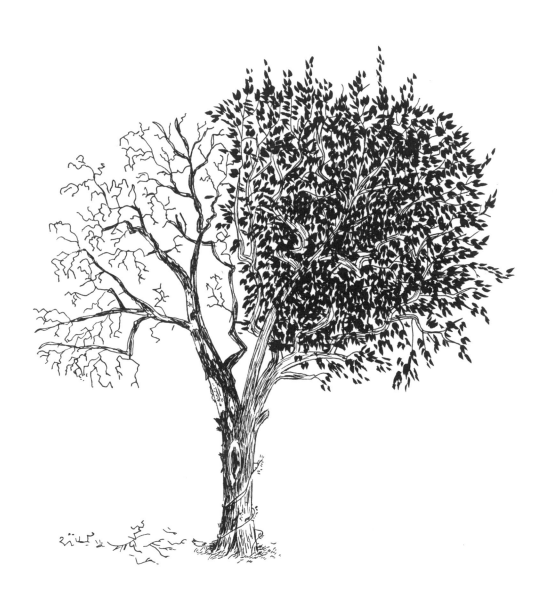

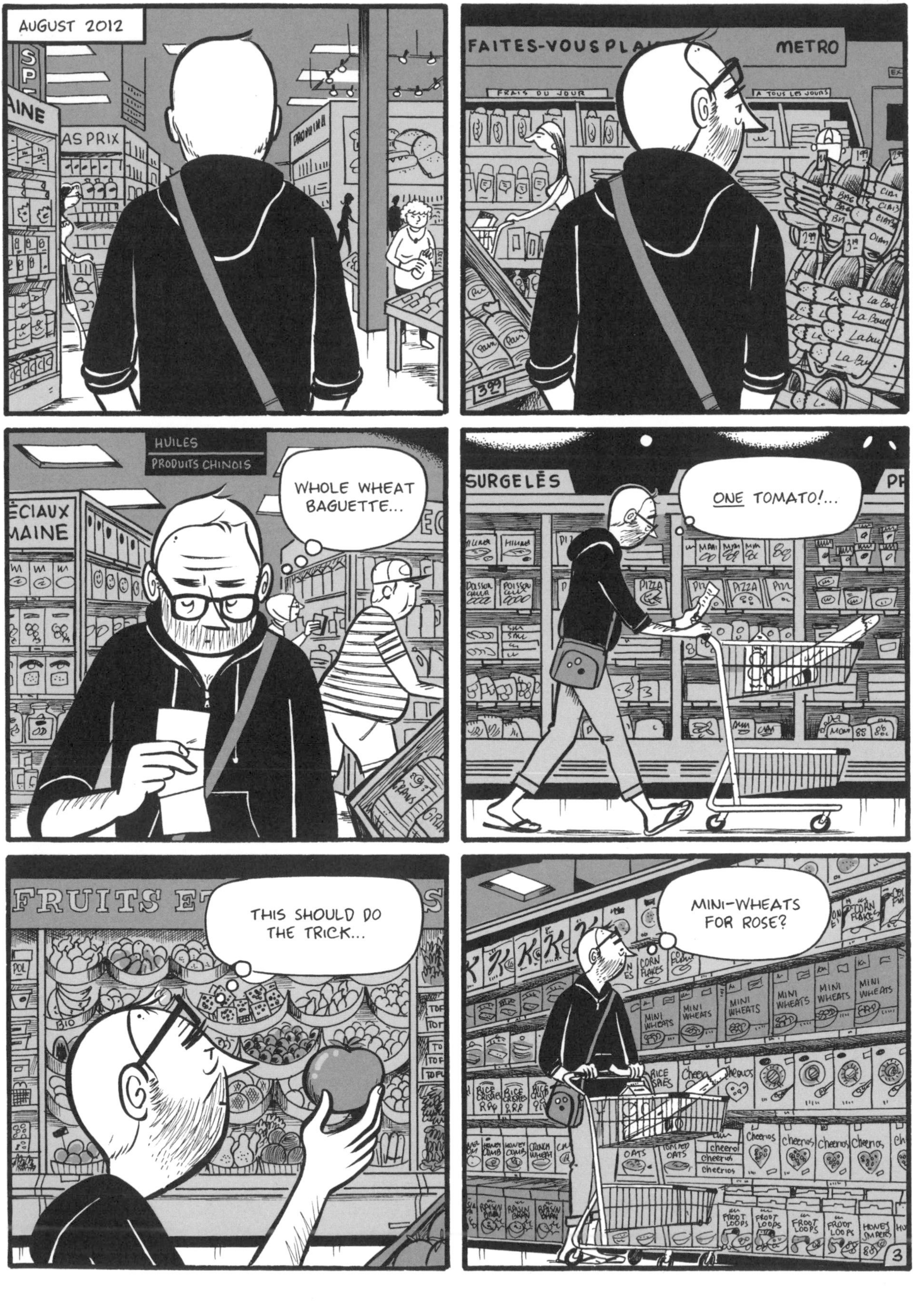
AUGUST 2012
METRO
HUILES
PRODUITS CHINOIS
WHOLE WHEAT BAGUETTE...
SURGELÉS
ONE TOMATO!...
FRUITS ET
THIS SHOULD DO THE TRICK...
MINI-WHEATS FOR ROSE?

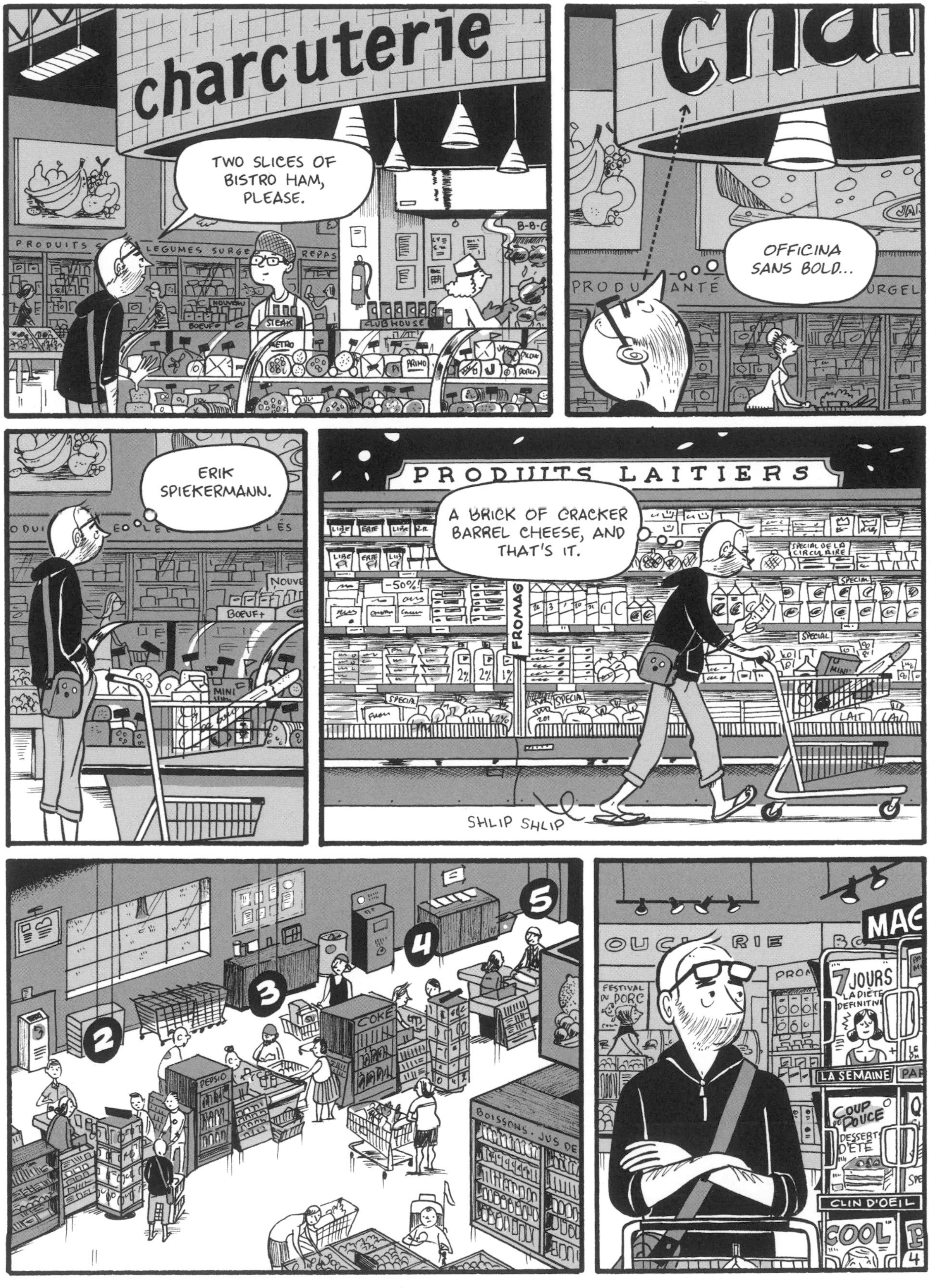
charcuterie
TWO SLICES OF BISTRO HAM, PLEASE.
OFFICINA SANS BOLD...
ERIK SPIEKERMANN.
PRODUITS LAITIERS
A BRICK OF CRACKER BARREL CHEESE, AND THAT'S IT.
FROMAG
SHLIP SHLIP
BOISSONS. JUS DE
FESTIVAL DU PORC
7 JOURS
LA DIÈTE DÉFINITIVE
LA SEMAINE
COUP POUCE
DESSERTS D'ÉTÉ
CLIN D'OEIL
COOL

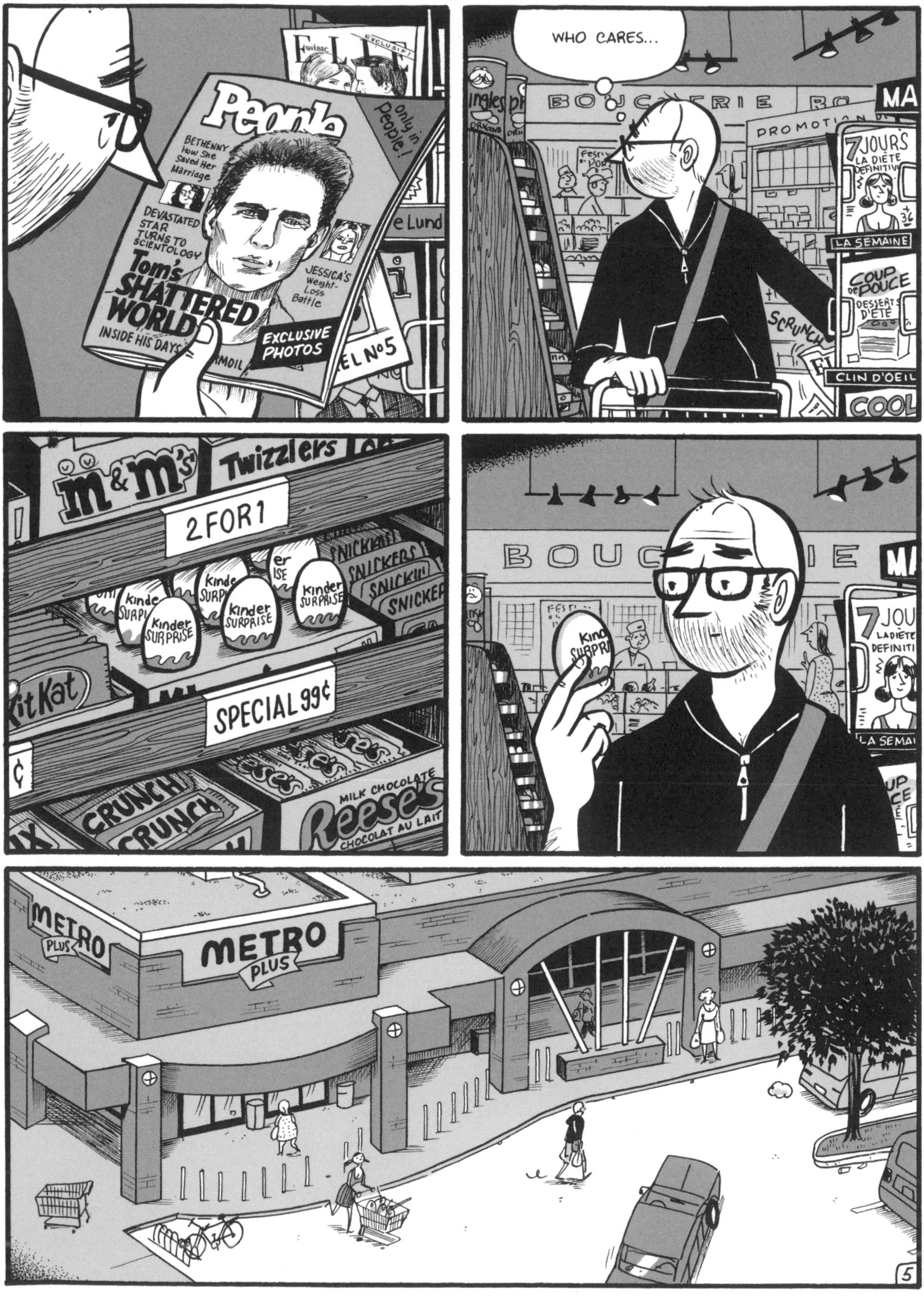
ELLE
QUÉBEC
EXCLUSIF!
People
only in People!
BETHENNY How She Saved Her Marriage
DEVASTATED STAR TURNS TO SCIENTOLOGY
Tom's SHATTERED WORLD
INSIDE HIS DAYS
JESSICA'S Weight-Loss Battle
EXCLUSIVE PHOTOS
WHO CARES...
BOUCHERIE
PROMOTION
7 JOURS
LA DIÈTE DÉFINITIVE
LA SEMAINE
COUP DE POUCE
DESSERTS D'ÉTÉ
SCRUNCH
CLIN D'OEIL
COOL
m&m's
Twizzlers
2 FOR 1
kinder SURPRISE
SNICKERS
KitKat
SPECIAL 99¢
CRUNCH
MILK CHOCOLATE
Reese's
CHOCOLAT AU LAIT
BOUC IE
7 JOURS
LA DIÈTE DÉFINITI
LA SEMAI
METRO PLUS
METRO PLUS

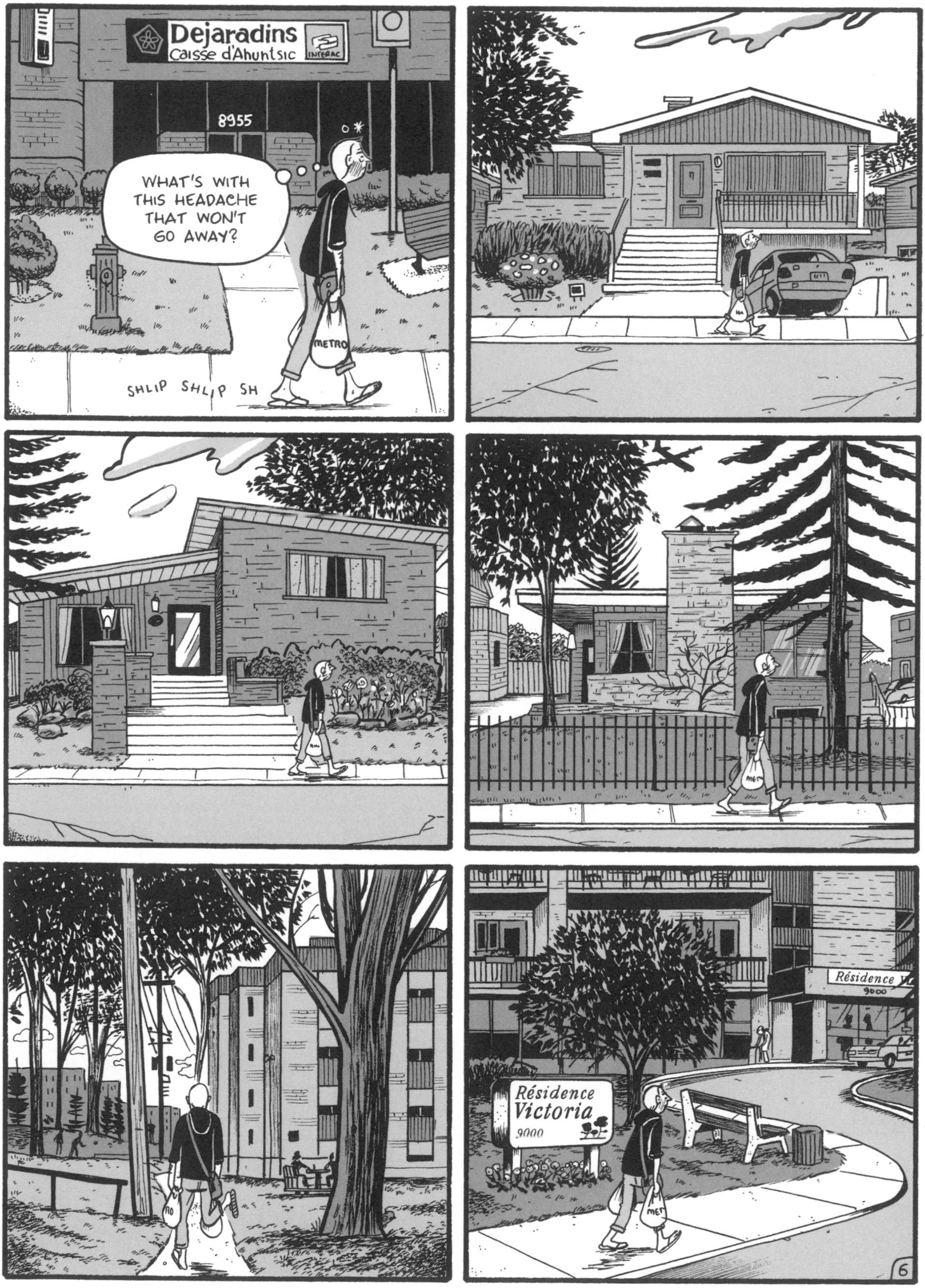
Dejaradins
Caisse d'Ahuntsic
INTERAC
8955
WHAT'S WITH THIS HEADACHE THAT WON'T GO AWAY?
METRO
SHLIP SHLIP SH
Résidence V
9000
Résidence Victoria
9000

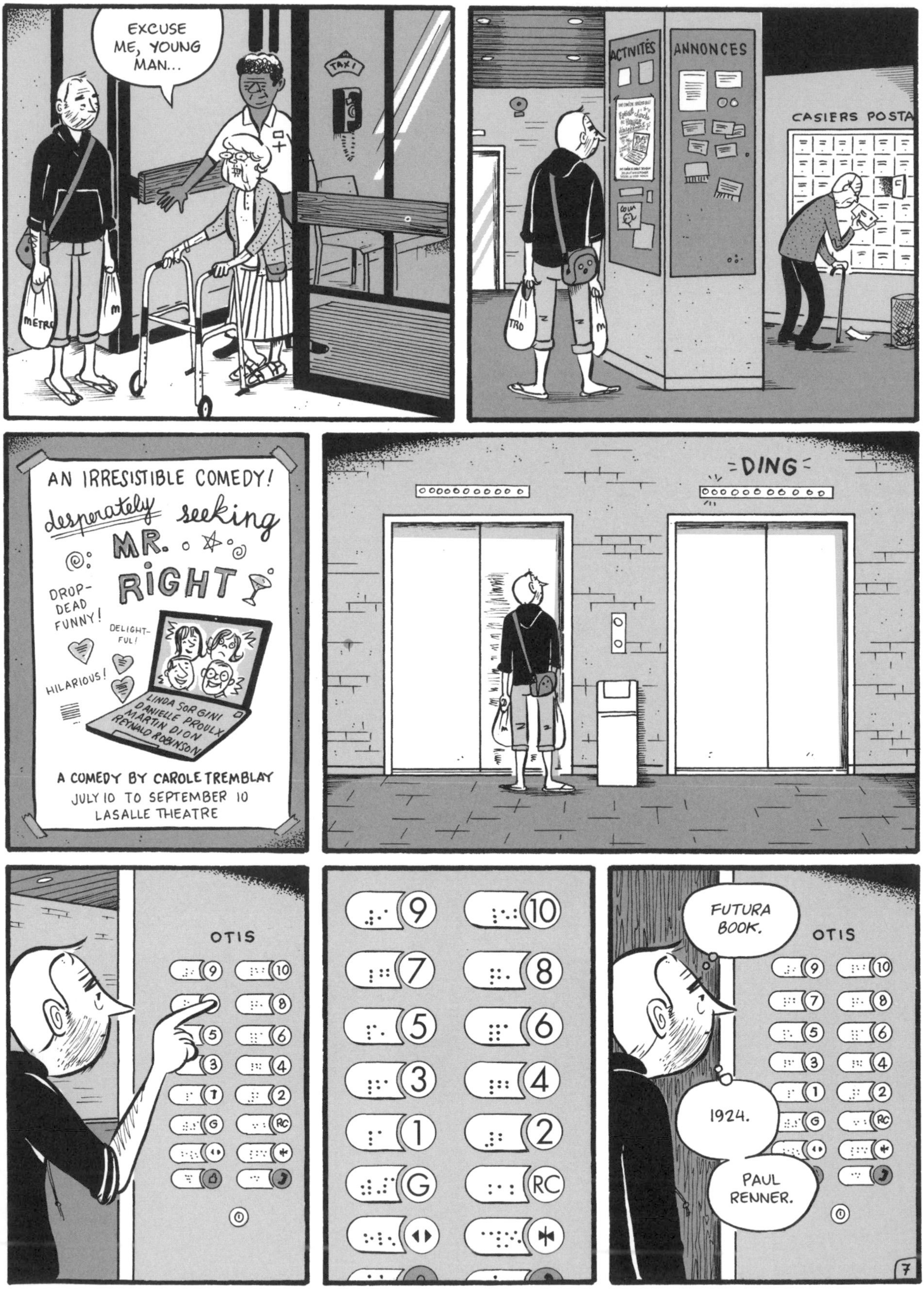
EXCUSE ME, YOUNG MAN...
TAXI
METRO
ACTIVITÉS
ANNONCES
CASIERS POSTA
AN IRRESISTIBLE COMEDY!
desperately seeking
MR. RIGHT
DROP-DEAD FUNNY!
DELIGHT-FUL!
HILARIOUS!
LINDA SORGINI
DANIELLE PROULX
MARTIN DION
REYNALD ROBINSON
A COMEDY BY CAROLE TREMBLAY
JULY 10 TO SEPTEMBER 10
LASALLE THEATRE
DING
OTIS
FUTURA BOOK.
OTIS
1924.
PAUL RENNER.

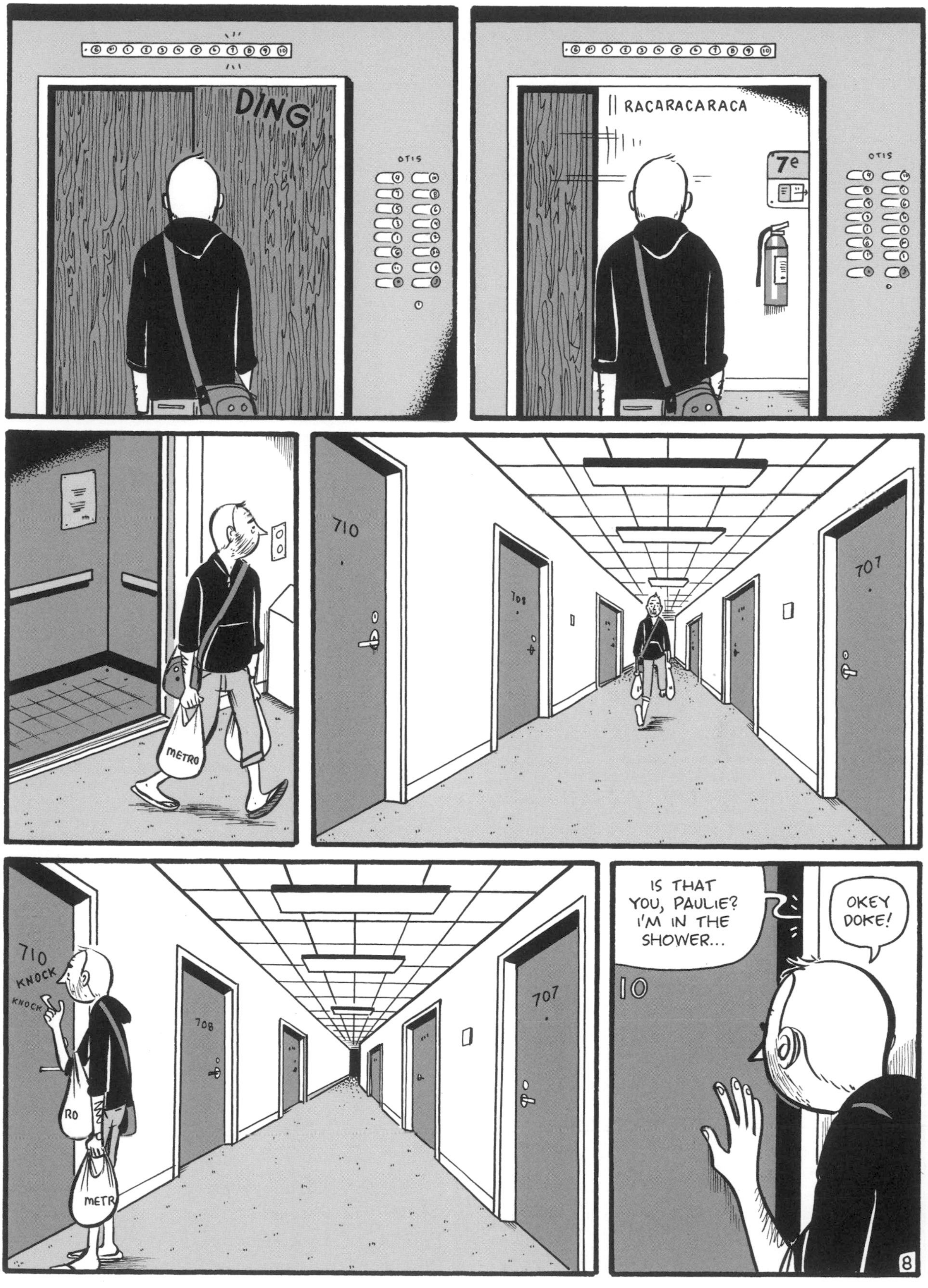
DING
OTIS
RACARACARACA
7e
OTIS
METRO
710
708
707
710
KNOCK
KNOCK
RO
METR
708
707
IS THAT YOU, PAULIE? I'M IN THE SHOWER...
OKEY DOKE!
10

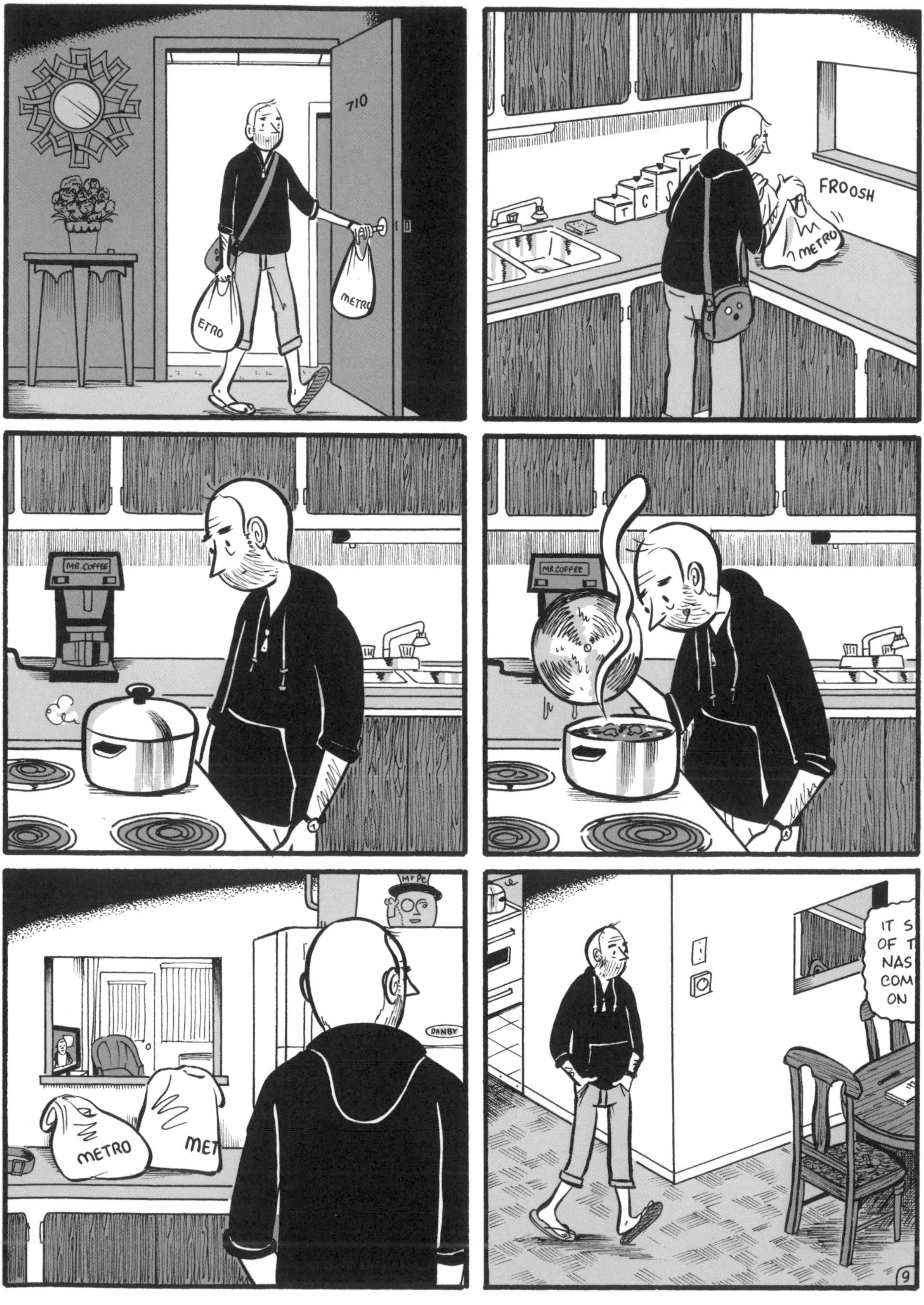
710
ETRO
METRO
T C S
FROOSH
METRO
MR. COFFEE
MR. COFFEE
Mr Pe
DANBY
METRO
MET
IT S
OF T
NAS
COM
ON

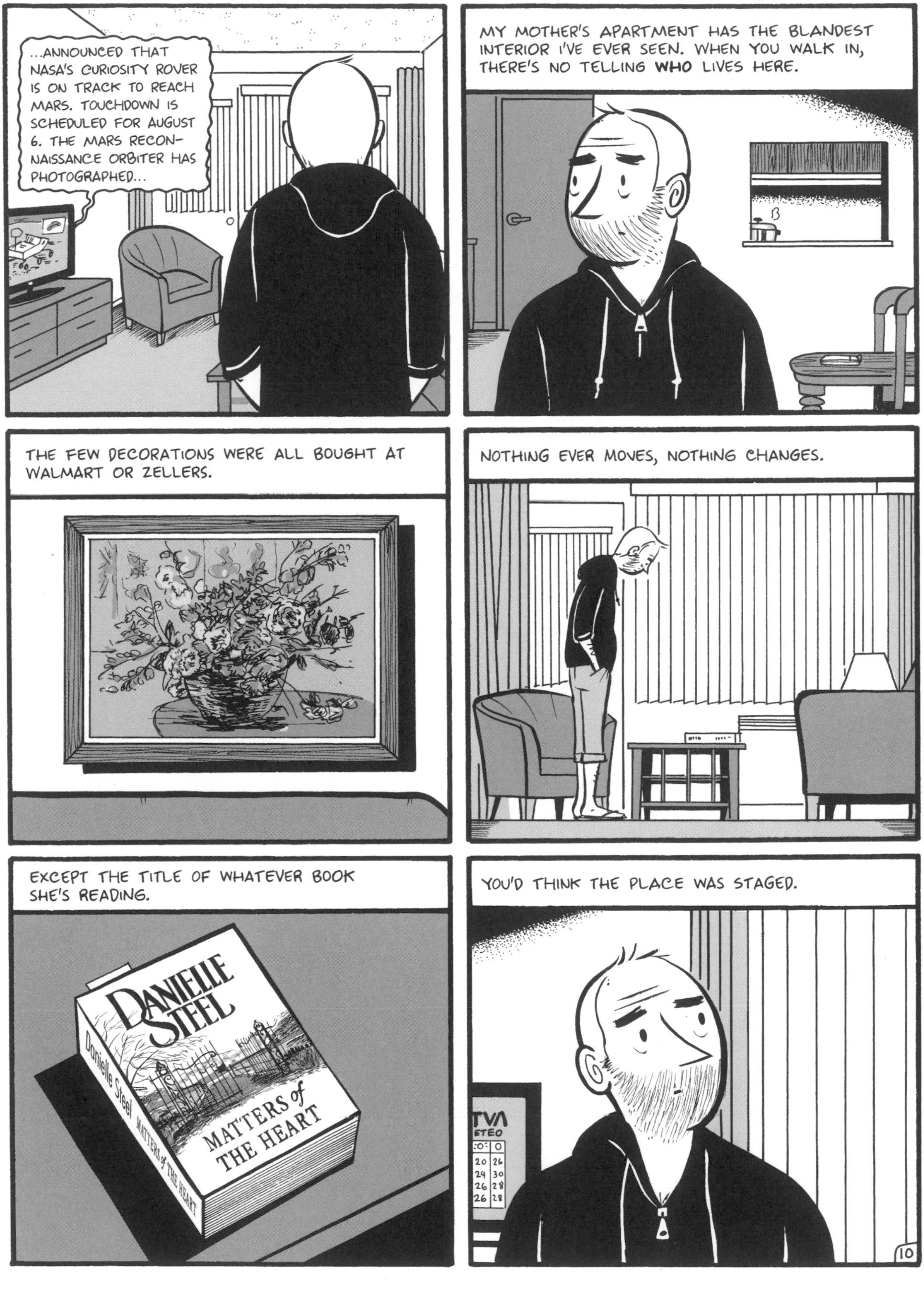
...ANNOUNCED THAT NASA'S CURIOSITY ROVER IS ON TRACK TO REACH MARS. TOUCHDOWN IS SCHEDULED FOR AUGUST 6. THE MARS RECON-NAISSANCE ORBITER HAS PHOTOGRAPHED...
MY MOTHER'S APARTMENT HAS THE BLANDEST INTERIOR I'VE EVER SEEN. WHEN YOU WALK IN, THERE'S NO TELLING **WHO** LIVES HERE.
THE FEW DECORATIONS WERE ALL BOUGHT AT WALMART OR ZELLERS.
NOTHING EVER MOVES, NOTHING CHANGES.
EXCEPT THE TITLE OF WHATEVER BOOK SHE'S READING.
DANIELLE STEEL
MATTERS of THE HEART
Danielle Steel MATTERS of THE HEART
YOU'D THINK THE PLACE WAS STAGED.
TVA

A MODEL UNIT.

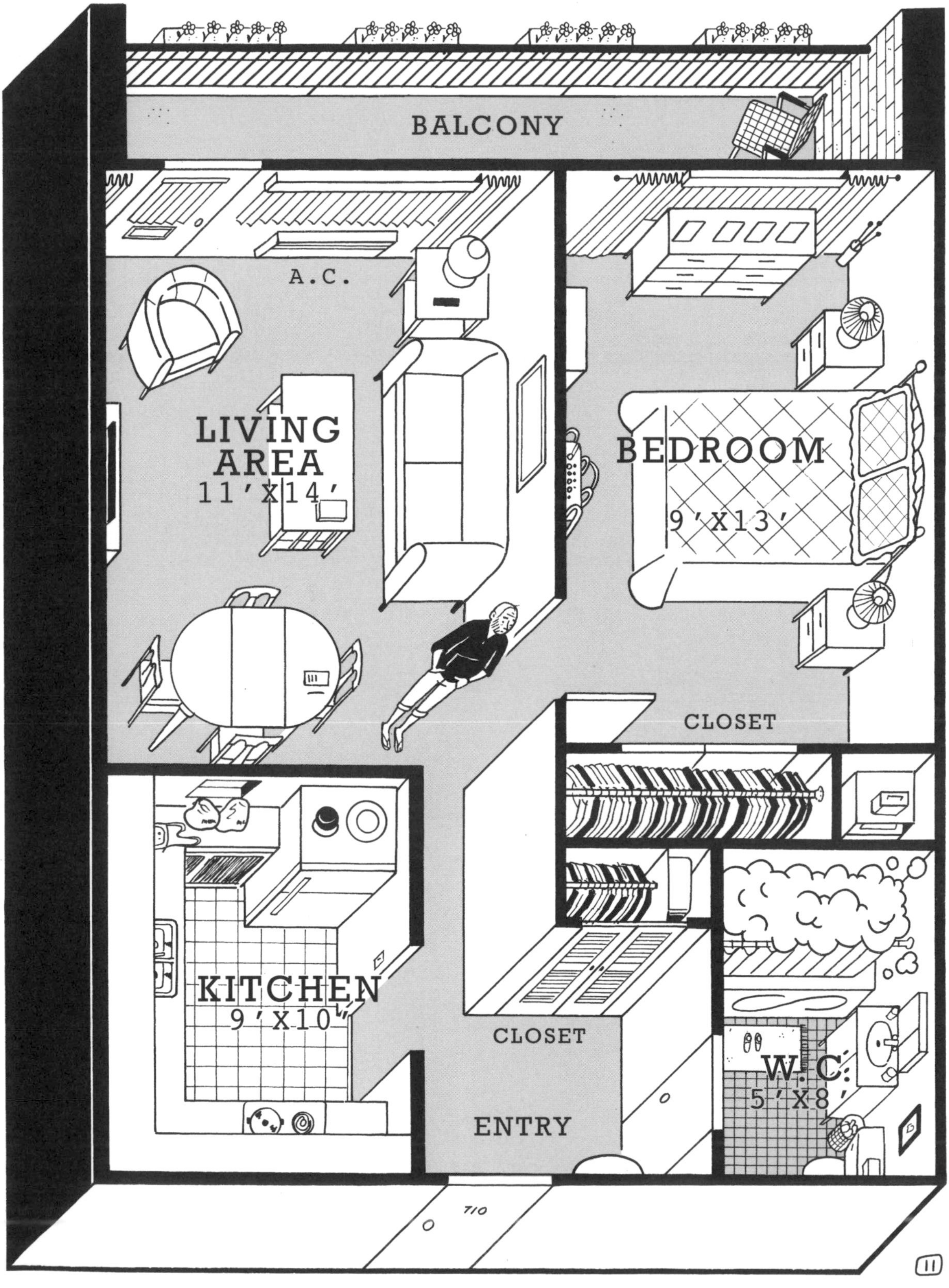

BALCONY
A.C.
LIVING AREA
11'X14'
BEDROOM
9'X13'
CLOSET
KITCHEN
9'X10"
CLOSET
W.C.
5'X8'
ENTRY
710

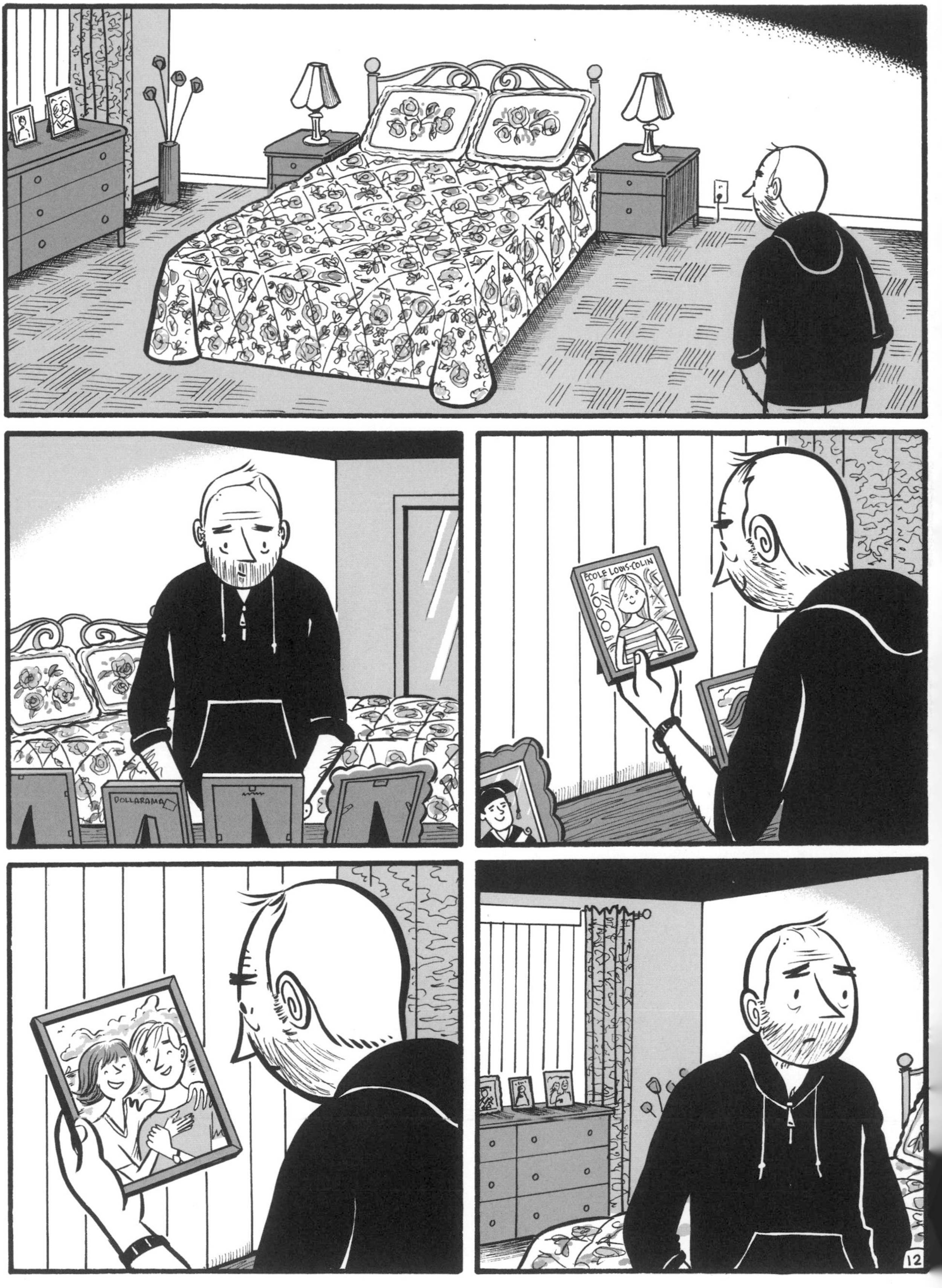
DOLLARAMA
ÉCOLE LOUIS-COLIN

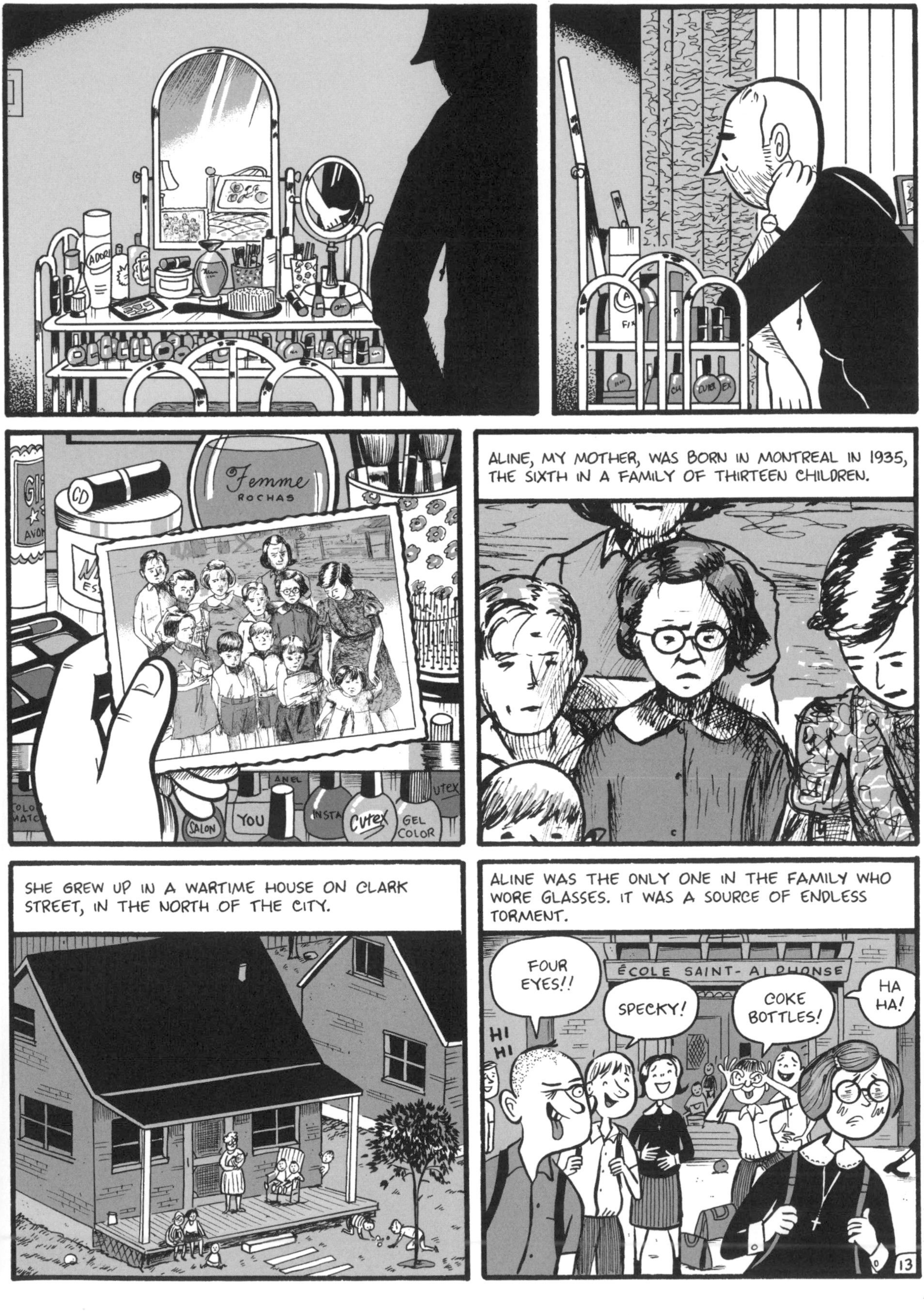
Femme
ROCHAS
YOU
SALON
Cutex
GEL COLOR
ALINE, MY MOTHER, WAS BORN IN MONTREAL IN 1935, THE SIXTH IN A FAMILY OF THIRTEEN CHILDREN.
SHE GREW UP IN A WARTIME HOUSE ON CLARK STREET, IN THE NORTH OF THE CITY.
ALINE WAS THE ONLY ONE IN THE FAMILY WHO WORE GLASSES. IT WAS A SOURCE OF ENDLESS TORMENT.
ÉCOLE SAINT-ALPHONSE
FOUR EYES!!
HI HI
SPECKY!
COKE BOTTLES!
HA HA!

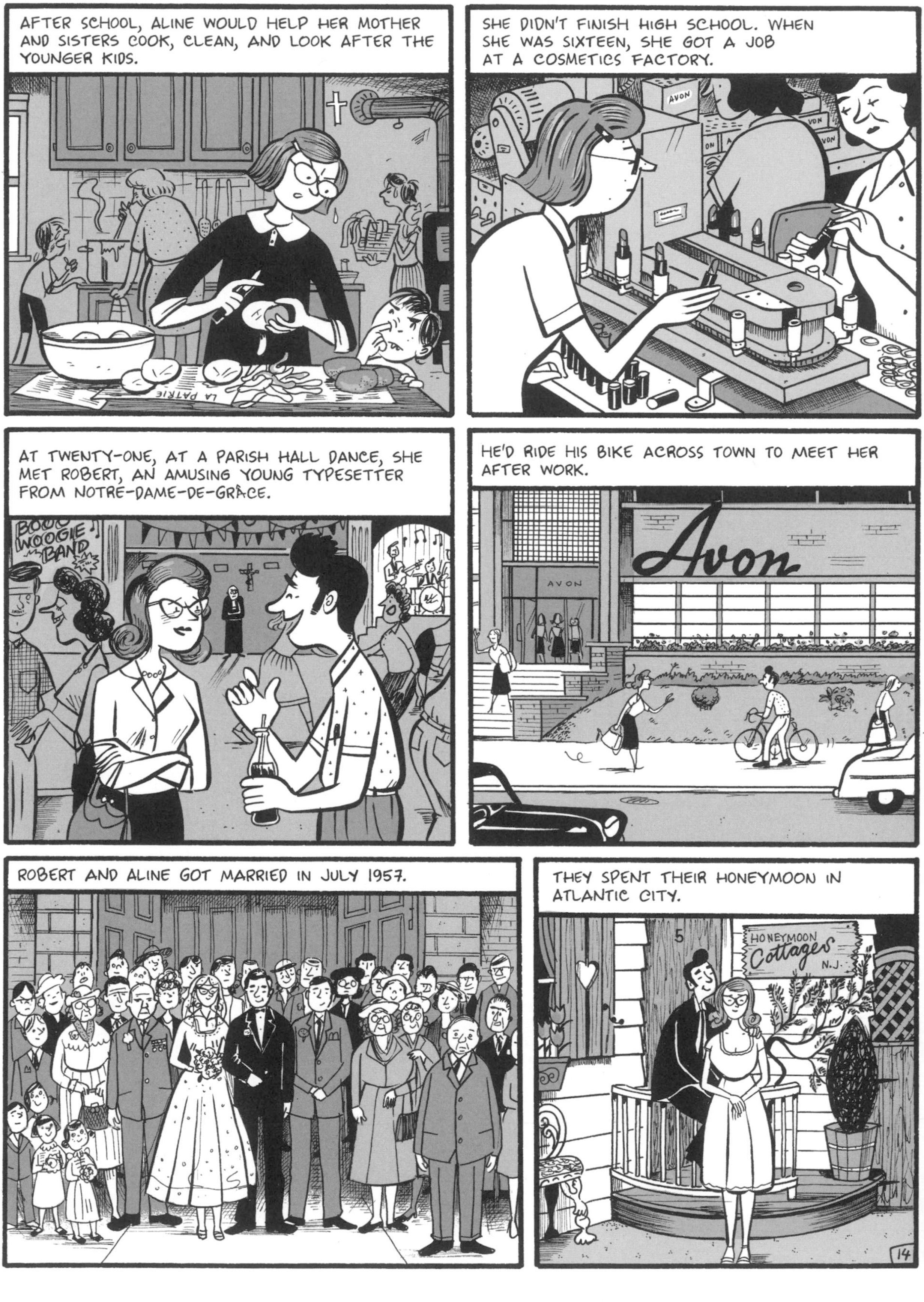
AFTER SCHOOL, ALINE WOULD HELP HER MOTHER AND SISTERS COOK, CLEAN, AND LOOK AFTER THE YOUNGER KIDS.
LA PATRIE
SHE DIDN'T FINISH HIGH SCHOOL. WHEN SHE WAS SIXTEEN, SHE GOT A JOB AT A COSMETICS FACTORY.
AVON
AT TWENTY-ONE, AT A PARISH HALL DANCE, SHE MET ROBERT, AN AMUSING YOUNG TYPESETTER FROM NOTRE-DAME-DE-GRÂCE.
WOOGIE BAND
HE'D RIDE HIS BIKE ACROSS TOWN TO MEET HER AFTER WORK.
Avon
AVON
ROBERT AND ALINE GOT MARRIED IN JULY 1957.
THEY SPENT THEIR HONEYMOON IN ATLANTIC CITY.
5
HONEYMOON Cottages N.J.

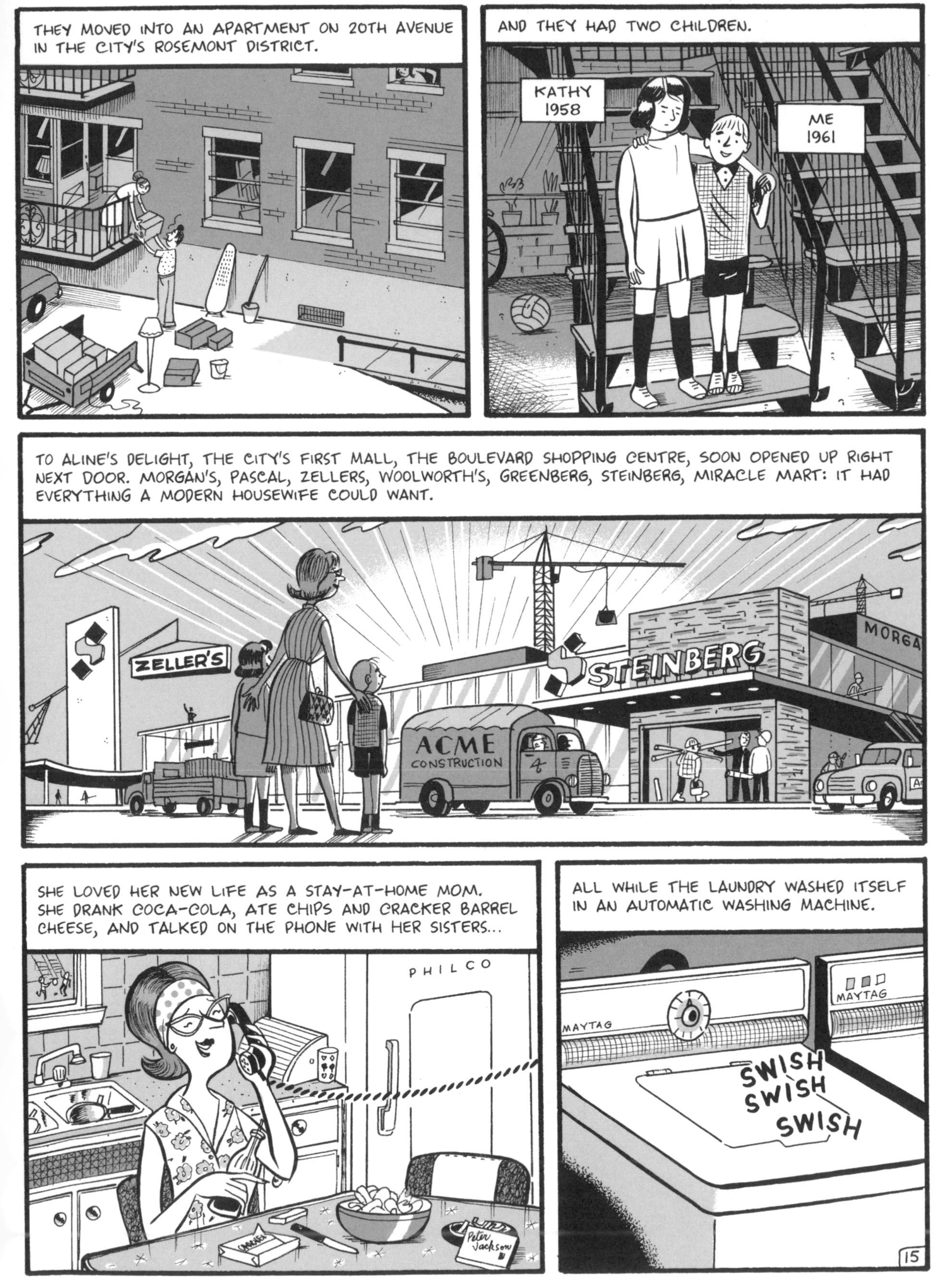
THEY MOVED INTO AN APARTMENT ON 20TH AVENUE IN THE CITY'S ROSEMONT DISTRICT.
AND THEY HAD TWO CHILDREN.
KATHY 1958
ME 1961
TO ALINE'S DELIGHT, THE CITY'S FIRST MALL, THE BOULEVARD SHOPPING CENTRE, SOON OPENED UP RIGHT NEXT DOOR. MORGAN'S, PASCAL, ZELLERS, WOOLWORTH'S, GREENBERG, STEINBERG, MIRACLE MART: IT HAD EVERYTHING A MODERN HOUSEWIFE COULD WANT.
ZELLER'S
STEINBERG
MORGA
ACME CONSTRUCTION
SHE LOVED HER NEW LIFE AS A STAY-AT-HOME MOM. SHE DRANK COCA-COLA, ATE CHIPS AND CRACKER BARREL CHEESE, AND TALKED ON THE PHONE WITH HER SISTERS...
PHILCO
Peter Jackson
ALL WHILE THE LAUNDRY WASHED ITSELF IN AN AUTOMATIC WASHING MACHINE.
MAYTAG
MAYTAG
SWISH SWISH SWISH

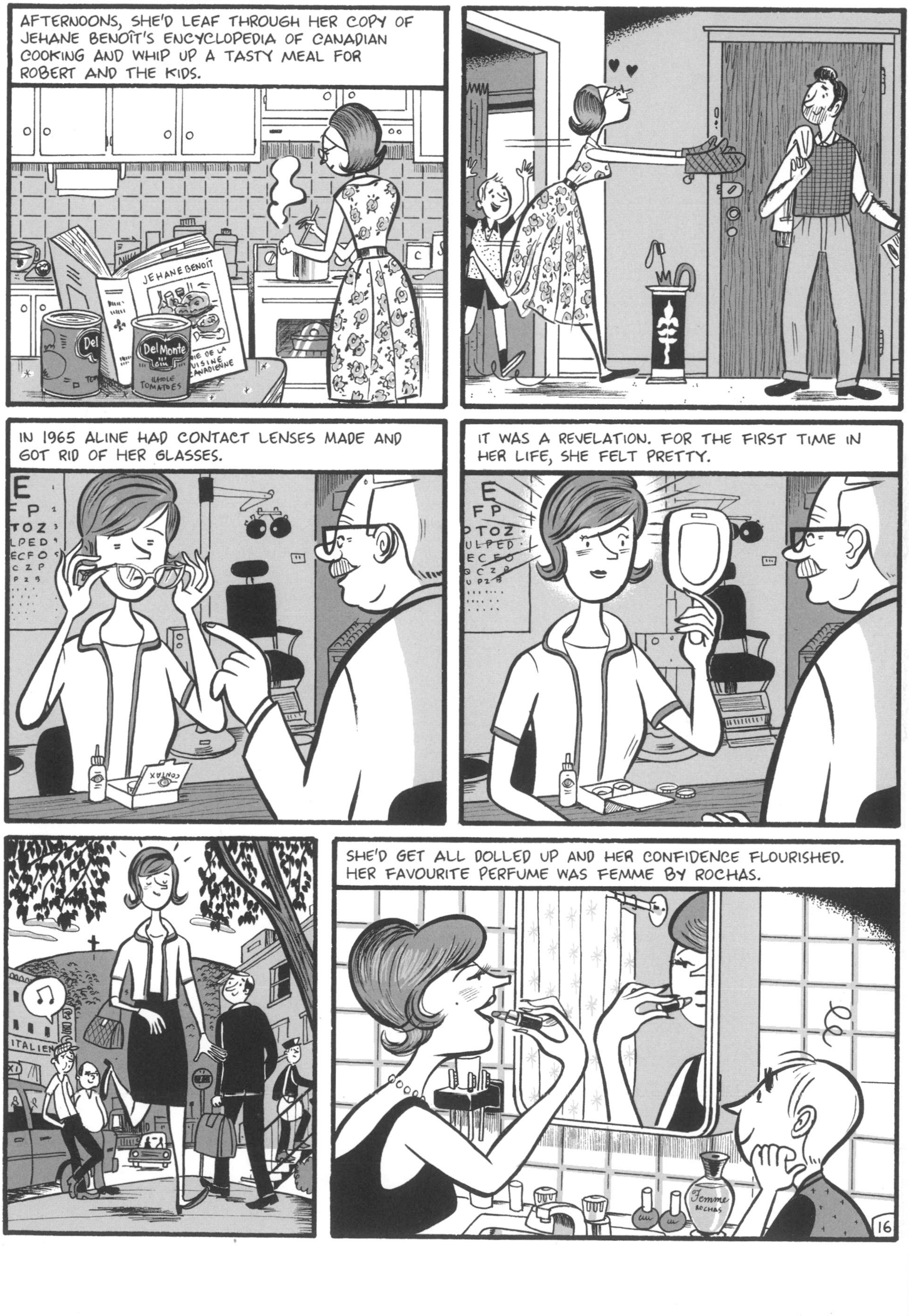
AFTERNOONS, SHE'D LEAF THROUGH HER COPY OF JEHANE BENOÎT'S ENCYCLOPEDIA OF CANADIAN COOKING AND WHIP UP A TASTY MEAL FOR ROBERT AND THE KIDS.
JEHANE BENOÎT
Del Monte
WHOLE TOMATOES
IN 1965 ALINE HAD CONTACT LENSES MADE AND GOT RID OF HER GLASSES.
IT WAS A REVELATION. FOR THE FIRST TIME IN HER LIFE, SHE FELT PRETTY.
ITALIEN
SHE'D GET ALL DOLLED UP AND HER CONFIDENCE FLOURISHED. HER FAVOURITE PERFUME WAS FEMME BY ROCHAS.
Femme
ROCHAS
16

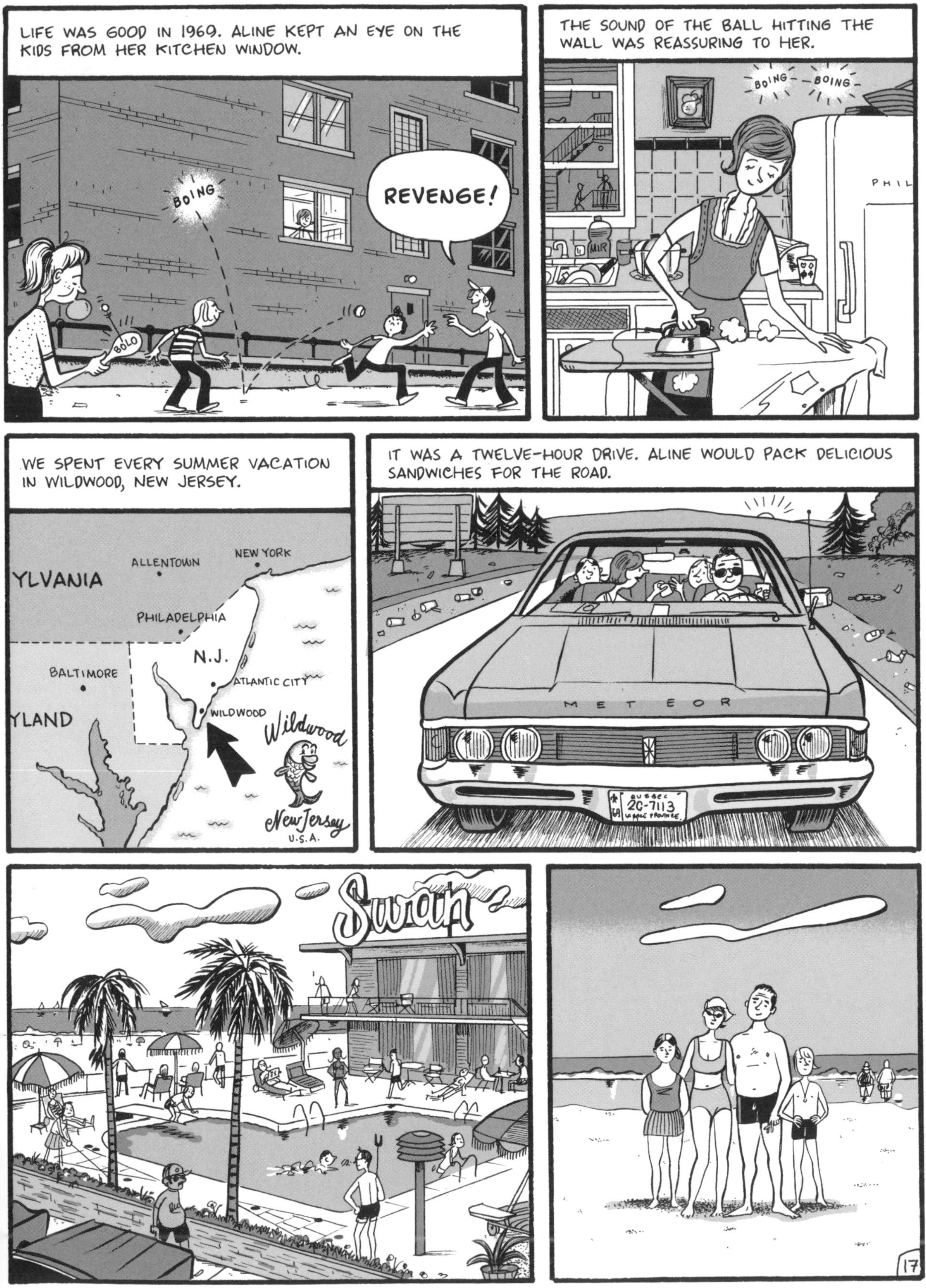
LIFE WAS GOOD IN 1969. ALINE KEPT AN EYE ON THE KIDS FROM HER KITCHEN WINDOW.
BOING
BOLO
REVENGE!
THE SOUND OF THE BALL HITTING THE WALL WAS REASSURING TO HER.
BOING — BOING
MIR
PHIL
WE SPENT EVERY SUMMER VACATION IN WILDWOOD, NEW JERSEY.
YLVANIA
ALLENTOWN
NEW YORK
PHILADELPHIA
N.J.
BALTIMORE
ATLANTIC CITY
WILDWOOD
YLAND
Wildwood
New Jersey
U.S.A.
IT WAS A TWELVE-HOUR DRIVE. ALINE WOULD PACK DELICIOUS SANDWICHES FOR THE ROAD.
METEOR
2C-7113
Swan

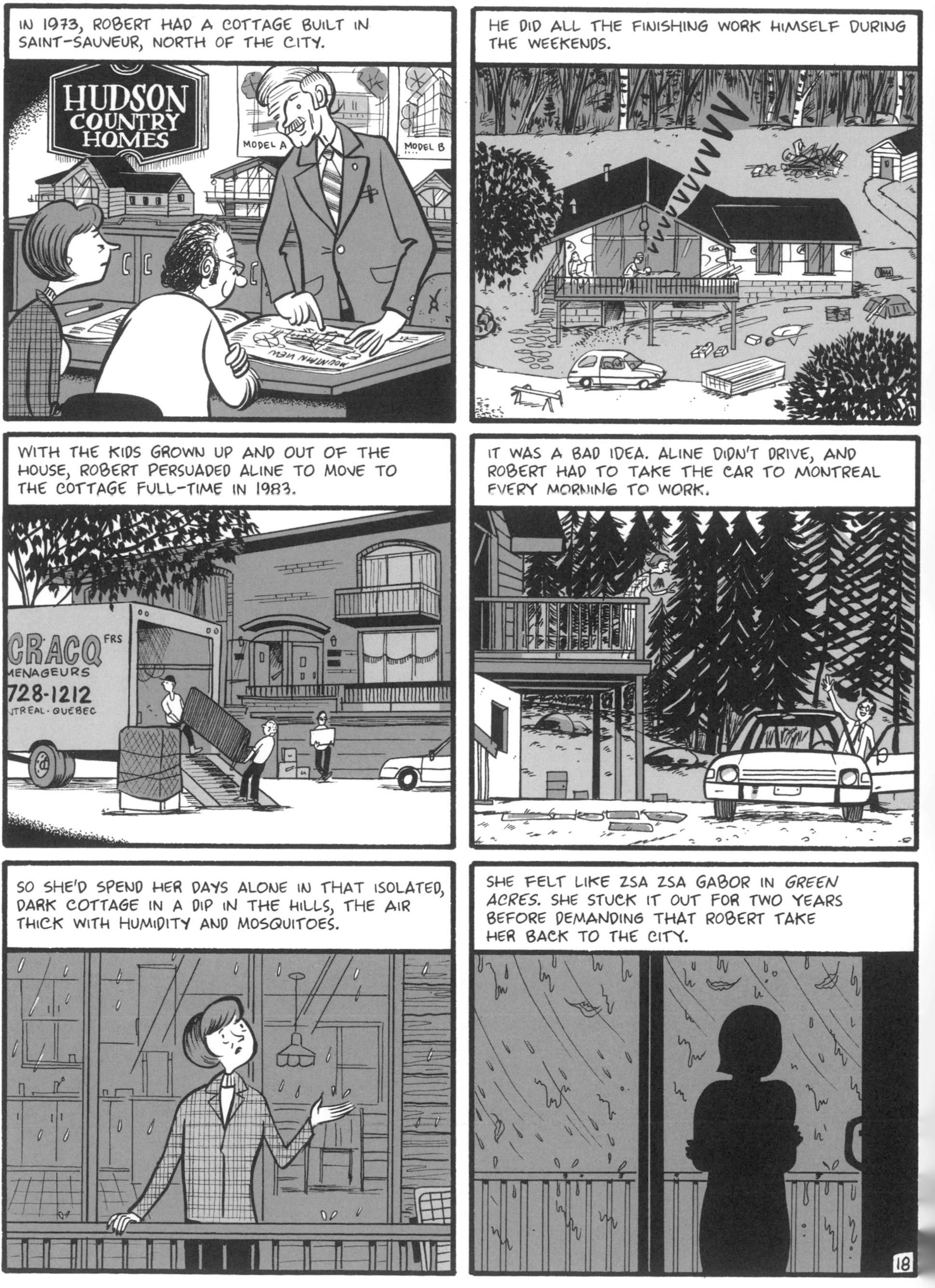
IN 1973, ROBERT HAD A COTTAGE BUILT IN SAINT-SAUVEUR, NORTH OF THE CITY.
HUDSON COUNTRY HOMES
MODEL A
MODEL B
HE DID ALL THE FINISHING WORK HIMSELF DURING THE WEEKENDS.
WITH THE KIDS GROWN UP AND OUT OF THE HOUSE, ROBERT PERSUADED ALINE TO MOVE TO THE COTTAGE FULL-TIME IN 1983.
CRACQ FRS
MENAGEURS
728-1212
NTREAL-QUEBEC
IT WAS A BAD IDEA. ALINE DIDN'T DRIVE, AND ROBERT HAD TO TAKE THE CAR TO MONTREAL EVERY MORNING TO WORK.
SO SHE'D SPEND HER DAYS ALONE IN THAT ISOLATED, DARK COTTAGE IN A DIP IN THE HILLS, THE AIR THICK WITH HUMIDITY AND MOSQUITOES.
SHE FELT LIKE ZSA ZSA GABOR IN *GREEN ACRES*. SHE STUCK IT OUT FOR TWO YEARS BEFORE DEMANDING THAT ROBERT TAKE HER BACK TO THE CITY.

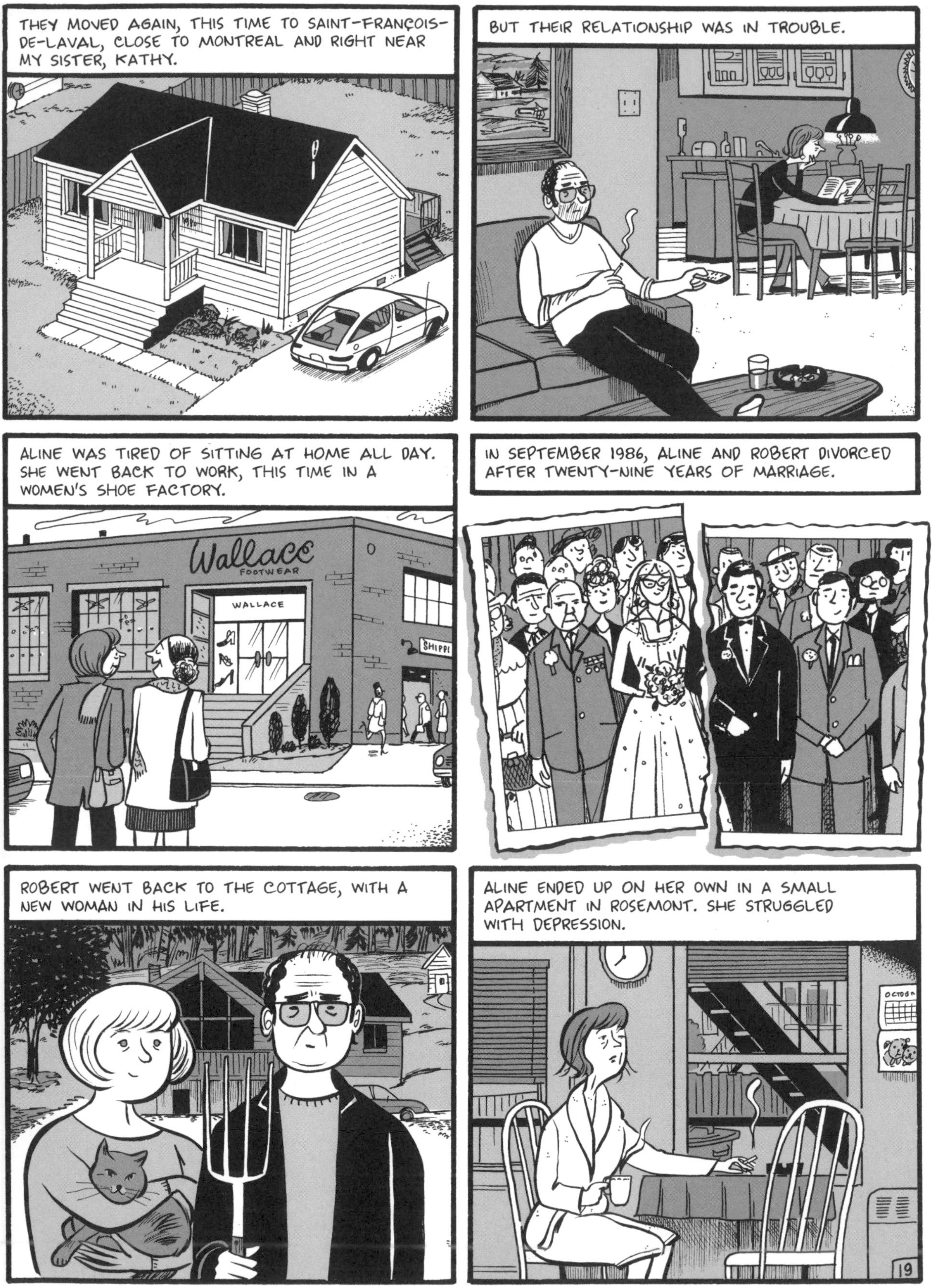
THEY MOVED AGAIN, THIS TIME TO SAINT-FRANÇOIS-DE-LAVAL, CLOSE TO MONTREAL AND RIGHT NEAR MY SISTER, KATHY.
BUT THEIR RELATIONSHIP WAS IN TROUBLE.
ALINE WAS TIRED OF SITTING AT HOME ALL DAY. SHE WENT BACK TO WORK, THIS TIME IN A WOMEN'S SHOE FACTORY.
Wallace
FOOTWEAR
WALLACE
IN SEPTEMBER 1986, ALINE AND ROBERT DIVORCED AFTER TWENTY-NINE YEARS OF MARRIAGE.
ROBERT WENT BACK TO THE COTTAGE, WITH A NEW WOMAN IN HIS LIFE.
ALINE ENDED UP ON HER OWN IN A SMALL APARTMENT IN ROSEMONT. SHE STRUGGLED WITH DEPRESSION.

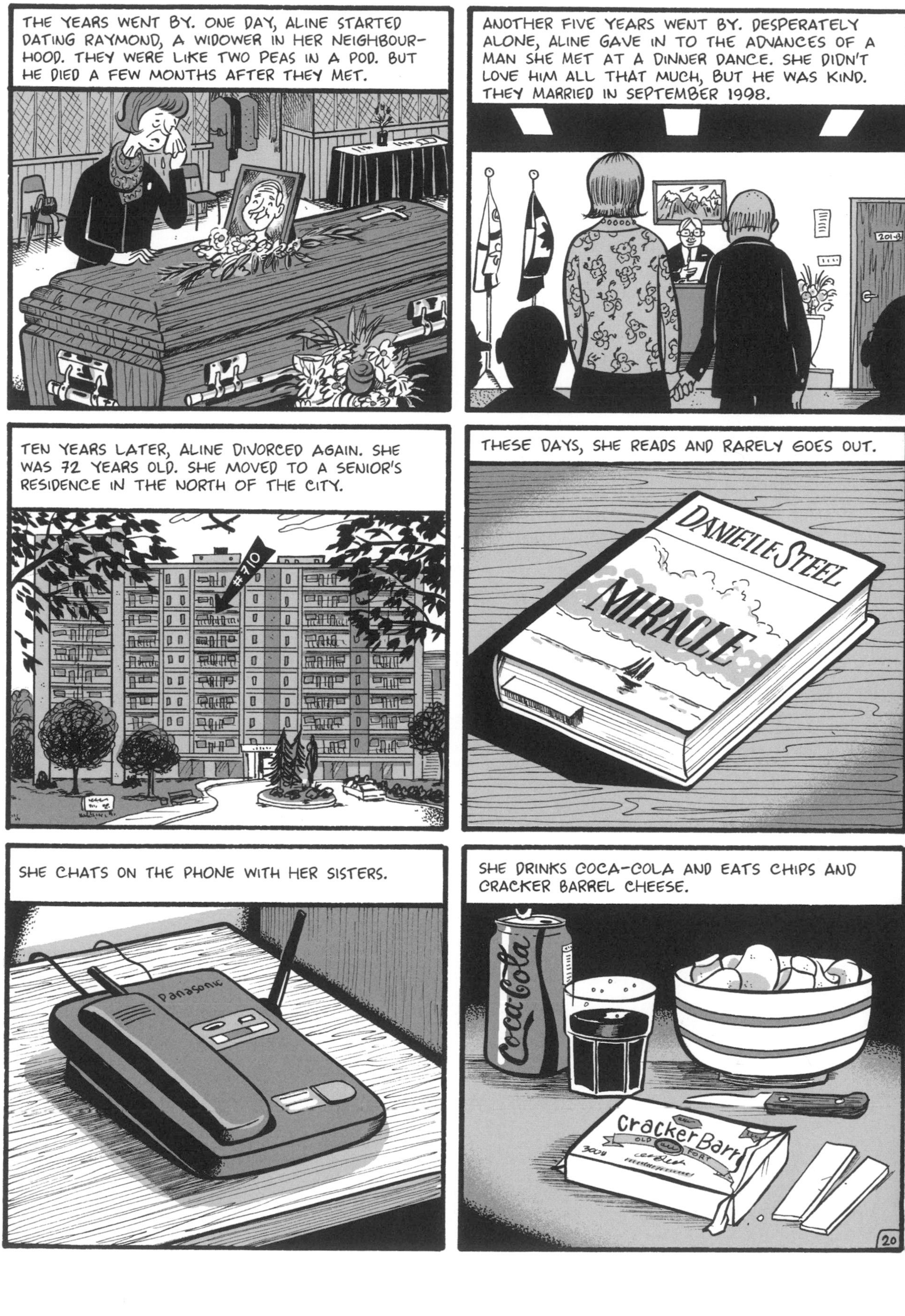
THE YEARS WENT BY. ONE DAY, ALINE STARTED DATING RAYMOND, A WIDOWER IN HER NEIGHBOURHOOD. THEY WERE LIKE TWO PEAS IN A POD. BUT HE DIED A FEW MONTHS AFTER THEY MET.
ANOTHER FIVE YEARS WENT BY. DESPERATELY ALONE, ALINE GAVE IN TO THE ADVANCES OF A MAN SHE MET AT A DINNER DANCE. SHE DIDN'T LOVE HIM ALL THAT MUCH, BUT HE WAS KIND. THEY MARRIED IN SEPTEMBER 1998.
TEN YEARS LATER, ALINE DIVORCED AGAIN. SHE WAS 72 YEARS OLD. SHE MOVED TO A SENIOR'S RESIDENCE IN THE NORTH OF THE CITY.
#710
THESE DAYS, SHE READS AND RARELY GOES OUT.
DANIELLE STEEL
MIRACLE
SHE CHATS ON THE PHONE WITH HER SISTERS.
Panasonic
SHE DRINKS COCA-COLA AND EATS CHIPS AND CRACKER BARREL CHEESE.
Coca-Cola
CrackerBarr
OLD
FORT

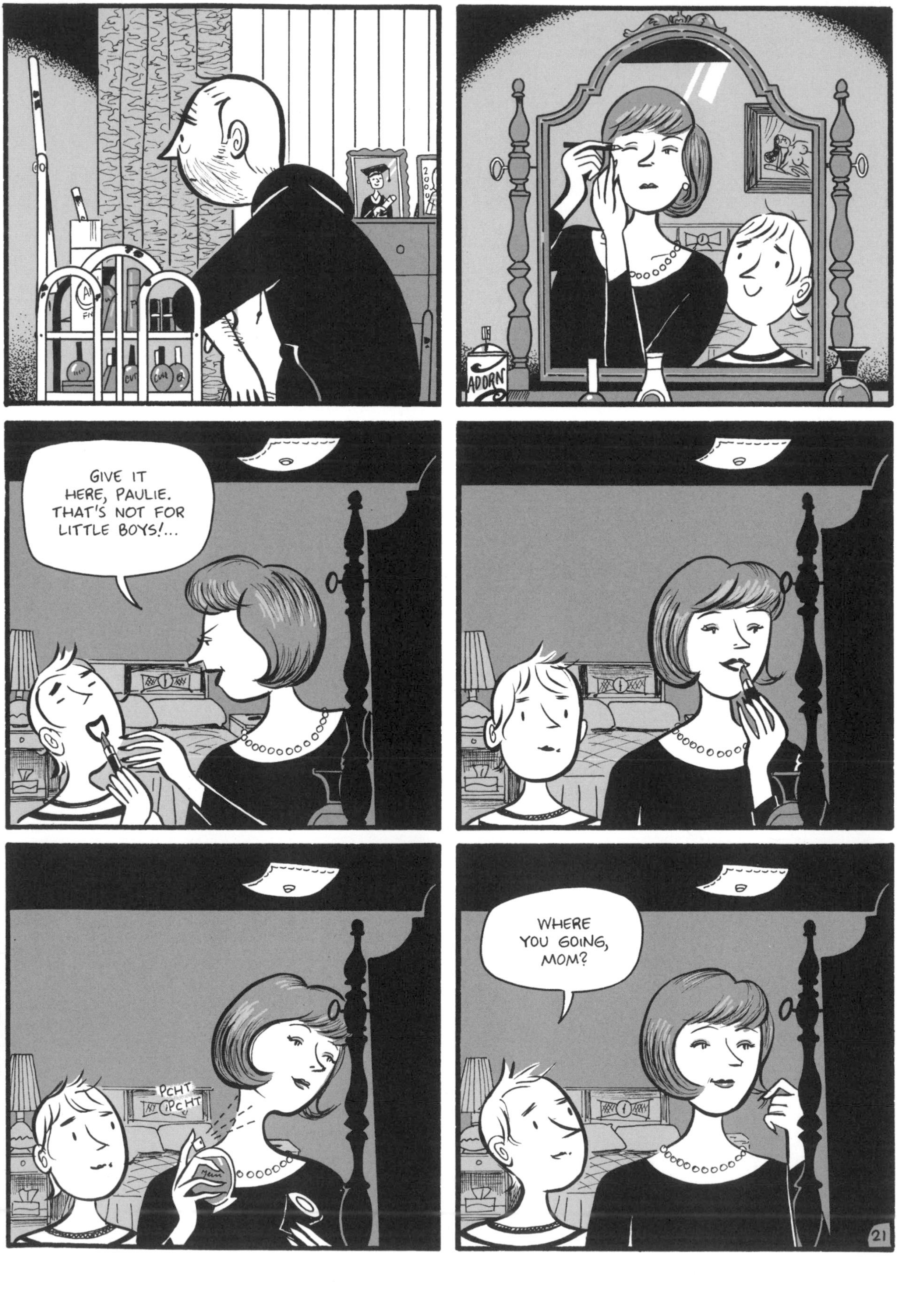
ADORN
GIVE IT HERE, PAULIE. THAT'S NOT FOR LITTLE BOYS!...
PCHT
PCHT
WHERE YOU GOING, MOM?

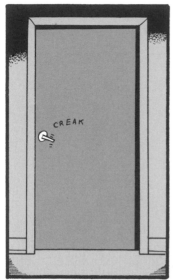

CREAK

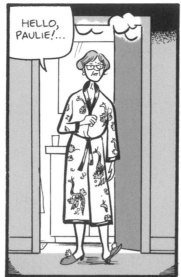

HELLO, PAULIE!...

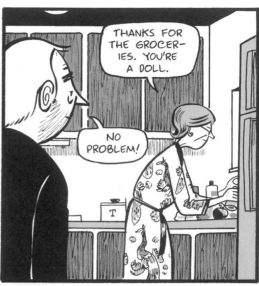

THANKS FOR THE GROCERIES. YOU'RE A DOLL.

NO PROBLEM!

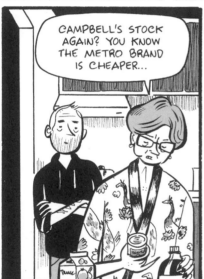

CAMPBELL'S STOCK AGAIN? YOU KNOW THE METRO BRAND IS CHEAPER...

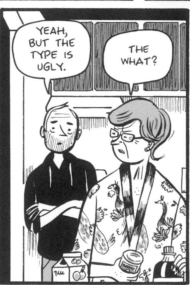

YEAH, BUT THE TYPE IS UGLY.

THE WHAT?

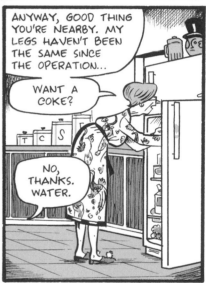

ANYWAY, GOOD THING YOU'RE NEARBY. MY LEGS HAVEN'T BEEN THE SAME SINCE THE OPERATION...

WANT A COKE?

NO, THANKS. WATER.

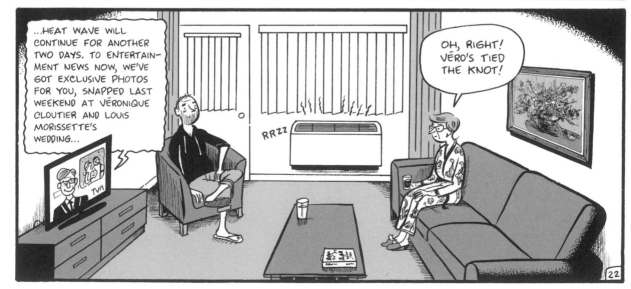

...HEAT WAVE WILL CONTINUE FOR ANOTHER TWO DAYS. TO ENTERTAINMENT NEWS NOW, WE'VE GOT EXCLUSIVE PHOTOS FOR YOU, SNAPPED LAST WEEKEND AT VÉRONIQUE CLOUTIER AND LOUIS MORISSETTE'S WEDDING...

RRZZ

OH, RIGHT! VÉRO'S TIED THE KNOT!

22

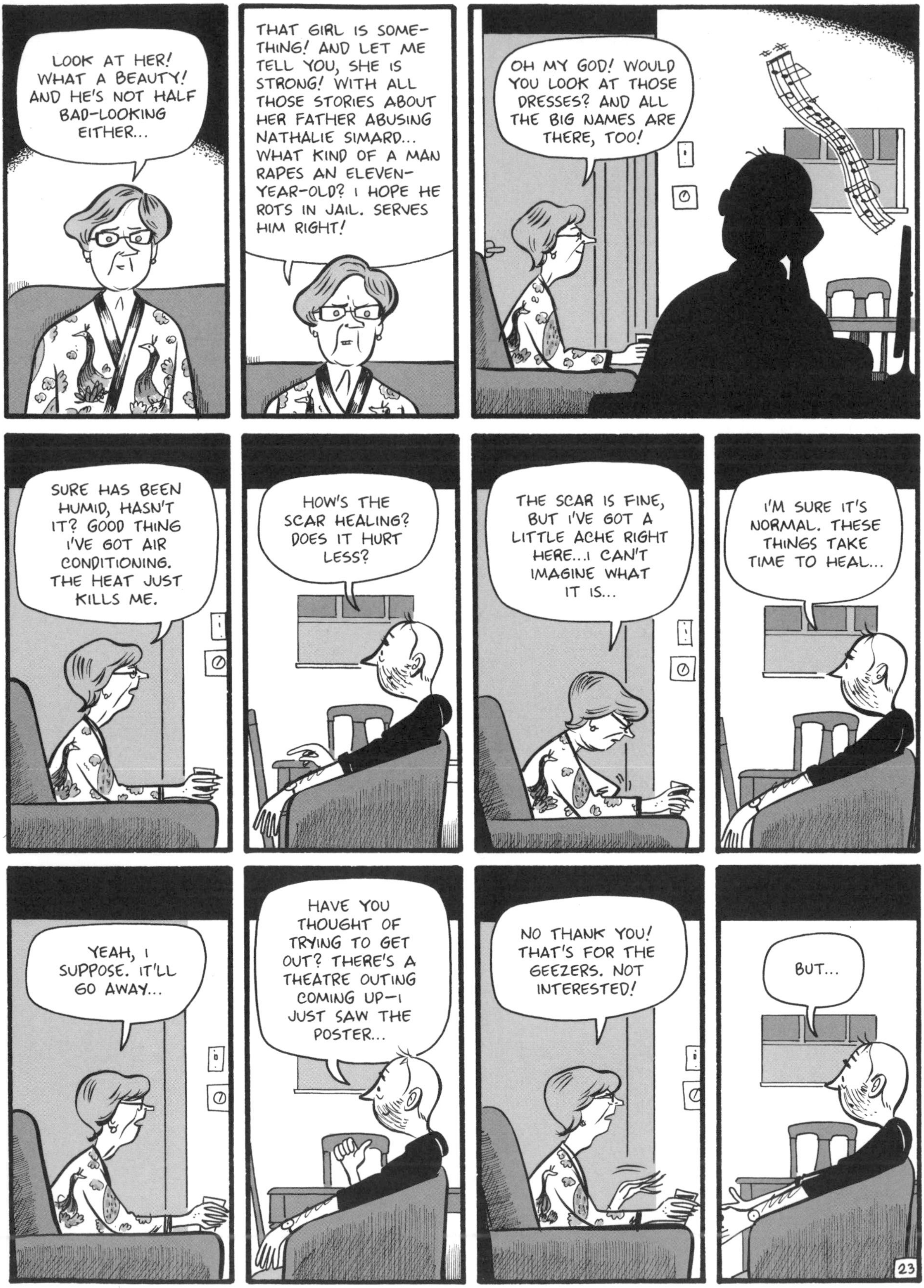
LOOK AT HER! WHAT A BEAUTY! AND HE'S NOT HALF BAD-LOOKING EITHER...
THAT GIRL IS SOMETHING! AND LET ME TELL YOU, SHE IS STRONG! WITH ALL THOSE STORIES ABOUT HER FATHER ABUSING NATHALIE SIMARD... WHAT KIND OF A MAN RAPES AN ELEVEN-YEAR-OLD? I HOPE HE ROTS IN JAIL. SERVES HIM RIGHT!
OH MY GOD! WOULD YOU LOOK AT THOSE DRESSES? AND ALL THE BIG NAMES ARE THERE, TOO!
SURE HAS BEEN HUMID, HASN'T IT? GOOD THING I'VE GOT AIR CONDITIONING. THE HEAT JUST KILLS ME.
HOW'S THE SCAR HEALING? DOES IT HURT LESS?
THE SCAR IS FINE, BUT I'VE GOT A LITTLE ACHE RIGHT HERE... I CAN'T IMAGINE WHAT IT IS...
I'M SURE IT'S NORMAL. THESE THINGS TAKE TIME TO HEAL...
YEAH, I SUPPOSE. IT'LL GO AWAY...
HAVE YOU THOUGHT OF TRYING TO GET OUT? THERE'S A THEATRE OUTING COMING UP—I JUST SAW THE POSTER...
NO THANK YOU! THAT'S FOR THE GEEZERS. NOT INTERESTED!
BUT...

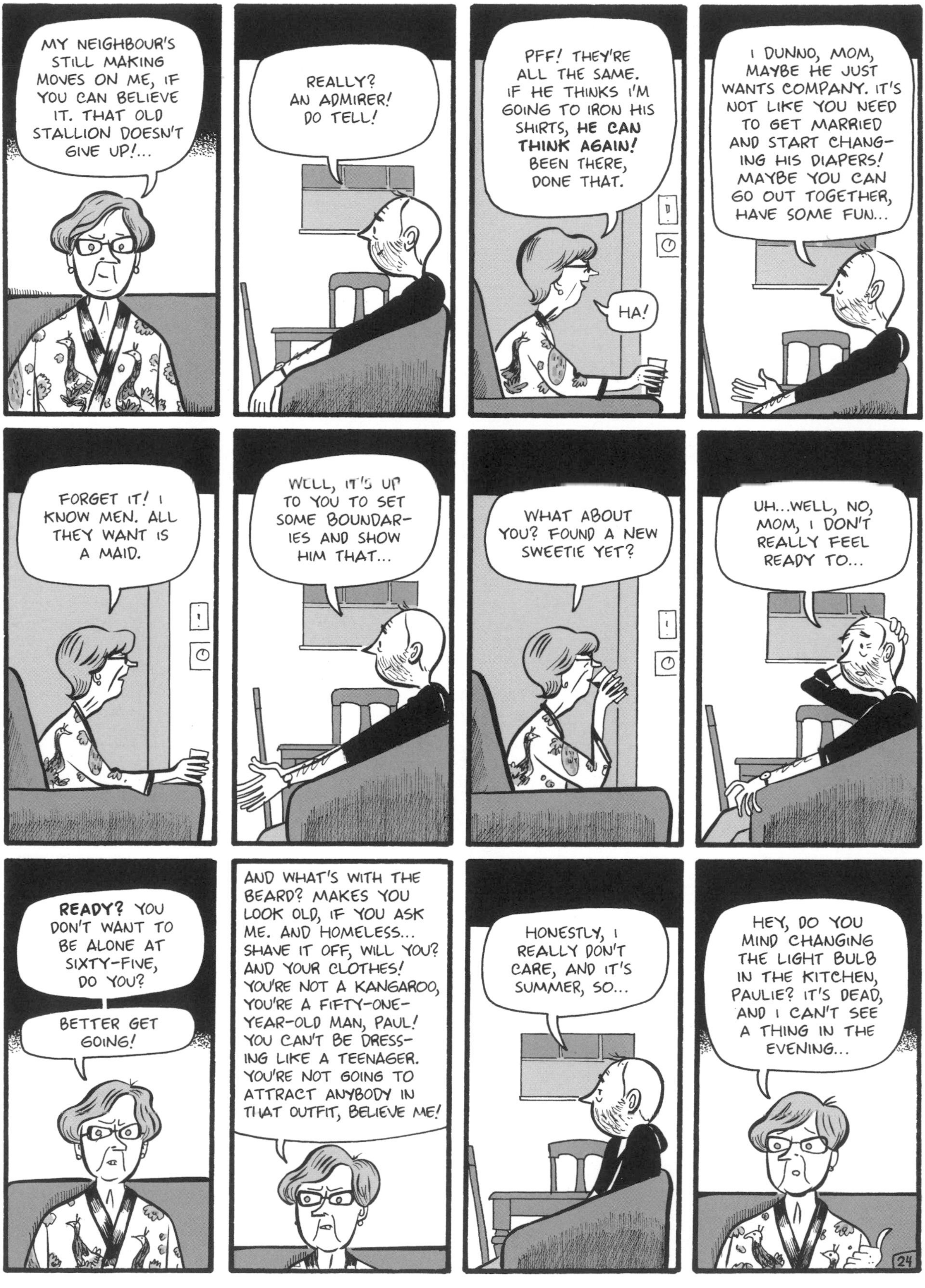
MY NEIGHBOUR'S STILL MAKING MOVES ON ME, IF YOU CAN BELIEVE IT. THAT OLD STALLION DOESN'T GIVE UP!...
REALLY? AN ADMIRER! DO TELL!
PFF! THEY'RE ALL THE SAME. IF HE THINKS I'M GOING TO IRON HIS SHIRTS, **HE CAN THINK AGAIN!** BEEN THERE, DONE THAT.
HA!
I DUNNO, MOM, MAYBE HE JUST WANTS COMPANY. IT'S NOT LIKE YOU NEED TO GET MARRIED AND START CHANGING HIS DIAPERS! MAYBE YOU CAN GO OUT TOGETHER, HAVE SOME FUN...
FORGET IT! I KNOW MEN. ALL THEY WANT IS A MAID.
WELL, IT'S UP TO YOU TO SET SOME BOUNDARIES AND SHOW HIM THAT...
WHAT ABOUT YOU? FOUND A NEW SWEETIE YET?
UH...WELL, NO, MOM, I DON'T REALLY FEEL READY TO...
READY? YOU DON'T WANT TO BE ALONE AT SIXTY-FIVE, DO YOU?
BETTER GET GOING!
AND WHAT'S WITH THE BEARD? MAKES YOU LOOK OLD, IF YOU ASK ME. AND HOMELESS... SHAVE IT OFF, WILL YOU? AND YOUR CLOTHES! YOU'RE NOT A KANGAROO, YOU'RE A FIFTY-ONE-YEAR-OLD MAN, PAUL! YOU CAN'T BE DRESSING LIKE A TEENAGER. YOU'RE NOT GOING TO ATTRACT ANYBODY IN THAT OUTFIT, BELIEVE ME!
HONESTLY, I REALLY DON'T CARE, AND IT'S SUMMER, SO...
HEY, DO YOU MIND CHANGING THE LIGHT BULB IN THE KITCHEN, PAULIE? IT'S DEAD, AND I CAN'T SEE A THING IN THE EVENING...
24

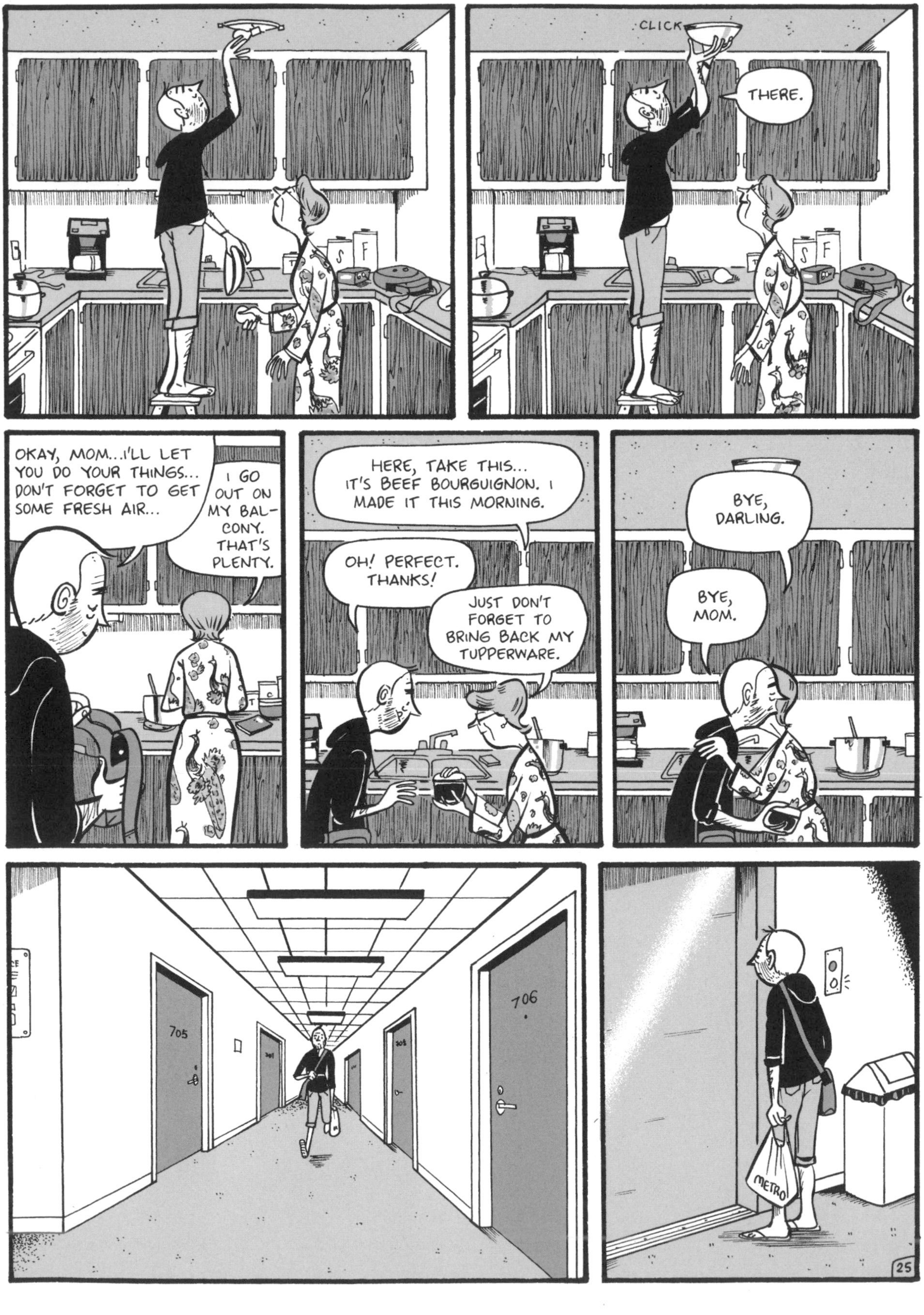
CLICK
THERE.
OKAY, MOM... I'LL LET YOU DO YOUR THINGS... DON'T FORGET TO GET SOME FRESH AIR...
I GO OUT ON MY BALCONY. THAT'S PLENTY.
HERE, TAKE THIS... IT'S BEEF BOURGUIGNON. I MADE IT THIS MORNING.
OH! PERFECT. THANKS!
JUST DON'T FORGET TO BRING BACK MY TUPPERWARE.
BYE, DARLING.
BYE, MOM.
705
706
METRO

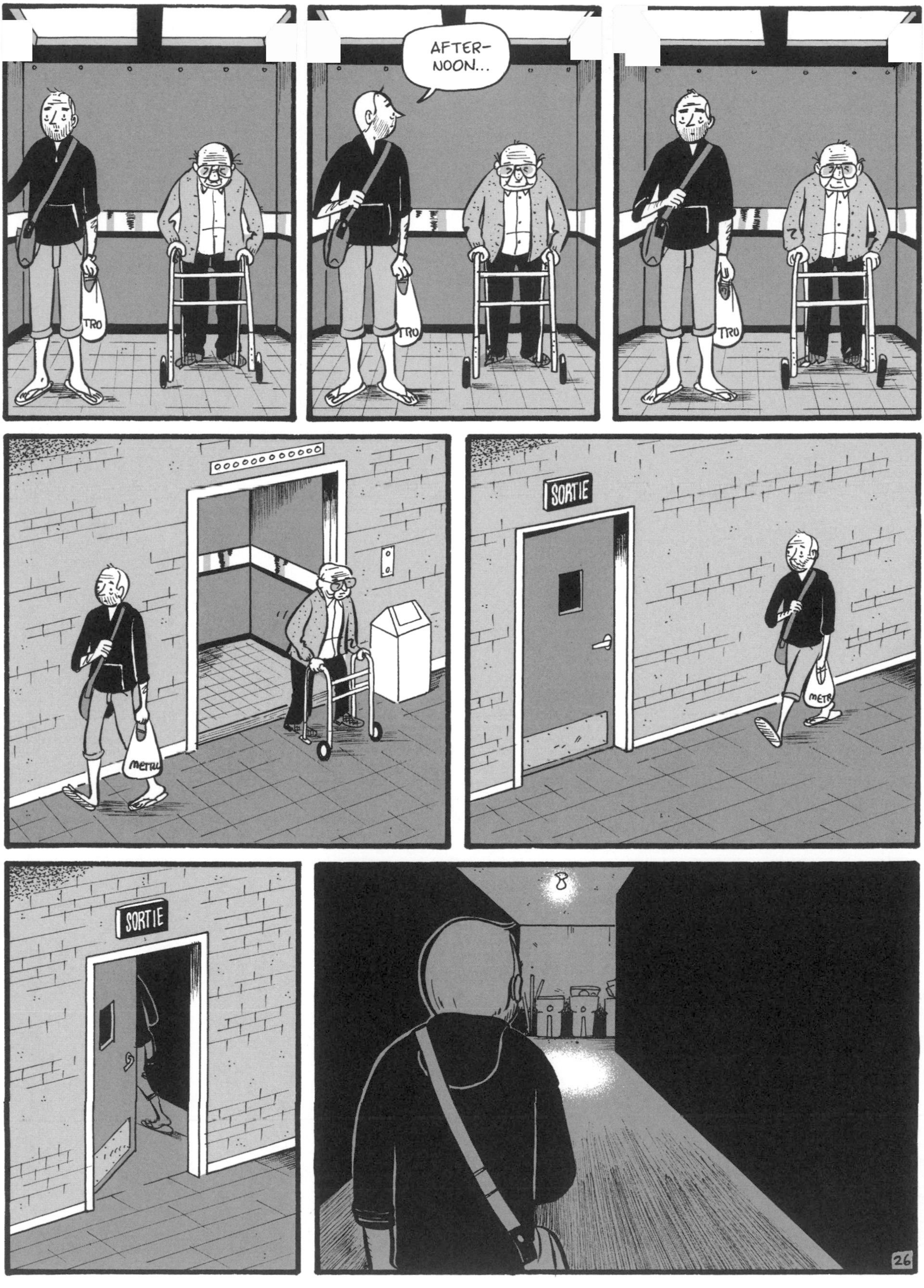
TRO
AFTER-
NOON...
TRO
TRO
METRU
SORTIE
METR
SORTIE

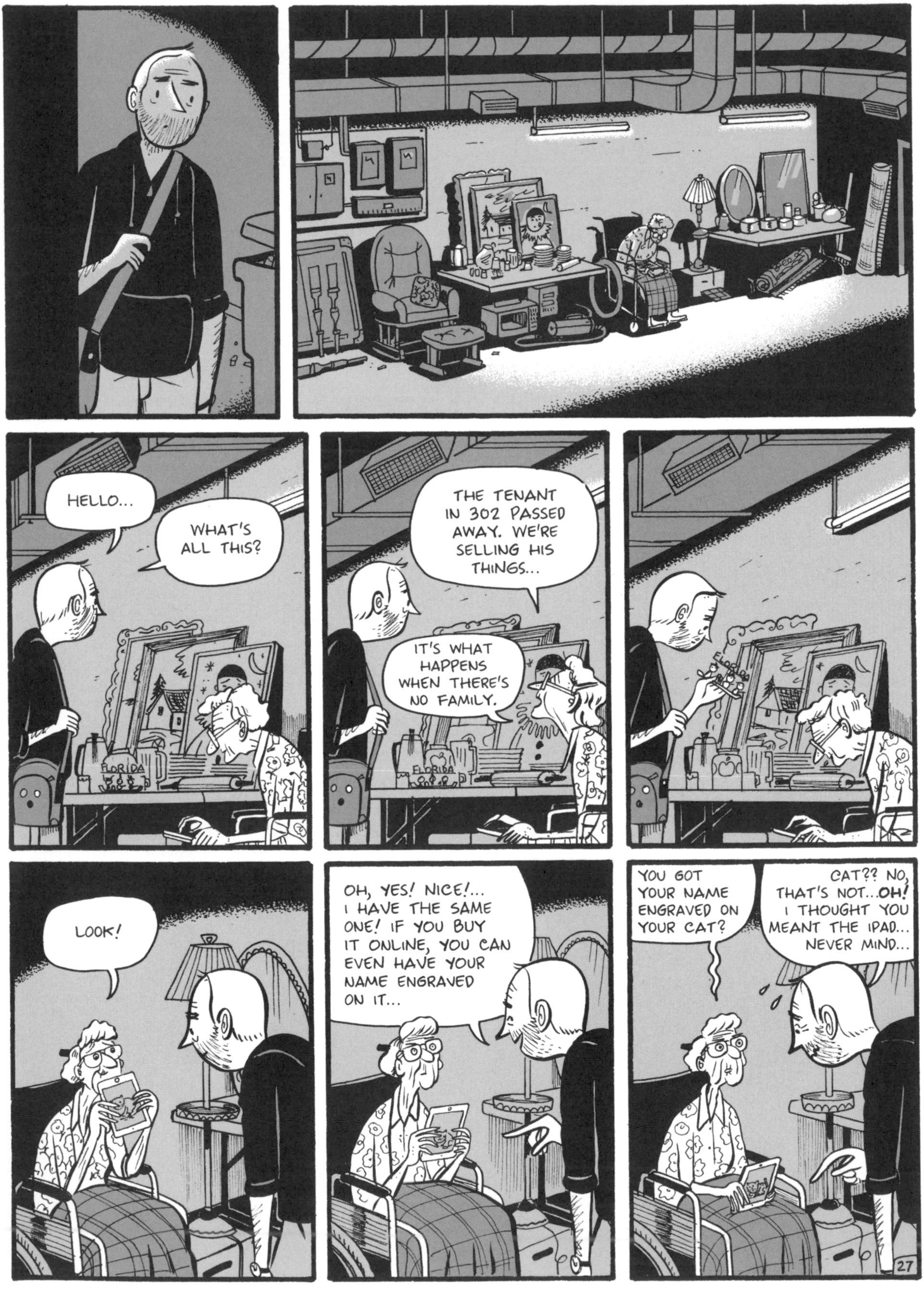

HELLO...
WHAT'S ALL THIS?
THE TENANT IN 302 PASSED AWAY. WE'RE SELLING HIS THINGS...
IT'S WHAT HAPPENS WHEN THERE'S NO FAMILY.
LOOK!
OH, YES! NICE!... I HAVE THE SAME ONE! IF YOU BUY IT ONLINE, YOU CAN EVEN HAVE YOUR NAME ENGRAVED ON IT...
YOU GOT YOUR NAME ENGRAVED ON YOUR CAT?
CAT?? NO, THAT'S NOT...**OH!** I THOUGHT YOU MEANT THE IPAD... NEVER MIND...

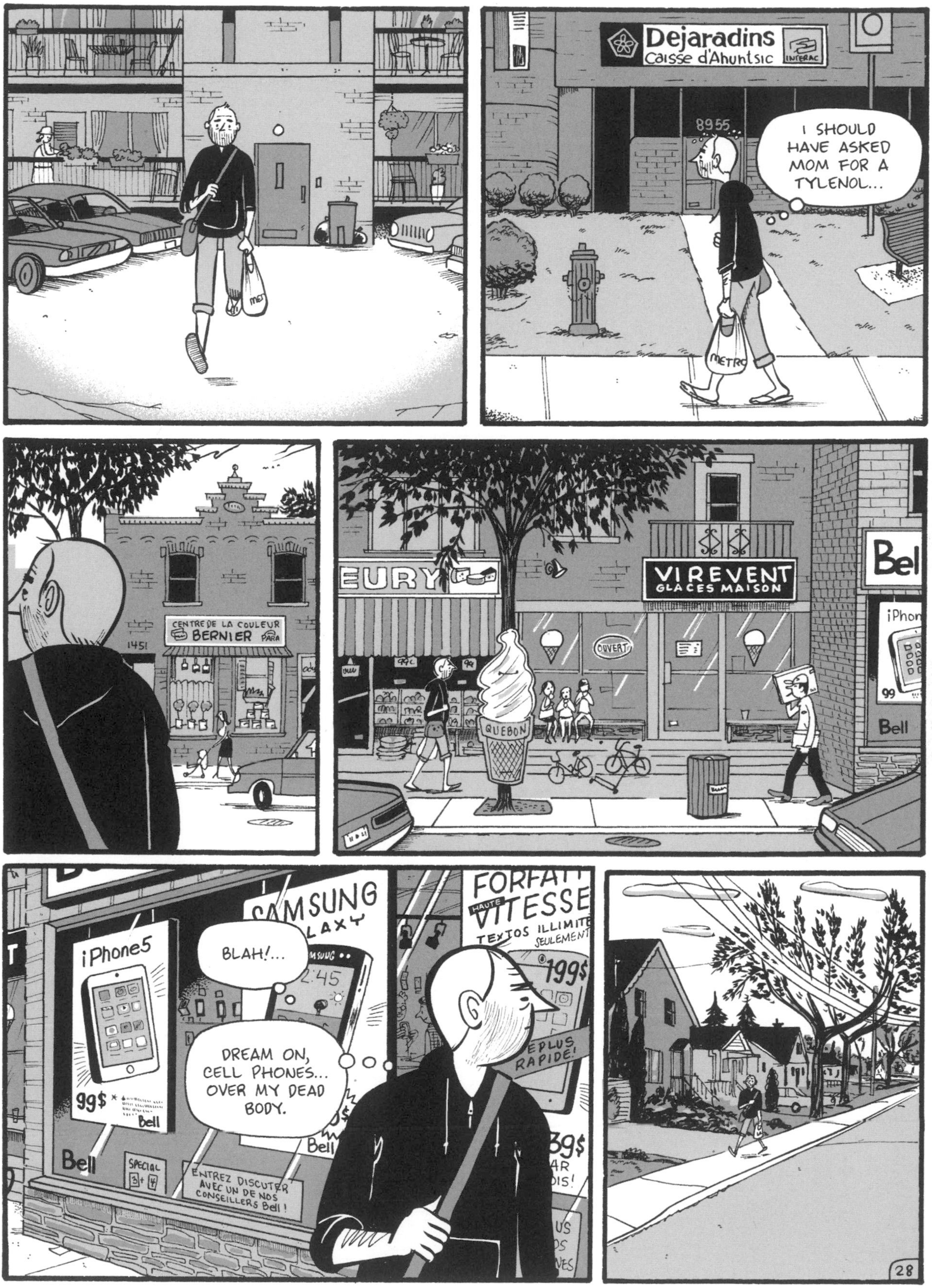
Dejaradins
Caisse d'Ahuntsic
INTERAC
8955
I SHOULD HAVE ASKED MOM FOR A TYLENOL...
METRO
CENTRE DE LA COULEUR
BERNIER
1451
VIREVENT
GLACES MAISON
OUVERT
QUEBON
iPhone5
99$
Bell
BLAH!...
DREAM ON, CELL PHONES... OVER MY DEAD BODY.
HAUTE
VITESSE
SEULEMENT
199$
SPECIAL
ENTREZ DISCUTER AVEC UN DE NOS CONSEILLERS Bell !

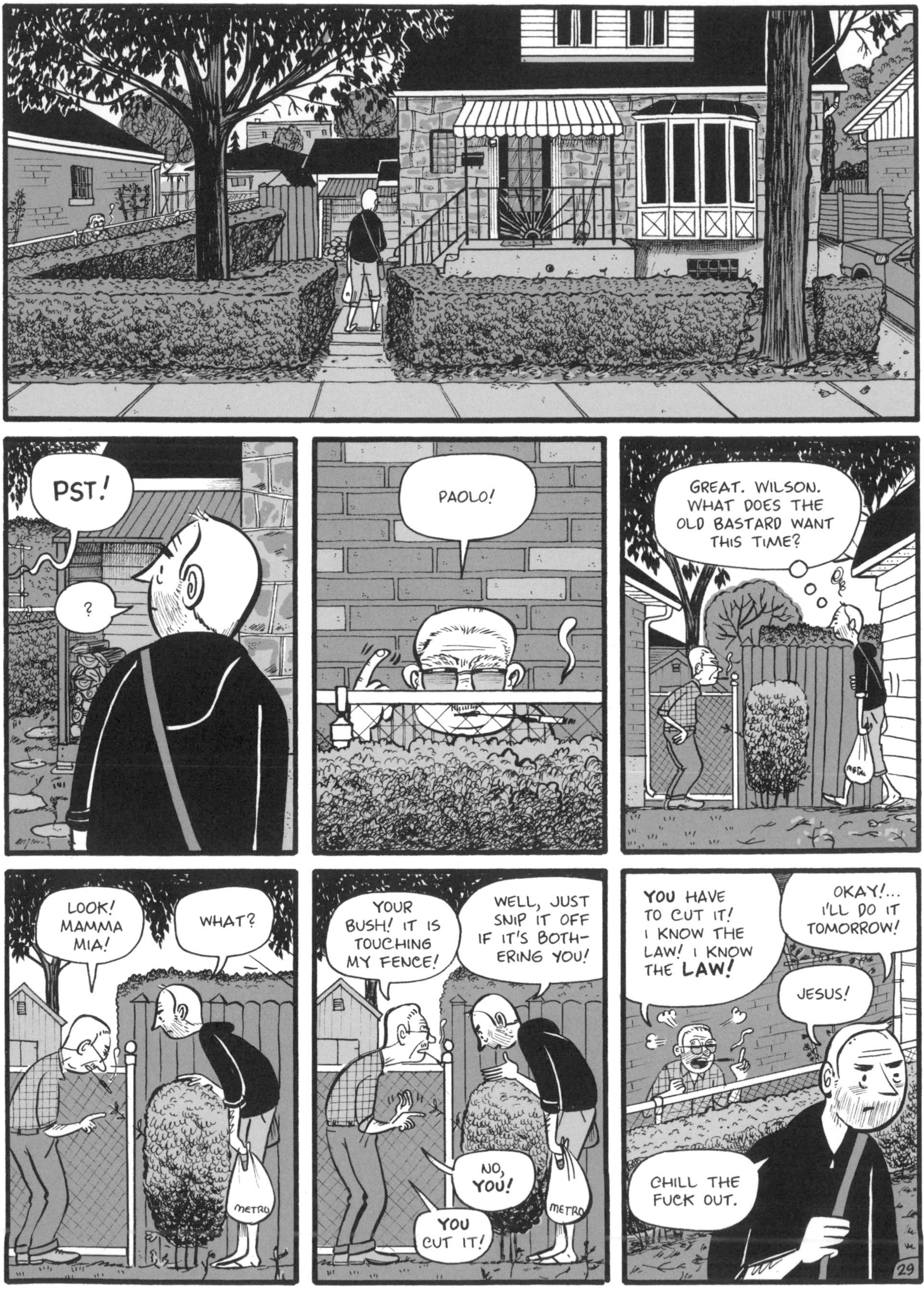
PST!
?
PAOLO!
GREAT. WILSON. WHAT DOES THE OLD BASTARD WANT THIS TIME?
LOOK! MAMMA MIA!
WHAT?
METRO
YOUR BUSH! IT IS TOUCHING MY FENCE!
WELL, JUST SNIP IT OFF IF IT'S BOTHERING YOU!
NO, YOU!
YOU CUT IT!
METRO
YOU HAVE TO CUT IT! I KNOW THE LAW! I KNOW THE LAW!
OKAY!... I'LL DO IT TOMORROW!
JESUS!
CHILL THE FUCK OUT.

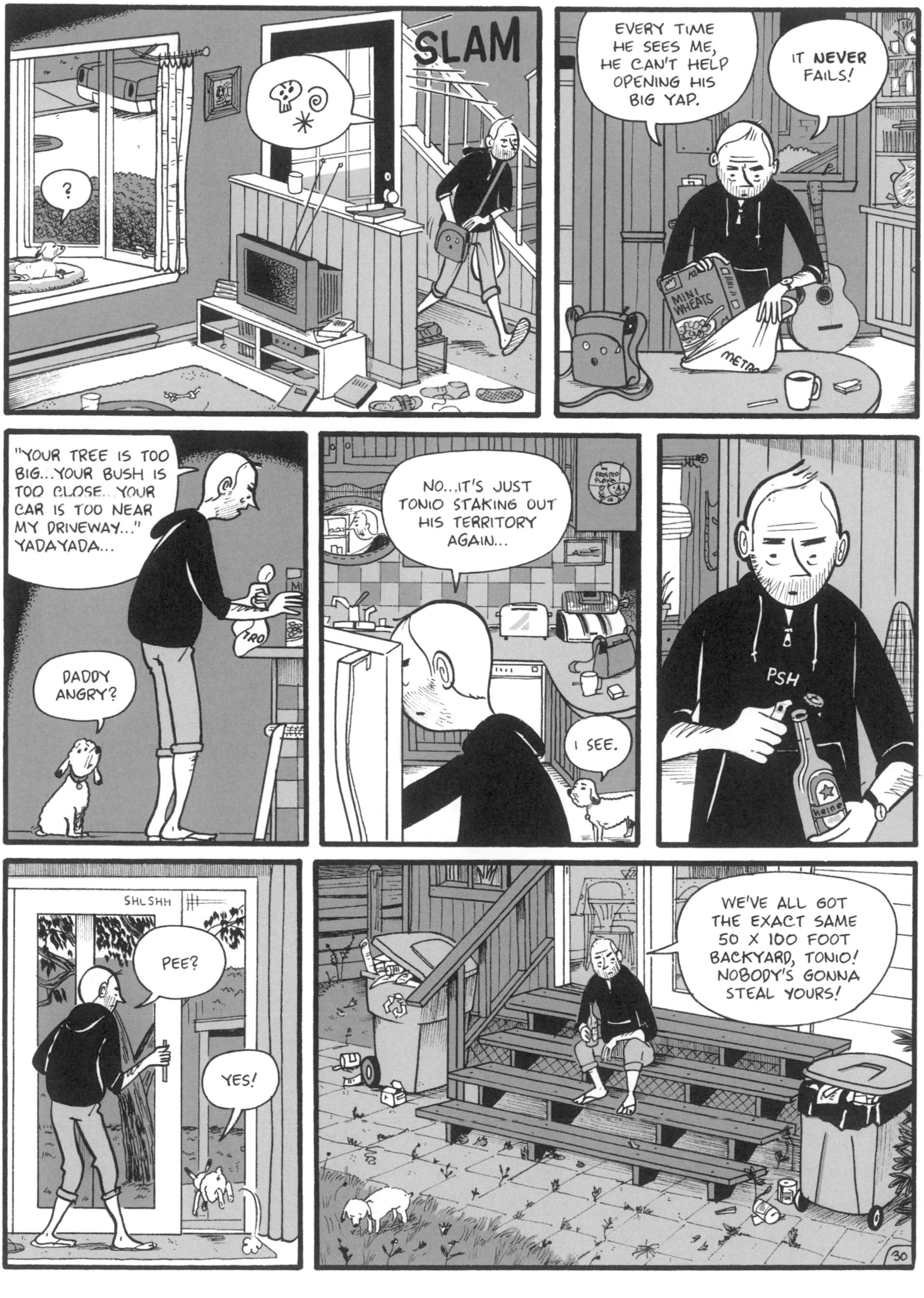

SLAM
?
EVERY TIME HE SEES ME, HE CAN'T HELP OPENING HIS BIG YAP.
IT **NEVER** FAILS!
MINI WHEATS
METRO
"YOUR TREE IS TOO BIG... YOUR BUSH IS TOO CLOSE... YOUR CAR IS TOO NEAR MY DRIVEWAY..." YADAYADA...
DADDY ANGRY?
NO... IT'S JUST TONIO STAKING OUT HIS TERRITORY AGAIN...
I SEE.
PSH
SHLSHH
PEE?
YES!
WE'VE ALL GOT THE EXACT SAME 50 X 100 FOOT BACKYARD, TONIO! NOBODY'S GONNA STEAL YOURS!

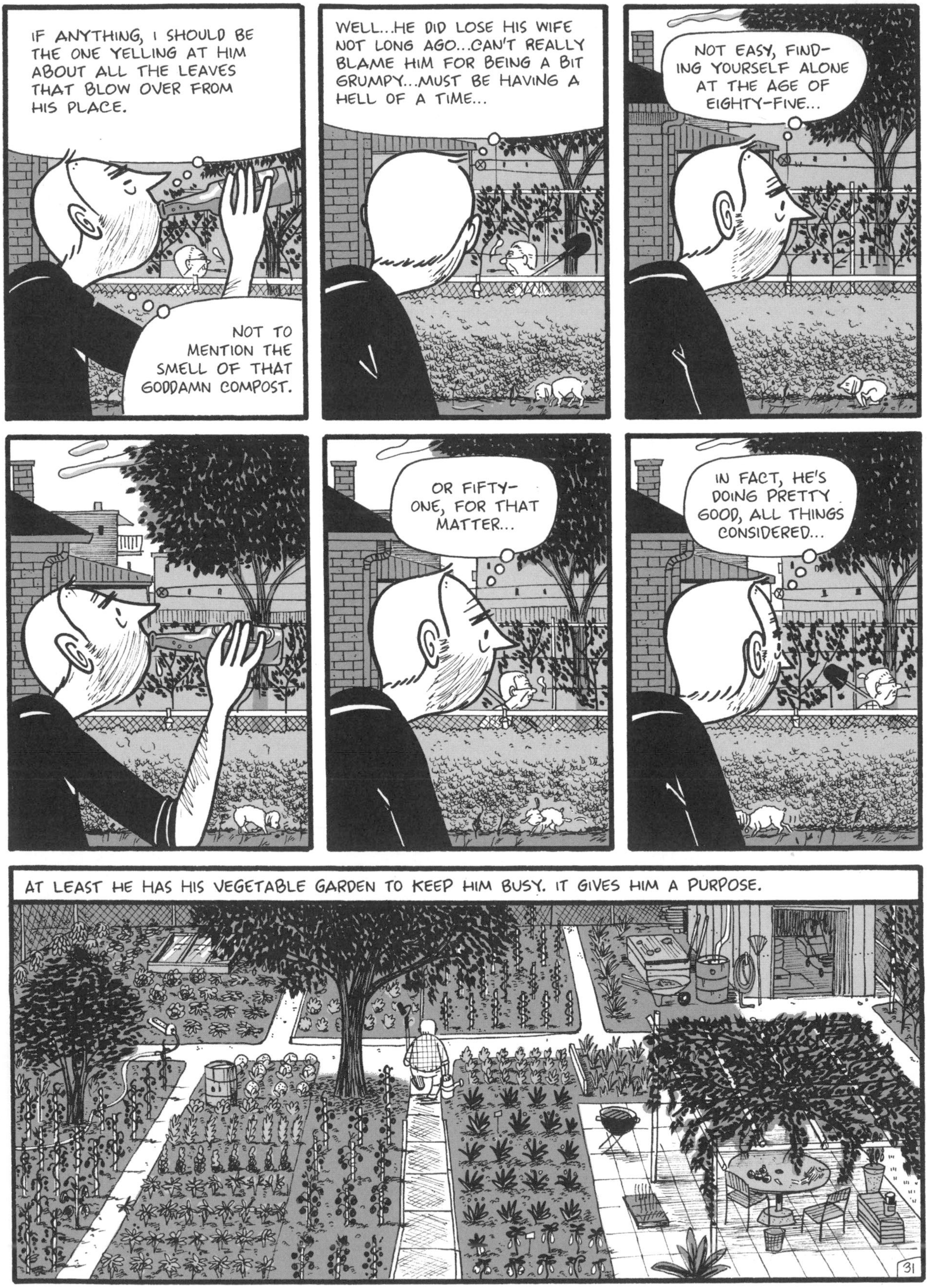

IF ANYTHING, I SHOULD BE THE ONE YELLING AT HIM ABOUT ALL THE LEAVES THAT BLOW OVER FROM HIS PLACE.
NOT TO MENTION THE SMELL OF THAT GODDAMN COMPOST.
WELL...HE DID LOSE HIS WIFE NOT LONG AGO...CAN'T REALLY BLAME HIM FOR BEING A BIT GRUMPY...MUST BE HAVING A HELL OF A TIME...
NOT EASY, FINDING YOURSELF ALONE AT THE AGE OF EIGHTY-FIVE...
OR FIFTY-ONE, FOR THAT MATTER...
IN FACT, HE'S DOING PRETTY GOOD, ALL THINGS CONSIDERED...
AT LEAST HE HAS HIS VEGETABLE GARDEN TO KEEP HIM BUSY. IT GIVES HIM A PURPOSE.

TONIO WAS BORN TO GROW VEGETABLES. HE HAS ALL THE ATTRIBUTES OF A SUPER-GARDENER:

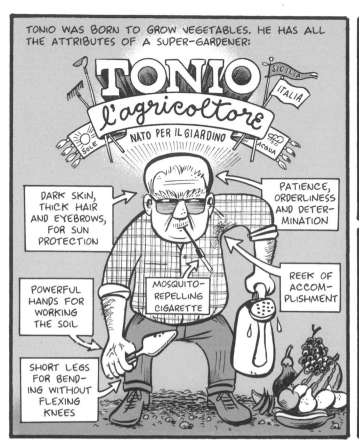

TONIO
l'agricoltore
NATO PER IL GIARDINO
SICILIA • ITALIA
SOLE • ACQUA

DARK SKIN, THICK HAIR AND EYEBROWS, FOR SUN PROTECTION

PATIENCE, ORDERLINESS AND DETERMINATION

POWERFUL HANDS FOR WORKING THE SOIL

MOSQUITO-REPELLING CIGARETTE

REEK OF ACCOMPLISHMENT

SHORT LEGS FOR BENDING WITHOUT FLEXING KNEES

EVERY SPRING IN MID-APRIL, TONIO SPREADS HIS OWN CAREFULLY CALIBRATED COMPOST OVER THE WHOLE GARDEN.

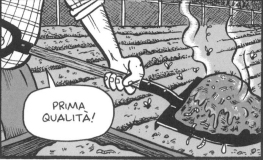

PRIMA QUALITÀ!

AND HE PLACES EACH PLANT (STARTED FROM SEED) IN THE OPTIMAL LOCATION.

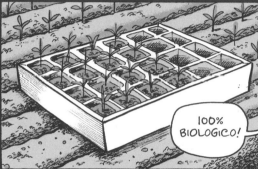

100% BIOLOGICO!

EVERY VARIETY IS PLANTED WITH CAREFUL CONSIDERATION FOR THE PREVAILING WINDS, THE ANGLE OF THE SUN, AND SOIL DRAINAGE.

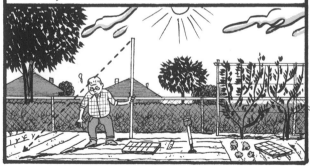

ONCE THE MASTER PLAN IS COMPLETE, HE'S ROOTED TO THAT BACKYARD.

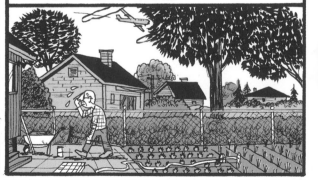

FROM HIS LOOKOUT, HE KEEPS WATCH OVER HIS VEGETABLE KINGDOM 24/7...

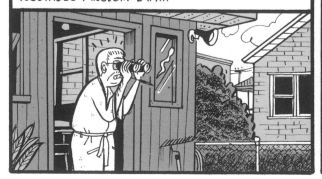

EXAMINING EVERY NEW LEAF, EVERY BUD, EVERY INSECT.

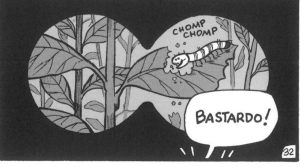

CHOMP CHOMP

BASTARDO!

32

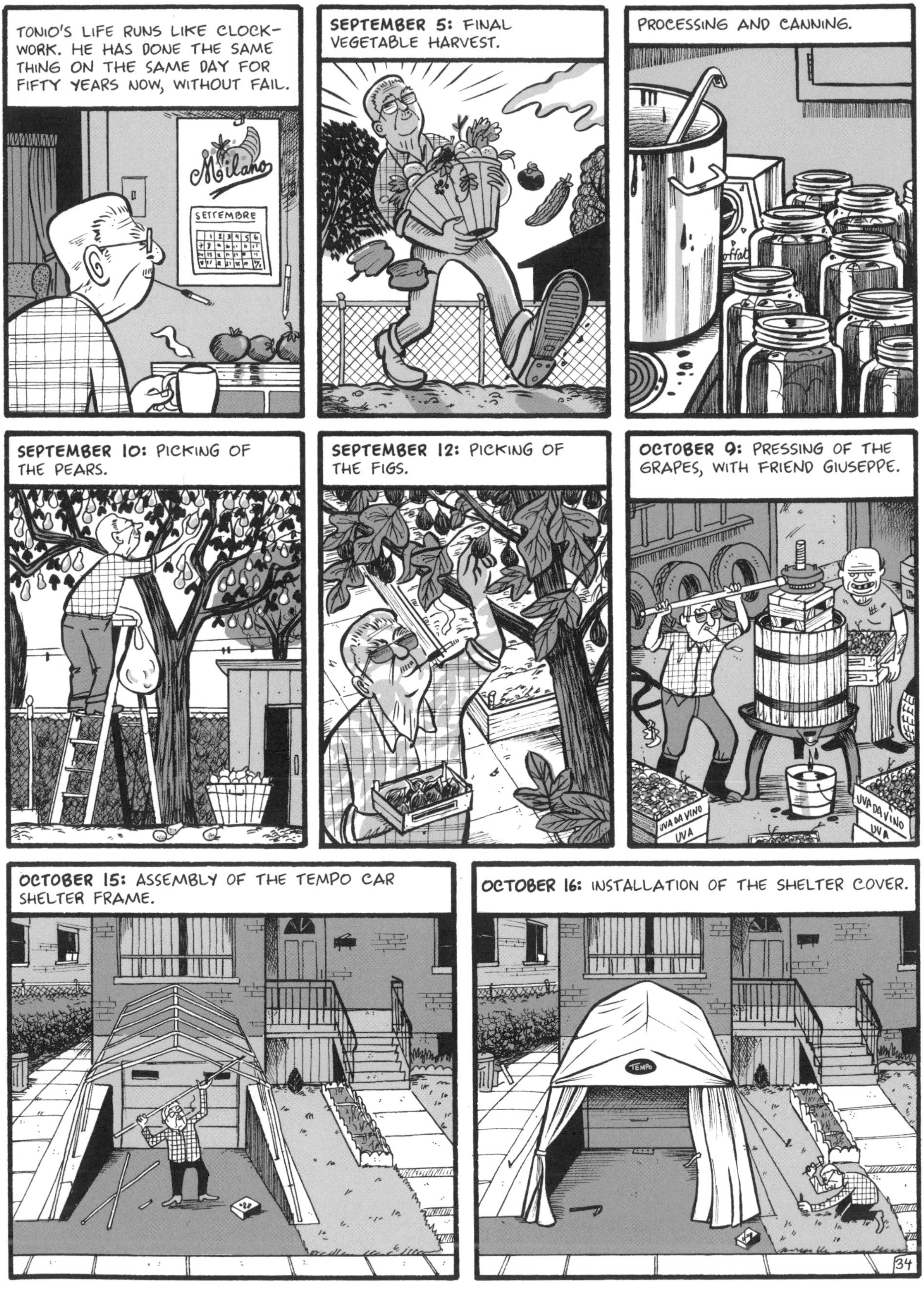
TONIO'S LIFE RUNS LIKE CLOCKWORK. HE HAS DONE THE SAME THING ON THE SAME DAY FOR FIFTY YEARS NOW, WITHOUT FAIL.
Milano
SETTEMBRE
SEPTEMBER 5: FINAL VEGETABLE HARVEST.
PROCESSING AND CANNING.
SEPTEMBER 10: PICKING OF THE PEARS.
SEPTEMBER 12: PICKING OF THE FIGS.
OCTOBER 9: PRESSING OF THE GRAPES, WITH FRIEND GIUSEPPE.
UVA DA VINO
UVA
UVA DA VINO
UVA
OCTOBER 15: ASSEMBLY OF THE TEMPO CAR SHELTER FRAME.
OCTOBER 16: INSTALLATION OF THE SHELTER COVER.
TEMPO

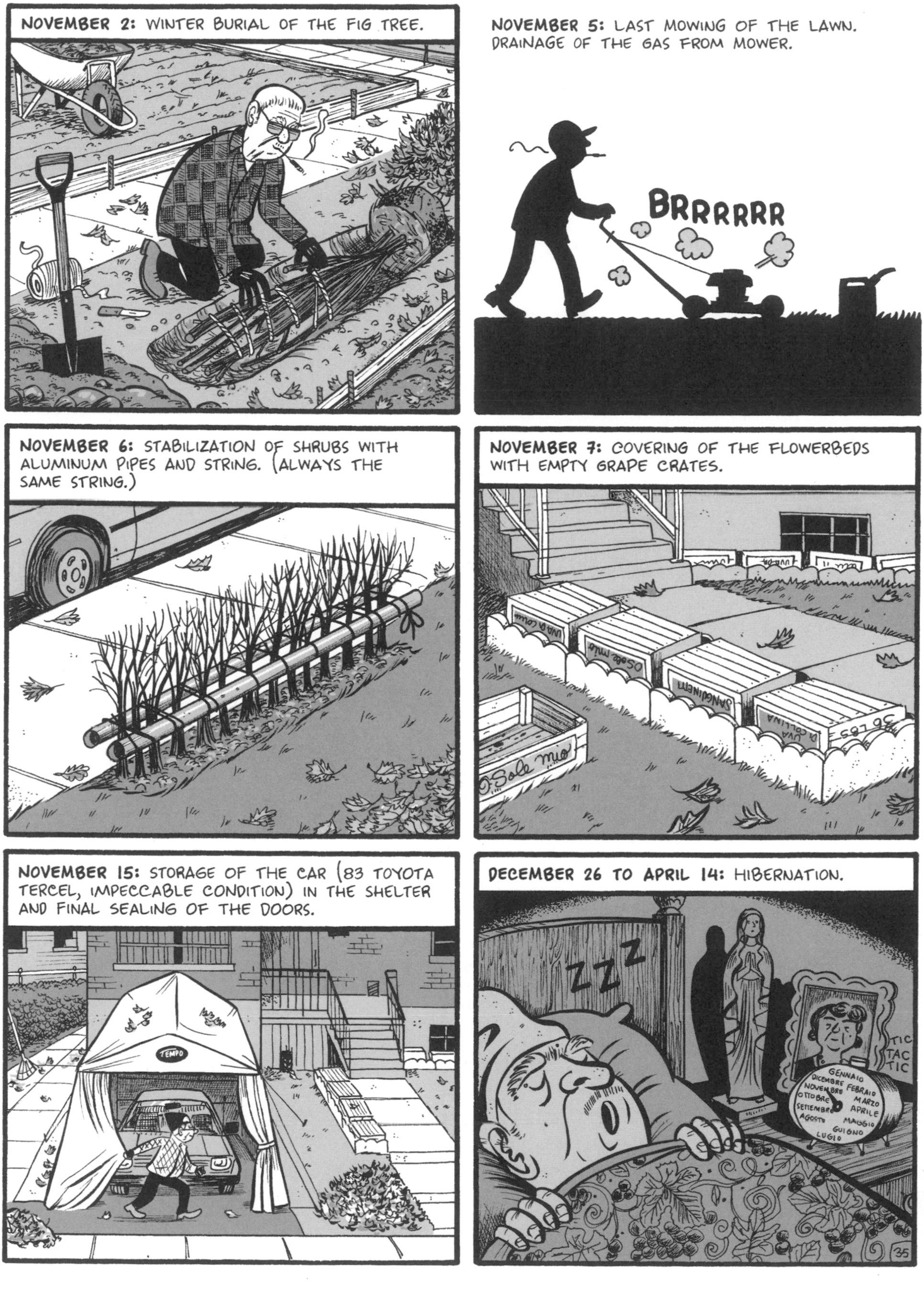
NOVEMBER 2: WINTER BURIAL OF THE FIG TREE.
NOVEMBER 5: LAST MOWING OF THE LAWN. DRAINAGE OF THE GAS FROM MOWER.
BRRRRRRR
NOVEMBER 6: STABILIZATION OF SHRUBS WITH ALUMINUM PIPES AND STRING. (ALWAYS THE SAME STRING.)
NOVEMBER 7: COVERING OF THE FLOWERBEDS WITH EMPTY GRAPE CRATES.
O Sole mio
NOVEMBER 15: STORAGE OF THE CAR (83 TOYOTA TERCEL, IMPECCABLE CONDITION) IN THE SHELTER AND FINAL SEALING OF THE DOORS.
TEMPO
DECEMBER 26 TO APRIL 14: HIBERNATION.
ZZZ
TIC TAC TIC
GENNAIO FEBRAIO MARZO APRILE MAGGIO GUIGNO LUGLO AGOSTO SETTEMBRE OTTOBRE NOVEMBRE DICEMBRE

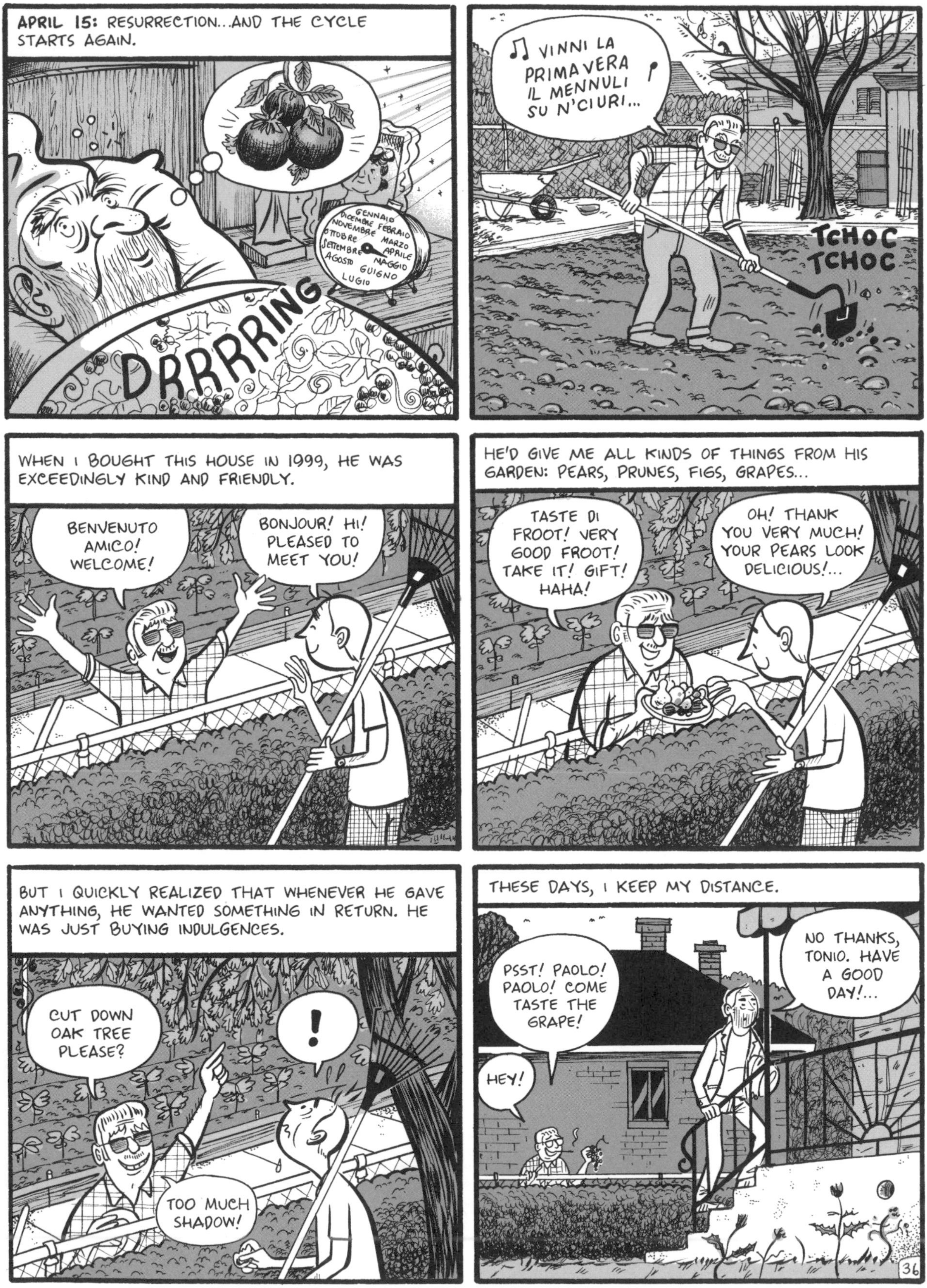
APRIL 15: RESURRECTION...AND THE CYCLE STARTS AGAIN.
GENNAIO DICEMBRE FEBRAIO NOVEMBRE MARZO OTTOBRE APRILE SETTEMBRE MAGGIO AGOSTO GUIGNO LUGIO
DRRRRING
♫ VINNI LA PRIMAVERA IL MENNULI SU N'CIURI...
TCHOC TCHOC
WHEN I BOUGHT THIS HOUSE IN 1999, HE WAS EXCEEDINGLY KIND AND FRIENDLY.
BENVENUTO AMICO! WELCOME!
BONJOUR! HI! PLEASED TO MEET YOU!
HE'D GIVE ME ALL KINDS OF THINGS FROM HIS GARDEN: PEARS, PRUNES, FIGS, GRAPES...
TASTE DI FROOT! VERY GOOD FROOT! TAKE IT! GIFT! HAHA!
OH! THANK YOU VERY MUCH! YOUR PEARS LOOK DELICIOUS!...
BUT I QUICKLY REALIZED THAT WHENEVER HE GAVE ANYTHING, HE WANTED SOMETHING IN RETURN. HE WAS JUST BUYING INDULGENCES.
CUT DOWN OAK TREE PLEASE?
!
TOO MUCH SHADOW!
THESE DAYS, I KEEP MY DISTANCE.
HEY!
PSST! PAOLO! PAOLO! COME TASTE THE GRAPE!
NO THANKS, TONIO. HAVE A GOOD DAY!...

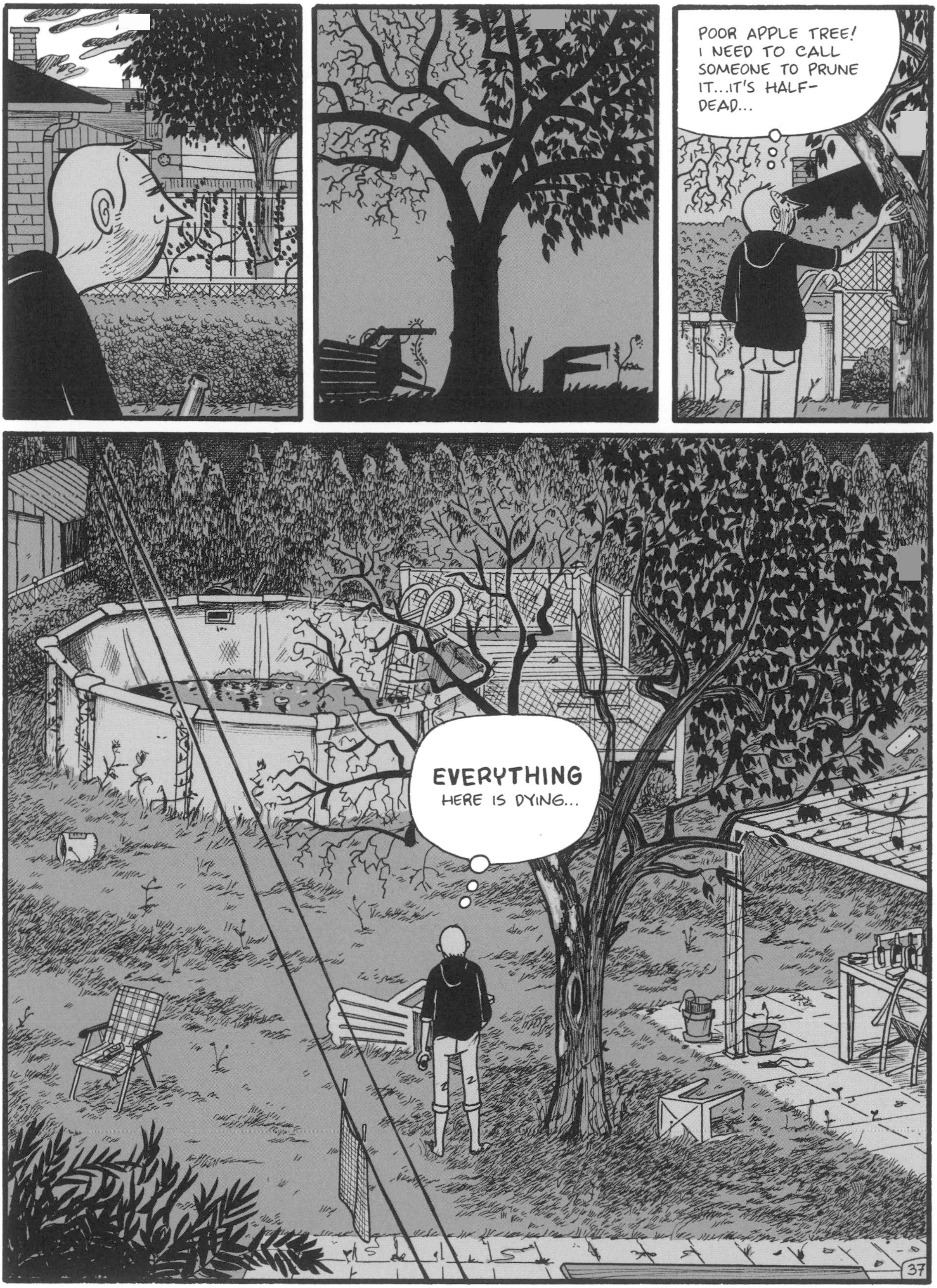
POOR APPLE TREE! I NEED TO CALL SOMEONE TO PRUNE IT...IT'S HALF-DEAD...
EVERYTHING HERE IS DYING...

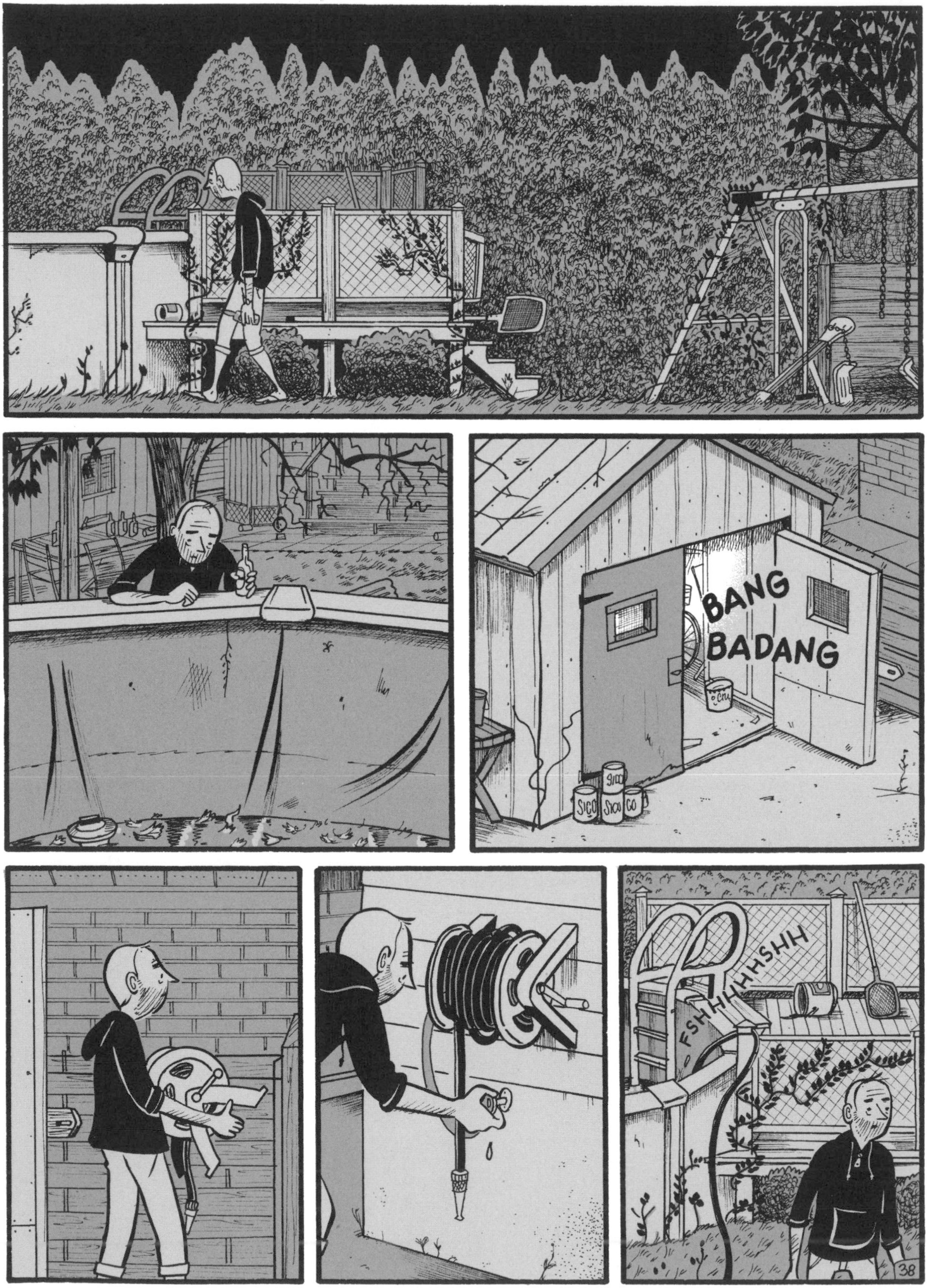
BANG
BADANG
SICO
FSHHHHHSHH

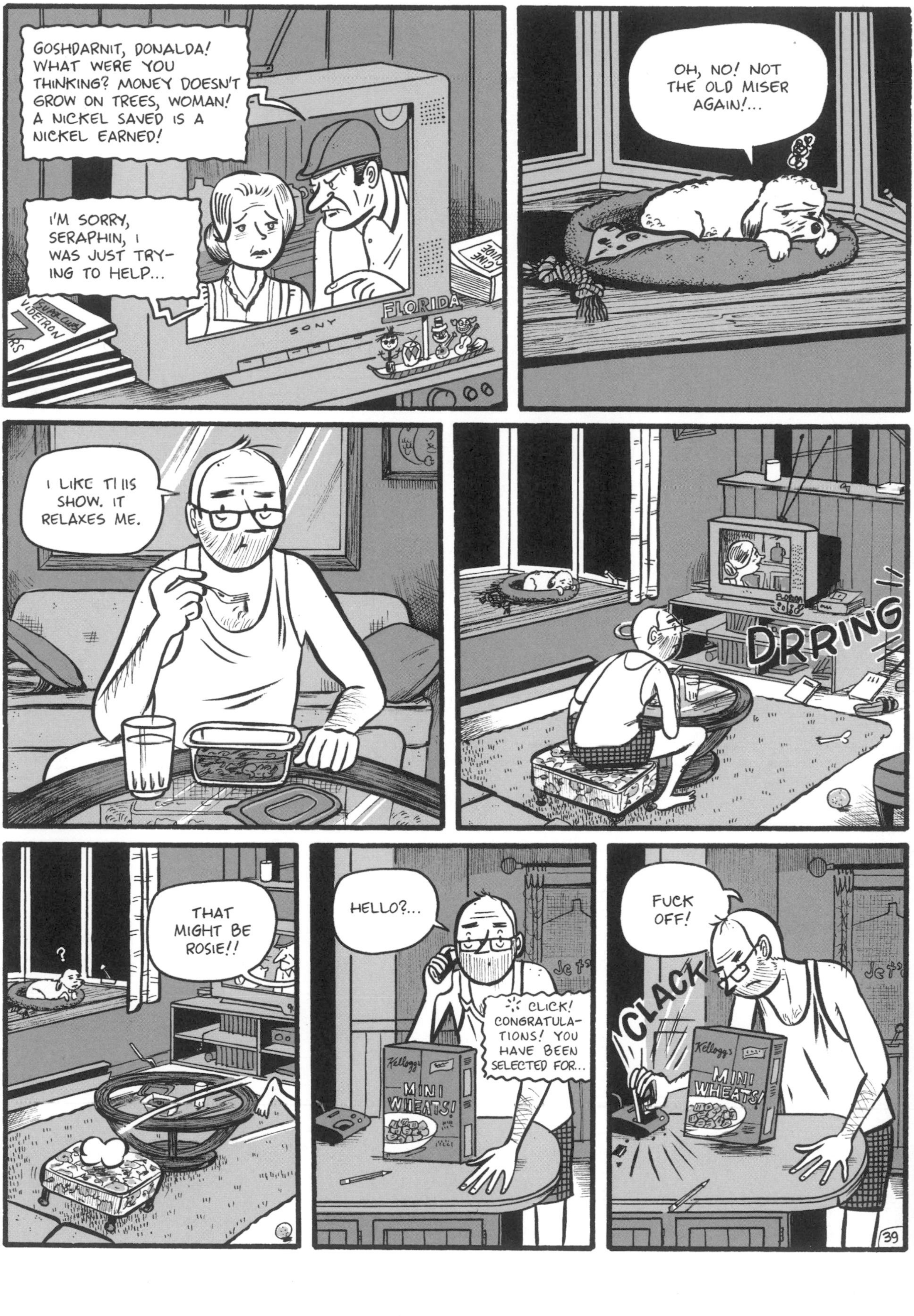
GOSHDARNIT, DONALDA! WHAT WERE YOU THINKING? MONEY DOESN'T GROW ON TREES, WOMAN! A NICKEL SAVED IS A NICKEL EARNED!
I'M SORRY, SERAPHIN, I WAS JUST TRY-ING TO HELP...
SONY
FLORIDA
OH, NO! NOT THE OLD MISER AGAIN!...
I LIKE THIS SHOW. IT RELAXES ME.
DRRING
THAT MIGHT BE ROSIE!!
HELLO?...
CLICK! CONGRATULA-TIONS! YOU HAVE BEEN SELECTED FOR...
Kellogg's
MINI WHEATS!
FUCK OFF!
CLACK

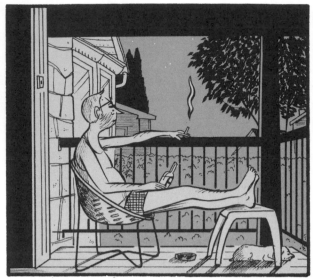

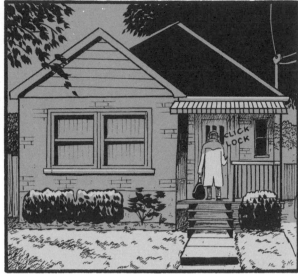

"MISTER STOGIE." THE GUY ACROSS THE STREET. ABOUT SEVENTY YEARS OLD. WEARS A WIG AND LIVES ALONE.

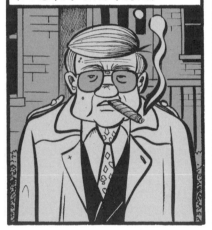

I DON'T KNOW HIS NAME. HE'S NEVER SPOKEN TO ME.

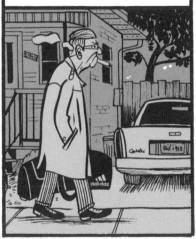

EVERY EVENING AT 9 PM, HE STEPS OUT WITH A BIG BLACK SPORTS BAG, GETS INTO HIS CADILLAC, AND DOESN'T REAPPEAR UNTIL TWO IN THE MORNING.

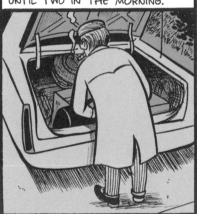

WHAT THE HELL DOES HE DO ALL NIGHT?

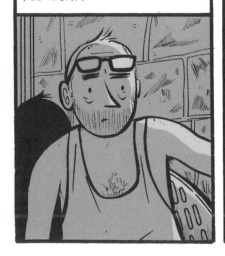

RUN DRUGS? WEAPONS? PROSTITUTES? WHO KNOWS...

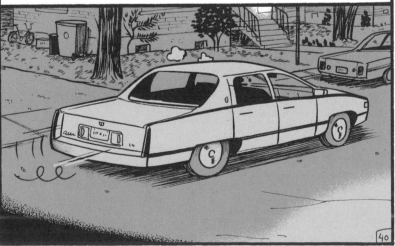

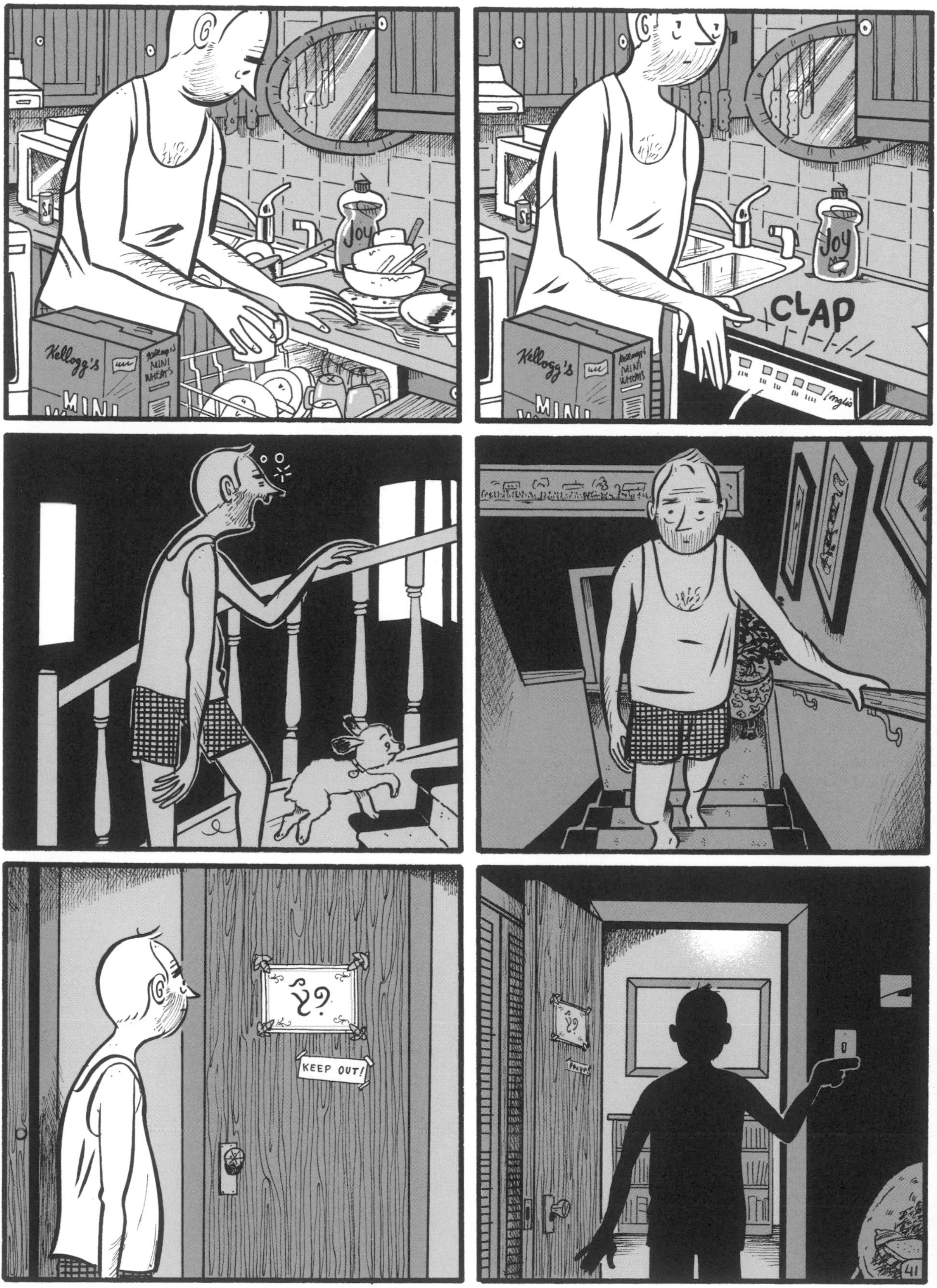
Kellogg's
MINI WHEATS
JOY
CLAP
¿?
KEEP OUT!

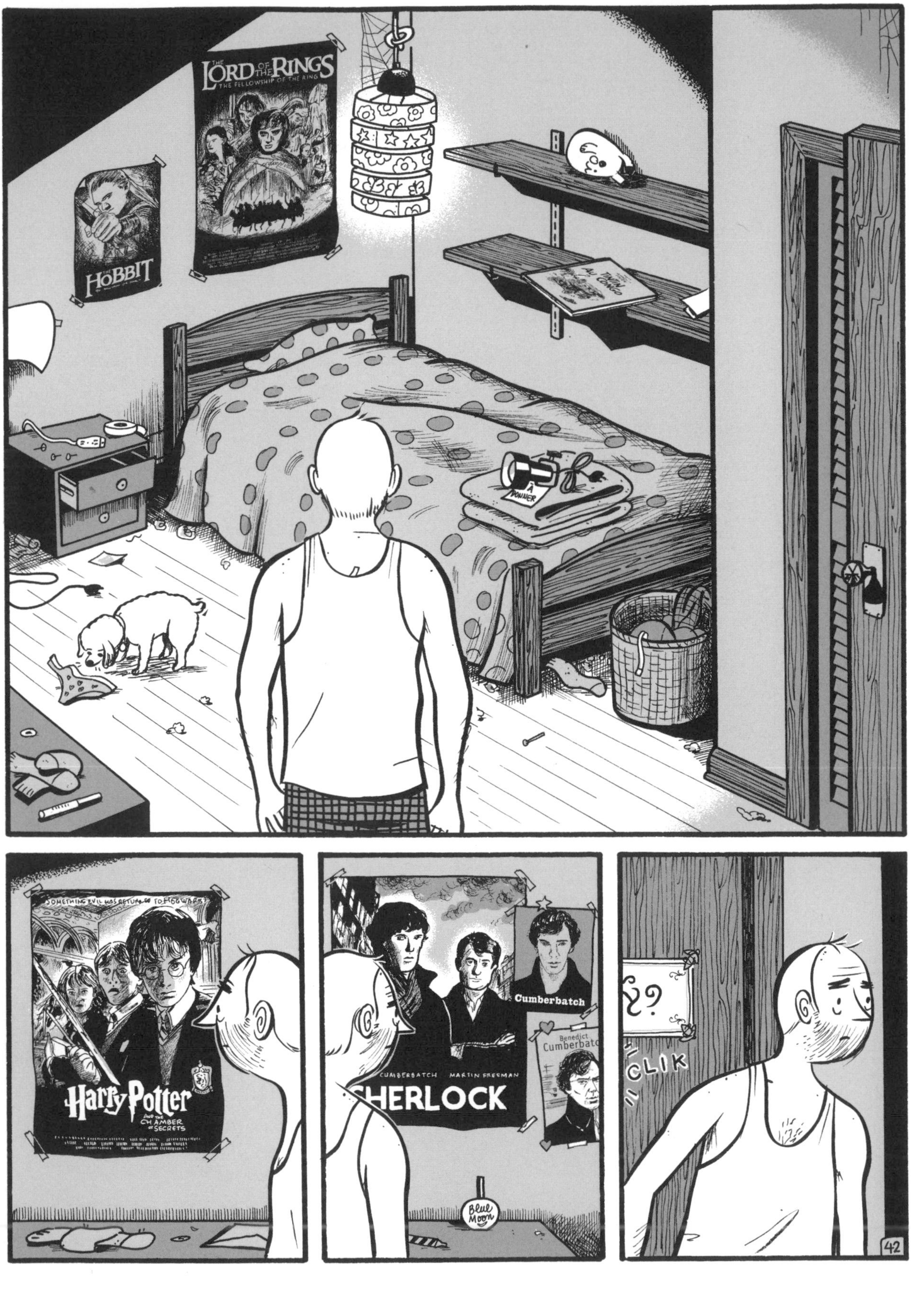
THE LORD OF THE RINGS
THE FELLOWSHIP OF THE RING
THE HOBBIT
TINTIN AU CONGO
À DONNER
SOMETHING EVIL HAS RETURNED TO HOGWARTS
Harry Potter and the CHAMBER of SECRETS
CUMBERBATCH MARTIN FREEMAN
HERLOCK
Cumberbatch
Benedict Cumberbatc
Blue Moon
?
CLIK

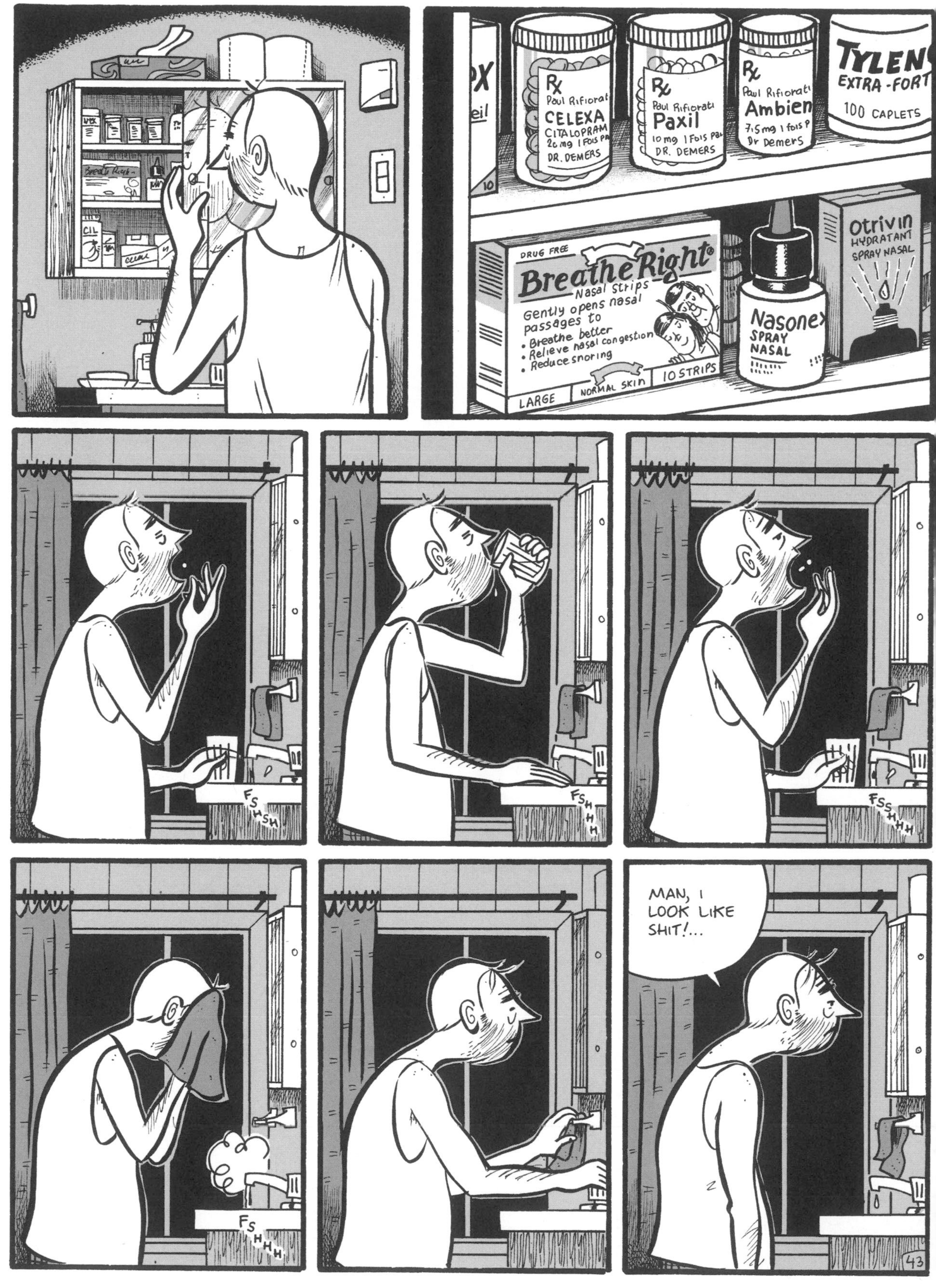
Rx
Paul Rifiorati
CELEXA
CITALOPRAM
20 mg 1 Fois Pa
DR. DEMERS
Rx
Paul Rifiorati
Paxil
10 mg 1 Fois Pa
DR. DEMERS
Rx
Paul Rifiorati
Ambien
7,5 mg 1 Fois P
Dr Demers
TYLEN
EXTRA-FORT
100 CAPLETS
DRUG FREE
Breathe Right®
Nasal Strips
Gently opens nasal passages to
• Breathe better
• Relieve nasal congestion
• Reduce snoring
LARGE
NORMAL SKIN
10 STRIPS
Nasonex
SPRAY
NASAL
Otrivin
HYDRATANT
SPRAY NASAL
FSHSH
FSHHH
FSSHHH
FSHHH
MAN, I LOOK LIKE SHIT!...

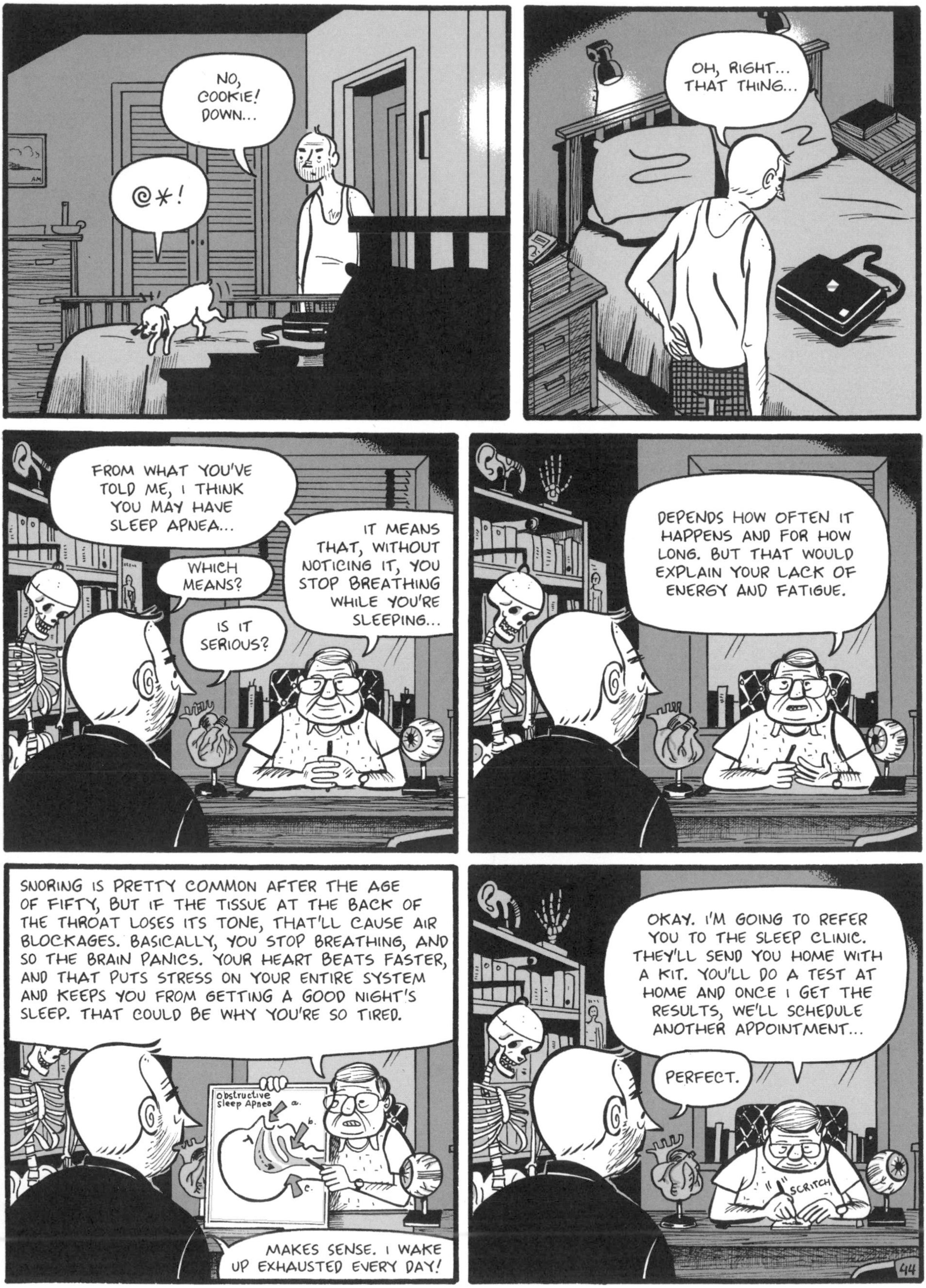
NO, COOKIE! DOWN...
@*!
OH, RIGHT... THAT THING...
FROM WHAT YOU'VE TOLD ME, I THINK YOU MAY HAVE SLEEP APNEA...
WHICH MEANS?
IT MEANS THAT, WITHOUT NOTICING IT, YOU STOP BREATHING WHILE YOU'RE SLEEPING...
IS IT SERIOUS?
DEPENDS HOW OFTEN IT HAPPENS AND FOR HOW LONG. BUT THAT WOULD EXPLAIN YOUR LACK OF ENERGY AND FATIGUE.
SNORING IS PRETTY COMMON AFTER THE AGE OF FIFTY, BUT IF THE TISSUE AT THE BACK OF THE THROAT LOSES ITS TONE, THAT'LL CAUSE AIR BLOCKAGES. BASICALLY, YOU STOP BREATHING, AND SO THE BRAIN PANICS. YOUR HEART BEATS FASTER, AND THAT PUTS STRESS ON YOUR ENTIRE SYSTEM AND KEEPS YOU FROM GETTING A GOOD NIGHT'S SLEEP. THAT COULD BE WHY YOU'RE SO TIRED.
Obstructive Sleep Apnea
a.
b.
c.
MAKES SENSE. I WAKE UP EXHAUSTED EVERY DAY!
OKAY. I'M GOING TO REFER YOU TO THE SLEEP CLINIC. THEY'LL SEND YOU HOME WITH A KIT. YOU'LL DO A TEST AT HOME AND ONCE I GET THE RESULTS, WE'LL SCHEDULE ANOTHER APPOINTMENT...
PERFECT.
SCRITCH

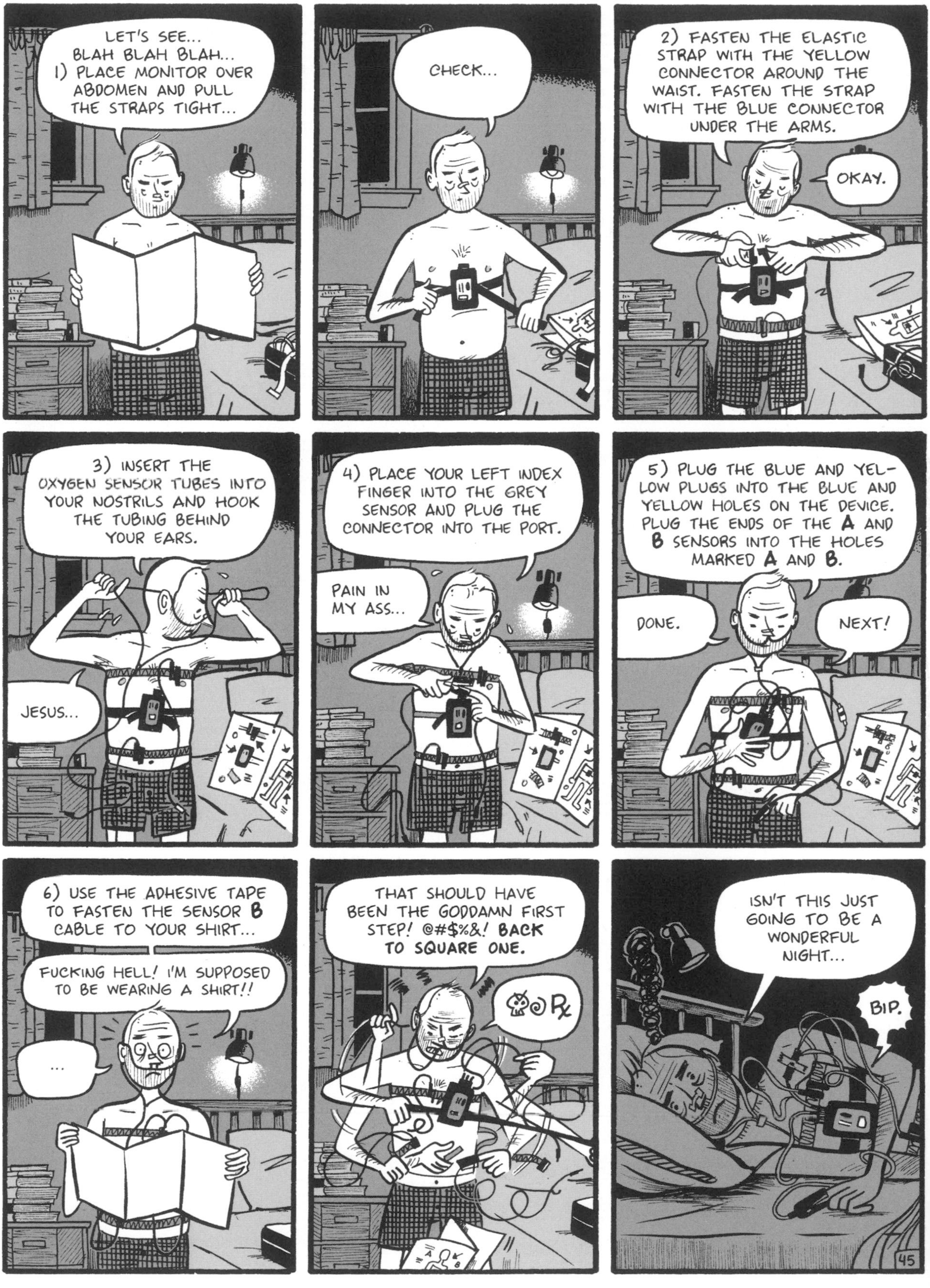
LET'S SEE... BLAH BLAH BLAH... 1) PLACE MONITOR OVER ABDOMEN AND PULL THE STRAPS TIGHT...
CHECK...
2) FASTEN THE ELASTIC STRAP WITH THE YELLOW CONNECTOR AROUND THE WAIST. FASTEN THE STRAP WITH THE BLUE CONNECTOR UNDER THE ARMS.
OKAY.
3) INSERT THE OXYGEN SENSOR TUBES INTO YOUR NOSTRILS AND HOOK THE TUBING BEHIND YOUR EARS.
JESUS...
4) PLACE YOUR LEFT INDEX FINGER INTO THE GREY SENSOR AND PLUG THE CONNECTOR INTO THE PORT.
PAIN IN MY ASS...
5) PLUG THE BLUE AND YEL-LOW PLUGS INTO THE BLUE AND YELLOW HOLES ON THE DEVICE. PLUG THE ENDS OF THE **A** AND **B** SENSORS INTO THE HOLES MARKED **A** AND **B**.
DONE.
NEXT!
6) USE THE ADHESIVE TAPE TO FASTEN THE SENSOR **B** CABLE TO YOUR SHIRT...
FUCKING HELL! I'M SUPPOSED TO BE WEARING A SHIRT!!
...
THAT SHOULD HAVE BEEN THE GODDAMN FIRST STEP! @#$%&! **BACK TO SQUARE ONE.**
ISN'T THIS JUST GOING TO BE A WONDERFUL NIGHT...
BIP.

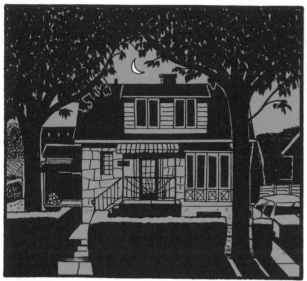

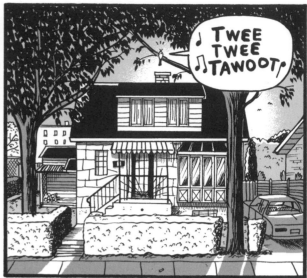

♪ TWEE TWEE ♪ TAWOOT ♪

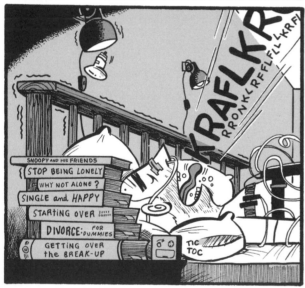

KRAFLKR RRONKLRFFLFLL·KRF

SNOOPY AND HIS FRIENDS
STOP BEING LONELY
WHY NOT ALONE?
SINGLE and HAPPY
STARTING OVER !!!!!
DIVORCE: FOR DUMMIES
GETTING OVER the BREAK-UP

TIC TOC

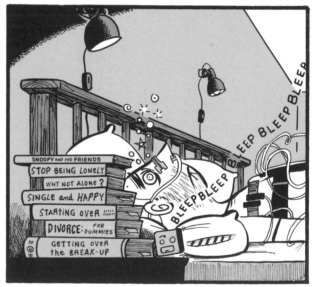

SNOOPY AND HIS FRIENDS
STOP BEING LONELY
WHY NOT ALONE?
SINGLE and HAPPY
STARTING OVER !!!!!
DIVORCE: FOR DUMMIES
GETTING OVER the BREAK-UP

BLEEP BLEEP BLEEP BLEEP BLEEP

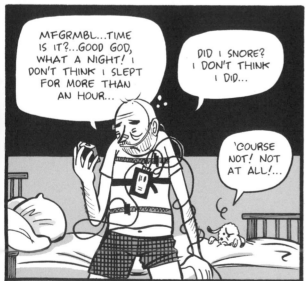

MFGRMBL...TIME IS IT?...GOOD GOD, WHAT A NIGHT! I DON'T THINK I SLEPT FOR MORE THAN AN HOUR...

DID I SNORE? I DON'T THINK I DID...

'COURSE NOT! NOT AT ALL!...

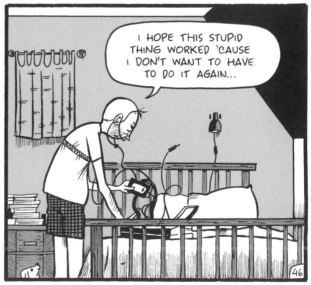

I HOPE THIS STUPID THING WORKED 'CAUSE I DON'T WANT TO HAVE TO DO IT AGAIN...

46

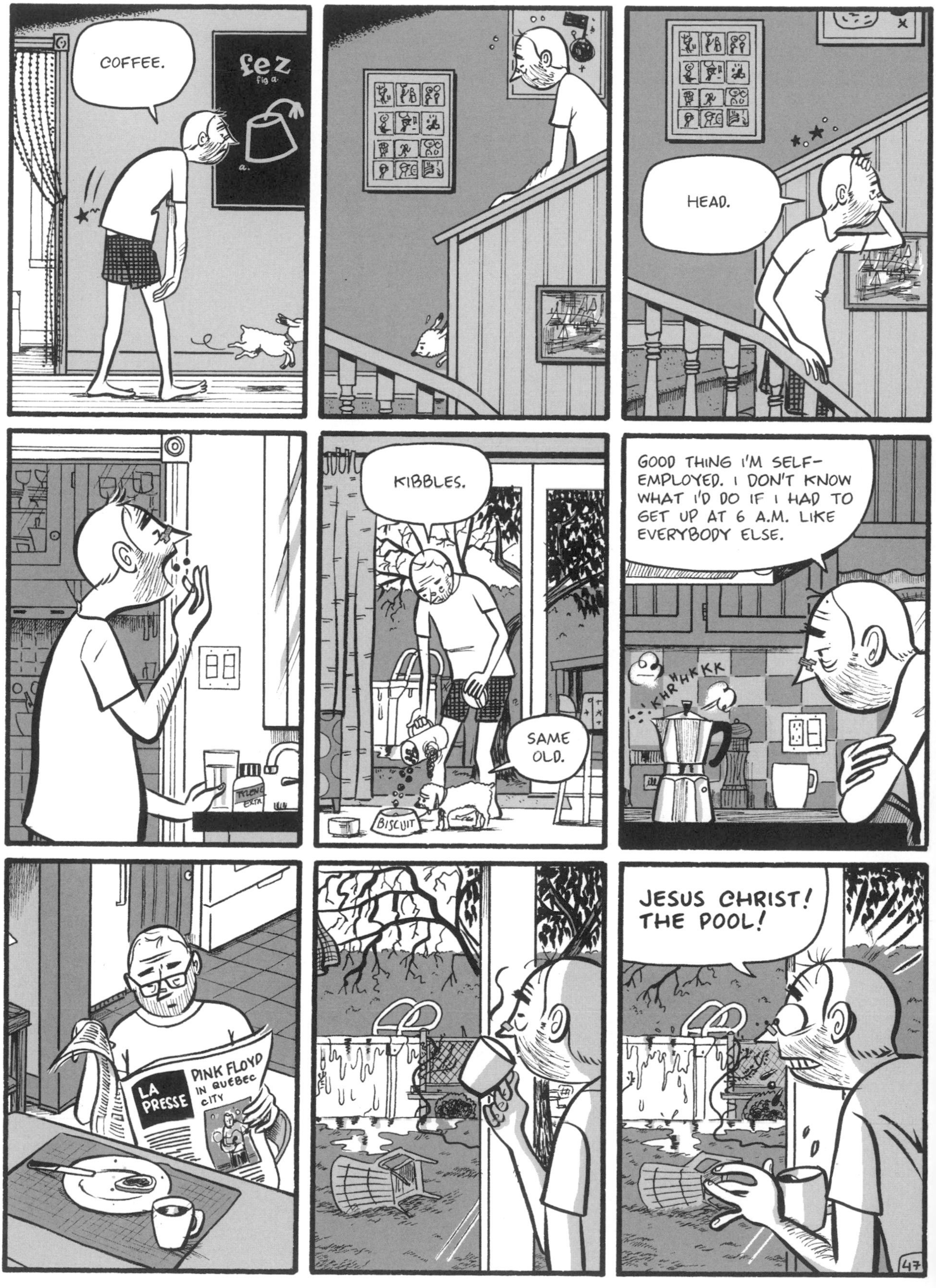
COFFEE.
fez
fig a.
a.
HEAD.
KIBBLES.
SAME OLD.
BISCUIT
GOOD THING I'M SELF-EMPLOYED. I DON'T KNOW WHAT I'D DO IF I HAD TO GET UP AT 6 A.M. LIKE EVERYBODY ELSE.
KHRHHKKK
LA PRESSE
PINK FLOYD IN QUEBEC CITY
JESUS CHRIST! THE POOL!

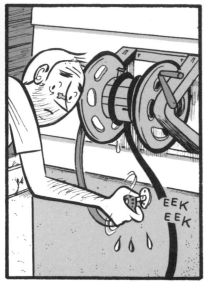

EEK EEK

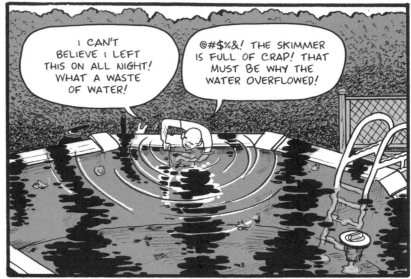

I CAN'T BELIEVE I LEFT THIS ON ALL NIGHT! WHAT A WASTE OF WATER!

@#$%&! THE SKIMMER IS FULL OF CRAP! THAT MUST BE WHY THE WATER OVERFLOWED!

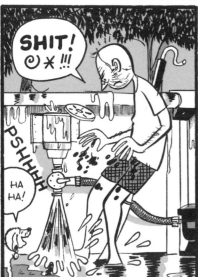

SHIT! ☺※!!!

PSHHH

HA HA!

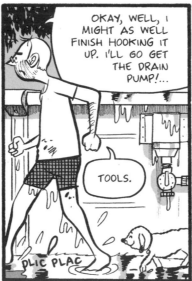

OKAY, WELL, I MIGHT AS WELL FINISH HOOKING IT UP. I'LL GO GET THE DRAIN PUMP!...

TOOLS.

PLIC PLAC

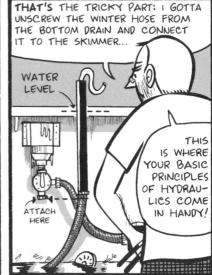

THAT'S THE TRICKY PART: I GOTTA UNSCREW THE WINTER HOSE FROM THE BOTTOM DRAIN AND CONNECT IT TO THE SKIMMER...

WATER LEVEL

ATTACH HERE

THIS IS WHERE YOUR BASIC PRINCIPLES OF HYDRAULICS COME IN HANDY!

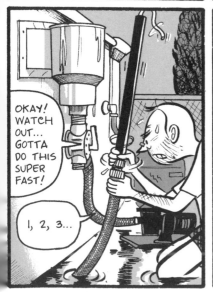

OKAY! WATCH OUT... GOTTA DO THIS SUPER FAST!

1, 2, 3...

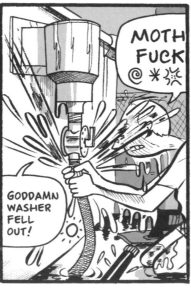

MOTH FUCK @※✸

GODDAMN WASHER FELL OUT!

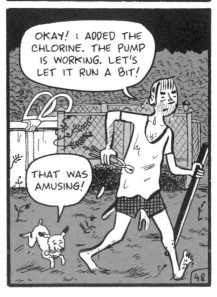

OKAY! I ADDED THE CHLORINE. THE PUMP IS WORKING. LET'S LET IT RUN A BIT!

THAT WAS AMUSING!

48

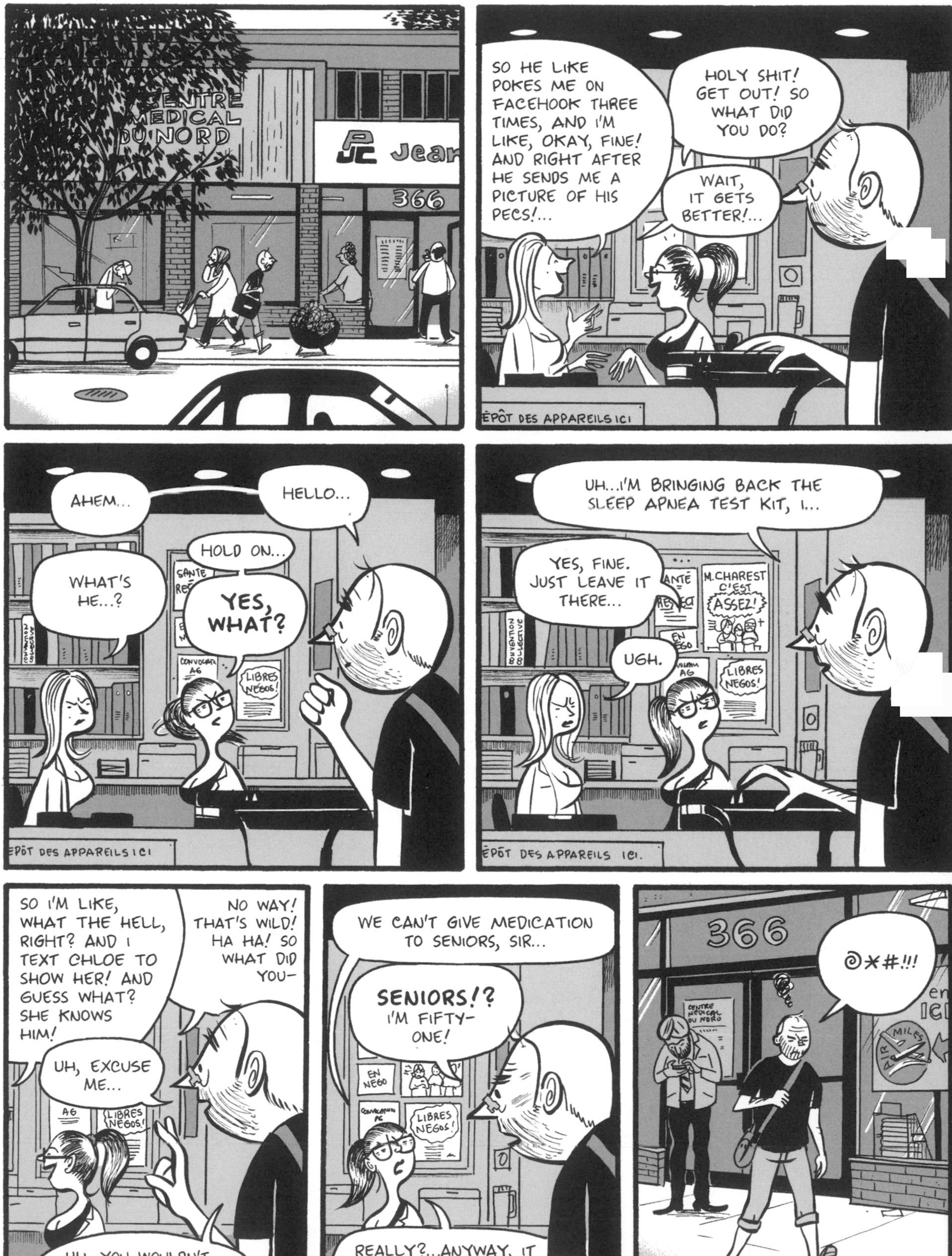

CENTRE MEDICAL DU NORD
PJC Jean
366
SO HE LIKE POKES ME ON FACEHOOK THREE TIMES, AND I'M LIKE, OKAY, FINE! AND RIGHT AFTER HE SENDS ME A PICTURE OF HIS PECS!...
HOLY SHIT! GET OUT! SO WHAT DID YOU DO?
WAIT, IT GETS BETTER!...
ÉPÔT DES APPAREILS ICI
AHEM...
HELLO...
WHAT'S HE...?
HOLD ON...
YES, WHAT?
LIBRES NEGOS!
ÉPÔT DES APPAREILS ICI
UH...I'M BRINGING BACK THE SLEEP APNEA TEST KIT, I...
YES, FINE. JUST LEAVE IT THERE...
M.CHAREST C'EST ASSEZ!
UGH.
LIBRES NEGOS!
ÉPÔT DES APPAREILS ICI.
SO I'M LIKE, WHAT THE HELL, RIGHT? AND I TEXT CHLOE TO SHOW HER! AND GUESS WHAT? SHE KNOWS HIM!
NO WAY! THAT'S WILD! HA HA! SO WHAT DID YOU-
UH, EXCUSE ME...
LIBRES NEGOS!
UH...YOU WOULDN'T HAPPEN TO HAVE A TYLENOL OR TWO, IT'S...
WE CAN'T GIVE MEDICATION TO SENIORS, SIR...
SENIORS!? I'M FIFTY-ONE!
EN NEGO
LIBRES NEGOS!
REALLY?...ANYWAY, IT DOESN'T MATTER. I'M NOT ALLOWED. SORRY.
366
@*#!!!
AIR MILES

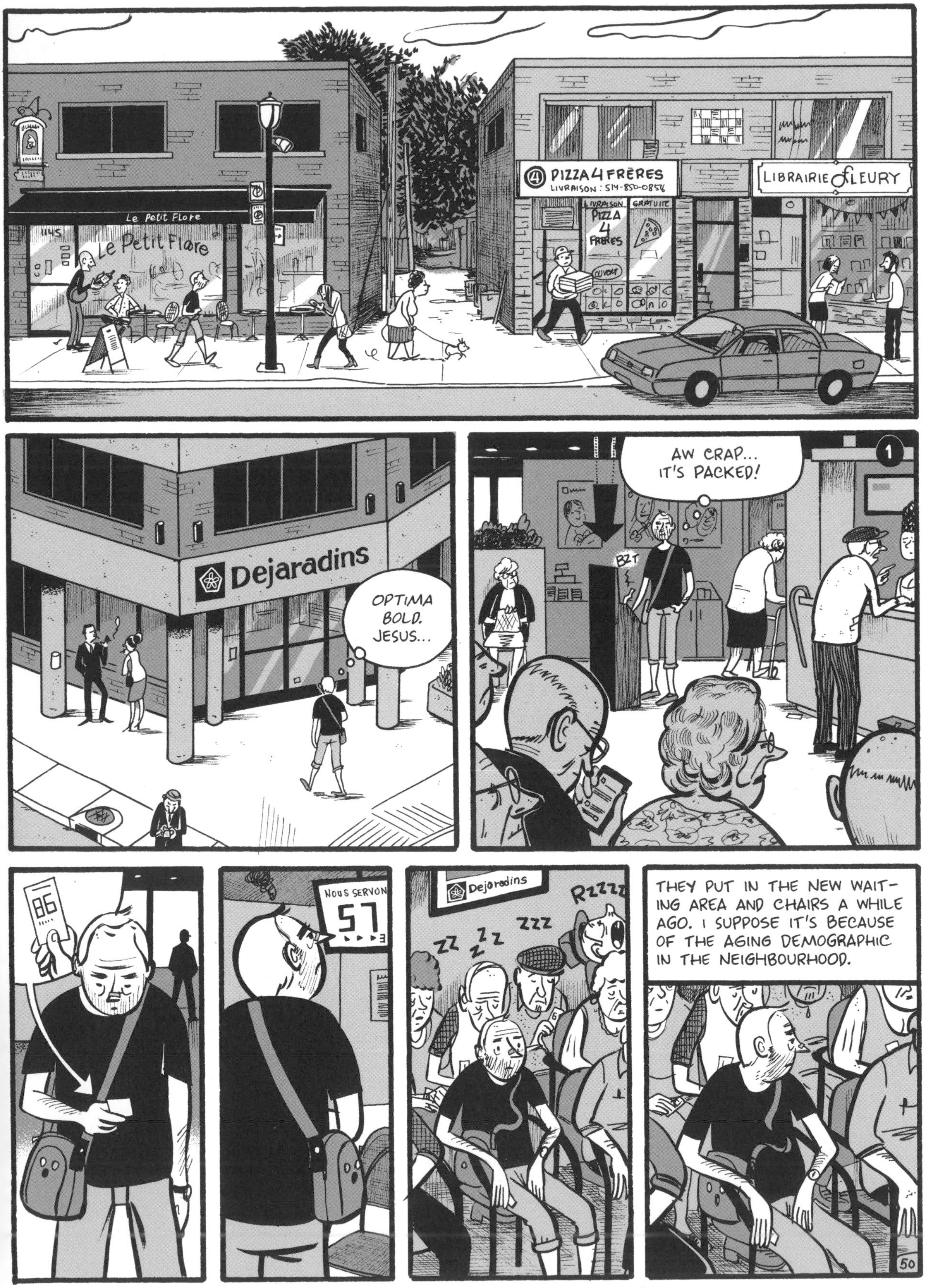

Le Petit Flore
445
Le Petit Flore
PIZZA 4 FRÈRES
LIVRAISON : 514-850-0856
LIVRAISON GRATUITE
PIZZA 4 FRÈRES
OUVERT
LIBRAIRIE FLEURY
Dejaradins
OPTIMA BOLD. JESUS...
1
AW CRAP... IT'S PACKED!
BZT
86
NOUS SERVON
57
Dejaradins
RZZZZ
ZZ Z Z ZZZ
THEY PUT IN THE NEW WAITING AREA AND CHAIRS A WHILE AGO. I SUPPOSE IT'S BECAUSE OF THE AGING DEMOGRAPHIC IN THE NEIGHBOURHOOD.

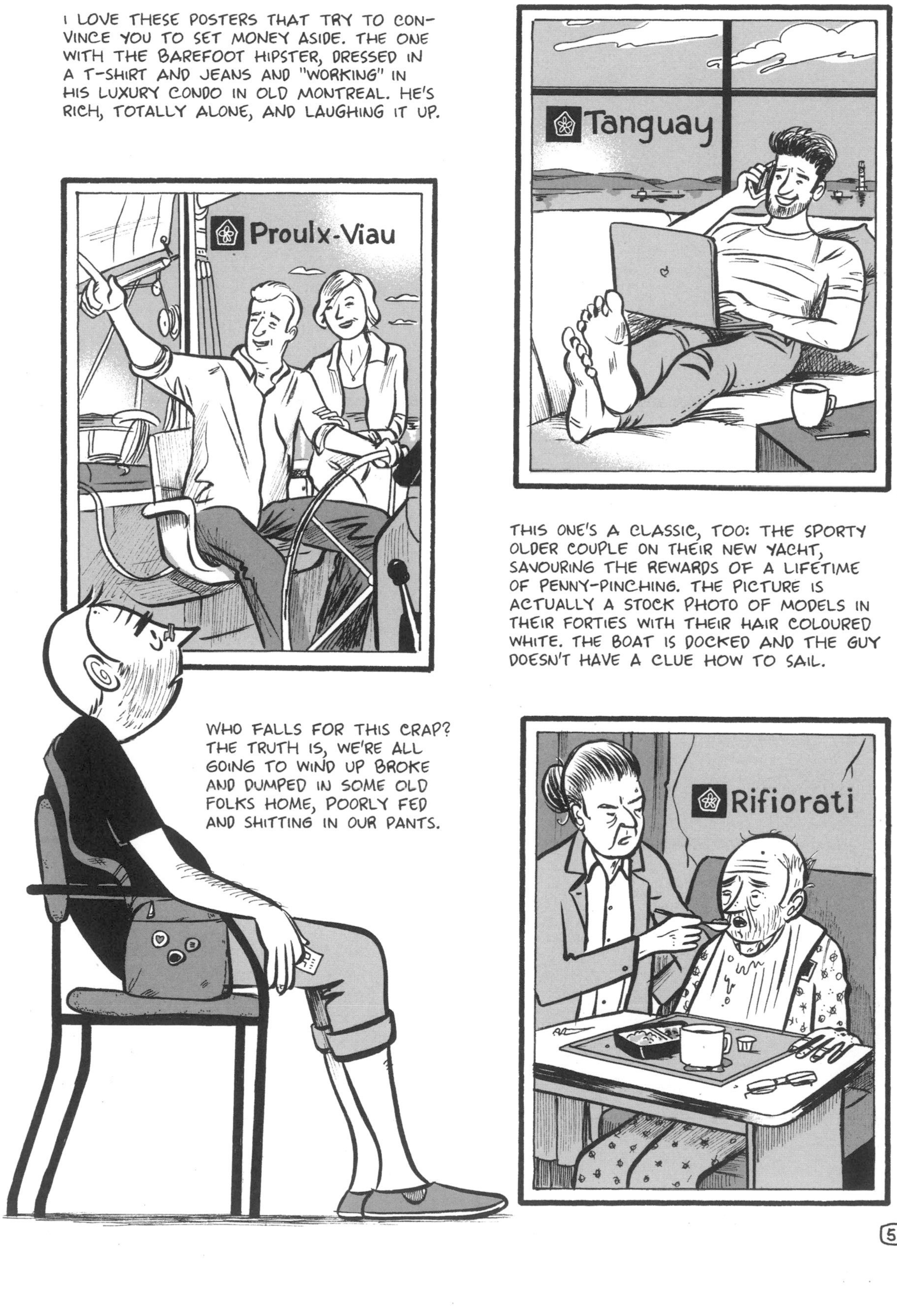
I LOVE THESE POSTERS THAT TRY TO CONVINCE YOU TO SET MONEY ASIDE. THE ONE WITH THE BAREFOOT HIPSTER, DRESSED IN A T-SHIRT AND JEANS AND "WORKING" IN HIS LUXURY CONDO IN OLD MONTREAL. HE'S RICH, TOTALLY ALONE, AND LAUGHING IT UP.
Tanguay
Proulx-Viau
THIS ONE'S A CLASSIC, TOO: THE SPORTY OLDER COUPLE ON THEIR NEW YACHT, SAVOURING THE REWARDS OF A LIFETIME OF PENNY-PINCHING. THE PICTURE IS ACTUALLY A STOCK PHOTO OF MODELS IN THEIR FORTIES WITH THEIR HAIR COLOURED WHITE. THE BOAT IS DOCKED AND THE GUY DOESN'T HAVE A CLUE HOW TO SAIL.
WHO FALLS FOR THIS CRAP? THE TRUTH IS, WE'RE ALL GOING TO WIND UP BROKE AND DUMPED IN SOME OLD FOLKS HOME, POORLY FED AND SHITTING IN OUR PANTS.
Rifiorati

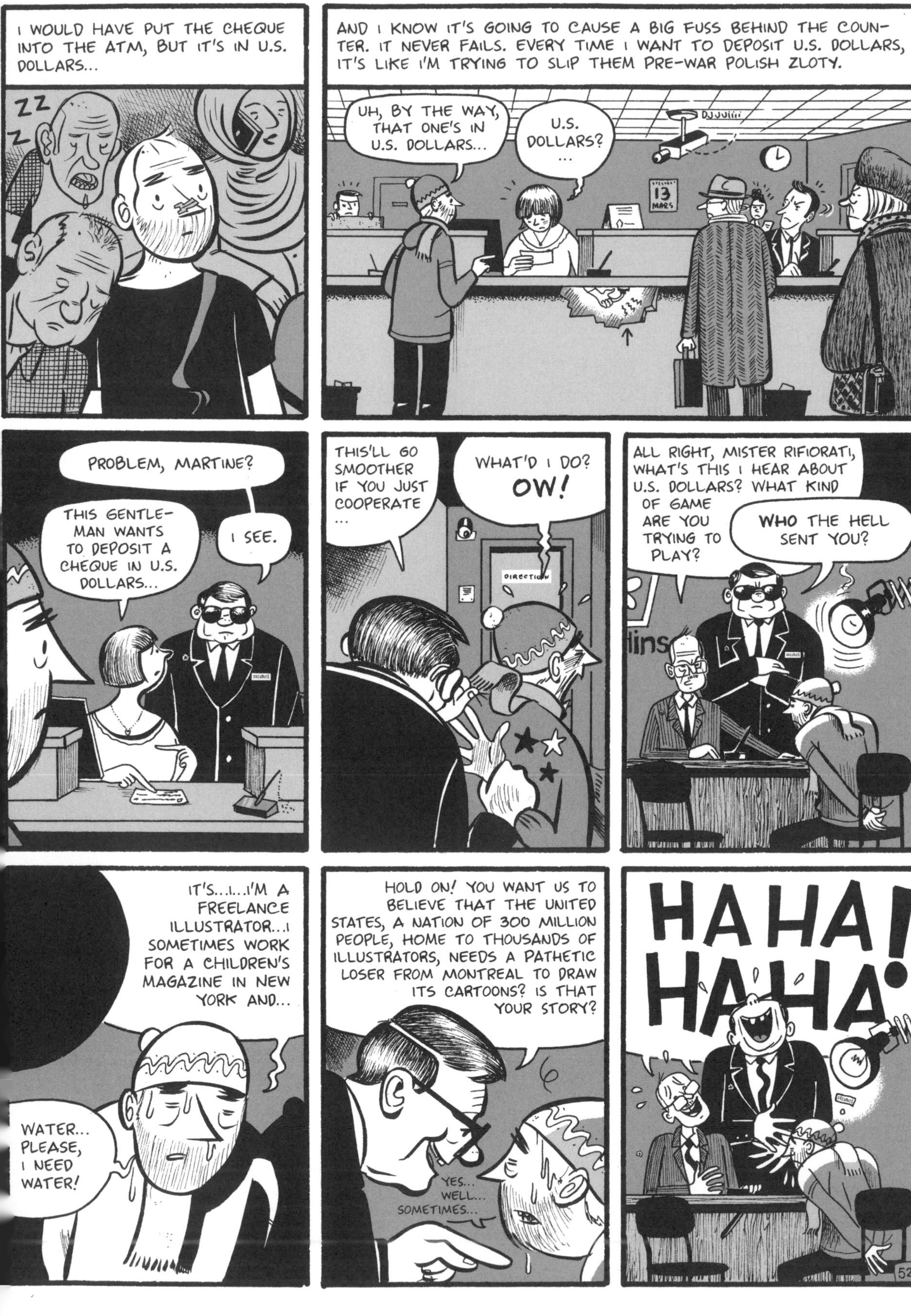
I WOULD HAVE PUT THE CHEQUE INTO THE ATM, BUT IT'S IN U.S. DOLLARS...
ZZ Z
AND I KNOW IT'S GOING TO CAUSE A BIG FUSS BEHIND THE COUNTER. IT NEVER FAILS. EVERY TIME I WANT TO DEPOSIT U.S. DOLLARS, IT'S LIKE I'M TRYING TO SLIP THEM PRE-WAR POLISH ZLOTY.
UH, BY THE WAY, THAT ONE'S IN U.S. DOLLARS...
U.S. DOLLARS? ...
DJJUiiii
13 MARS
PROBLEM, MARTINE?
THIS GENTLEMAN WANTS TO DEPOSIT A CHEQUE IN U.S. DOLLARS...
I SEE.
THIS'LL GO SMOOTHER IF YOU JUST COOPERATE ...
WHAT'D I DO? OW!
DIRECTION
ALL RIGHT, MISTER RIFIORATI, WHAT'S THIS I HEAR ABOUT U.S. DOLLARS? WHAT KIND OF GAME ARE YOU TRYING TO PLAY?
WHO THE HELL SENT YOU?
IT'S...I...I'M A FREELANCE ILLUSTRATOR...I SOMETIMES WORK FOR A CHILDREN'S MAGAZINE IN NEW YORK AND...
WATER... PLEASE, I NEED WATER!
HOLD ON! YOU WANT US TO BELIEVE THAT THE UNITED STATES, A NATION OF 300 MILLION PEOPLE, HOME TO THOUSANDS OF ILLUSTRATORS, NEEDS A PATHETIC LOSER FROM MONTREAL TO DRAW ITS CARTOONS? IS THAT YOUR STORY?
YES... WELL... SOMETIMES...
HAHA! HAHA!

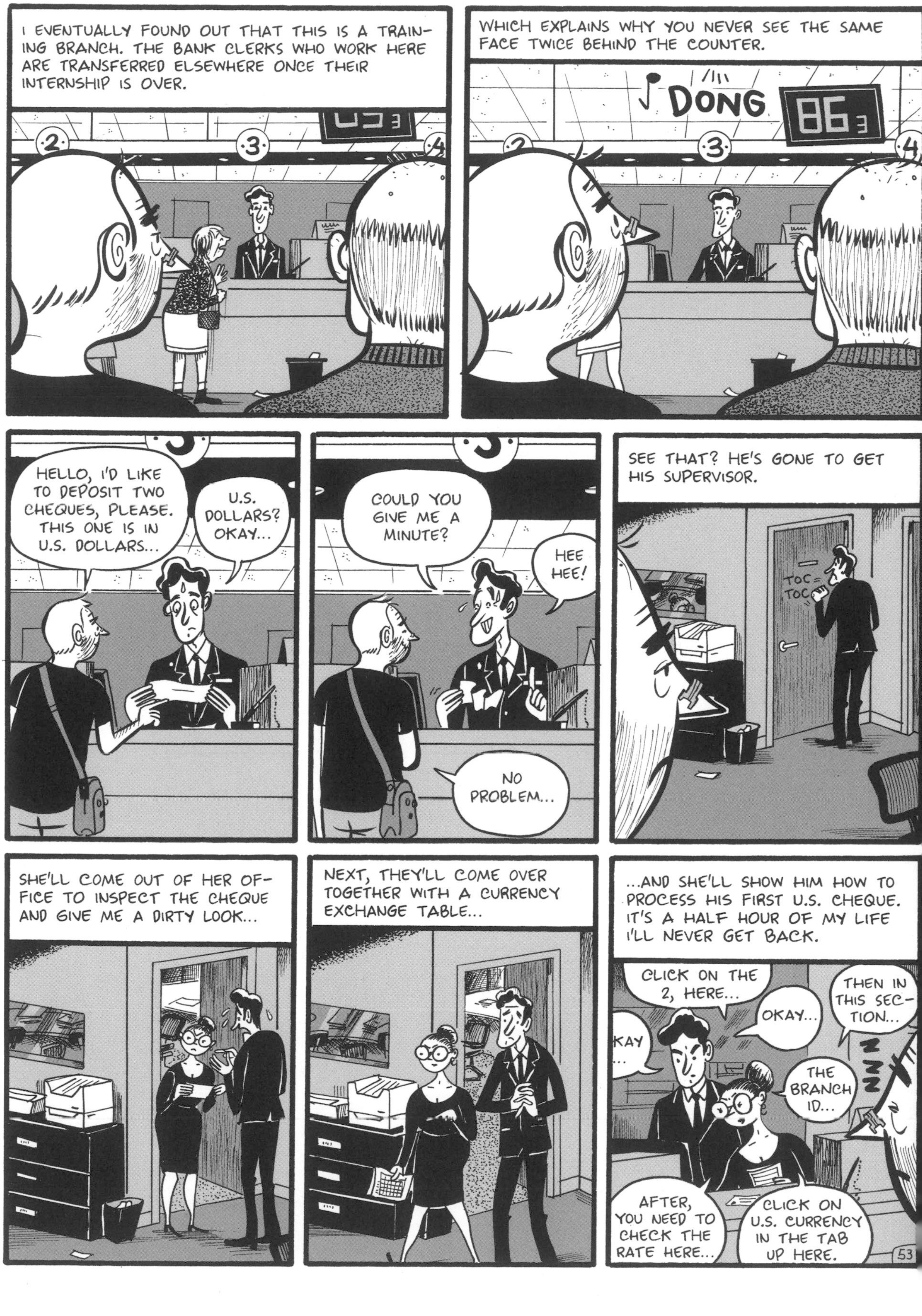
I EVENTUALLY FOUND OUT THAT THIS IS A TRAINING BRANCH. THE BANK CLERKS WHO WORK HERE ARE TRANSFERRED ELSEWHERE ONCE THEIR INTERNSHIP IS OVER.
WHICH EXPLAINS WHY YOU NEVER SEE THE SAME FACE TWICE BEHIND THE COUNTER.
DONG
86
HELLO, I'D LIKE TO DEPOSIT TWO CHEQUES, PLEASE. THIS ONE IS IN U.S. DOLLARS...
U.S. DOLLARS? OKAY...
COULD YOU GIVE ME A MINUTE?
HEE HEE!
NO PROBLEM...
SEE THAT? HE'S GONE TO GET HIS SUPERVISOR.
TOC TOC
SHE'LL COME OUT OF HER OFFICE TO INSPECT THE CHEQUE AND GIVE ME A DIRTY LOOK...
NEXT, THEY'LL COME OVER TOGETHER WITH A CURRENCY EXCHANGE TABLE...
...AND SHE'LL SHOW HIM HOW TO PROCESS HIS FIRST U.S. CHEQUE. IT'S A HALF HOUR OF MY LIFE I'LL NEVER GET BACK.
CLICK ON THE 2, HERE...
OKAY...
THEN IN THIS SECTION...
THE BRANCH ID...
ZZZ
AFTER, YOU NEED TO CHECK THE RATE HERE...
CLICK ON U.S. CURRENCY IN THE TAB UP HERE.

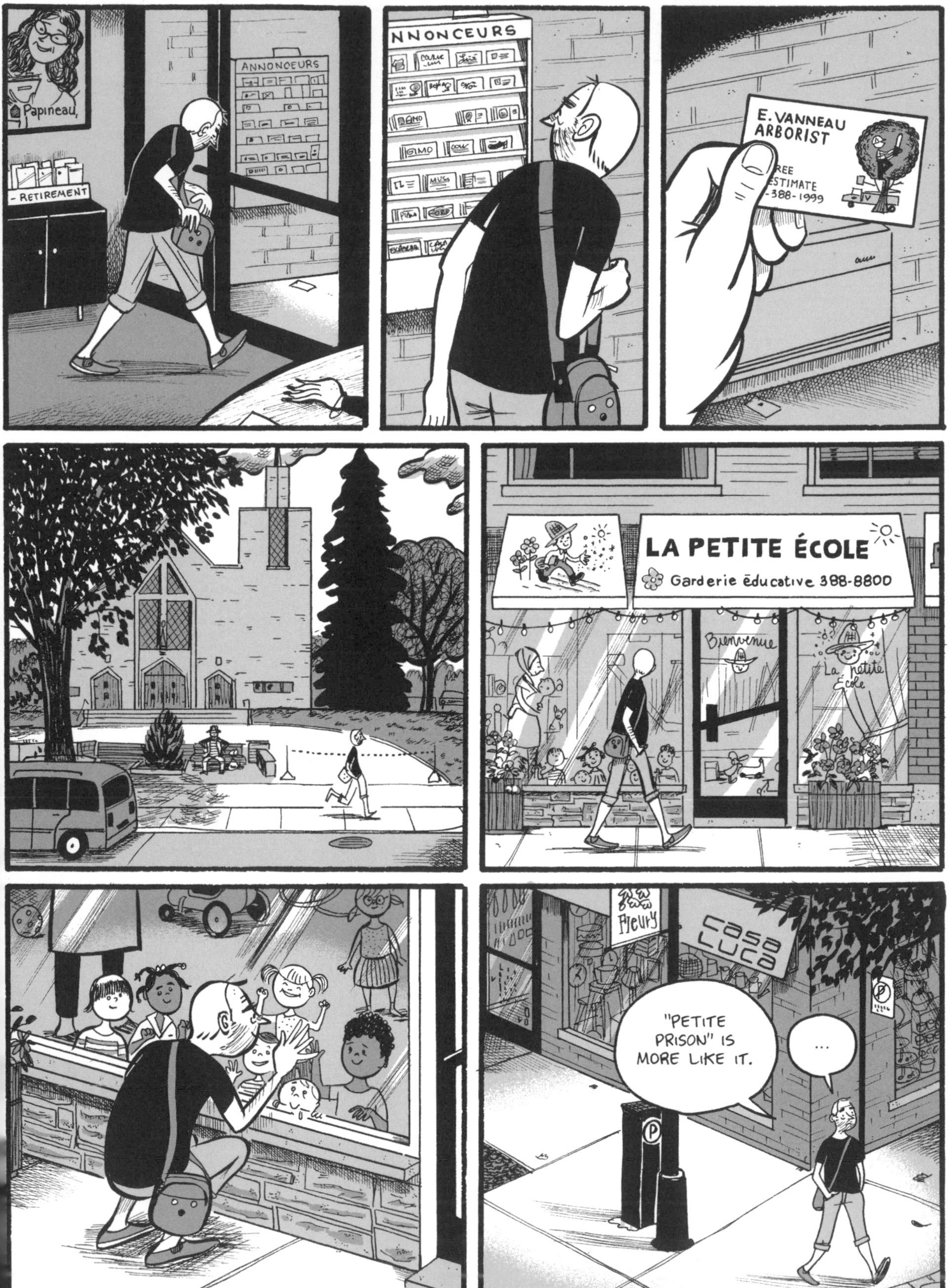
Papineau
ANNONCEURS
- RETIREMENT
NNONCEURS
E. VANNEAU
ARBORIST
LA PETITE ÉCOLE
Garderie éducative 388-8800
Bienvenue
La petite École
Fleury
casa Luca
"PETITE PRISON" IS MORE LIKE IT.
...

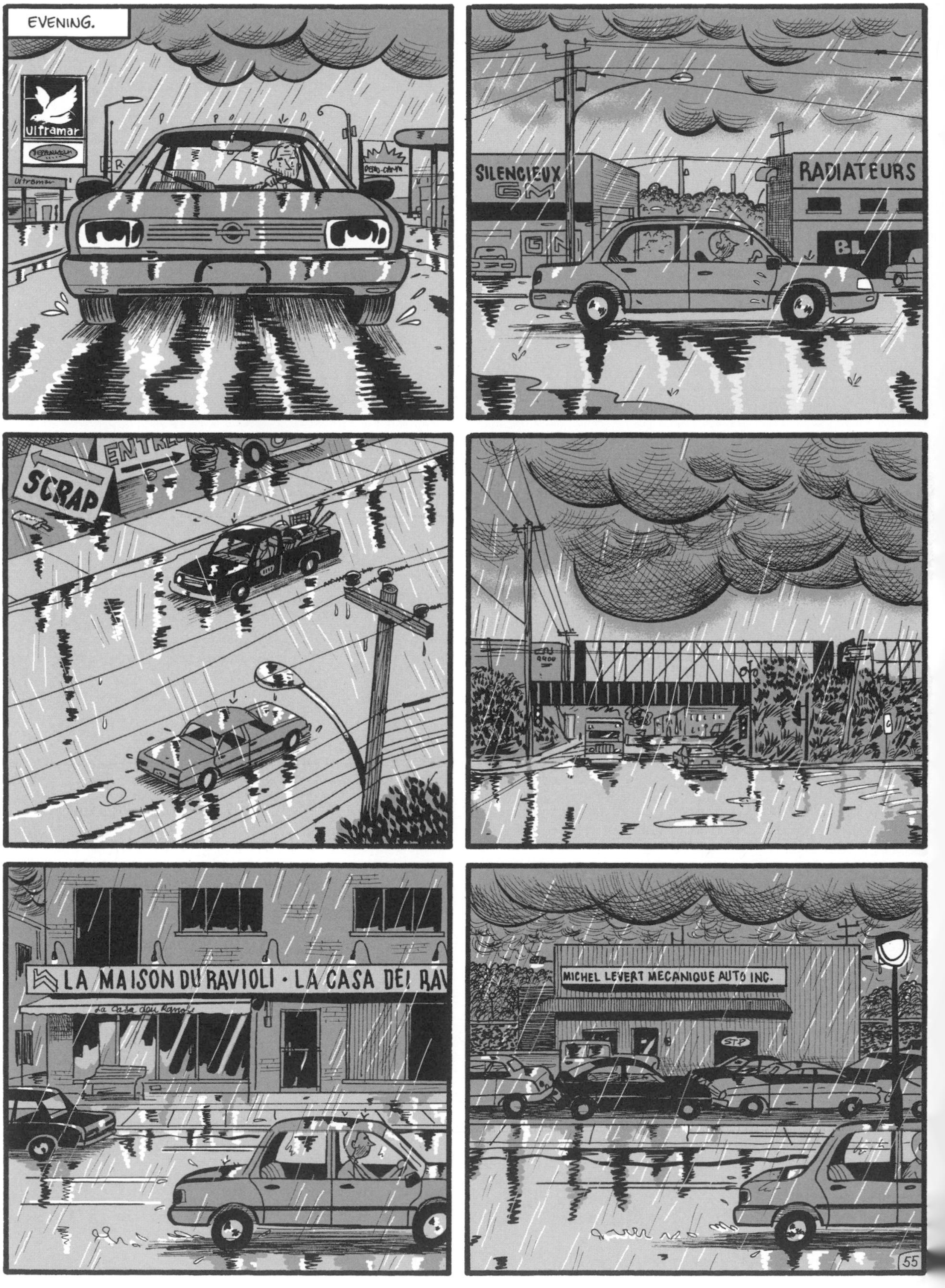
EVENING.
Ultramar
SILENCIEUX
GM
RADIATEURS
SCRAP
LA MAISON DU RAVIOLI · LA CASA DEI RAV
MICHEL LEVERT MECANIQUE AUTO INC.

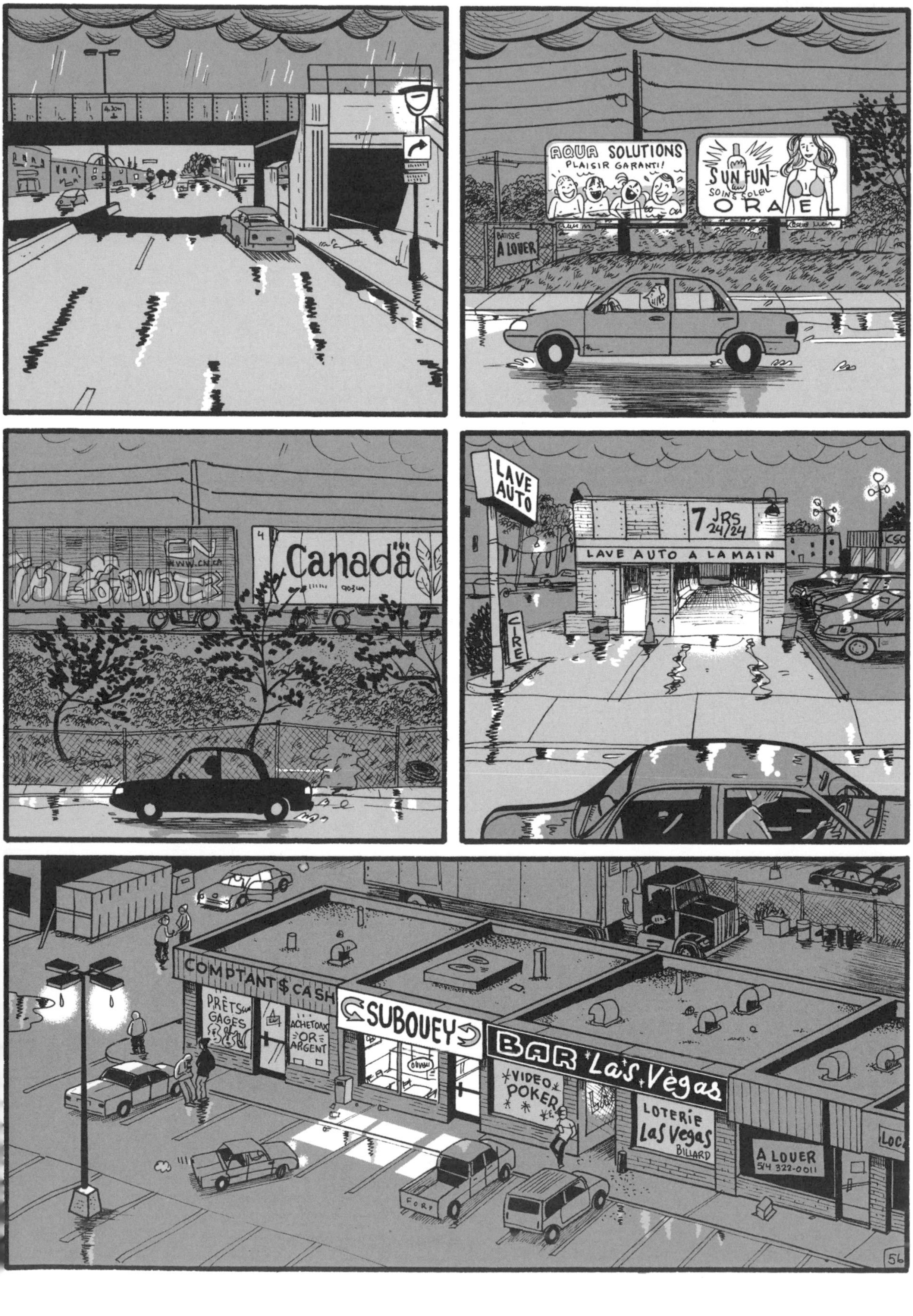
AQUA SOLUTIONS
PLAISIR GARANTI!
SUN FUN
SOINS SOLEIL
ORAEL
BÂTISSE
À LOUER
CN
WWW.CN.CA
Canada
LAVE AUTO
7 JRS 24/24
LAVE AUTO A LA MAIN
CIRE
COMPTANT $ CASH
PRÊTS SUR GAGES
ACHETONS OR ARGENT
SUBOUEY
BAR Las Vegas
VIDEO POKER
LOTERIE
LAS VEGAS
BILLARD
À LOUER
514 322-0011

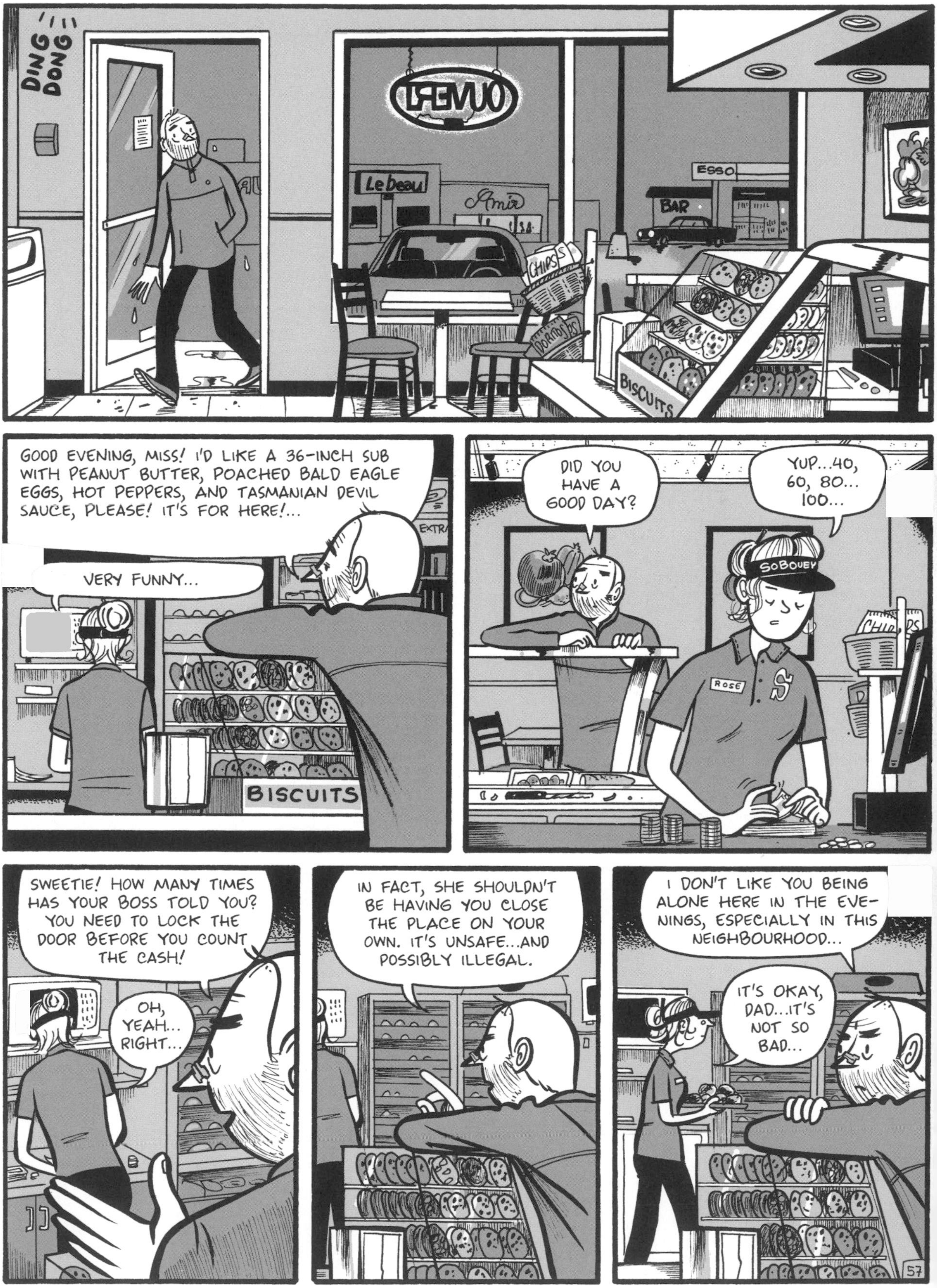
DING DONG
LEBEAU
Le beau
Amir
ESSO
BAR
CHIPS
DORITOS
BISCUITS
GOOD EVENING, MISS! I'D LIKE A 36-INCH SUB WITH PEANUT BUTTER, POACHED BALD EAGLE EGGS, HOT PEPPERS, AND TASMANIAN DEVIL SAUCE, PLEASE! IT'S FOR HERE!...
VERY FUNNY...
BISCUITS
DID YOU HAVE A GOOD DAY?
YUP...40, 60, 80... 100...
SOBOUEY
ROSE
SWEETIE! HOW MANY TIMES HAS YOUR BOSS TOLD YOU? YOU NEED TO LOCK THE DOOR BEFORE YOU COUNT THE CASH!
OH, YEAH... RIGHT...
IN FACT, SHE SHOULDN'T BE HAVING YOU CLOSE THE PLACE ON YOUR OWN. IT'S UNSAFE...AND POSSIBLY ILLEGAL.
I DON'T LIKE YOU BEING ALONE HERE IN THE EVENINGS, ESPECIALLY IN THIS NEIGHBOURHOOD...
IT'S OKAY, DAD...IT'S NOT SO BAD...

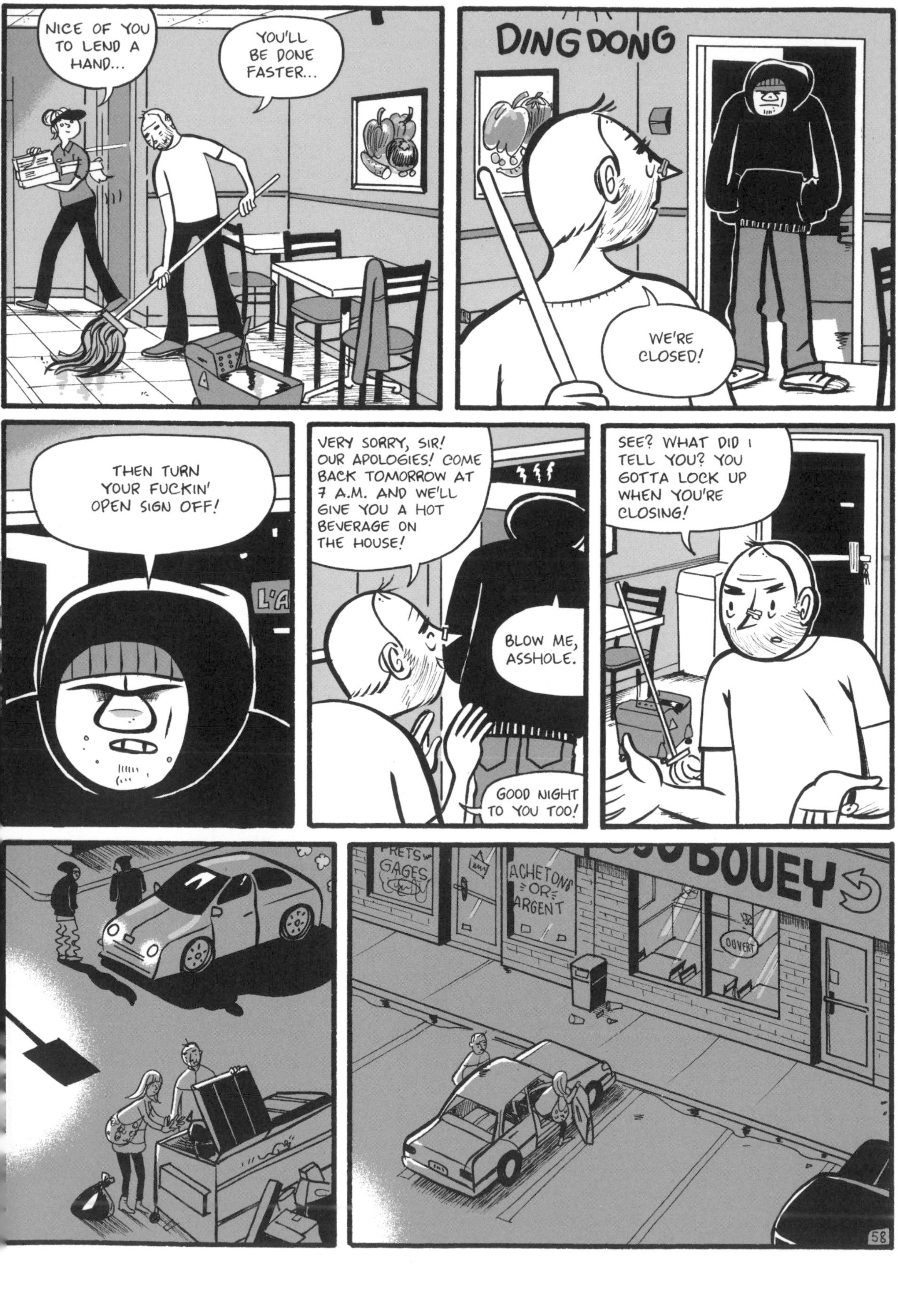
NICE OF YOU TO LEND A HAND...
YOU'LL BE DONE FASTER...
DING DONG
WE'RE CLOSED!
THEN TURN YOUR FUCKIN' OPEN SIGN OFF!
L'A
VERY SORRY, SIR! OUR APOLOGIES! COME BACK TOMORROW AT 7 A.M. AND WE'LL GIVE YOU A HOT BEVERAGE ON THE HOUSE!
BLOW ME, ASSHOLE.
GOOD NIGHT TO YOU TOO!
SEE? WHAT DID I TELL YOU? YOU GOTTA LOCK UP WHEN YOU'RE CLOSING!
PRETS GAGES
ACHETONS OR ARGENT
BOUEY
OUVERT

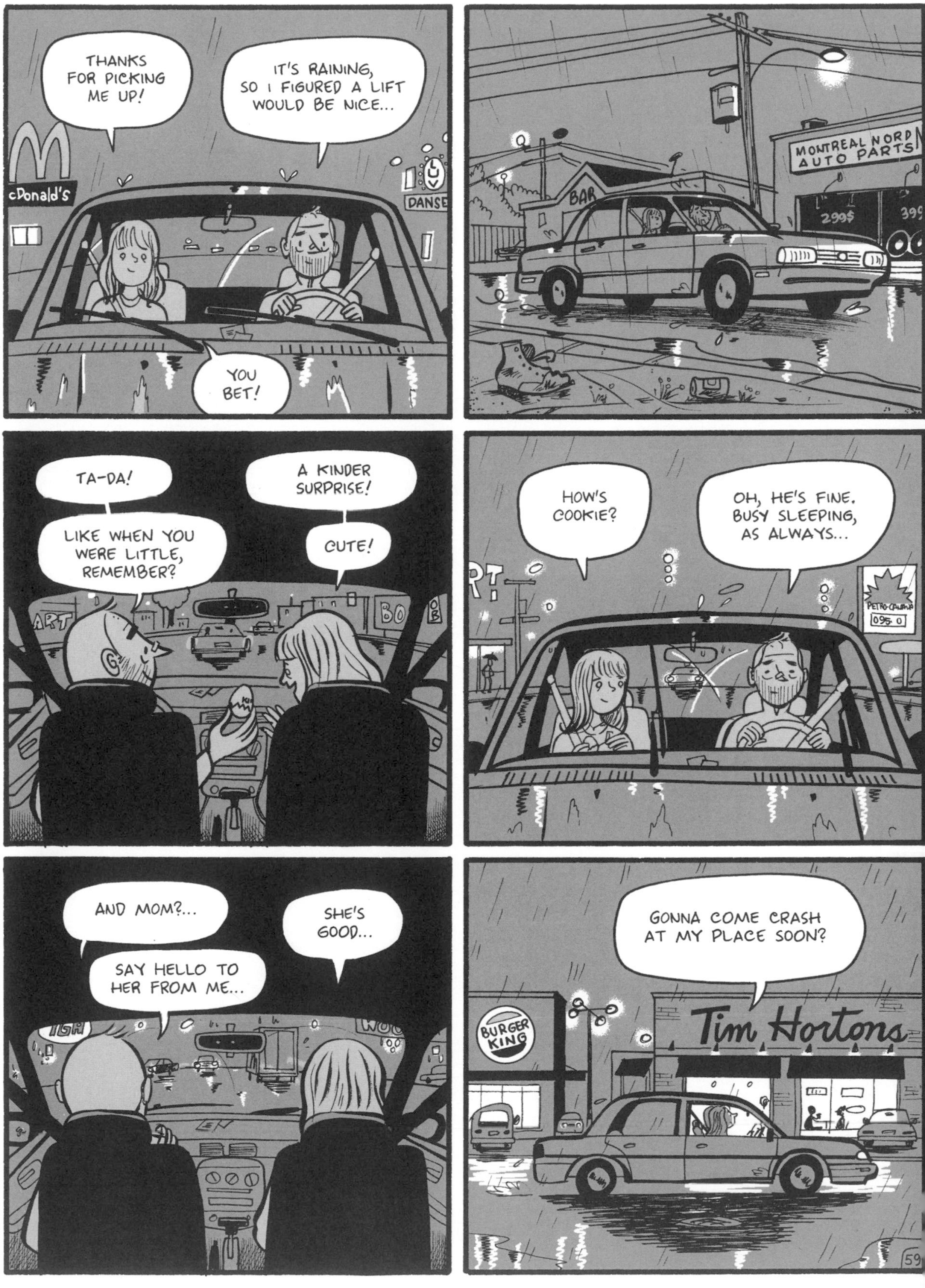
THANKS FOR PICKING ME UP!
IT'S RAINING, SO I FIGURED A LIFT WOULD BE NICE...
cDonald's
LUV
DANSE
YOU BET!
MONTREAL NORD AUTO PARTS
BAR
299$
TA-DA!
LIKE WHEN YOU WERE LITTLE, REMEMBER?
A KINDER SURPRISE!
CUTE!
HOW'S COOKIE?
OH, HE'S FINE. BUSY SLEEPING, AS ALWAYS...
AND MOM?...
SAY HELLO TO HER FROM ME...
SHE'S GOOD...
GONNA COME CRASH AT MY PLACE SOON?
BURGER KING
Tim Hortons

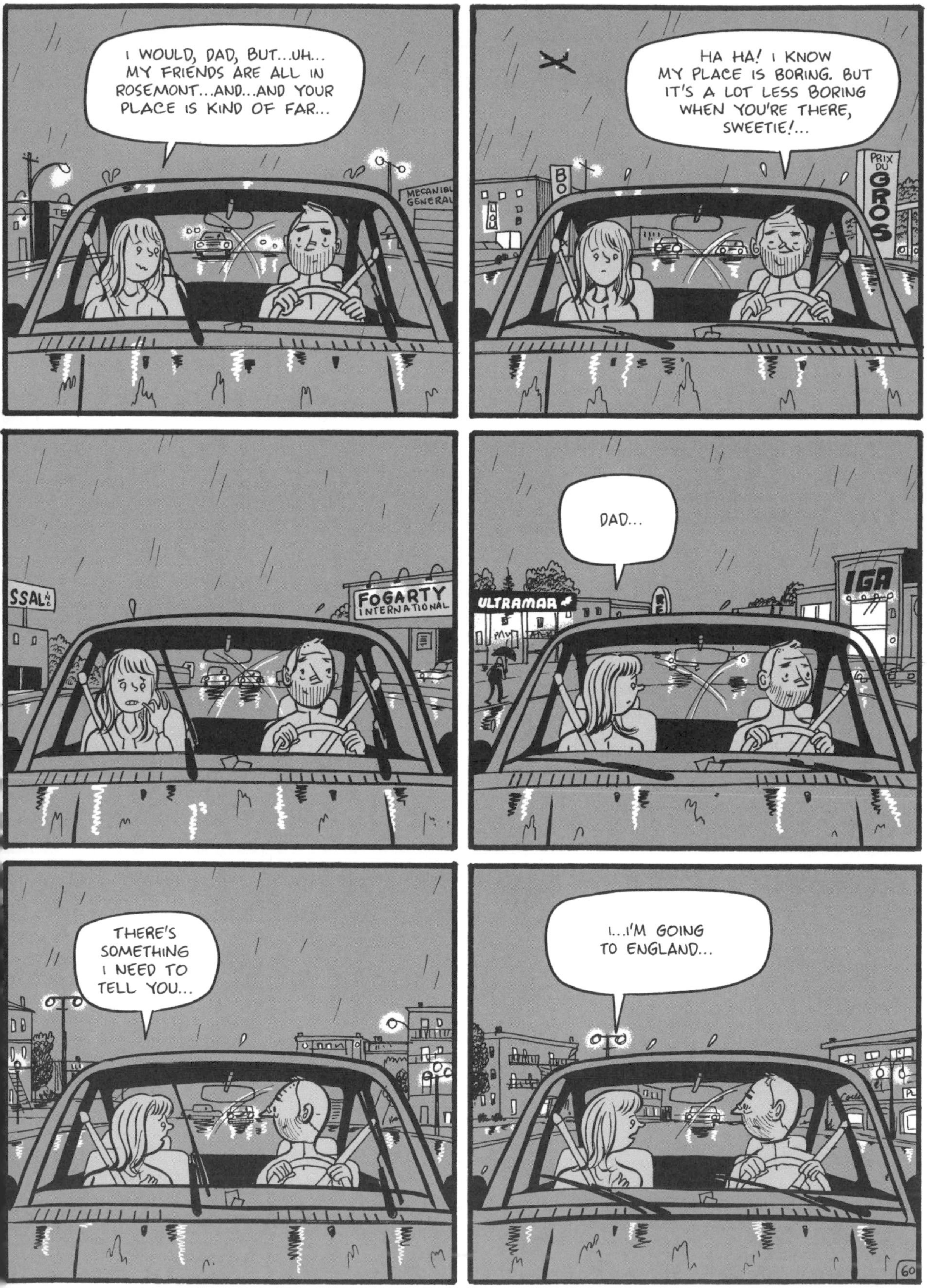
I WOULD, DAD, BUT...UH... MY FRIENDS ARE ALL IN ROSEMONT...AND...AND YOUR PLACE IS KIND OF FAR...
HA HA! I KNOW MY PLACE IS BORING. BUT IT'S A LOT LESS BORING WHEN YOU'RE THERE, SWEETIE!...
PRIX DU GROS
FOGARTY INTERNATIONAL
DAD...
ULTRAMAR
IGA
THERE'S SOMETHING I NEED TO TELL YOU...
I...I'M GOING TO ENGLAND...

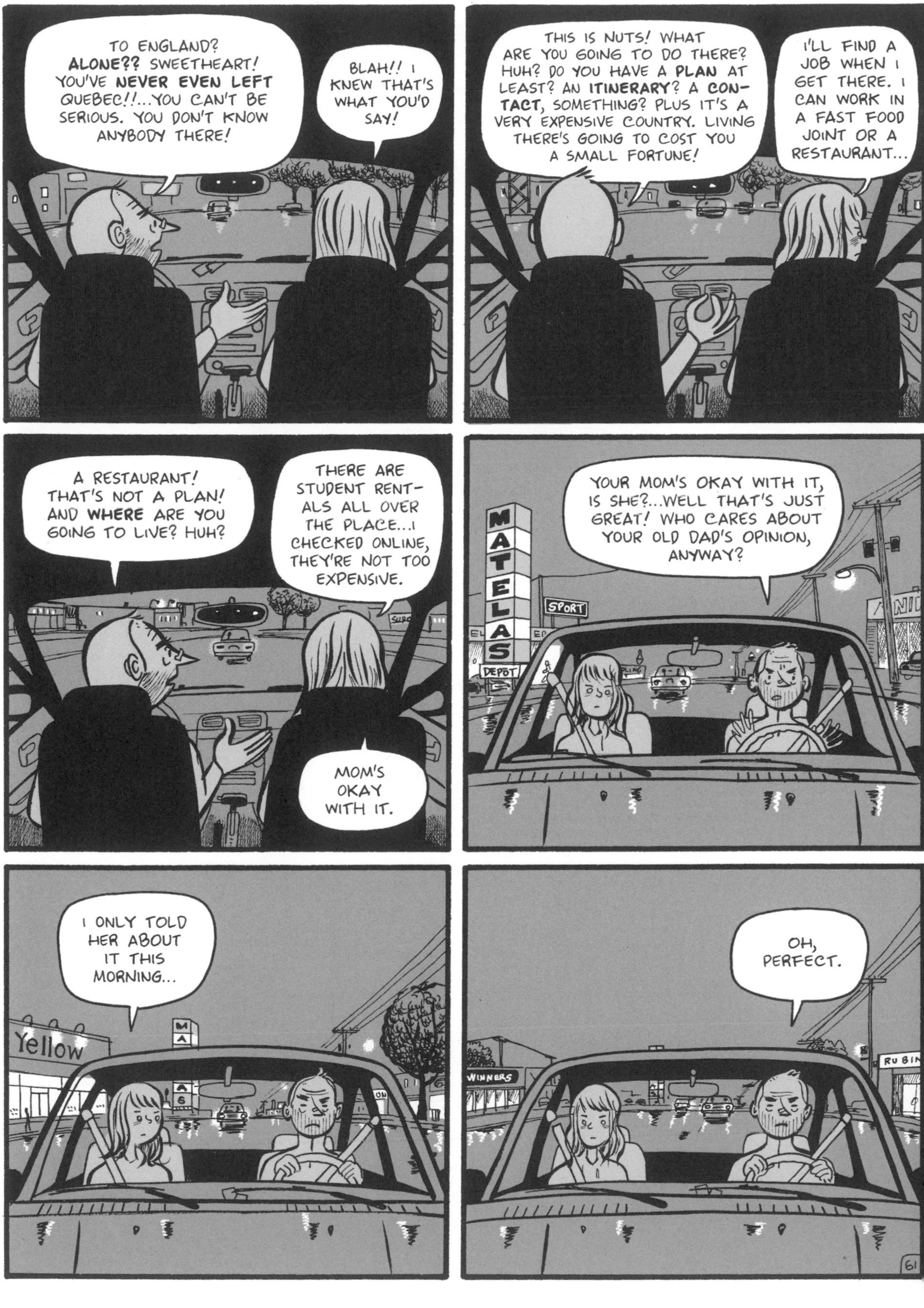
TO ENGLAND? **ALONE??** SWEETHEART! YOU'VE **NEVER EVEN LEFT** QUEBEC!!...YOU CAN'T BE SERIOUS. YOU DON'T KNOW ANYBODY THERE!
BLAH!! I KNEW THAT'S WHAT YOU'D SAY!
THIS IS NUTS! WHAT ARE YOU GOING TO DO THERE? HUH? DO YOU HAVE A **PLAN** AT LEAST? AN **ITINERARY**? A **CONTACT**, SOMETHING? PLUS IT'S A VERY EXPENSIVE COUNTRY. LIVING THERE'S GOING TO COST YOU A SMALL FORTUNE!
I'LL FIND A JOB WHEN I GET THERE. I CAN WORK IN A FAST FOOD JOINT OR A RESTAURANT...
A RESTAURANT! THAT'S NOT A PLAN! AND **WHERE** ARE YOU GOING TO LIVE? HUH?
THERE ARE STUDENT RENTALS ALL OVER THE PLACE...I CHECKED ONLINE, THEY'RE NOT TOO EXPENSIVE.
MOM'S OKAY WITH IT.
MATELAS
SPORT
DEPOT
YOUR MOM'S OKAY WITH IT, IS SHE?...WELL THAT'S JUST GREAT! WHO CARES ABOUT YOUR OLD DAD'S OPINION, ANYWAY?
I ONLY TOLD HER ABOUT IT THIS MORNING...
Yellow
WINNERS
OH, PERFECT.

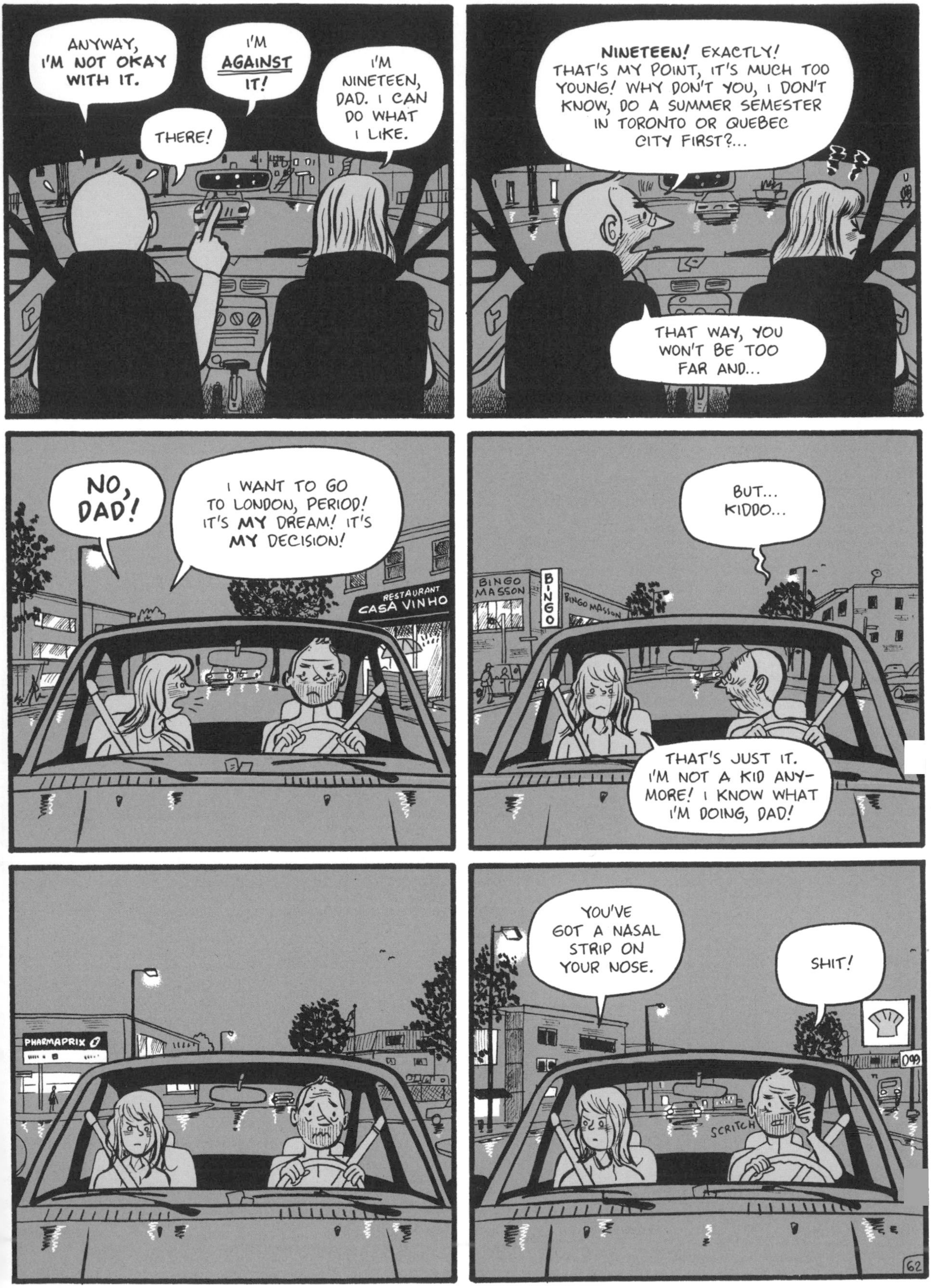
ANYWAY, I'M NOT OKAY WITH IT.
THERE!
I'M AGAINST IT!
I'M NINETEEN, DAD. I CAN DO WHAT I LIKE.
NINETEEN! EXACTLY! THAT'S MY POINT, IT'S MUCH TOO YOUNG! WHY DON'T YOU, I DON'T KNOW, DO A SUMMER SEMESTER IN TORONTO OR QUEBEC CITY FIRST?...
THAT WAY, YOU WON'T BE TOO FAR AND...
NO, DAD!
I WANT TO GO TO LONDON, PERIOD! IT'S MY DREAM! IT'S MY DECISION!
RESTAURANT CASA VINHO
BINGO MASSON
BINGO
BINGO MASSON
BUT... KIDDO...
THAT'S JUST IT. I'M NOT A KID ANYMORE! I KNOW WHAT I'M DOING, DAD!
PHARMAPRIX
YOU'VE GOT A NASAL STRIP ON YOUR NOSE.
SHIT!
SCRITCH

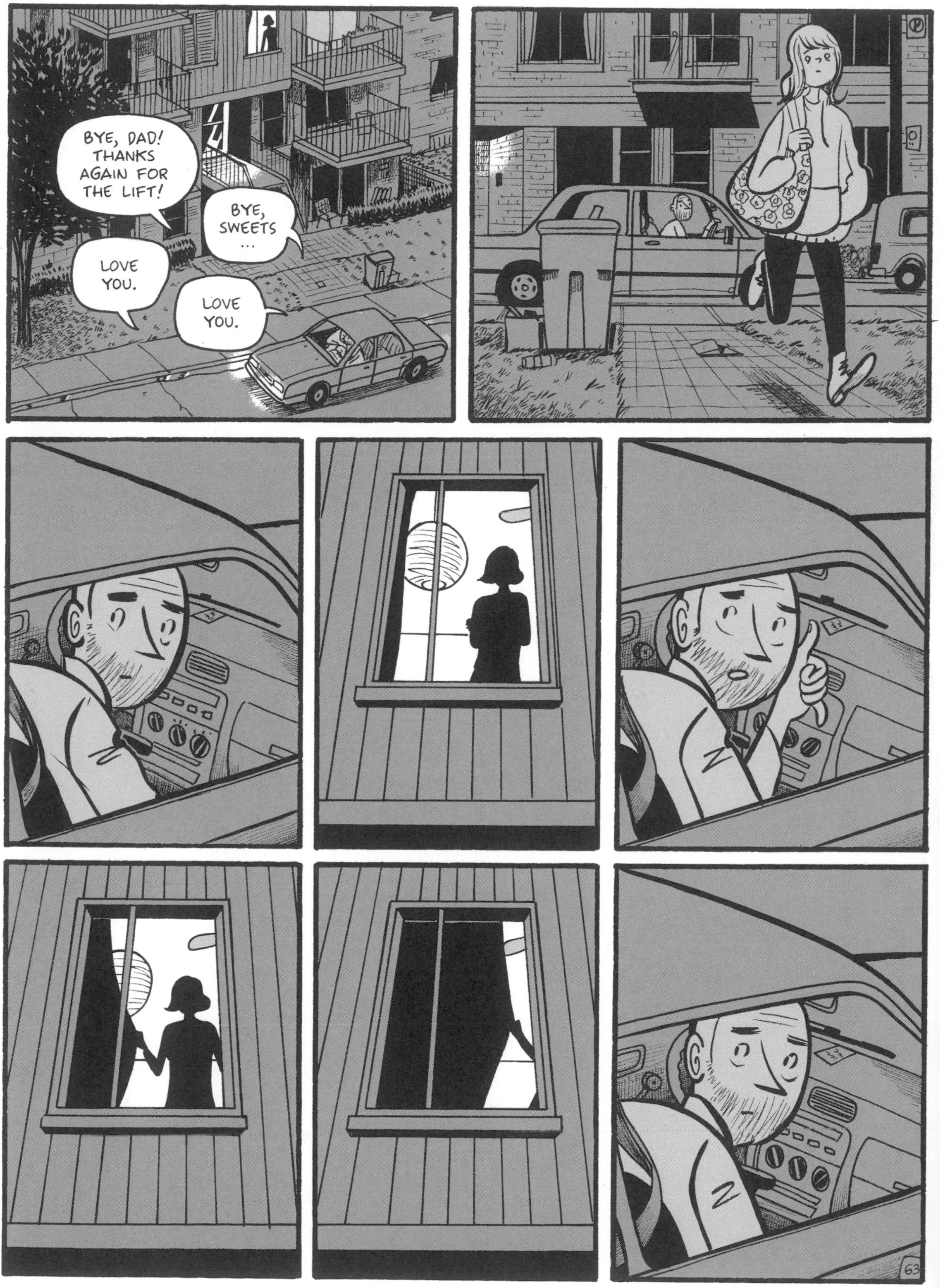
BYE, DAD! THANKS AGAIN FOR THE LIFT!
BYE, SWEETS ...
LOVE YOU.
LOVE YOU.

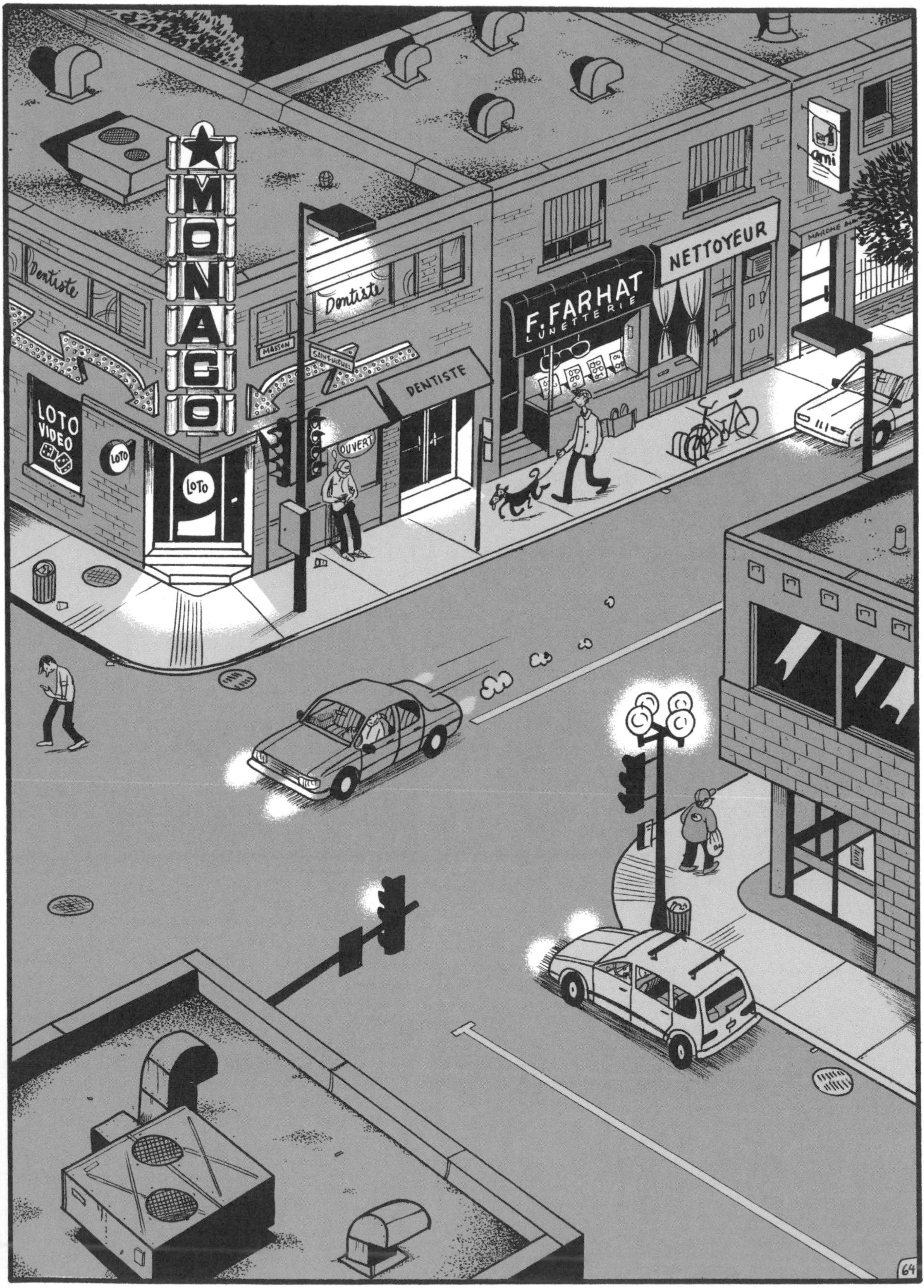
MONACO
Dentiste
Dentiste
MASSON
SAINT-MICHEL
LOTO
VIDEO
LOTO
LOTO
OUVERT
DENTISTE
F. FARHAT
LUNETTERIE
NETTOYEUR
ami

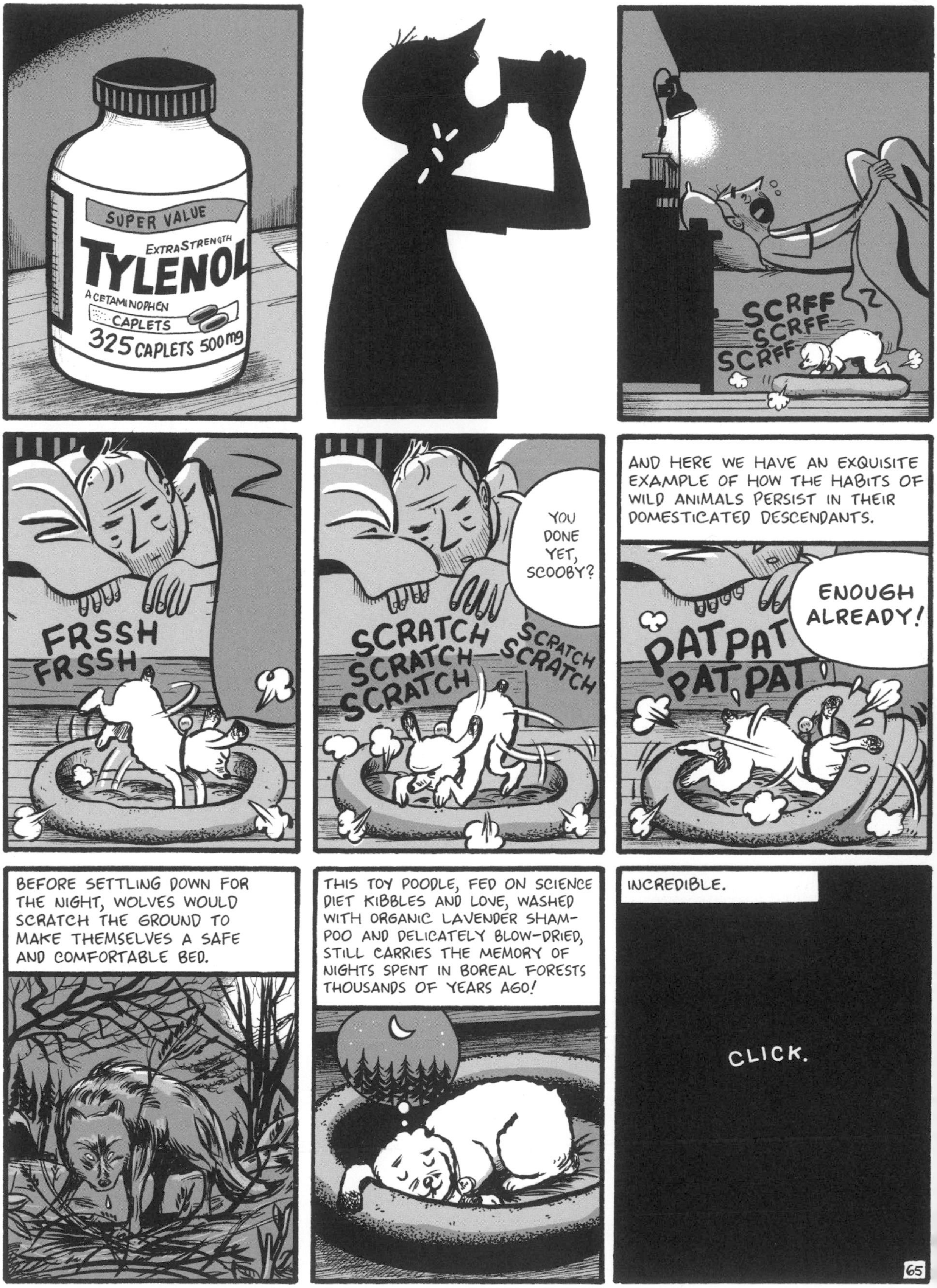
SUPER VALUE
EXTRASTRENGTH
TYLENOL
ACETAMINOPHEN
CAPLETS
325 CAPLETS 500mg
SCRFF SCRFF SCRFF
Z
FRSSH FRSSH
YOU DONE YET, SCOOBY?
SCRATCH SCRATCH SCRATCH
SCRATCH SCRATCH
AND HERE WE HAVE AN EXQUISITE EXAMPLE OF HOW THE HABITS OF WILD ANIMALS PERSIST IN THEIR DOMESTICATED DESCENDANTS.
ENOUGH ALREADY!
PATPAT PAT PAT
BEFORE SETTLING DOWN FOR THE NIGHT, WOLVES WOULD SCRATCH THE GROUND TO MAKE THEMSELVES A SAFE AND COMFORTABLE BED.
THIS TOY POODLE, FED ON SCIENCE DIET KIBBLES AND LOVE, WASHED WITH ORGANIC LAVENDER SHAMPOO AND DELICATELY BLOW-DRIED, STILL CARRIES THE MEMORY OF NIGHTS SPENT IN BOREAL FORESTS THOUSANDS OF YEARS AGO!
INCREDIBLE.
CLICK.

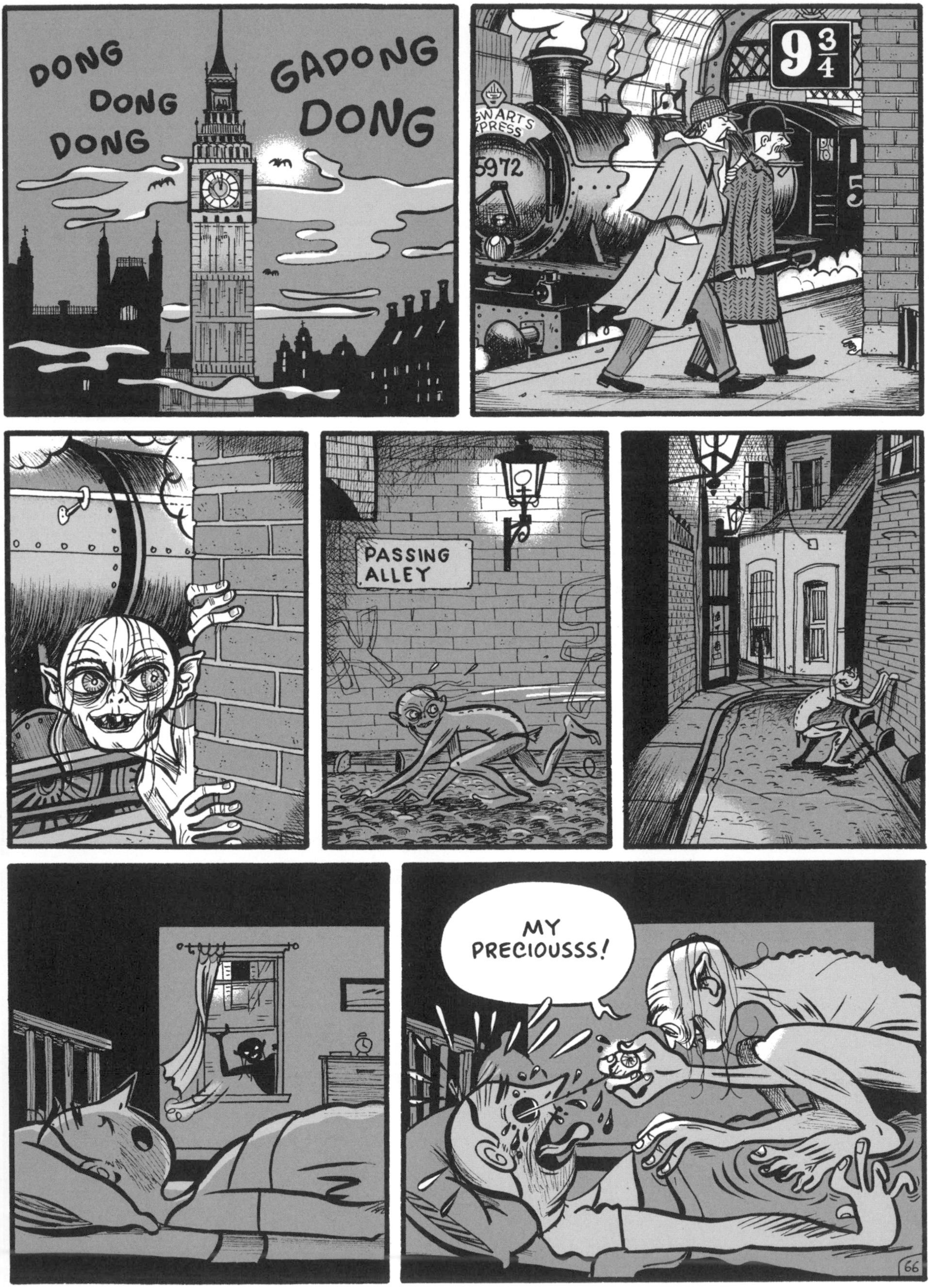
DONG
DONG
DONG
GADONG
DONG
9 3/4
PASSING
ALLEY
MY PRECIOUSSS!

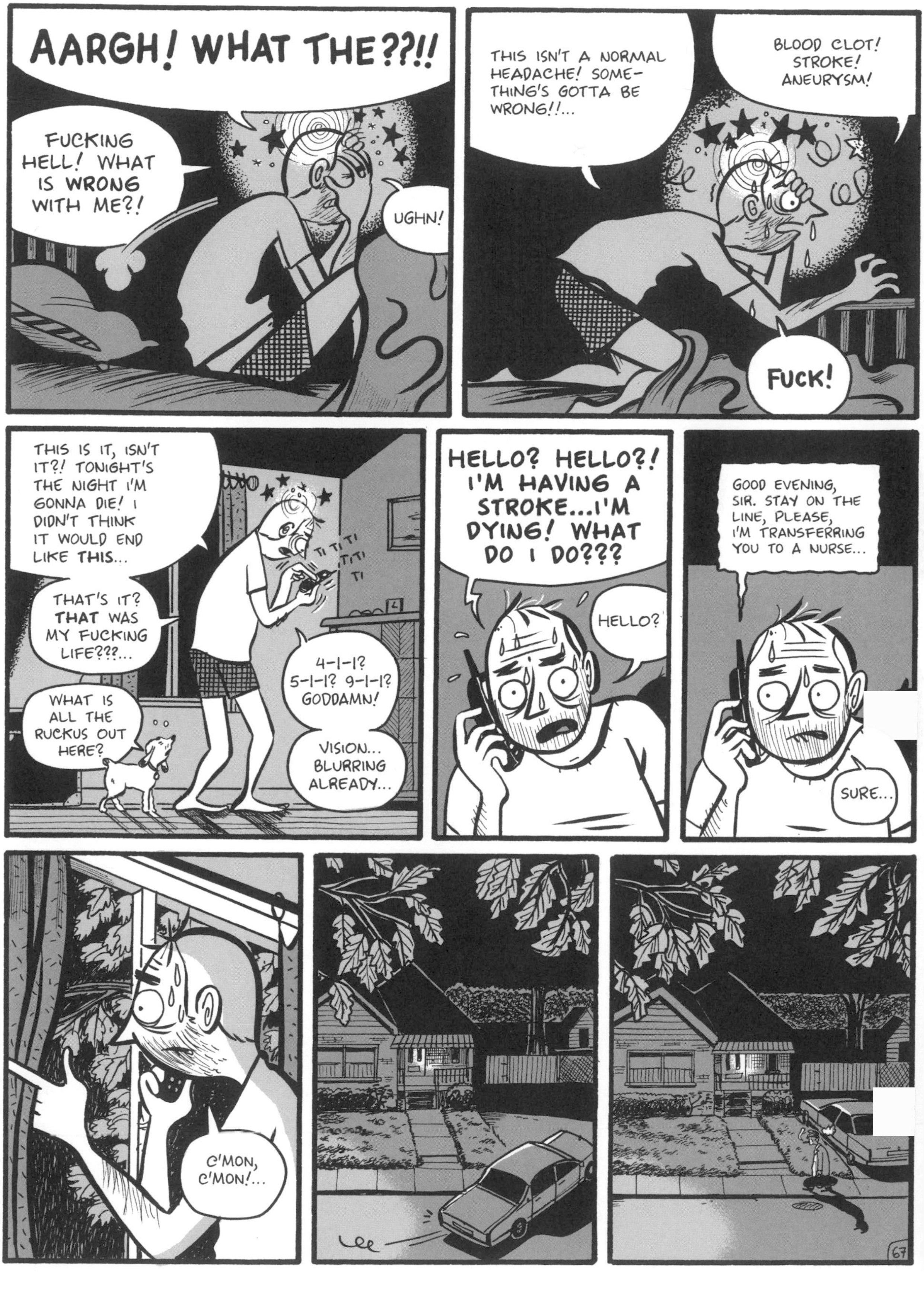
AARGH! WHAT THE??!!
FUCKING HELL! WHAT IS WRONG WITH ME?!
UGHN!
THIS ISN'T A NORMAL HEADACHE! SOMETHING'S GOTTA BE WRONG!!...
BLOOD CLOT! STROKE! ANEURYSM!
FUCK!
THIS IS IT, ISN'T IT?! TONIGHT'S THE NIGHT I'M GONNA DIE! I DIDN'T THINK IT WOULD END LIKE THIS...
TI TI TI TI TI TI
THAT'S IT? THAT WAS MY FUCKING LIFE???...
4-1-1? 5-1-1? 9-1-1? GODDAMN!
WHAT IS ALL THE RUCKUS OUT HERE?
VISION... BLURRING ALREADY...
HELLO? HELLO?! I'M HAVING A STROKE...I'M DYING! WHAT DO I DO???
HELLO?
GOOD EVENING, SIR. STAY ON THE LINE, PLEASE, I'M TRANSFERRING YOU TO A NURSE...
SURE...
C'MON, C'MON!...

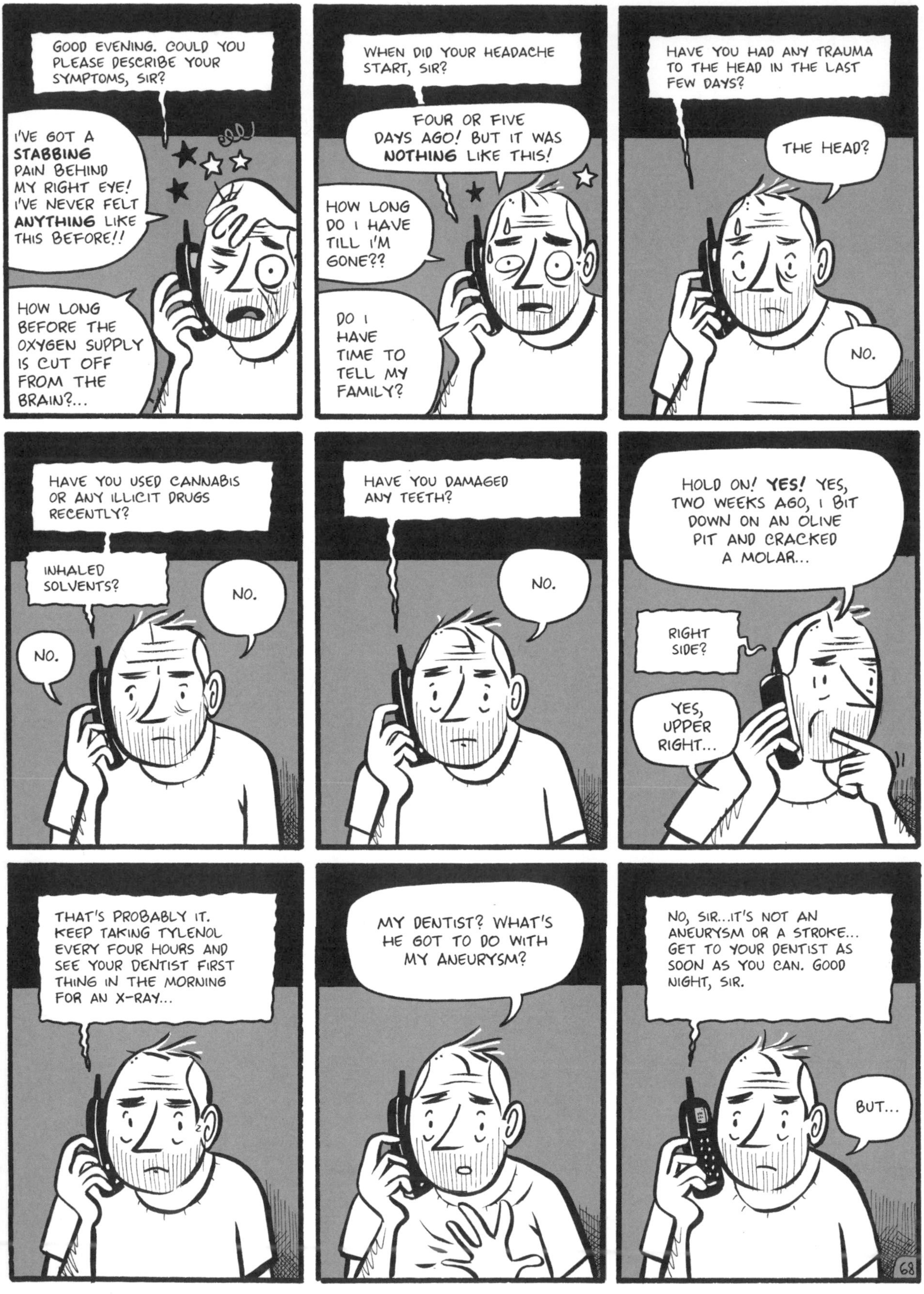
GOOD EVENING. COULD YOU PLEASE DESCRIBE YOUR SYMPTOMS, SIR?
I'VE GOT A **STABBING** PAIN BEHIND MY RIGHT EYE! I'VE NEVER FELT **ANYTHING** LIKE THIS BEFORE!!
HOW LONG BEFORE THE OXYGEN SUPPLY IS CUT OFF FROM THE BRAIN?...
WHEN DID YOUR HEADACHE START, SIR?
FOUR OR FIVE DAYS AGO! BUT IT WAS **NOTHING** LIKE THIS!
HOW LONG DO I HAVE TILL I'M GONE??
DO I HAVE TIME TO TELL MY FAMILY?
HAVE YOU HAD ANY TRAUMA TO THE HEAD IN THE LAST FEW DAYS?
THE HEAD?
NO.
HAVE YOU USED CANNABIS OR ANY ILLICIT DRUGS RECENTLY?
NO.
INHALED SOLVENTS?
NO.
HAVE YOU DAMAGED ANY TEETH?
NO.
HOLD ON! **YES!** YES, TWO WEEKS AGO, I BIT DOWN ON AN OLIVE PIT AND CRACKED A MOLAR...
RIGHT SIDE?
YES, UPPER RIGHT...
THAT'S PROBABLY IT. KEEP TAKING TYLENOL EVERY FOUR HOURS AND SEE YOUR DENTIST FIRST THING IN THE MORNING FOR AN X-RAY...
MY DENTIST? WHAT'S HE GOT TO DO WITH MY ANEURYSM?
NO, SIR...IT'S NOT AN ANEURYSM OR A STROKE... GET TO YOUR DENTIST AS SOON AS YOU CAN. GOOD NIGHT, SIR.
BUT...

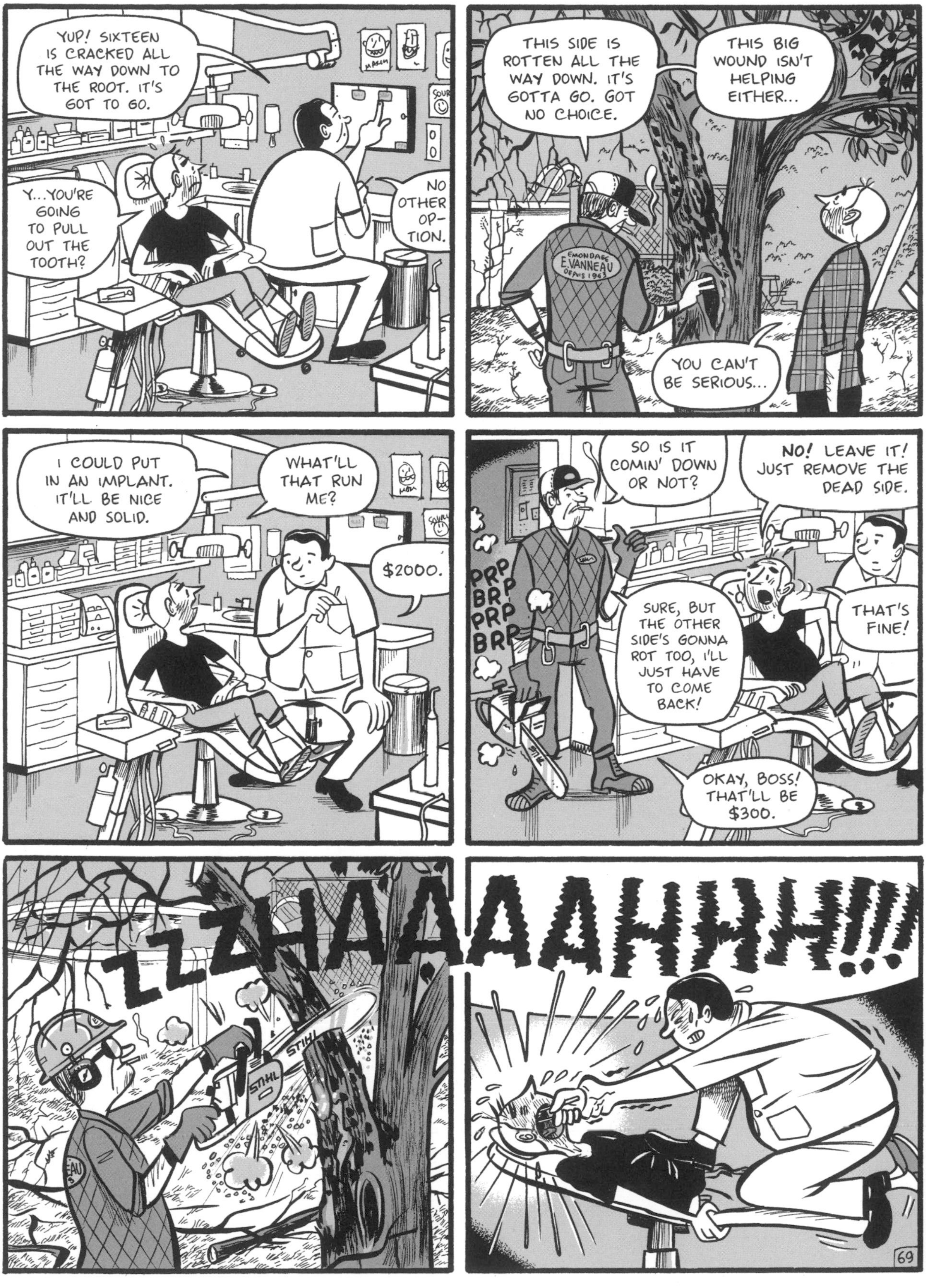
YUP! SIXTEEN IS CRACKED ALL THE WAY DOWN TO THE ROOT. IT'S GOT TO GO.
Y...YOU'RE GOING TO PULL OUT THE TOOTH?
NO OTHER OP-TION.
THIS SIDE IS ROTTEN ALL THE WAY DOWN. IT'S GOTTA GO. GOT NO CHOICE.
THIS BIG WOUND ISN'T HELPING EITHER...
ÉMONDAGE E.VANNEAU DEPUIS 1963
YOU CAN'T BE SERIOUS...
I COULD PUT IN AN IMPLANT. IT'LL BE NICE AND SOLID.
WHAT'LL THAT RUN ME?
$2000.
SO IS IT COMIN' DOWN OR NOT?
NO! LEAVE IT! JUST REMOVE THE DEAD SIDE.
PRP BRP PRP BRP
SURE, BUT THE OTHER SIDE'S GONNA ROT TOO, I'LL JUST HAVE TO COME BACK!
THAT'S FINE!
OKAY, BOSS! THAT'LL BE $300.
ZZZHAAAAHHH!!!!
STIHL

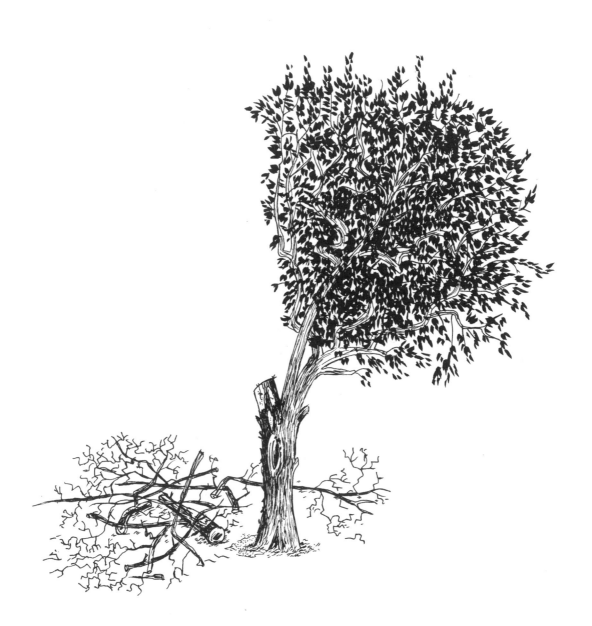

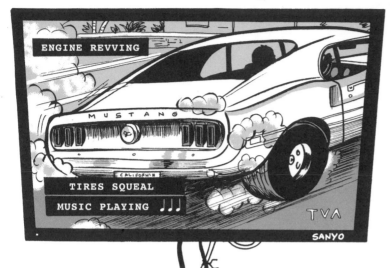

ENGINE REVVING

MUSTANG

CALIFORNIA

TIRES SQUEAL

MUSIC PLAYING ♪♪♪

TVA

SANYO

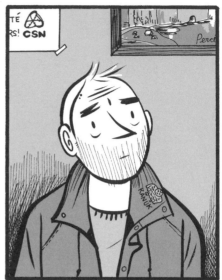

CSN

Perce

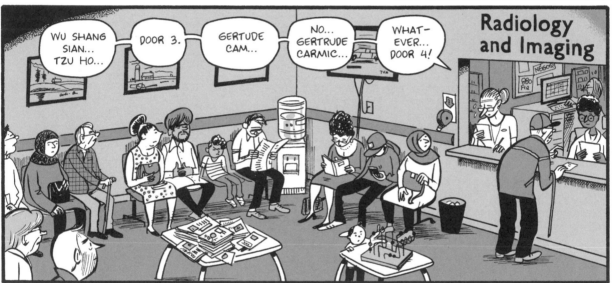

WU SHANG SIAN... TZU HO...

DOOR 3.

GERTUDE CAM...

NO... GERTRUDE CARMIC...

WHAT-EVER... DOOR 4!

Radiology and Imaging

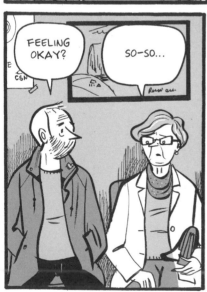

FEELING OKAY?

SO-SO...

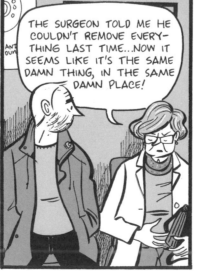

THE SURGEON TOLD ME HE COULDN'T REMOVE EVERY-THING LAST TIME...NOW IT SEEMS LIKE IT'S THE SAME DAMN THING, IN THE SAME DAMN PLACE!

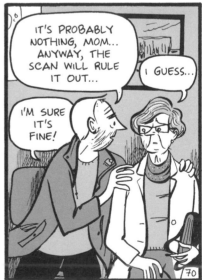

IT'S PROBABLY NOTHING, MOM... ANYWAY, THE SCAN WILL RULE IT OUT...

I GUESS...

I'M SURE IT'S FINE!

70

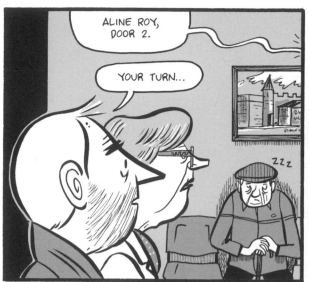

ALINE ROY, DOOR 2.

YOUR TURN...

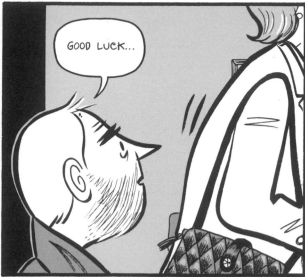

GOOD LUCK...

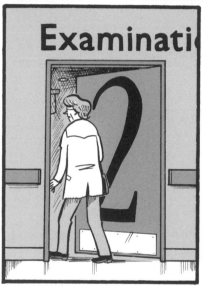

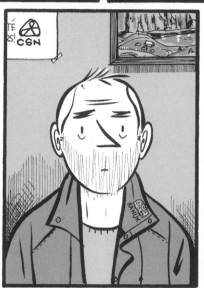

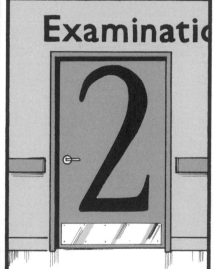

Examinati

Examinati

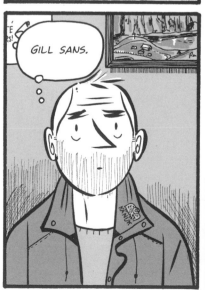

GILL SANS.

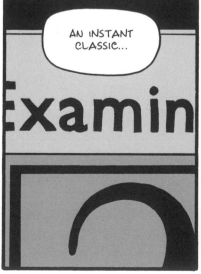

AN INSTANT CLASSIC...

Examin

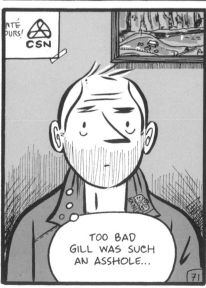

CSN

TOO BAD GILL WAS SUCH AN ASSHOLE...

71

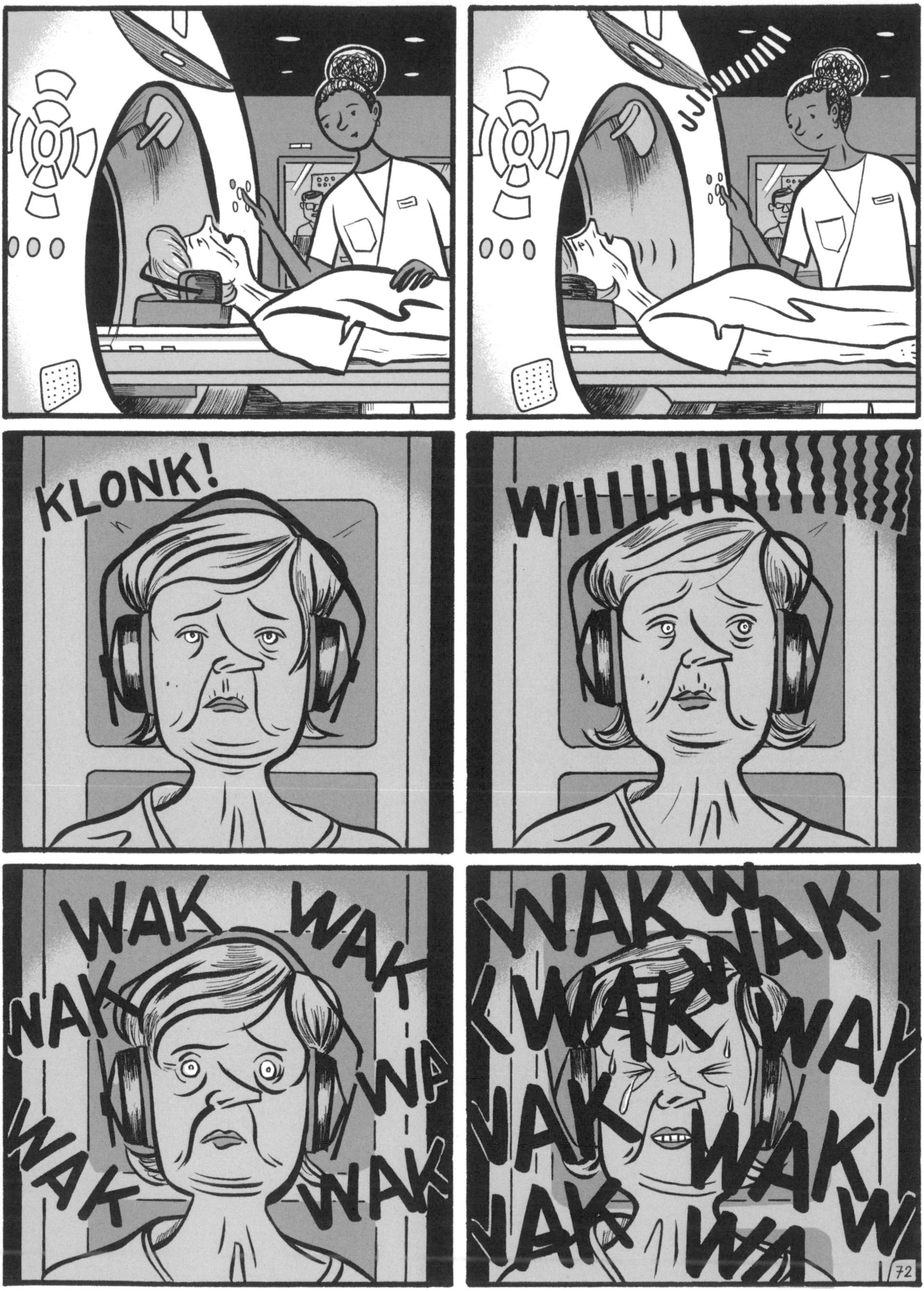
KLONK!
WIIIIIIII
WAK
WAK
WAK
WAK
WAK
WAK
WAK
WAK
WAK
WAK
WAK
WAK

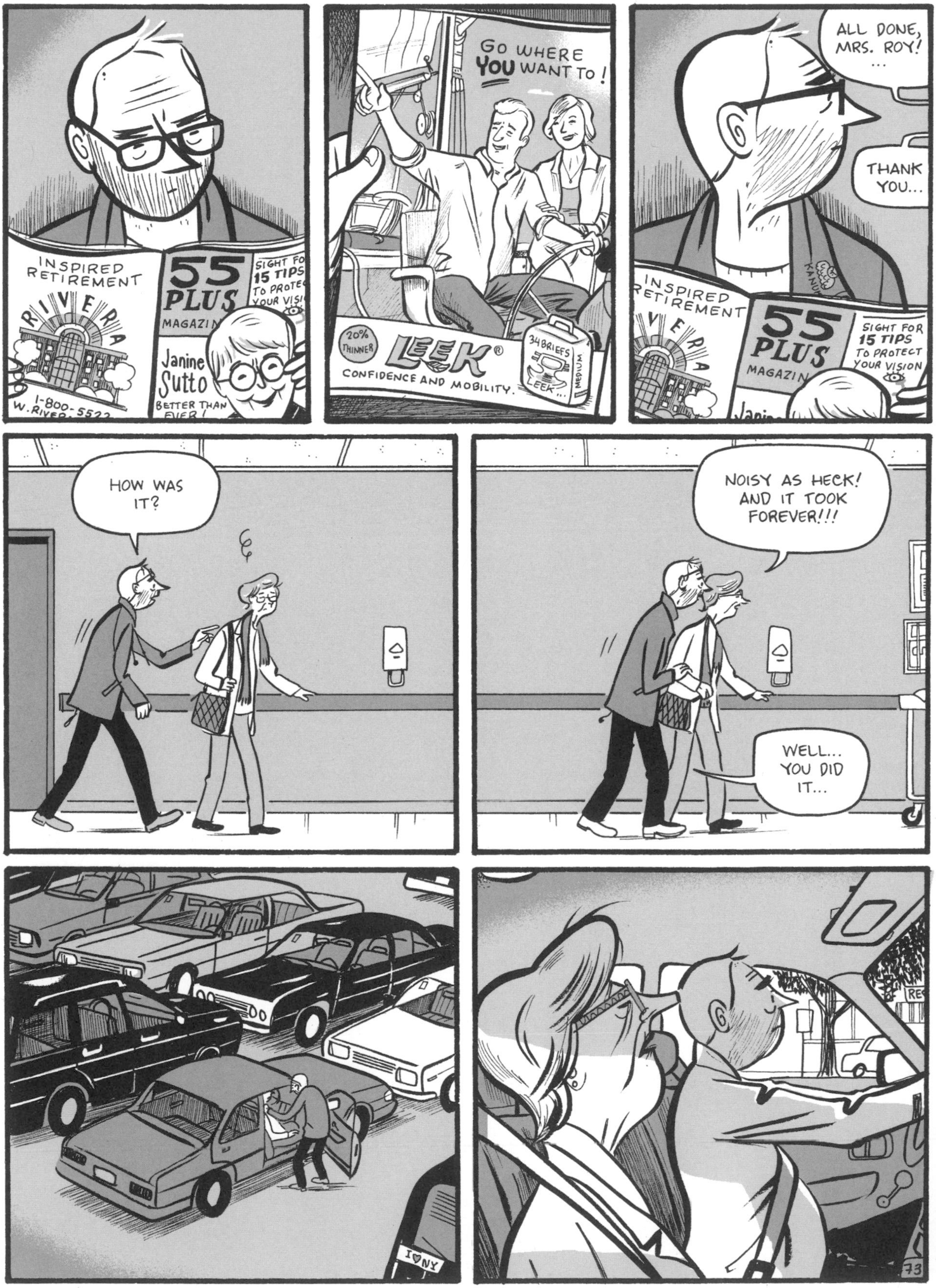
INSPIRED RETIREMENT
RIVERA
55 PLUS MAGAZIN
SIGHT FOR 15 TIPS TO PROTEC YOUR VISI
Janine Sutto
BETTER THAN
GO WHERE YOU WANT TO!
20% THINNER
LEEK®
CONFIDENCE AND MOBILITY.
34 BRIEFS
MEDIUM
LEEK...
ALL DONE, MRS. ROY! ...
THANK YOU...
INSPIRED RETIREMENT
55 PLUS MAGAZIN
SIGHT FOR 15 TIPS TO PROTECT YOUR VISION
HOW WAS IT?
NOISY AS HECK! AND IT TOOK FOREVER!!!
WELL... YOU DID IT...
I♥NY

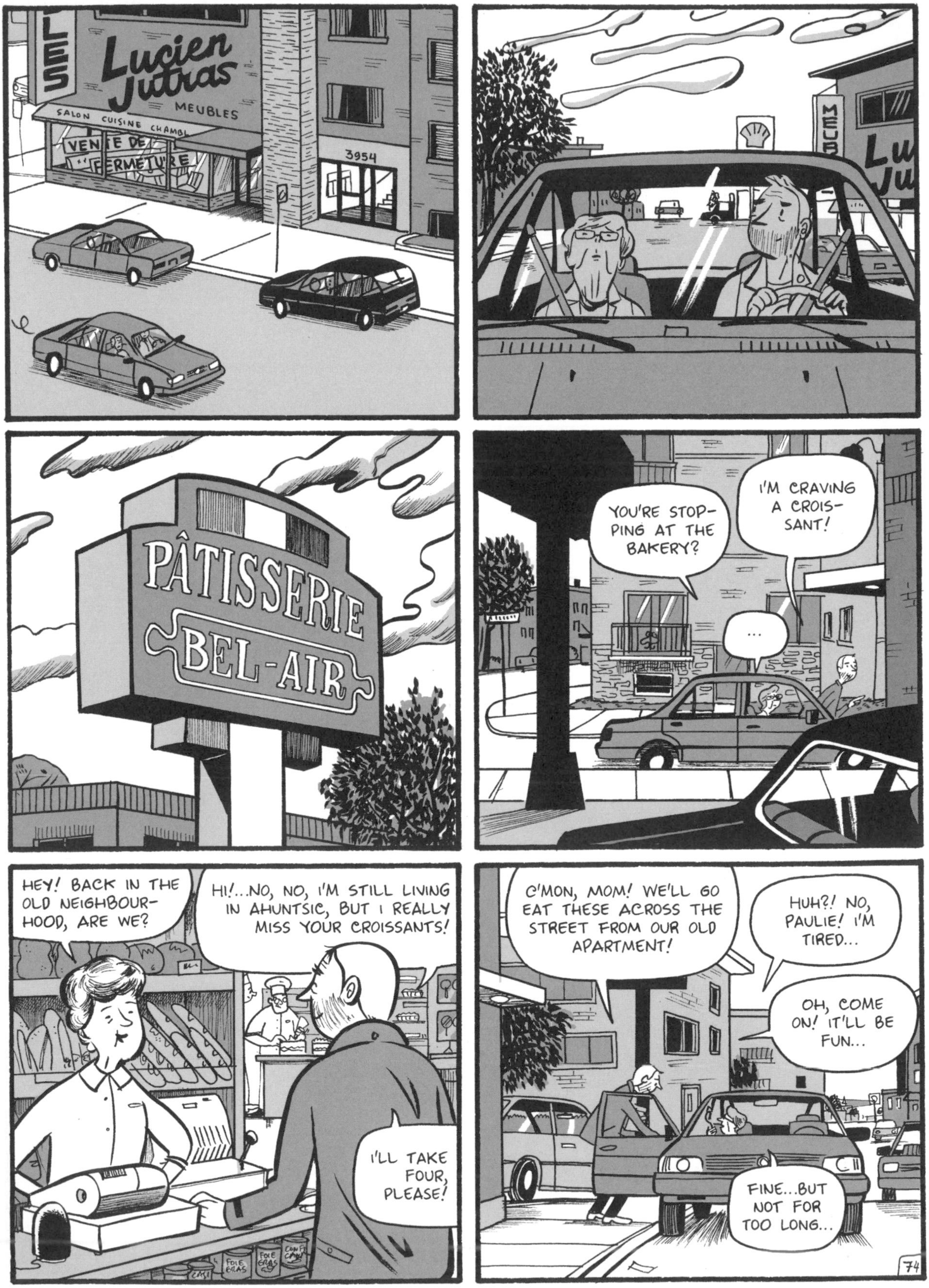
LES
Lucien Jutras
MEUBLES
SALON CUISINE CHAMB
VENTE DE FERMETURE
3954
MEUB
Lu Ju
PÂTISSERIE
BEL-AIR
YOU'RE STOPPING AT THE BAKERY?
I'M CRAVING A CROISSANT!
...
HEY! BACK IN THE OLD NEIGHBOURHOOD, ARE WE?
HI!...NO, NO, I'M STILL LIVING IN AHUNTSIC, BUT I REALLY MISS YOUR CROISSANTS!
I'LL TAKE FOUR, PLEASE!
FOIE GRAS
C'MON, MOM! WE'LL GO EAT THESE ACROSS THE STREET FROM OUR OLD APARTMENT!
HUH?! NO, PAULIE! I'M TIRED...
OH, COME ON! IT'LL BE FUN...
FINE...BUT NOT FOR TOO LONG...
74

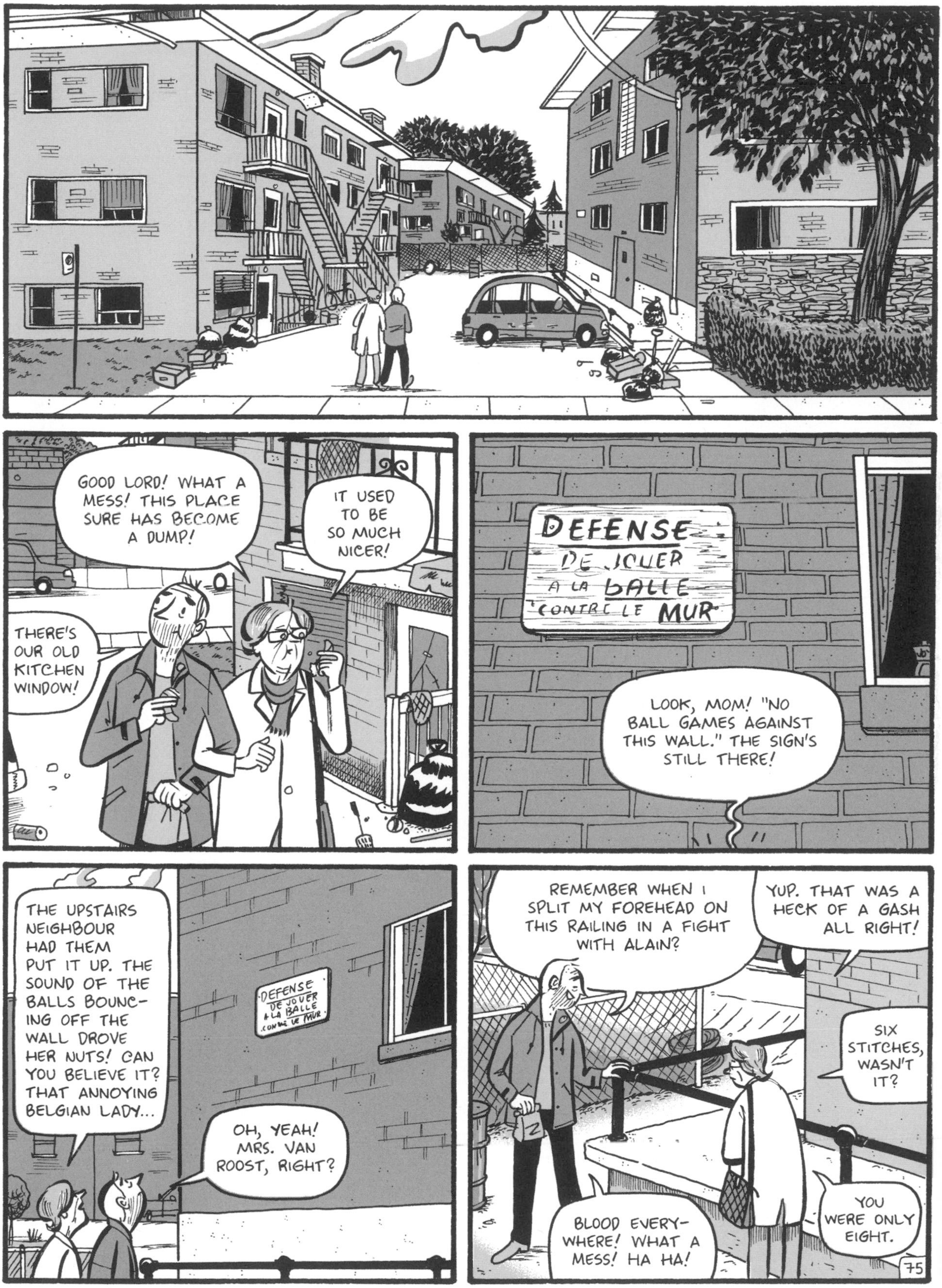

GOOD LORD! WHAT A MESS! THIS PLACE SURE HAS BECOME A DUMP!
IT USED TO BE SO MUCH NICER!
THERE'S OUR OLD KITCHEN WINDOW!
DEFENSE DE JOUER A LA BALLE CONTRE LE MUR
LOOK, MOM! "NO BALL GAMES AGAINST THIS WALL." THE SIGN'S STILL THERE!
THE UPSTAIRS NEIGHBOUR HAD THEM PUT IT UP. THE SOUND OF THE BALLS BOUNC-ING OFF THE WALL DROVE HER NUTS! CAN YOU BELIEVE IT? THAT ANNOYING BELGIAN LADY...
DEFENSE DE JOUER A LA BALLE CONTRE LE MUR
OH, YEAH! MRS. VAN ROOST, RIGHT?
REMEMBER WHEN I SPLIT MY FOREHEAD ON THIS RAILING IN A FIGHT WITH ALAIN?
YUP. THAT WAS A HECK OF A GASH ALL RIGHT!
SIX STITCHES, WASN'T IT?
BLOOD EVERY-WHERE! WHAT A MESS! HA HA!
YOU WERE ONLY EIGHT.

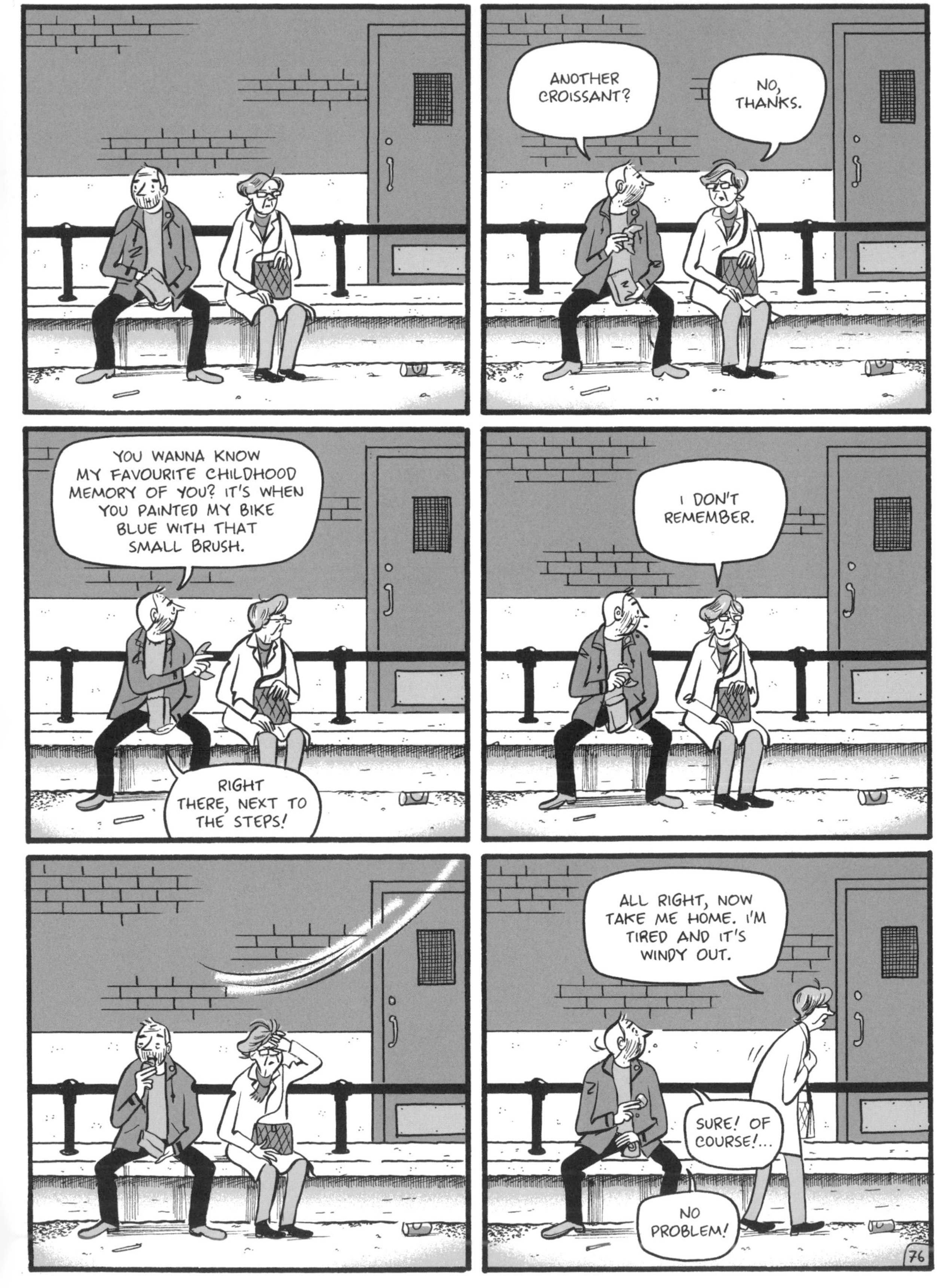
ANOTHER CROISSANT?
NO, THANKS.
YOU WANNA KNOW MY FAVOURITE CHILDHOOD MEMORY OF YOU? IT'S WHEN YOU PAINTED MY BIKE BLUE WITH THAT SMALL BRUSH.
RIGHT THERE, NEXT TO THE STEPS!
I DON'T REMEMBER.
ALL RIGHT, NOW TAKE ME HOME. I'M TIRED AND IT'S WINDY OUT.
SURE! OF COURSE!...
NO PROBLEM!
76

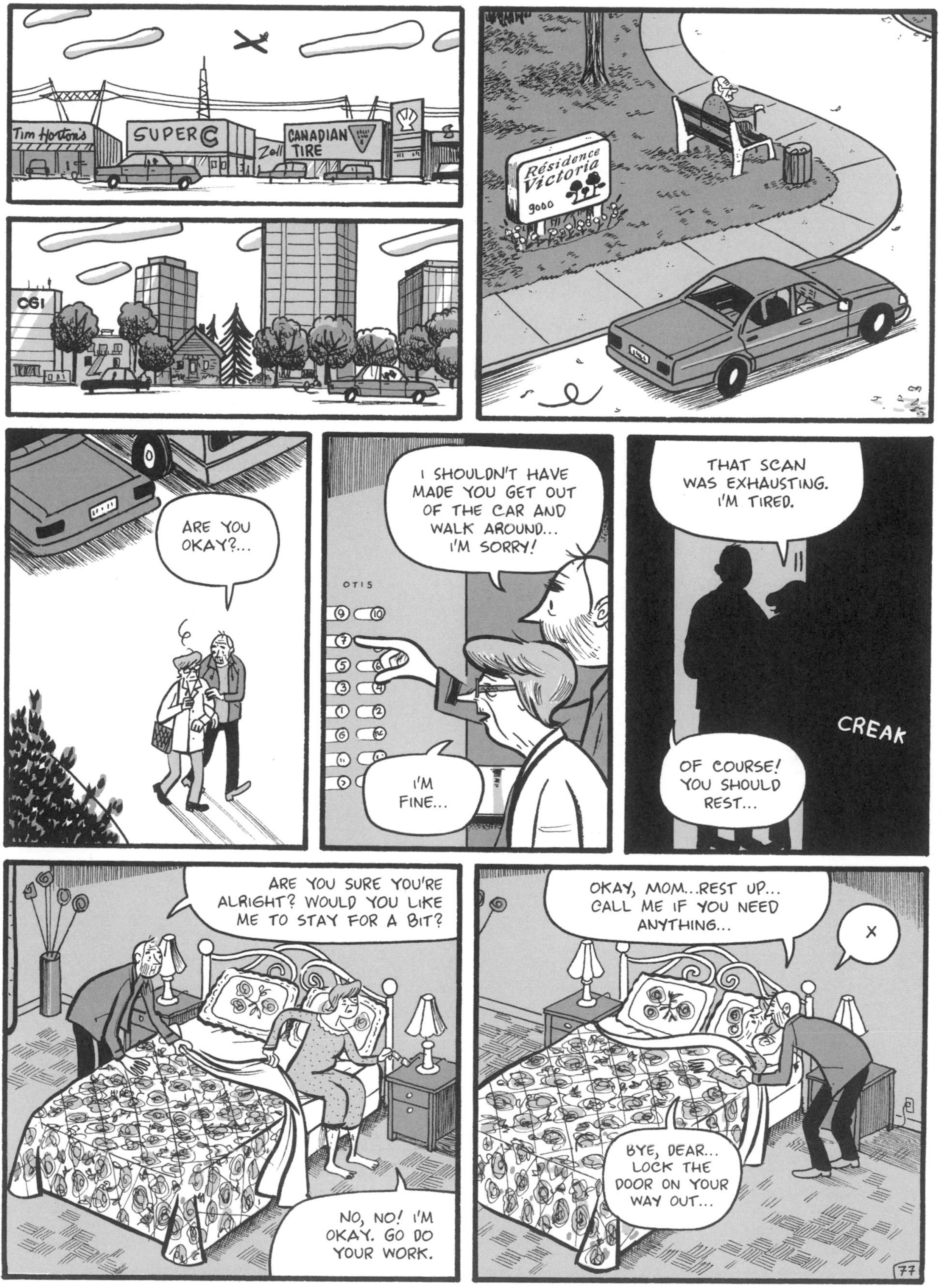

Tim Horton's
SUPER C
CANADIAN TIRE
CGI
Résidence Victoria
9000
ARE YOU OKAY?...
OTIS
I SHOULDN'T HAVE MADE YOU GET OUT OF THE CAR AND WALK AROUND... I'M SORRY!
I'M FINE...
THAT SCAN WAS EXHAUSTING. I'M TIRED.
CREAK
OF COURSE! YOU SHOULD REST...
ARE YOU SURE YOU'RE ALRIGHT? WOULD YOU LIKE ME TO STAY FOR A BIT?
NO, NO! I'M OKAY. GO DO YOUR WORK.
OKAY, MOM...REST UP... CALL ME IF YOU NEED ANYTHING...
X
BYE, DEAR... LOCK THE DOOR ON YOUR WAY OUT...

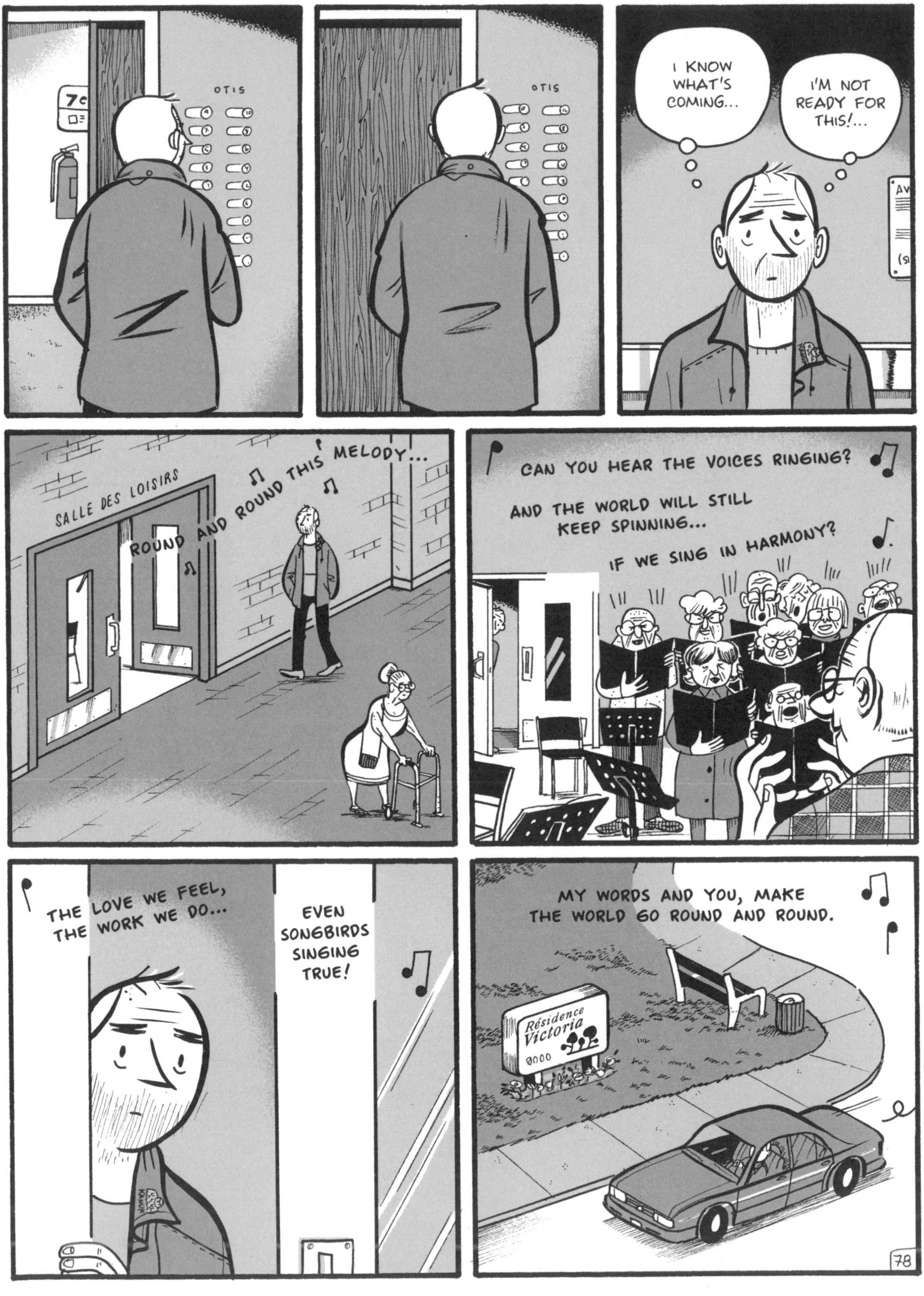
OTIS
OTIS
I KNOW WHAT'S COMING...
I'M NOT READY FOR THIS!...
SALLE DES LOISIRS
ROUND AND ROUND THIS MELODY...
CAN YOU HEAR THE VOICES RINGING?
AND THE WORLD WILL STILL KEEP SPINNING...
IF WE SING IN HARMONY?
THE LOVE WE FEEL, THE WORK WE DO...
EVEN SONGBIRDS SINGING TRUE!
MY WORDS AND YOU, MAKE THE WORLD GO ROUND AND ROUND.
Résidence Victoria
8000

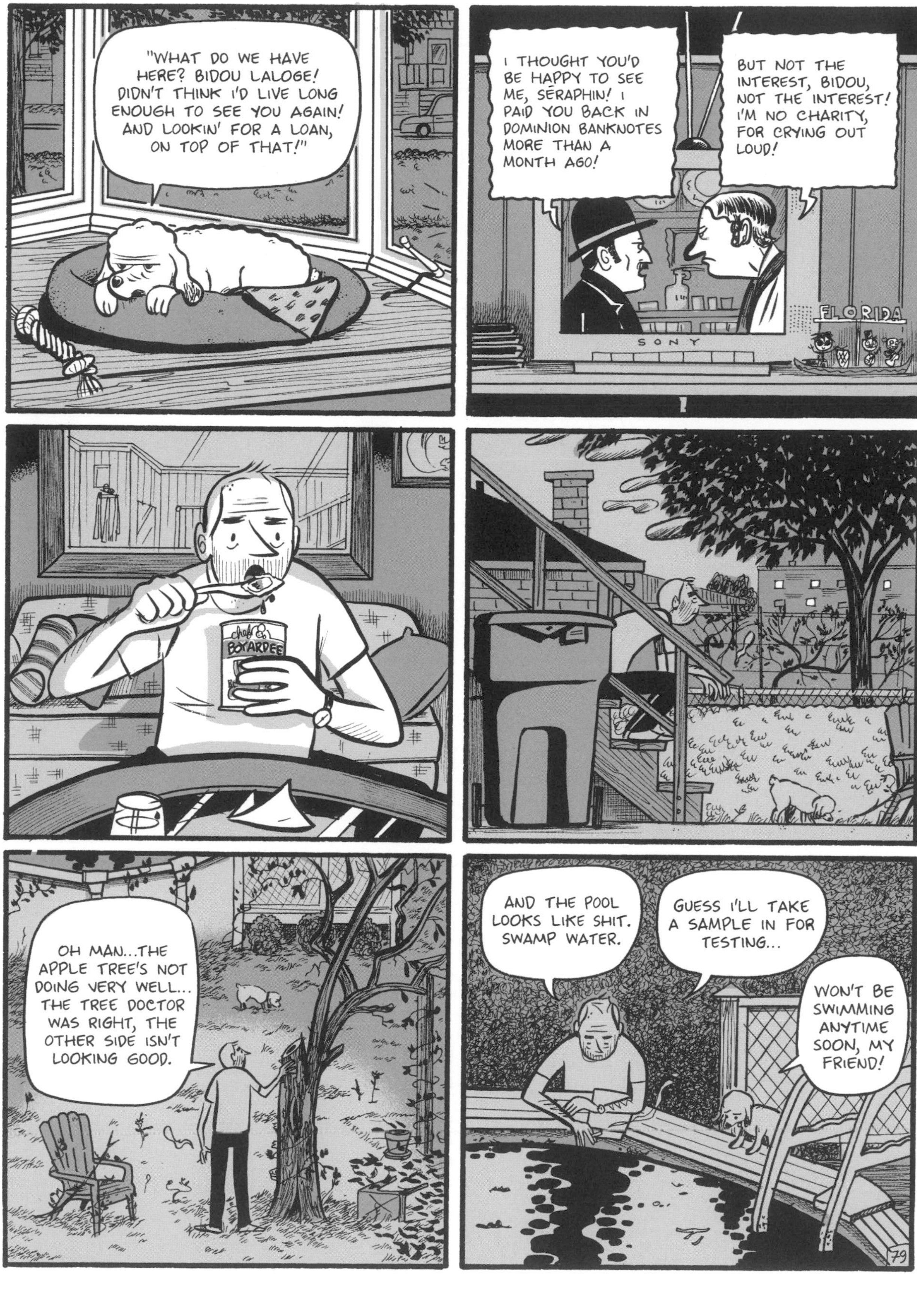
"WHAT DO WE HAVE HERE? BIDOU LALOGE! DIDN'T THINK I'D LIVE LONG ENOUGH TO SEE YOU AGAIN! AND LOOKIN' FOR A LOAN, ON TOP OF THAT!"
I THOUGHT YOU'D BE HAPPY TO SEE ME, SÉRAPHIN! I PAID YOU BACK IN DOMINION BANKNOTES MORE THAN A MONTH AGO!
BUT NOT THE INTEREST, BIDOU, NOT THE INTEREST! I'M NO CHARITY, FOR CRYING OUT LOUD!
FLORIDA
SONY
BOYARDEE
OH MAN...THE APPLE TREE'S NOT DOING VERY WELL... THE TREE DOCTOR WAS RIGHT, THE OTHER SIDE ISN'T LOOKING GOOD.
AND THE POOL LOOKS LIKE SHIT. SWAMP WATER.
GUESS I'LL TAKE A SAMPLE IN FOR TESTING...
WON'T BE SWIMMING ANYTIME SOON, MY FRIEND!

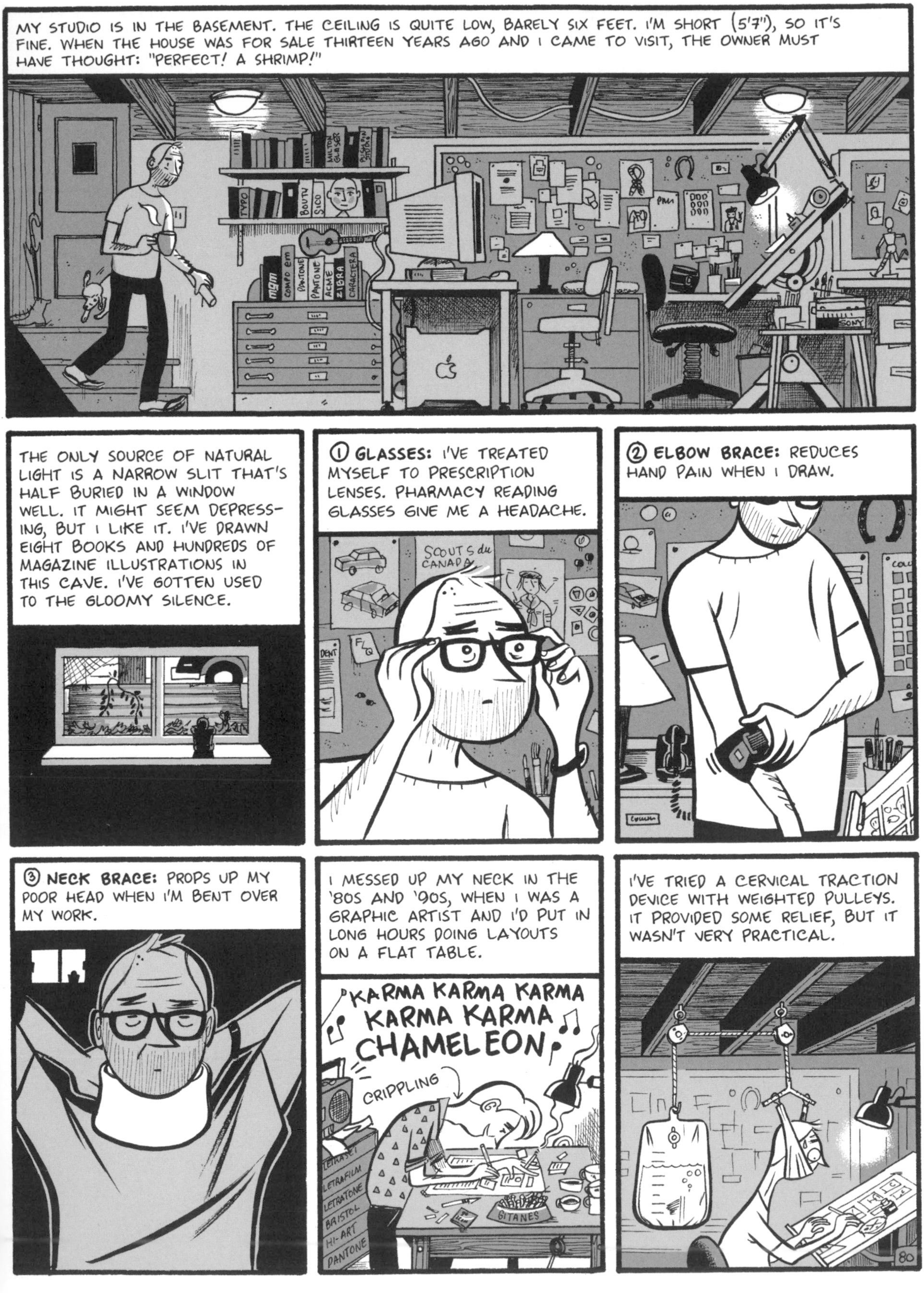
MY STUDIO IS IN THE BASEMENT. THE CEILING IS QUITE LOW, BARELY SIX FEET. I'M SHORT (5'7"), SO IT'S FINE. WHEN THE HOUSE WAS FOR SALE THIRTEEN YEARS AGO AND I CAME TO VISIT, THE OWNER MUST HAVE THOUGHT: "PERFECT! A SHRIMP!"
TYPO
BOUTV SICO
MILTON GLASER
COMPO em
PANTONE
PANTONE
ACME
ZIBRA
CARACTERA
SONY
THE ONLY SOURCE OF NATURAL LIGHT IS A NARROW SLIT THAT'S HALF BURIED IN A WINDOW WELL. IT MIGHT SEEM DEPRESSING, BUT I LIKE IT. I'VE DRAWN EIGHT BOOKS AND HUNDREDS OF MAGAZINE ILLUSTRATIONS IN THIS CAVE. I'VE GOTTEN USED TO THE GLOOMY SILENCE.
① GLASSES: I'VE TREATED MYSELF TO PRESCRIPTION LENSES. PHARMACY READING GLASSES GIVE ME A HEADACHE.
SCOUTS du CANADA
② ELBOW BRACE: REDUCES HAND PAIN WHEN I DRAW.
③ NECK BRACE: PROPS UP MY POOR HEAD WHEN I'M BENT OVER MY WORK.
I MESSED UP MY NECK IN THE '80S AND '90S, WHEN I WAS A GRAPHIC ARTIST AND I'D PUT IN LONG HOURS DOING LAYOUTS ON A FLAT TABLE.
KARMA KARMA KARMA KARMA KARMA CHAMELEON
CRIPPLING
LETRASET
LETRAFILM
LETRATONE
BRISTOL
HI-ART
PANTONE
GITANES
I'VE TRIED A CERVICAL TRACTION DEVICE WITH WEIGHTED PULLEYS. IT PROVIDED SOME RELIEF, BUT IT WASN'T VERY PRACTICAL.

ONE OF MY FAVOURITE STEPS IN MAKING COMICS IS DRAWING THE PANEL BORDERS.

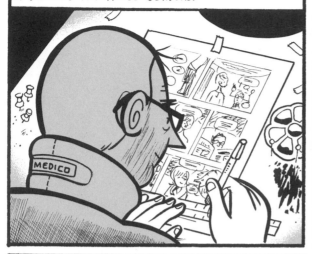

IT'S BRAINLESS, BUT I LOVE IT. THERE'S SOMETHING DEEPLY SATISFYING ABOUT DRAWING STRAIGHT LINES.

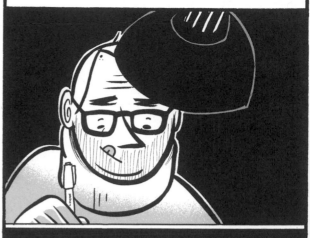

ARTISTS HAVE ALWAYS OBSESSED ABOUT DRAWING PERFECT LINES. FOR CENTURIES, THE ONLY WAY TO DO IT WAS WITH A RULING PEN. BUT IT'S A DIFFICULT TOOL TO USE.

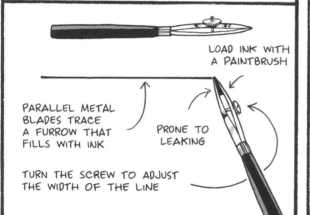

LOAD INK WITH A PAINTBRUSH

PARALLEL METAL BLADES TRACE A FURROW THAT FILLS WITH INK

PRONE TO LEAKING

TURN THE SCREW TO ADJUST THE WIDTH OF THE LINE

IN 1934, THE MANUFACTURER PELIKAN TRADEMARKED THE GRAPHOS, A TECHNICAL FOUNTAIN PEN.

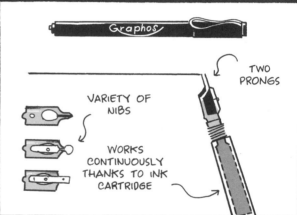

Graphos

TWO PRONGS

VARIETY OF NIBS

WORKS CONTINUOUSLY THANKS TO INK CARTRIDGE

THEN, IN 1953, ROTRING LAUNCHED A REVOLUTIONARY TECHNICAL PEN, THE RAPIDOGRAPH. IT WAS IMMEDIATELY ADOPTED BY MOST GRAPHIC DESIGN AND TECHNICAL DRAWING STUDIOS.

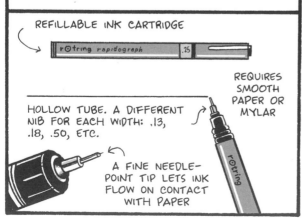

REFILLABLE INK CARTRIDGE

rOtring rapidograph .25

REQUIRES SMOOTH PAPER OR MYLAR

HOLLOW TUBE. A DIFFERENT NIB FOR EACH WIDTH: .13, .18, .50, ETC.

A FINE NEEDLE-POINT TIP LETS INK FLOW ON CONTACT WITH PAPER

rOtring

BUT RAPIDOS CAN BE TEMPERAMENTAL, TOO. IF YOU DON'T USE THEM REGULARLY, LOOK OUT. THEY'LL DRY UP AND CLOG, SO THEN YOU NEED TO TAKE THEM APART AND CLEAN EVERYTHING, WHICH IS A HUGE PAIN IN THE ASS.

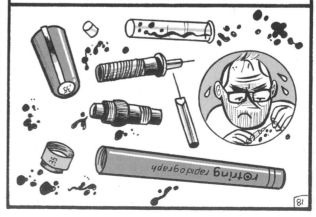

rOtring rapidograph

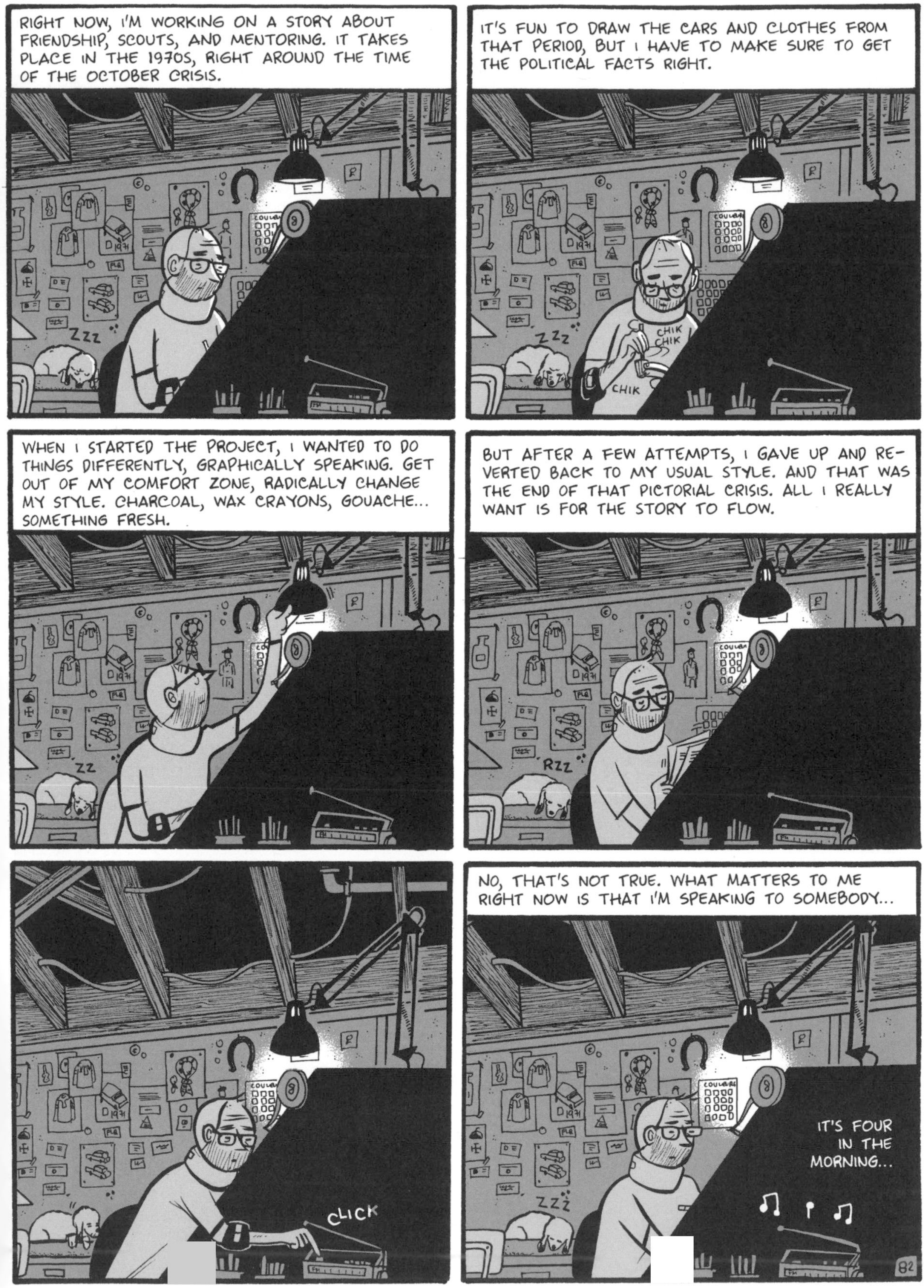
RIGHT NOW, I'M WORKING ON A STORY ABOUT FRIENDSHIP, SCOUTS, AND MENTORING. IT TAKES PLACE IN THE 1970S, RIGHT AROUND THE TIME OF THE OCTOBER CRISIS.
ZZZ
IT'S FUN TO DRAW THE CARS AND CLOTHES FROM THAT PERIOD, BUT I HAVE TO MAKE SURE TO GET THE POLITICAL FACTS RIGHT.
ZZZ
CHIK CHIK
CHIK
WHEN I STARTED THE PROJECT, I WANTED TO DO THINGS DIFFERENTLY, GRAPHICALLY SPEAKING. GET OUT OF MY COMFORT ZONE, RADICALLY CHANGE MY STYLE. CHARCOAL, WAX CRAYONS, GOUACHE... SOMETHING FRESH.
ZZ
BUT AFTER A FEW ATTEMPTS, I GAVE UP AND REVERTED BACK TO MY USUAL STYLE. AND THAT WAS THE END OF THAT PICTORIAL CRISIS. ALL I REALLY WANT IS FOR THE STORY TO FLOW.
RZZ
CLICK
NO, THAT'S NOT TRUE. WHAT MATTERS TO ME RIGHT NOW IS THAT I'M SPEAKING TO SOMEBODY...
IT'S FOUR IN THE MORNING...
ZZZ

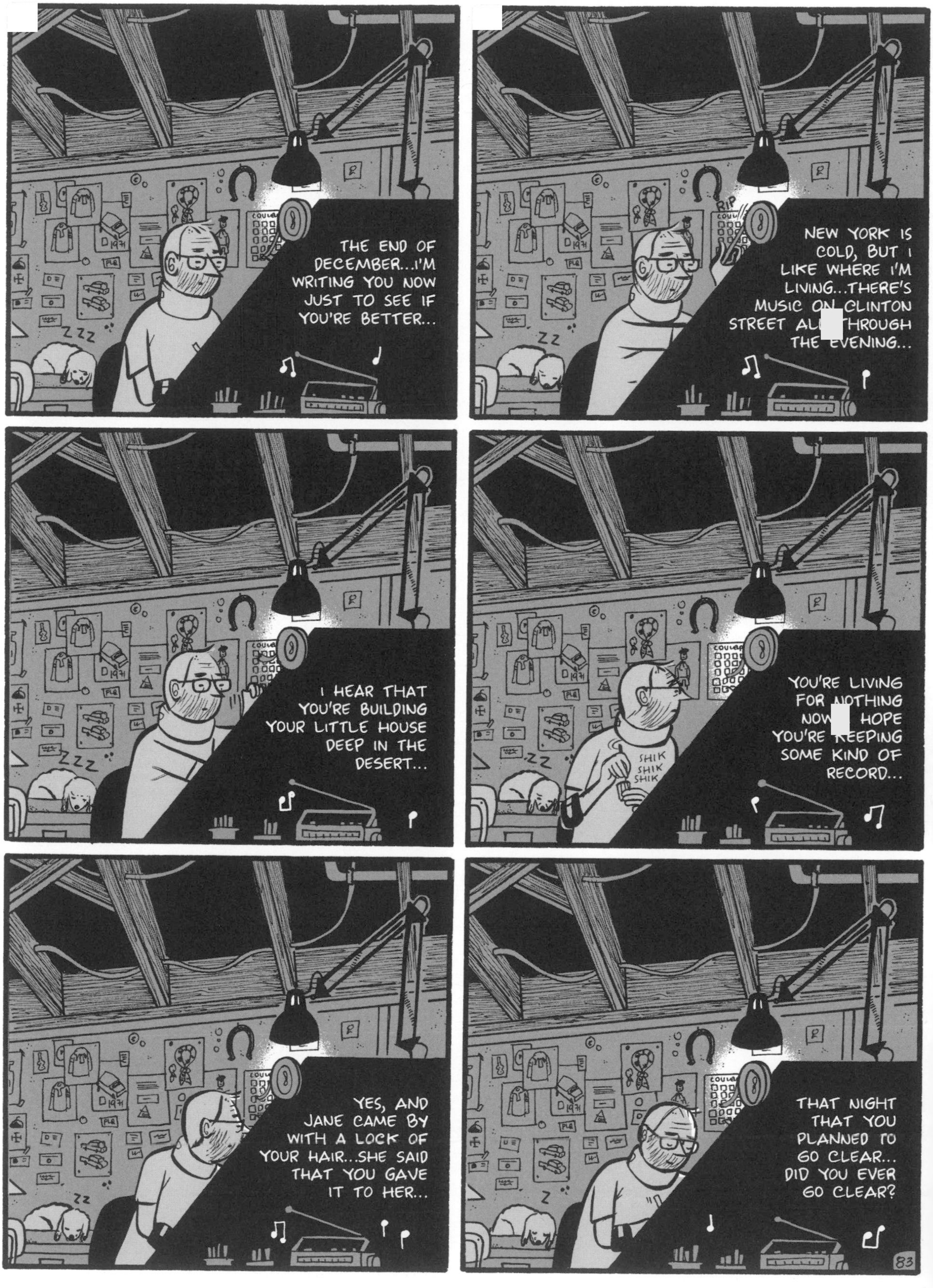
THE END OF DECEMBER...I'M WRITING YOU NOW JUST TO SEE IF YOU'RE BETTER...
ZZZ
NEW YORK IS COLD, BUT I LIKE WHERE I'M LIVING...THERE'S MUSIC ON CLINTON STREET AL THROUGH THE EVENING...
RIP
ZZ
I HEAR THAT YOU'RE BUILDING YOUR LITTLE HOUSE DEEP IN THE DESERT...
ZZZ
YOU'RE LIVING FOR NOTHING NOW HOPE YOU'RE KEEPING SOME KIND OF RECORD...
SHIK SHIK SHIK
ZZ
YES, AND JANE CAME BY WITH A LOCK OF YOUR HAIR...SHE SAID THAT YOU GAVE IT TO HER...
ZZ
THAT NIGHT THAT YOU PLANNED TO GO CLEAR... DID YOU EVER GO CLEAR?
Z

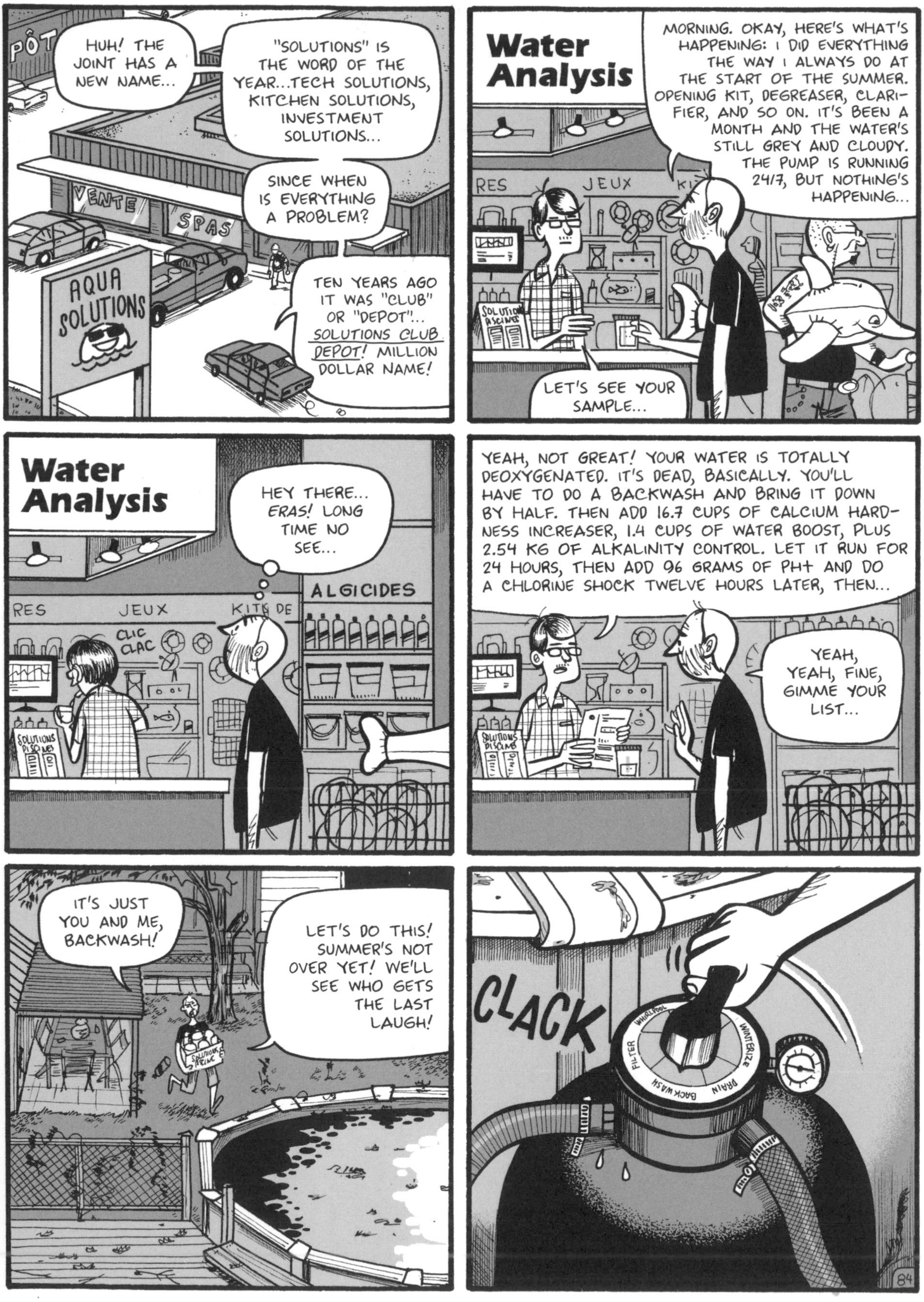
PÔT
HUH! THE JOINT HAS A NEW NAME...
"SOLUTIONS" IS THE WORD OF THE YEAR...TECH SOLUTIONS, KITCHEN SOLUTIONS, INVESTMENT SOLUTIONS...
SINCE WHEN IS EVERYTHING A PROBLEM?
VENTE
SPAS
AQUA SOLUTIONS
TEN YEARS AGO IT WAS "CLUB" OR "DEPOT"... SOLUTIONS CLUB DEPOT! MILLION DOLLAR NAME!
Water Analysis
MORNING. OKAY, HERE'S WHAT'S HAPPENING: I DID EVERYTHING THE WAY I ALWAYS DO AT THE START OF THE SUMMER. OPENING KIT, DEGREASER, CLARIFIER, AND SO ON. IT'S BEEN A MONTH AND THE WATER'S STILL GREY AND CLOUDY. THE PUMP IS RUNNING 24/7, BUT NOTHING'S HAPPENING...
RES
JEUX
LET'S SEE YOUR SAMPLE...
Water Analysis
HEY THERE... ERAS! LONG TIME NO SEE...
ALGICIDES
RES
JEUX
KITS DE
CLIC CLAC
SOLUTIONS PISCINES
YEAH, NOT GREAT! YOUR WATER IS TOTALLY DEOXYGENATED. IT'S DEAD, BASICALLY. YOU'LL HAVE TO DO A BACKWASH AND BRING IT DOWN BY HALF. THEN ADD 16.7 CUPS OF CALCIUM HARDNESS INCREASER, 1.4 CUPS OF WATER BOOST, PLUS 2.54 KG OF ALKALINITY CONTROL. LET IT RUN FOR 24 HOURS, THEN ADD 96 GRAMS OF PH+ AND DO A CHLORINE SHOCK TWELVE HOURS LATER, THEN...
YEAH, YEAH, FINE, GIMME YOUR LIST...
IT'S JUST YOU AND ME, BACKWASH!
LET'S DO THIS! SUMMER'S NOT OVER YET! WE'LL SEE WHO GETS THE LAST LAUGH!
CLACK
WHIRLPOOL
WINTERIZE
FILTER
BACKWASH
DRAIN

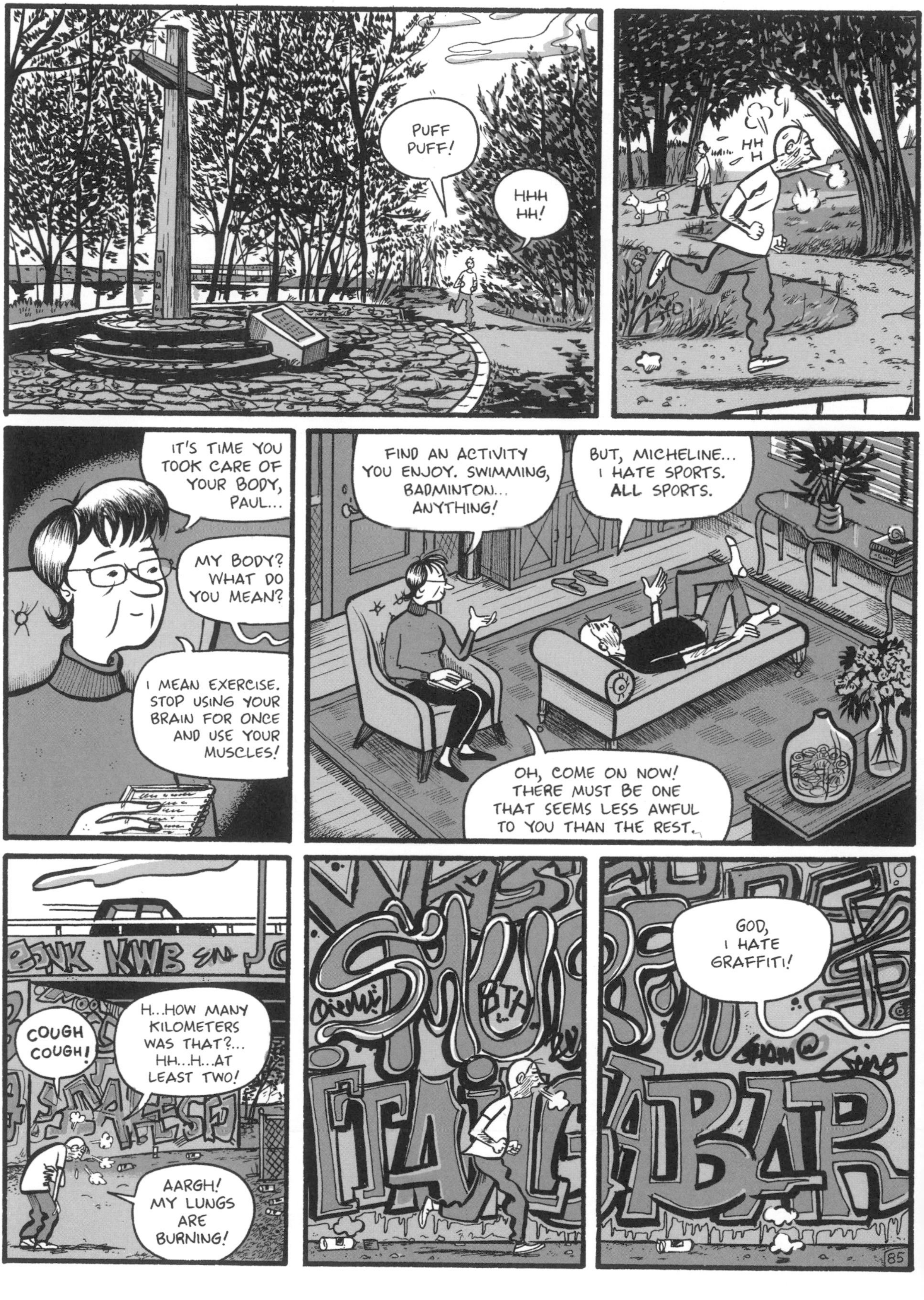
PUFF PUFF!
HHH HH!
HH H
IT'S TIME YOU TOOK CARE OF YOUR BODY, PAUL...
MY BODY? WHAT DO YOU MEAN?
I MEAN EXERCISE. STOP USING YOUR BRAIN FOR ONCE AND USE YOUR MUSCLES!
FIND AN ACTIVITY YOU ENJOY. SWIMMING, BADMINTON... ANYTHING!
BUT, MICHELINE... I HATE SPORTS. ALL SPORTS.
OH, COME ON NOW! THERE MUST BE ONE THAT SEEMS LESS AWFUL TO YOU THAN THE REST.
COUGH COUGH!
H...HOW MANY KILOMETERS WAS THAT?... HH...H...AT LEAST TWO!
AARGH! MY LUNGS ARE BURNING!
GOD, I HATE GRAFFITI!

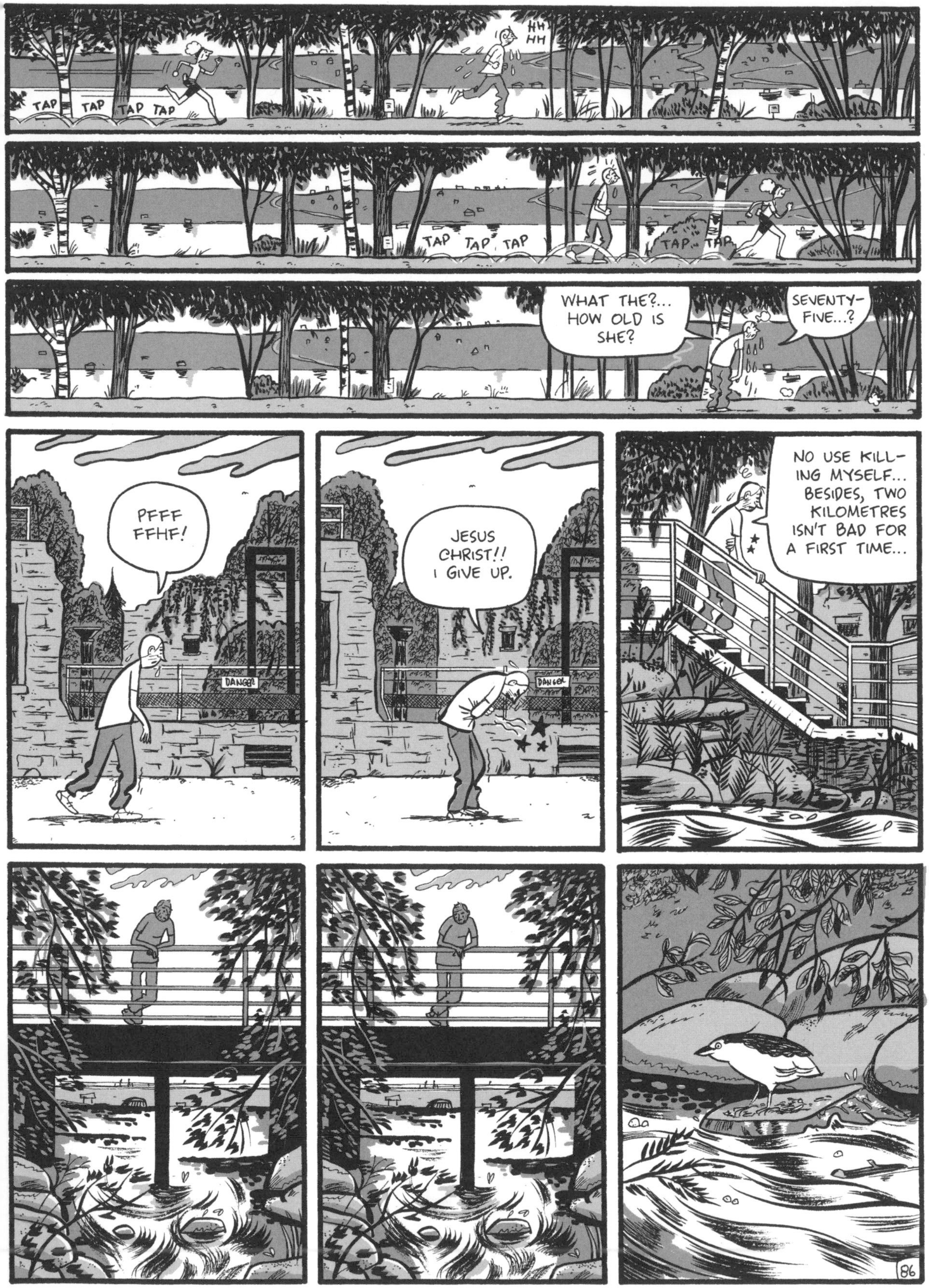
TAP TAP TAP TAP
HHHH
TAP TAP TAP
TAP TAP
WHAT THE?... HOW OLD IS SHE?
SEVENTY-FIVE...?
PFFF FFHF!
DANGER
JESUS CHRIST!! I GIVE UP.
DANGER
NO USE KILLING MYSELF... BESIDES, TWO KILOMETRES ISN'T BAD FOR A FIRST TIME...

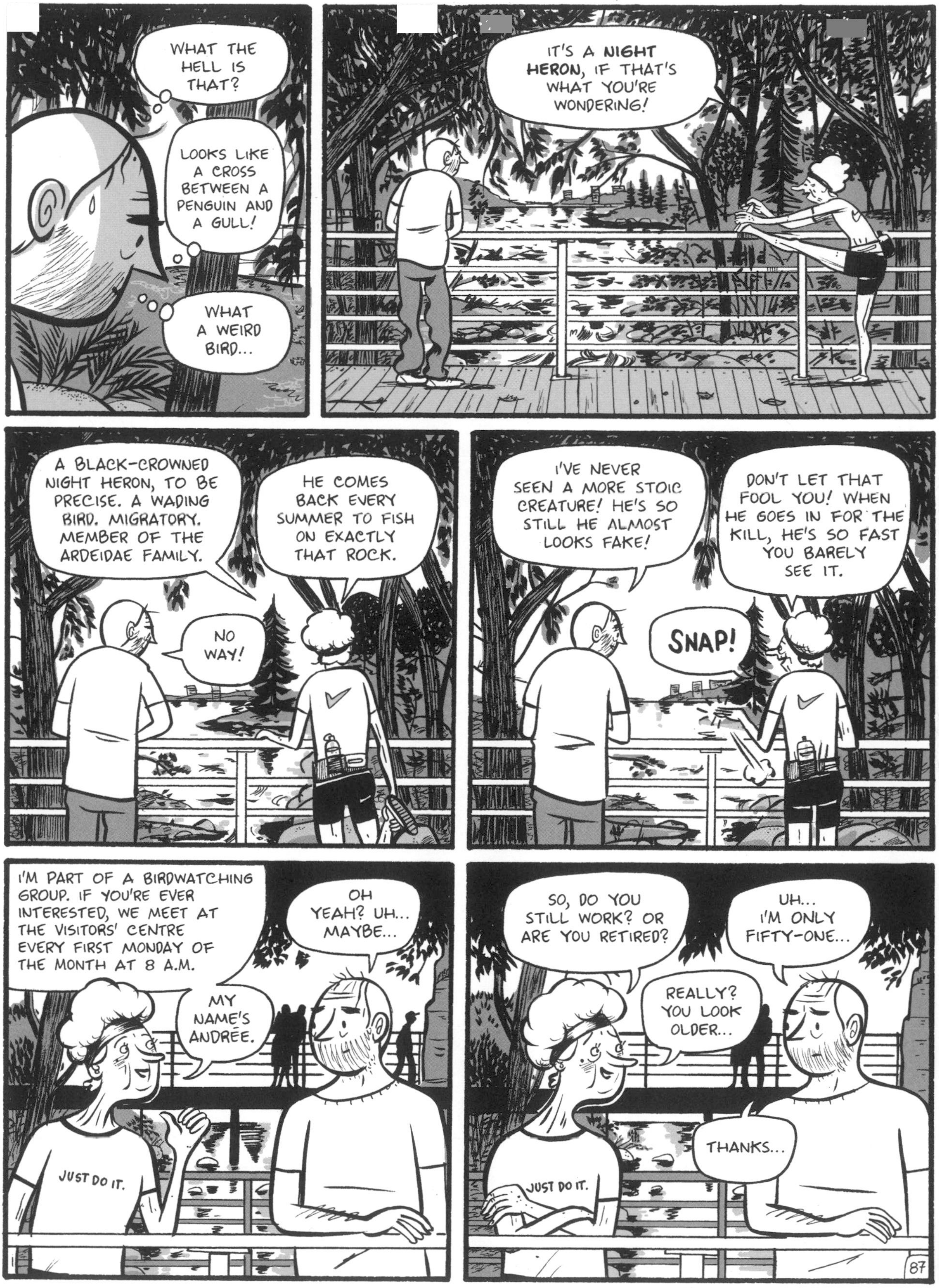
WHAT THE HELL IS THAT?
LOOKS LIKE A CROSS BETWEEN A PENGUIN AND A GULL!
WHAT A WEIRD BIRD...
IT'S A **NIGHT HERON**, IF THAT'S WHAT YOU'RE WONDERING!
A BLACK-CROWNED NIGHT HERON, TO BE PRECISE. A WADING BIRD. MIGRATORY. MEMBER OF THE ARDEIDAE FAMILY.
HE COMES BACK EVERY SUMMER TO FISH ON EXACTLY THAT ROCK.
NO WAY!
I'VE NEVER SEEN A MORE STOIC CREATURE! HE'S SO STILL HE ALMOST LOOKS FAKE!
DON'T LET THAT FOOL YOU! WHEN HE GOES IN FOR THE KILL, HE'S SO FAST YOU BARELY SEE IT.
SNAP!
I'M PART OF A BIRDWATCHING GROUP. IF YOU'RE EVER INTERESTED, WE MEET AT THE VISITORS' CENTRE EVERY FIRST MONDAY OF THE MONTH AT 8 A.M.
OH YEAH? UH... MAYBE...
MY NAME'S ANDRÉE.
JUST DO IT.
SO, DO YOU STILL WORK? OR ARE YOU RETIRED?
UH... I'M ONLY FIFTY-ONE...
REALLY? YOU LOOK OLDER...
THANKS...
JUST DO IT.

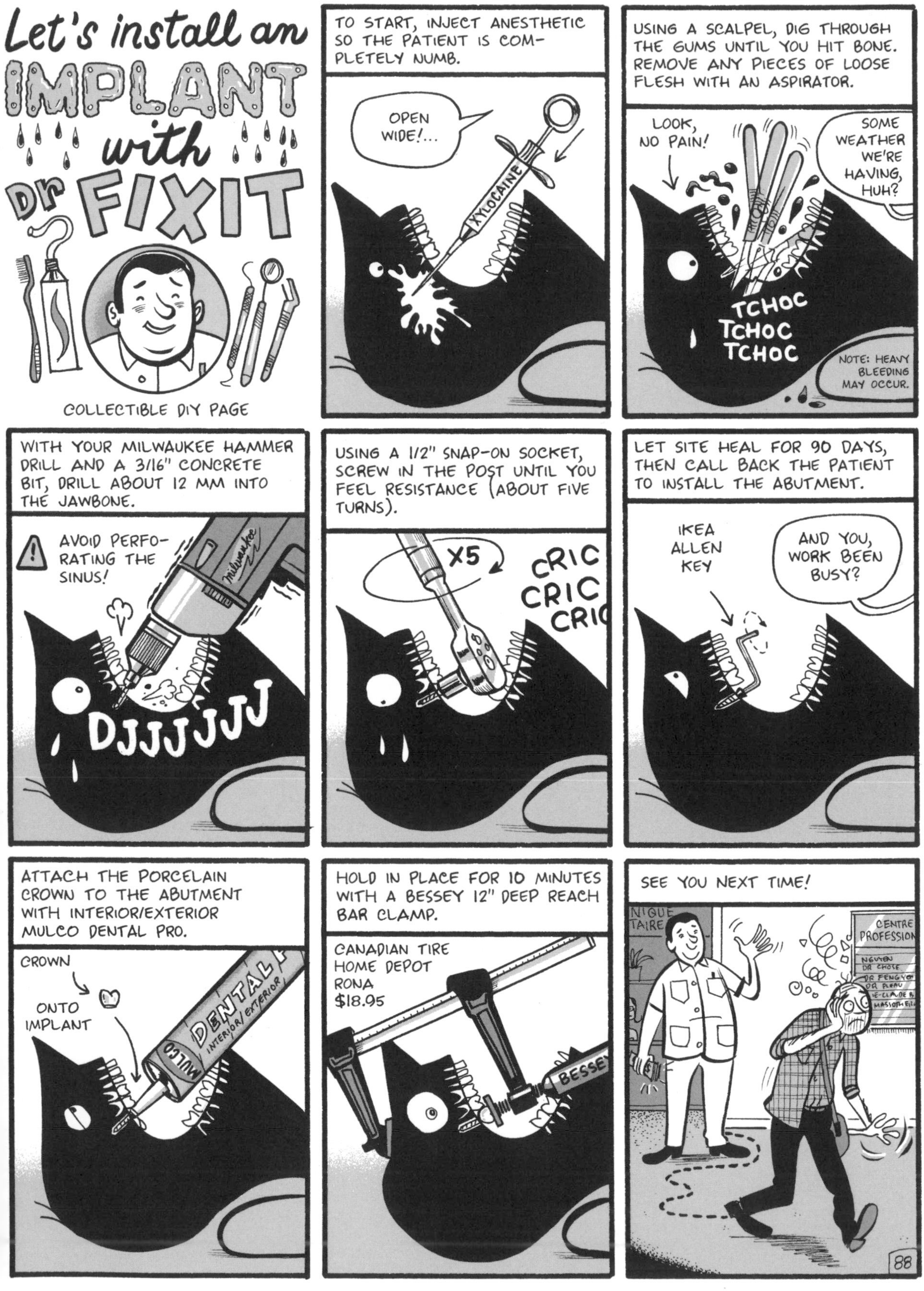

Let's install an IMPLANT with Dr FIXIT

COLLECTIBLE DIY PAGE

TO START, INJECT ANESTHETIC SO THE PATIENT IS COMPLETELY NUMB.

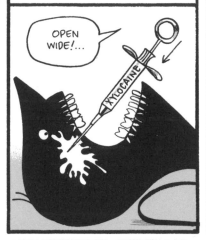

OPEN WIDE!...

XYLOCAINE

USING A SCALPEL, DIG THROUGH THE GUMS UNTIL YOU HIT BONE. REMOVE ANY PIECES OF LOOSE FLESH WITH AN ASPIRATOR.

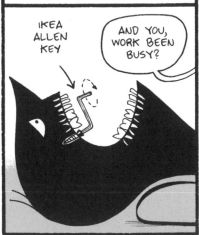

LOOK, NO PAIN!

SOME WEATHER WE'RE HAVING, HUH?

TCHOC TCHOC TCHOC

NOTE: HEAVY BLEEDING MAY OCCUR.

WITH YOUR MILWAUKEE HAMMER DRILL AND A 3/16" CONCRETE BIT, DRILL ABOUT 12 MM INTO THE JAWBONE.

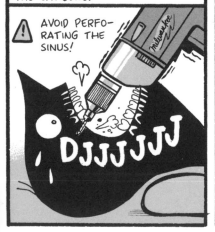

⚠ AVOID PERFORATING THE SINUS!

DJJJJJJ

USING A 1/2" SNAP-ON SOCKET, SCREW IN THE POST UNTIL YOU FEEL RESISTANCE (ABOUT FIVE TURNS).

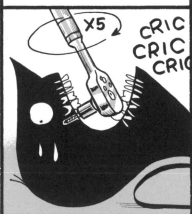

X5

CRIC CRIC CRIC

LET SITE HEAL FOR 90 DAYS, THEN CALL BACK THE PATIENT TO INSTALL THE ABUTMENT.

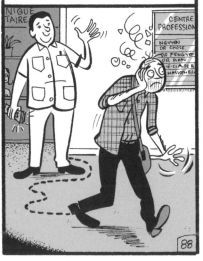

IKEA ALLEN KEY

AND YOU, WORK BEEN BUSY?

ATTACH THE PORCELAIN CROWN TO THE ABUTMENT WITH INTERIOR/EXTERIOR MULCO DENTAL PRO.

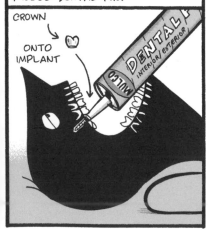

CROWN

ONTO IMPLANT

MULCO DENTAL INTERIOR/EXTERIOR

HOLD IN PLACE FOR 10 MINUTES WITH A BESSEY 12" DEEP REACH BAR CLAMP.

CANADIAN TIRE
HOME DEPOT
RONA
$18.95

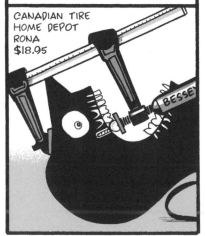

BESSEY

SEE YOU NEXT TIME!

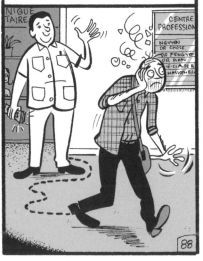

NIQUE TAIRE

CENTRE PROFESSION

NEUEN
DR CROSE
DR FENGYE
JE-PERAU
E-CLADE B
MASSOTHER

88

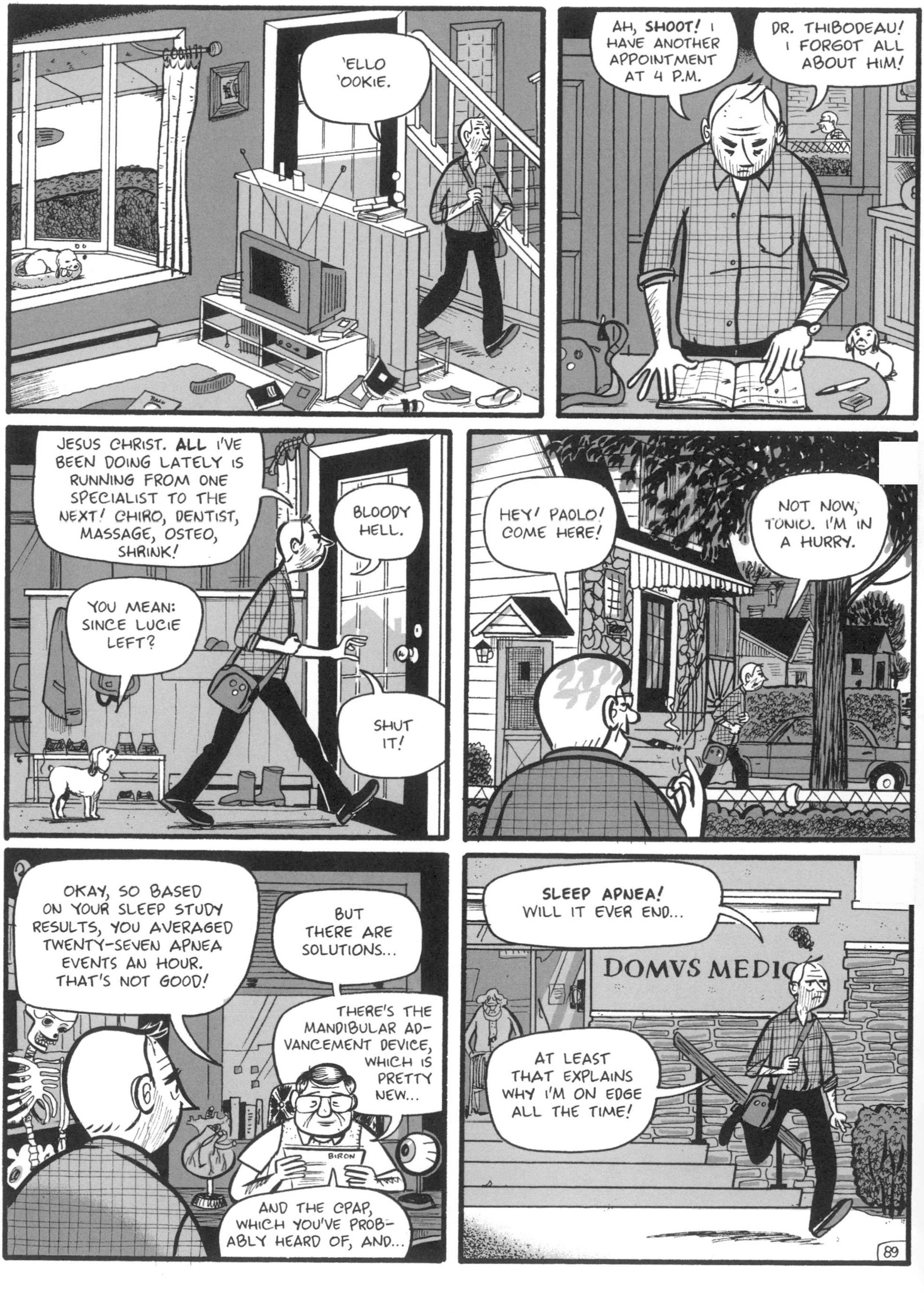
'ELLO 'OOKIE.
AH, SHOOT! I HAVE ANOTHER APPOINTMENT AT 4 P.M.
DR. THIBODEAU! I FORGOT ALL ABOUT HIM!
JESUS CHRIST. ALL I'VE BEEN DOING LATELY IS RUNNING FROM ONE SPECIALIST TO THE NEXT! CHIRO, DENTIST, MASSAGE, OSTEO, SHRINK!
BLOODY HELL.
YOU MEAN: SINCE LUCIE LEFT?
SHUT IT!
HEY! PAOLO! COME HERE!
NOT NOW, TONIO. I'M IN A HURRY.
OKAY, SO BASED ON YOUR SLEEP STUDY RESULTS, YOU AVERAGED TWENTY-SEVEN APNEA EVENTS AN HOUR. THAT'S NOT GOOD!
BUT THERE ARE SOLUTIONS...
THERE'S THE MANDIBULAR ADVANCEMENT DEVICE, WHICH IS PRETTY NEW...
BIRON
AND THE CPAP, WHICH YOU'VE PROBABLY HEARD OF, AND...
SLEEP APNEA! WILL IT EVER END...
DOMVS MEDIC
AT LEAST THAT EXPLAINS WHY I'M ON EDGE ALL THE TIME!

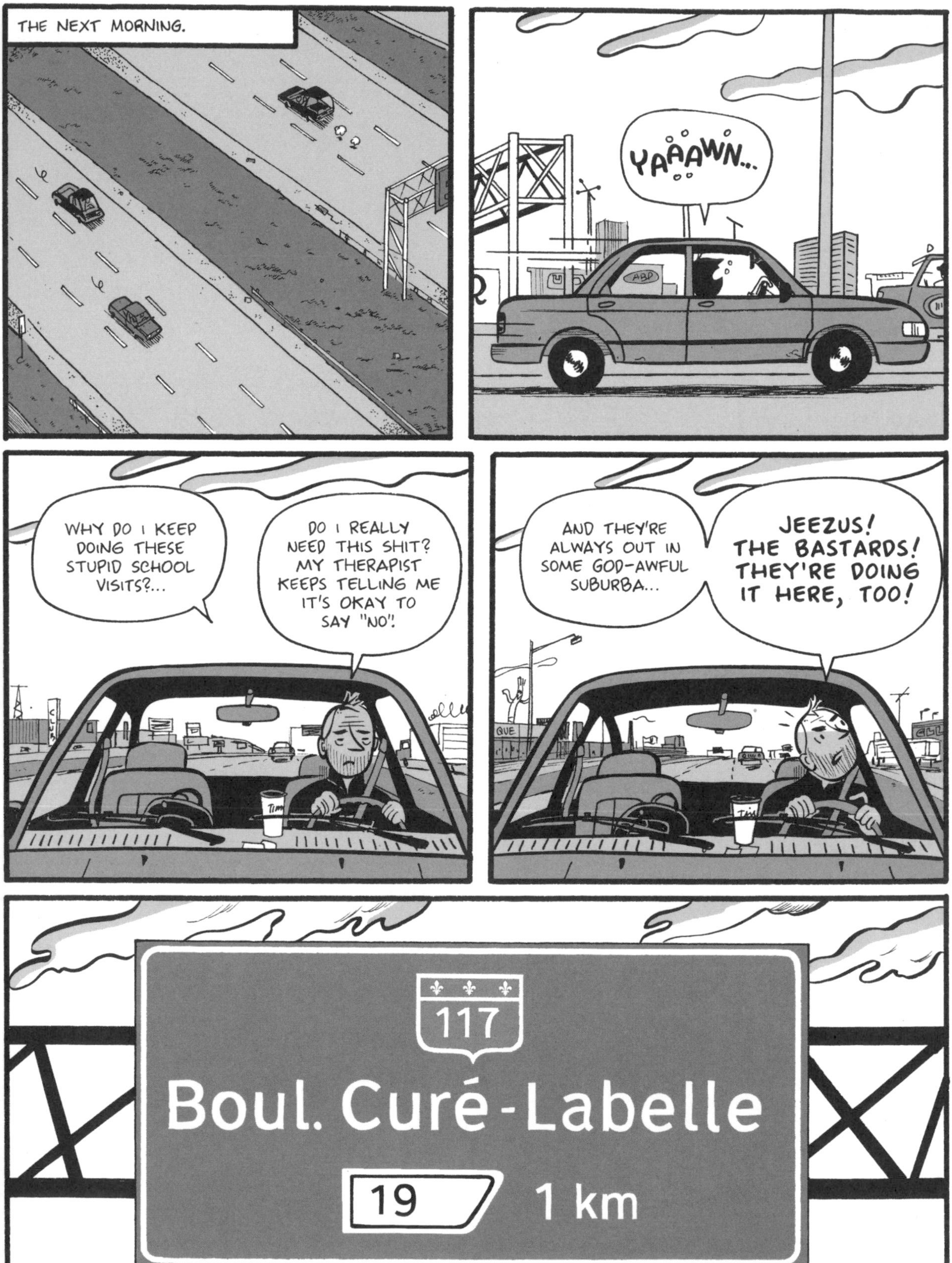
THE NEXT MORNING.
YAAAWN...
WHY DO I KEEP DOING THESE STUPID SCHOOL VISITS?...
DO I REALLY NEED THIS SHIT? MY THERAPIST KEEPS TELLING ME IT'S OKAY TO SAY "NO".
AND THEY'RE ALWAYS OUT IN SOME GOD-AWFUL SUBURBA...
JEEZUS! THE BASTARDS! THEY'RE DOING IT HERE, TOO!
117
Boul. Curé-Labelle
19
1 km

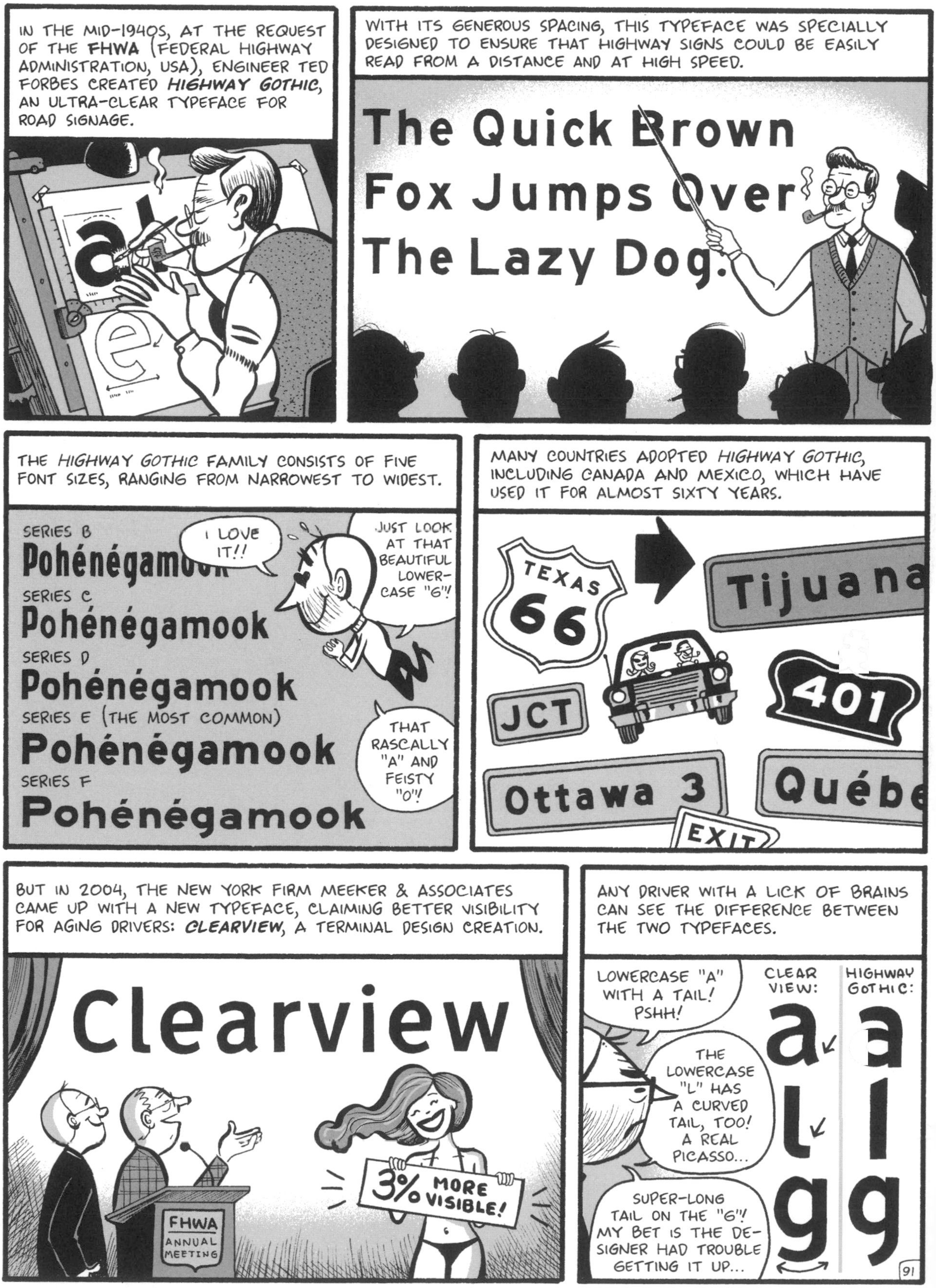
IN THE MID-1940S, AT THE REQUEST OF THE FHWA (FEDERAL HIGHWAY ADMINISTRATION, USA), ENGINEER TED FORBES CREATED HIGHWAY GOTHIC, AN ULTRA-CLEAR TYPEFACE FOR ROAD SIGNAGE.
WITH ITS GENEROUS SPACING, THIS TYPEFACE WAS SPECIALLY DESIGNED TO ENSURE THAT HIGHWAY SIGNS COULD BE EASILY READ FROM A DISTANCE AND AT HIGH SPEED.
The Quick Brown Fox Jumps Over The Lazy Dog.
THE HIGHWAY GOTHIC FAMILY CONSISTS OF FIVE FONT SIZES, RANGING FROM NARROWEST TO WIDEST.
SERIES B
Pohénégamook
SERIES C
Pohénégamook
SERIES D
Pohénégamook
SERIES E (THE MOST COMMON)
Pohénégamook
SERIES F
Pohénégamook
I LOVE IT!!
JUST LOOK AT THAT BEAUTIFUL LOWER-CASE "G"!
THAT RASCALLY "A" AND FEISTY "O"!
MANY COUNTRIES ADOPTED HIGHWAY GOTHIC, INCLUDING CANADA AND MEXICO, WHICH HAVE USED IT FOR ALMOST SIXTY YEARS.
TEXAS
66
Tijuana
401
JCT
Ottawa 3
Québe
EXIT
BUT IN 2004, THE NEW YORK FIRM MEEKER & ASSOCIATES CAME UP WITH A NEW TYPEFACE, CLAIMING BETTER VISIBILITY FOR AGING DRIVERS: CLEARVIEW, A TERMINAL DESIGN CREATION.
Clearview
FHWA ANNUAL MEETING
3% MORE VISIBLE!
ANY DRIVER WITH A LICK OF BRAINS CAN SEE THE DIFFERENCE BETWEEN THE TWO TYPEFACES.
LOWERCASE "A" WITH A TAIL! PSHH!
CLEAR VIEW:
HIGHWAY GOTHIC:
THE LOWERCASE "L" HAS A CURVED TAIL, TOO! A REAL PICASSO...
SUPER-LONG TAIL ON THE "G"! MY BET IS THE DE-SIGNER HAD TROUBLE GETTING IT UP...
a l g
a l g

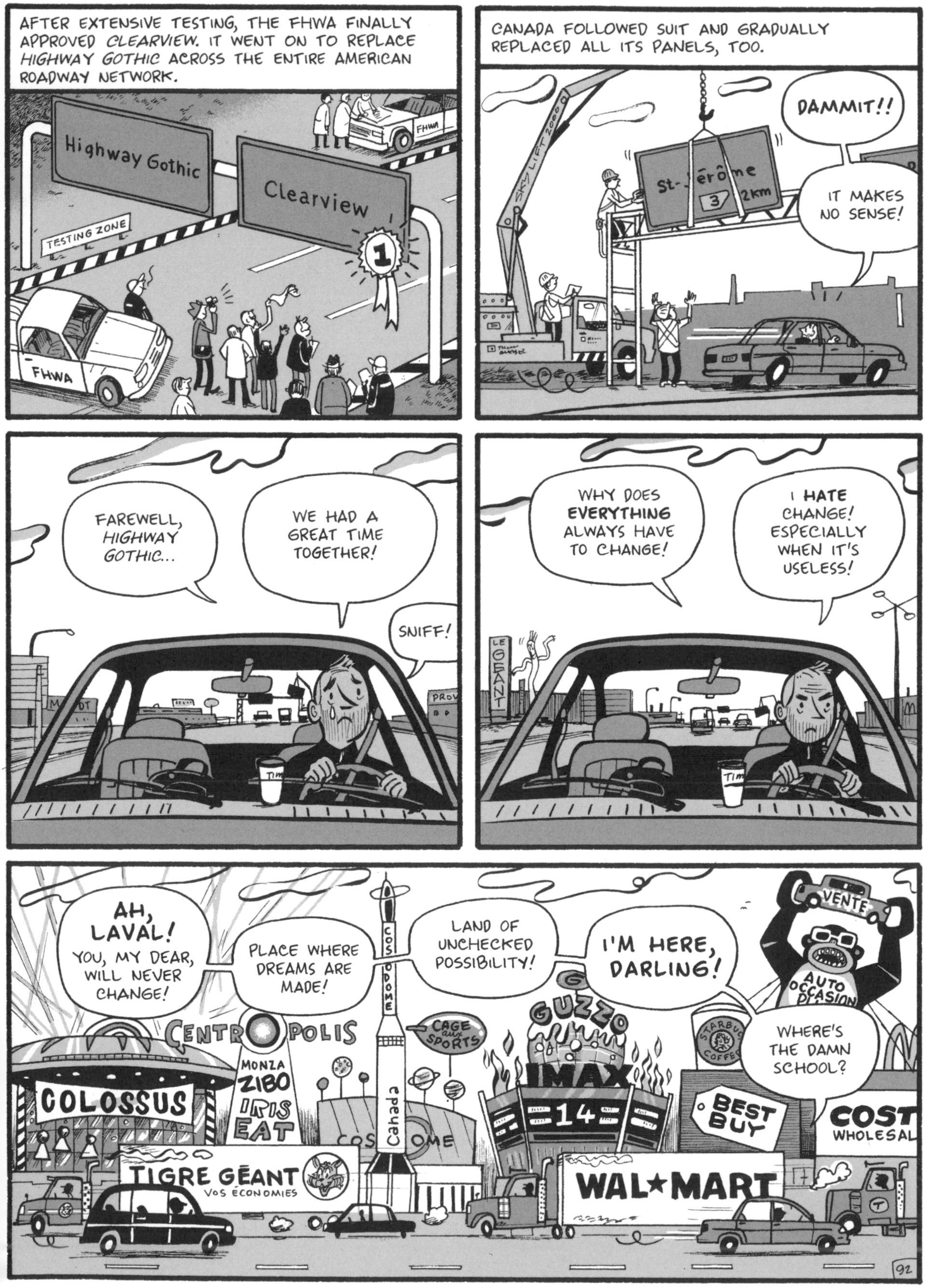
AFTER EXTENSIVE TESTING, THE FHWA FINALLY APPROVED CLEARVIEW. IT WENT ON TO REPLACE HIGHWAY GOTHIC ACROSS THE ENTIRE AMERICAN ROADWAY NETWORK.
FHWA
Highway Gothic
Clearview
TESTING ZONE
1
FHWA
CANADA FOLLOWED SUIT AND GRADUALLY REPLACED ALL ITS PANELS, TOO.
SKY LIFT 2000
DAMMIT!!
IT MAKES NO SENSE!
FAREWELL, HIGHWAY GOTHIC...
WE HAD A GREAT TIME TOGETHER!
SNIFF!
WHY DOES EVERYTHING ALWAYS HAVE TO CHANGE!
I HATE CHANGE! ESPECIALLY WHEN IT'S USELESS!
LE GÉANT
AH, LAVAL! YOU, MY DEAR, WILL NEVER CHANGE!
PLACE WHERE DREAMS ARE MADE!
LAND OF UNCHECKED POSSIBILITY!
I'M HERE, DARLING!
WHERE'S THE DAMN SCHOOL?
VENTE
AUTO OCCASION
GUZZO
CENTROPOLIS
COSMODOME
CAGE aux SPORTS
COLOSSUS
MONZA
ZIBO
IRIS
EAT
Canada
IMAX
14
BEST BUY
COST
WHOLESAL
TIGRE GÉANT
VOS ÉCONOMIES
WAL★MART

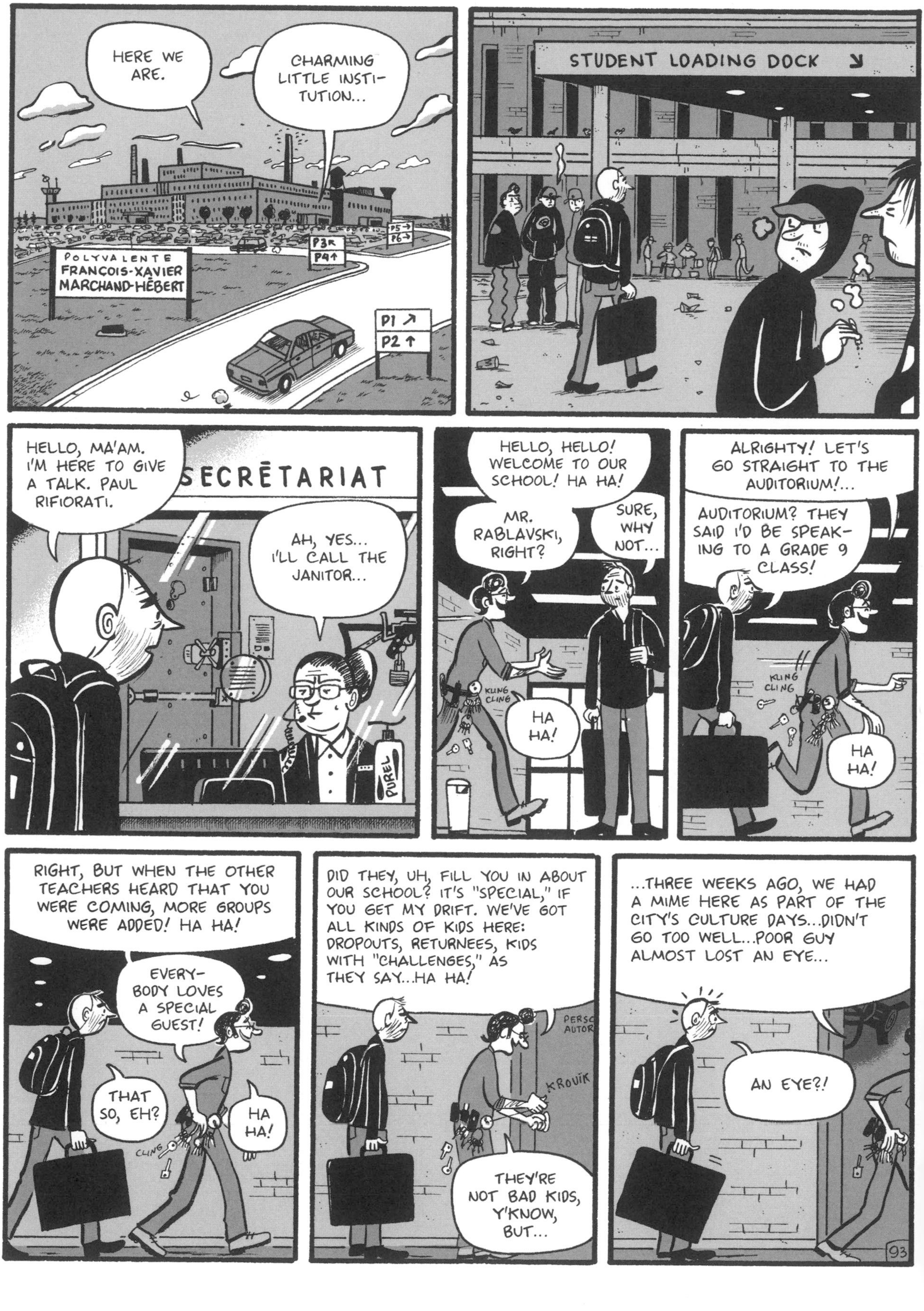
HERE WE ARE.
CHARMING LITTLE INSTITUTION...
POLYVALENTE FRANÇOIS-XAVIER MARCHAND-HÉBERT
P3R
P4↑
P5→
P6→
P1↗
P2↑
STUDENT LOADING DOCK ↘
HELLO, MA'AM. I'M HERE TO GIVE A TALK. PAUL RIFIORATI.
SECRÉTARIAT
AH, YES... I'LL CALL THE JANITOR...
PUREL
HELLO, HELLO! WELCOME TO OUR SCHOOL! HA HA!
MR. RABLAVSKI, RIGHT?
SURE, WHY NOT...
KLING CLING
HA HA!
ALRIGHTY! LET'S GO STRAIGHT TO THE AUDITORIUM!...
AUDITORIUM? THEY SAID I'D BE SPEAKING TO A GRADE 9 CLASS!
KLING CLING
HA HA!
RIGHT, BUT WHEN THE OTHER TEACHERS HEARD THAT YOU WERE COMING, MORE GROUPS WERE ADDED! HA HA!
EVERYBODY LOVES A SPECIAL GUEST!
THAT SO, EH?
HA HA!
CLING
DID THEY, UH, FILL YOU IN ABOUT OUR SCHOOL? IT'S "SPECIAL," IF YOU GET MY DRIFT. WE'VE GOT ALL KINDS OF KIDS HERE: DROPOUTS, RETURNEES, KIDS WITH "CHALLENGES," AS THEY SAY...HA HA!
KROUIK
THEY'RE NOT BAD KIDS, Y'KNOW, BUT...
...THREE WEEKS AGO, WE HAD A MIME HERE AS PART OF THE CITY'S CULTURE DAYS...DIDN'T GO TOO WELL...POOR GUY ALMOST LOST AN EYE...
AN EYE?!

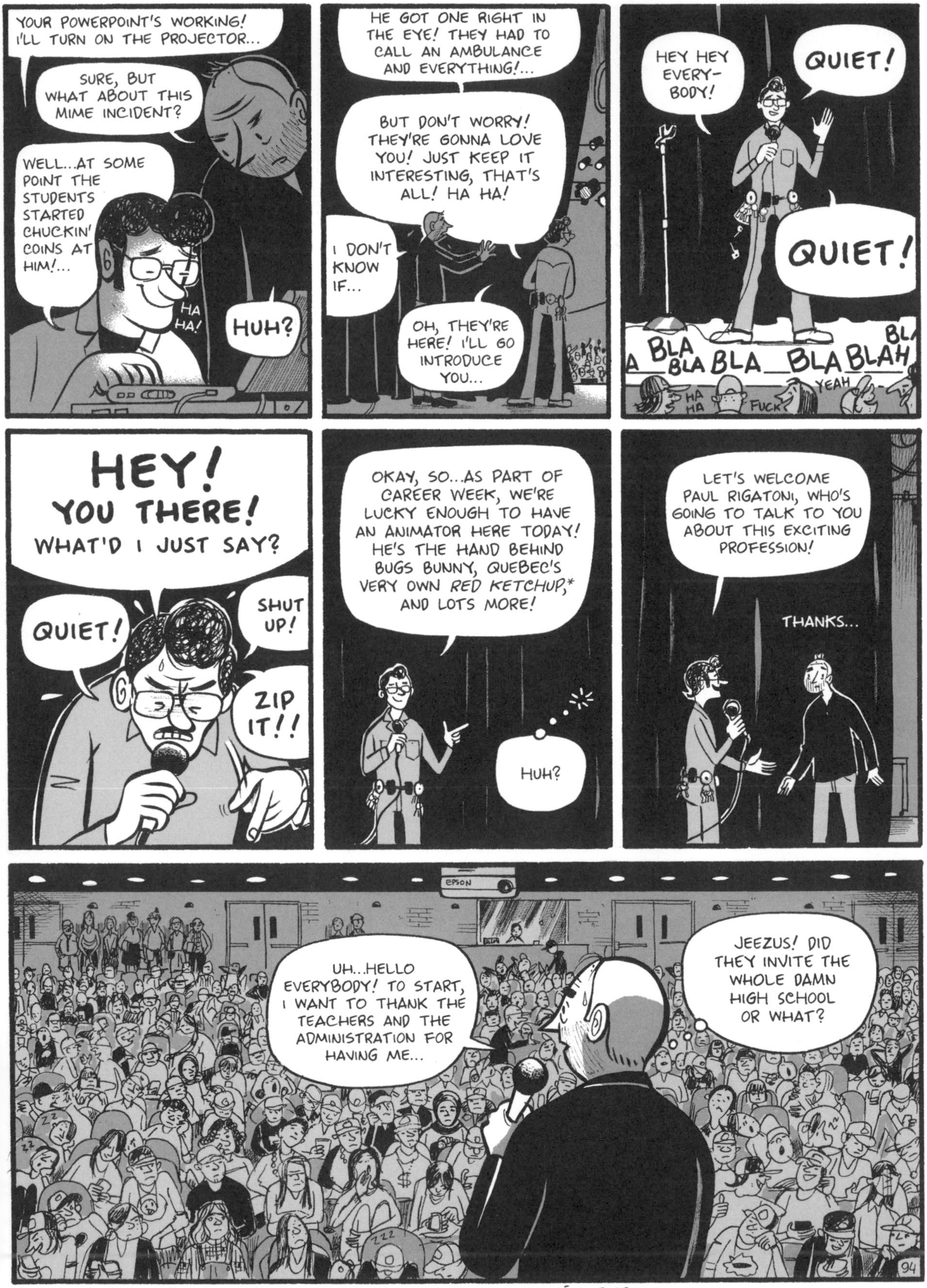
YOUR POWERPOINT'S WORKING! I'LL TURN ON THE PROJECTOR...
SURE, BUT WHAT ABOUT THIS MIME INCIDENT?
WELL...AT SOME POINT THE STUDENTS STARTED CHUCKIN' COINS AT HIM!...
HA HA!
HUH?
HE GOT ONE RIGHT IN THE EYE! THEY HAD TO CALL AN AMBULANCE AND EVERYTHING!...
BUT DON'T WORRY! THEY'RE GONNA LOVE YOU! JUST KEEP IT INTERESTING, THAT'S ALL! HA HA!
I DON'T KNOW IF...
OH, THEY'RE HERE! I'LL GO INTRODUCE YOU...
HEY HEY EVERY-BODY!
QUIET!
QUIET!
BLA BLA BLA BLA BLA BLAH BLA
HA HA
FUCK
YEAH
HEY! YOU THERE! WHAT'D I JUST SAY?
QUIET!
SHUT UP!
ZIP IT!!
OKAY, SO...AS PART OF CAREER WEEK, WE'RE LUCKY ENOUGH TO HAVE AN ANIMATOR HERE TODAY! HE'S THE HAND BEHIND BUGS BUNNY, QUEBEC'S VERY OWN *RED KETCHUP*,* AND LOTS MORE!
HUH?
LET'S WELCOME PAUL RIGATONI, WHO'S GOING TO TALK TO YOU ABOUT THIS EXCITING PROFESSION!
THANKS...
EPSON
UH...HELLO EVERYBODY! TO START, I WANT TO THANK THE TEACHERS AND THE ADMINISTRATION FOR HAVING ME...
JEEZUS! DID THEY INVITE THE WHOLE DAMN HIGH SCHOOL OR WHAT?
94

*A CULT QUEBEC COMIC BOOK SERIES, CREATED BY PIERRE FOURNIER AND RÉAL GODBOUT.

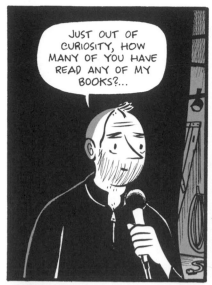

JUST OUT OF CURIOSITY, HOW MANY OF YOU HAVE READ ANY OF MY BOOKS?...

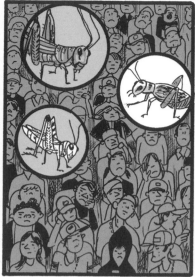

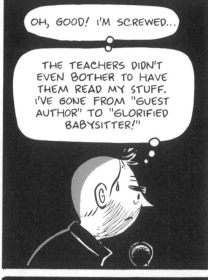

OH, GOOD! I'M SCREWED...

THE TEACHERS DIDN'T EVEN BOTHER TO HAVE THEM READ MY STUFF. I'VE GONE FROM "GUEST AUTHOR" TO "GLORIFIED BABYSITTER!"

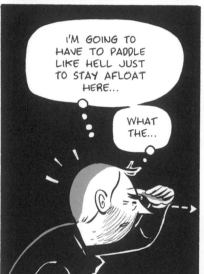

I'M GOING TO HAVE TO PADDLE LIKE HELL JUST TO STAY AFLOAT HERE...

WHAT THE...

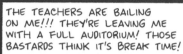

THE TEACHERS ARE BAILING ON ME!!! THEY'RE LEAVING ME WITH A FULL AUDITORIUM! THOSE BASTARDS THINK IT'S BREAK TIME!

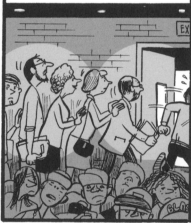

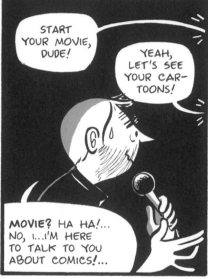

START YOUR MOVIE, DUDE!

YEAH, LET'S SEE YOUR CARTOONS!

MOVIE? HA HA!... NO, I...I'M HERE TO TALK TO YOU ABOUT COMICS!...

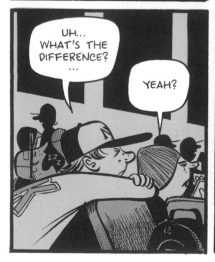

UH... WHAT'S THE DIFFERENCE? ...

YEAH?

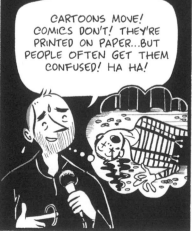

CARTOONS MOVE! COMICS DON'T! THEY'RE PRINTED ON PAPER...BUT PEOPLE OFTEN GET THEM CONFUSED! HA HA!

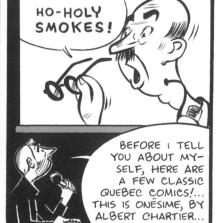

HO-HOLY SMOKES!

BEFORE I TELL YOU ABOUT MY-SELF, HERE ARE A FEW CLASSIC QUEBEC COMICS!... THIS IS ONÉSIME, BY ALBERT CHARTIER...

95

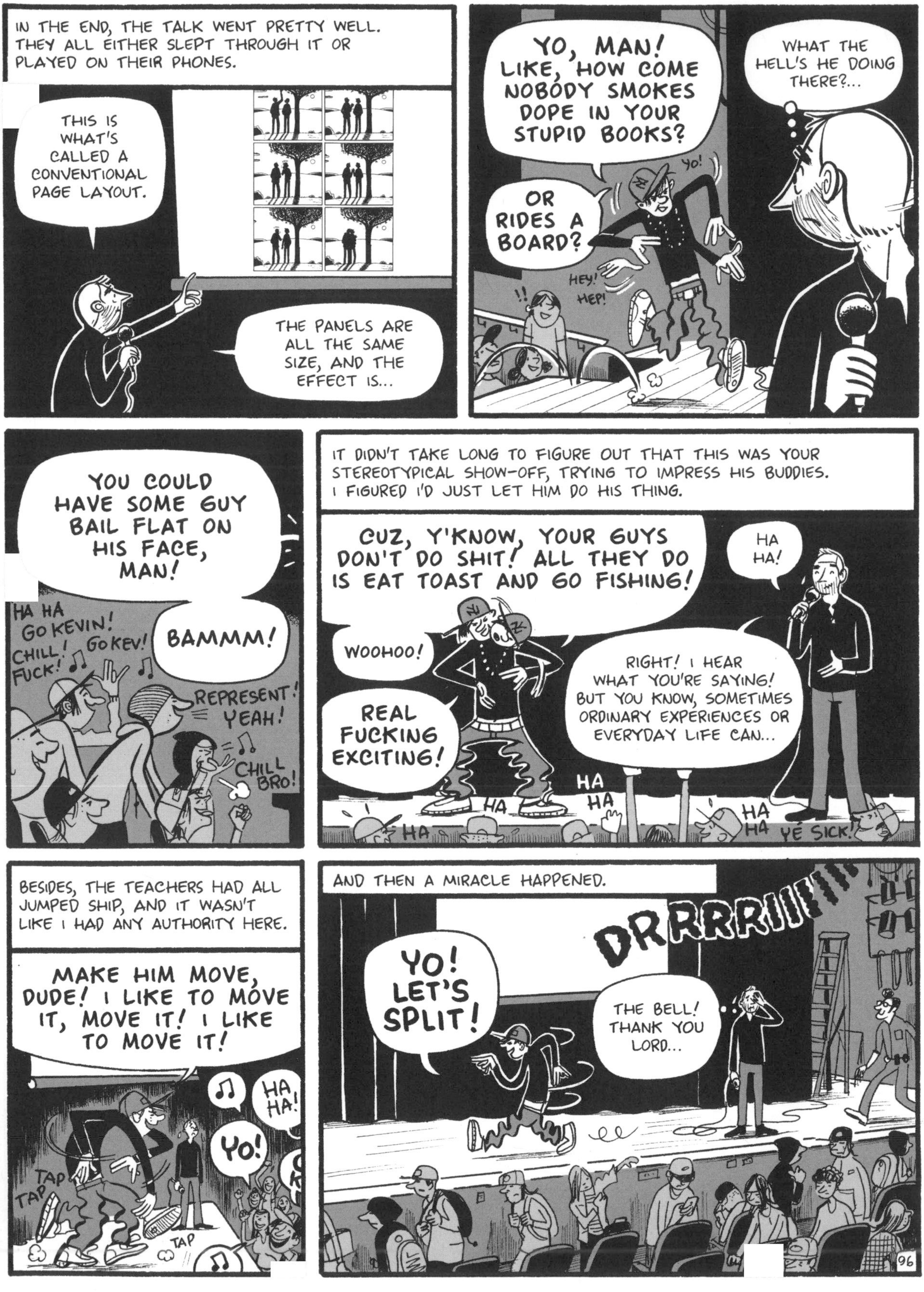
IN THE END, THE TALK WENT PRETTY WELL. THEY ALL EITHER SLEPT THROUGH IT OR PLAYED ON THEIR PHONES.
THIS IS WHAT'S CALLED A CONVENTIONAL PAGE LAYOUT.
THE PANELS ARE ALL THE SAME SIZE, AND THE EFFECT IS...
YO, MAN! LIKE, HOW COME NOBODY SMOKES DOPE IN YOUR STUPID BOOKS?
YO!
OR RIDES A BOARD?
HEY!
HEP!
WHAT THE HELL'S HE DOING THERE?...
YOU COULD HAVE SOME GUY BAIL FLAT ON HIS FACE, MAN!
BAMMM!
HA HA
GO KEVIN!
GO KEV!
CHILL!
FUCK!
REPRESENT!
YEAH!
CHILL BRO!
IT DIDN'T TAKE LONG TO FIGURE OUT THAT THIS WAS YOUR STEREOTYPICAL SHOW-OFF, TRYING TO IMPRESS HIS BUDDIES. I FIGURED I'D JUST LET HIM DO HIS THING.
CUZ, Y'KNOW, YOUR GUYS DON'T DO SHIT! ALL THEY DO IS EAT TOAST AND GO FISHING!
HA HA!
WOOHOO!
REAL FUCKING EXCITING!
RIGHT! I HEAR WHAT YOU'RE SAYING! BUT YOU KNOW, SOMETIMES ORDINARY EXPERIENCES OR EVERYDAY LIFE CAN...
HA HA
HA
HA
HA HA
YÉ SICK!
BESIDES, THE TEACHERS HAD ALL JUMPED SHIP, AND IT WASN'T LIKE I HAD ANY AUTHORITY HERE.
MAKE HIM MOVE, DUDE! I LIKE TO MOVE IT, MOVE IT! I LIKE TO MOVE IT!
HA HA!
YO!
TAP TAP
TAP
AND THEN A MIRACLE HAPPENED.
DRRRRIIII
YO! LET'S SPLIT!
THE BELL! THANK YOU LORD...
96

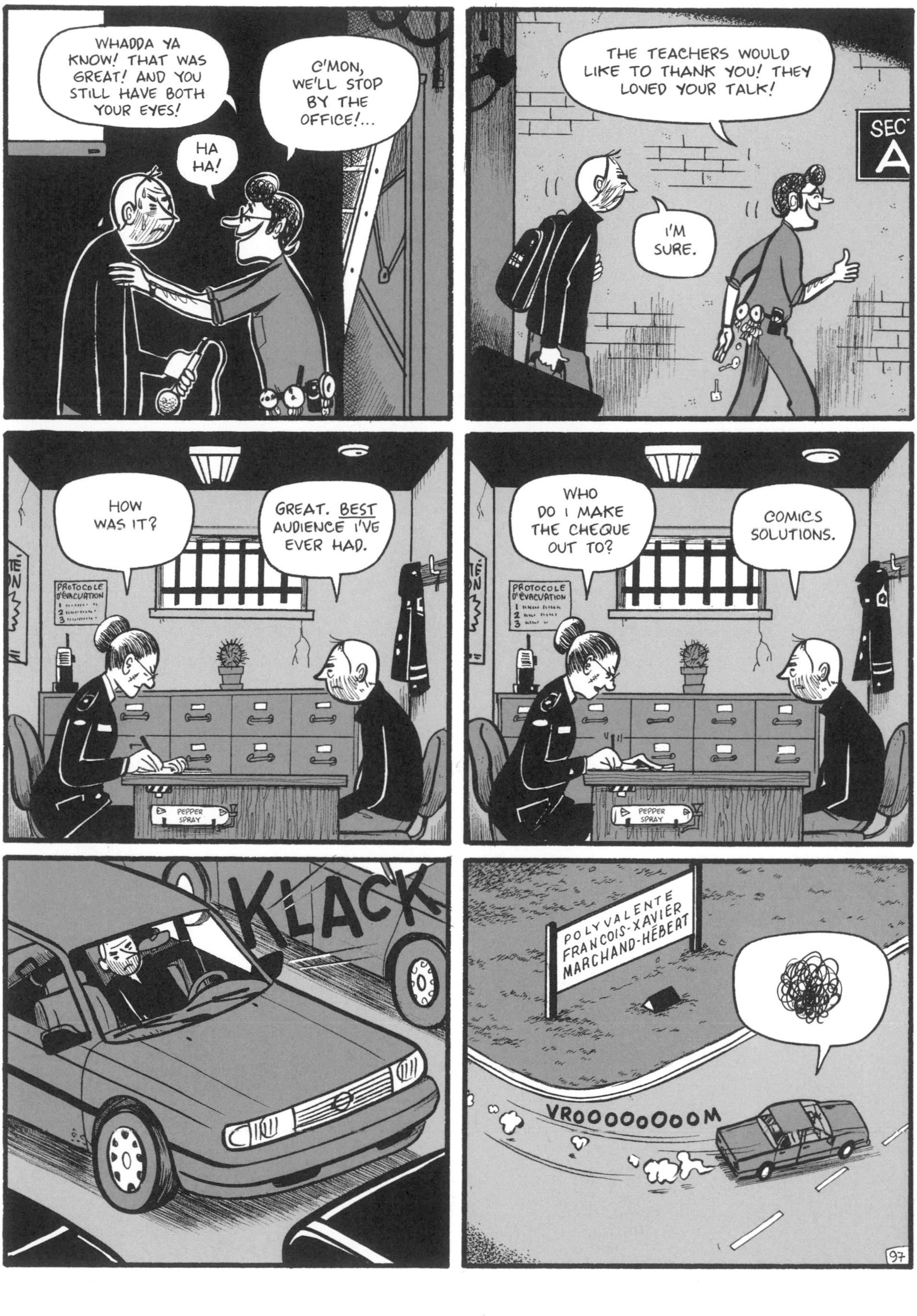
WHADDA YA KNOW! THAT WAS GREAT! AND YOU STILL HAVE BOTH YOUR EYES!
C'MON, WE'LL STOP BY THE OFFICE!...
HA HA!
THE TEACHERS WOULD LIKE TO THANK YOU! THEY LOVED YOUR TALK!
SECT A
I'M SURE.
HOW WAS IT?
GREAT. BEST AUDIENCE I'VE EVER HAD.
PROTOCOLE D'ÉVACUATION
PEPPER SPRAY
WHO DO I MAKE THE CHEQUE OUT TO?
COMICS SOLUTIONS.
PROTOCOLE D'ÉVACUATION
PEPPER SPRAY
KLACK
POLYVALENTE FRANCOIS-XAVIER MARCHAND-HÉBERT
VROOOOOOOOM

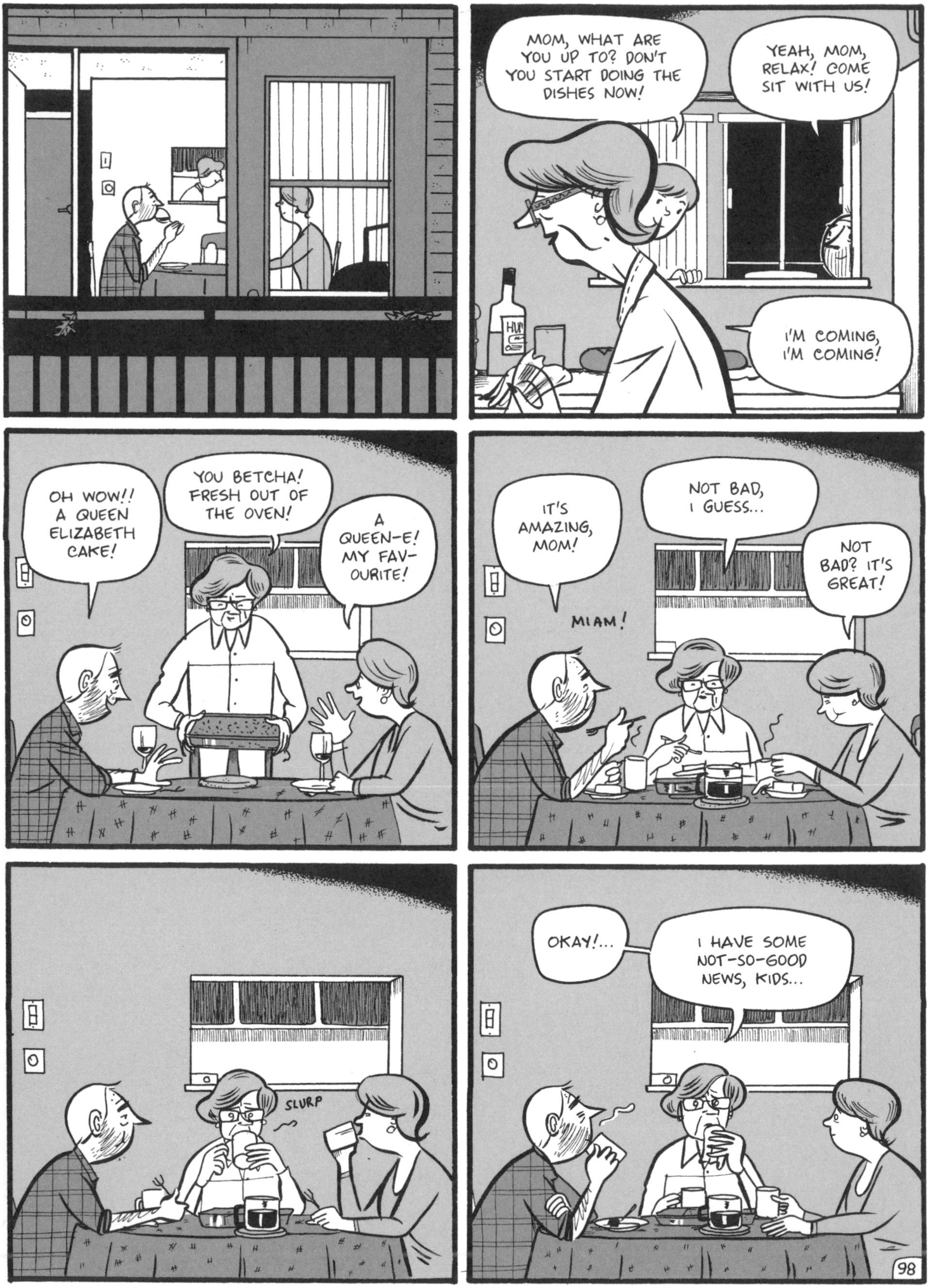
MOM, WHAT ARE YOU UP TO? DON'T YOU START DOING THE DISHES NOW!
YEAH, MOM, RELAX! COME SIT WITH US!
I'M COMING, I'M COMING!
OH WOW!! A QUEEN ELIZABETH CAKE!
YOU BETCHA! FRESH OUT OF THE OVEN!
A QUEEN-E! MY FAV-OURITE!
IT'S AMAZING, MOM!
MIAM!
NOT BAD, I GUESS...
NOT BAD? IT'S GREAT!
SLURP
OKAY!...
I HAVE SOME NOT-SO-GOOD NEWS, KIDS...

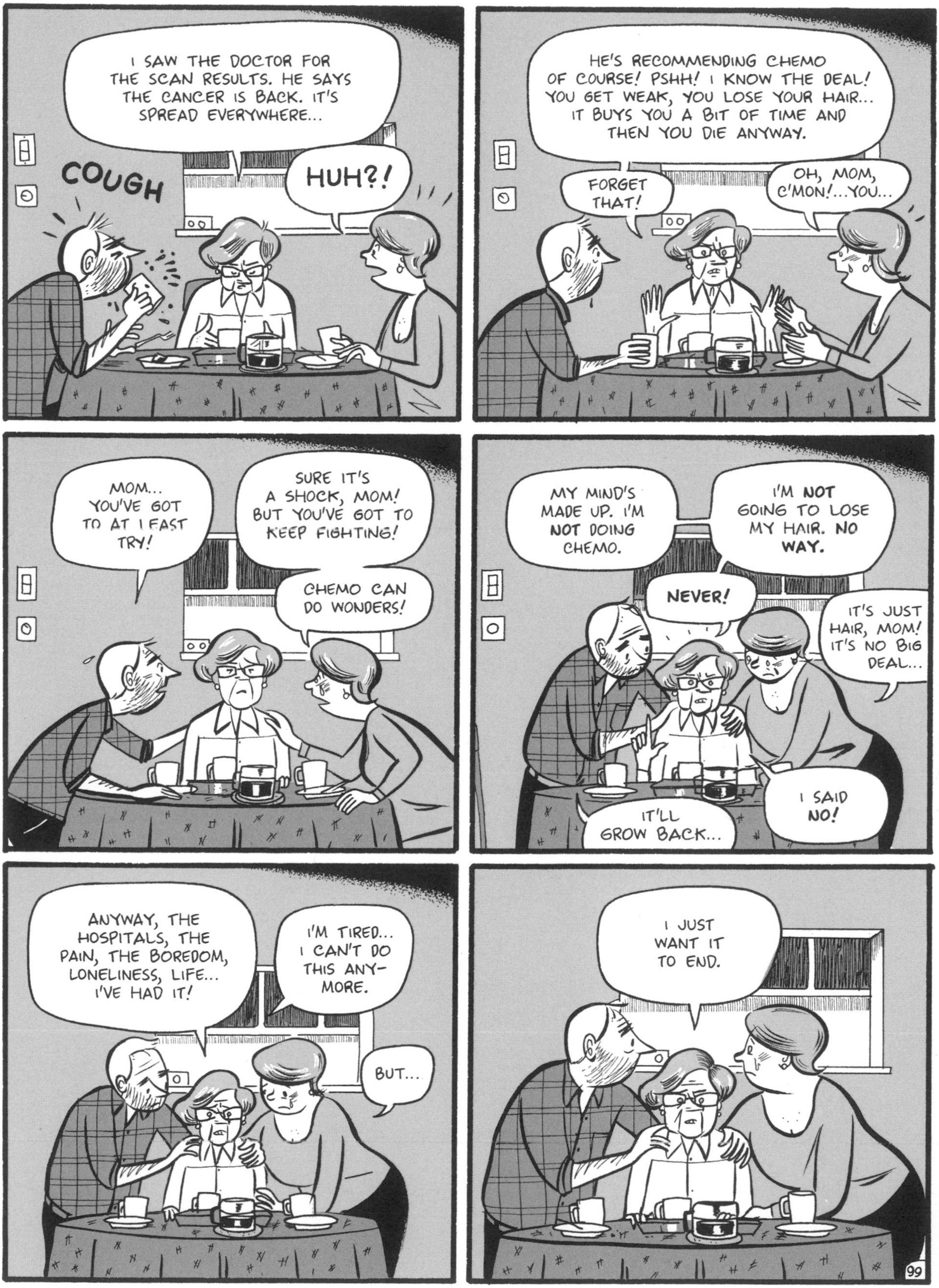
I SAW THE DOCTOR FOR THE SCAN RESULTS. HE SAYS THE CANCER IS BACK. IT'S SPREAD EVERYWHERE...
COUGH
HUH?!
HE'S RECOMMENDING CHEMO OF COURSE! PSHH! I KNOW THE DEAL! YOU GET WEAK, YOU LOSE YOUR HAIR... IT BUYS YOU A BIT OF TIME AND THEN YOU DIE ANYWAY.
FORGET THAT!
OH, MOM, C'MON!... YOU...
MOM... YOU'VE GOT TO AT LEAST TRY!
SURE IT'S A SHOCK, MOM! BUT YOU'VE GOT TO KEEP FIGHTING!
CHEMO CAN DO WONDERS!
MY MIND'S MADE UP. I'M **NOT** DOING CHEMO.
I'M **NOT** GOING TO LOSE MY HAIR. **NO WAY.**
NEVER!
IT'S JUST HAIR, MOM! IT'S NO BIG DEAL...
IT'LL GROW BACK...
I SAID **NO!**
ANYWAY, THE HOSPITALS, THE PAIN, THE BOREDOM, LONELINESS, LIFE... I'VE HAD IT!
I'M TIRED... I CAN'T DO THIS ANY-MORE.
BUT...
I JUST WANT IT TO END.

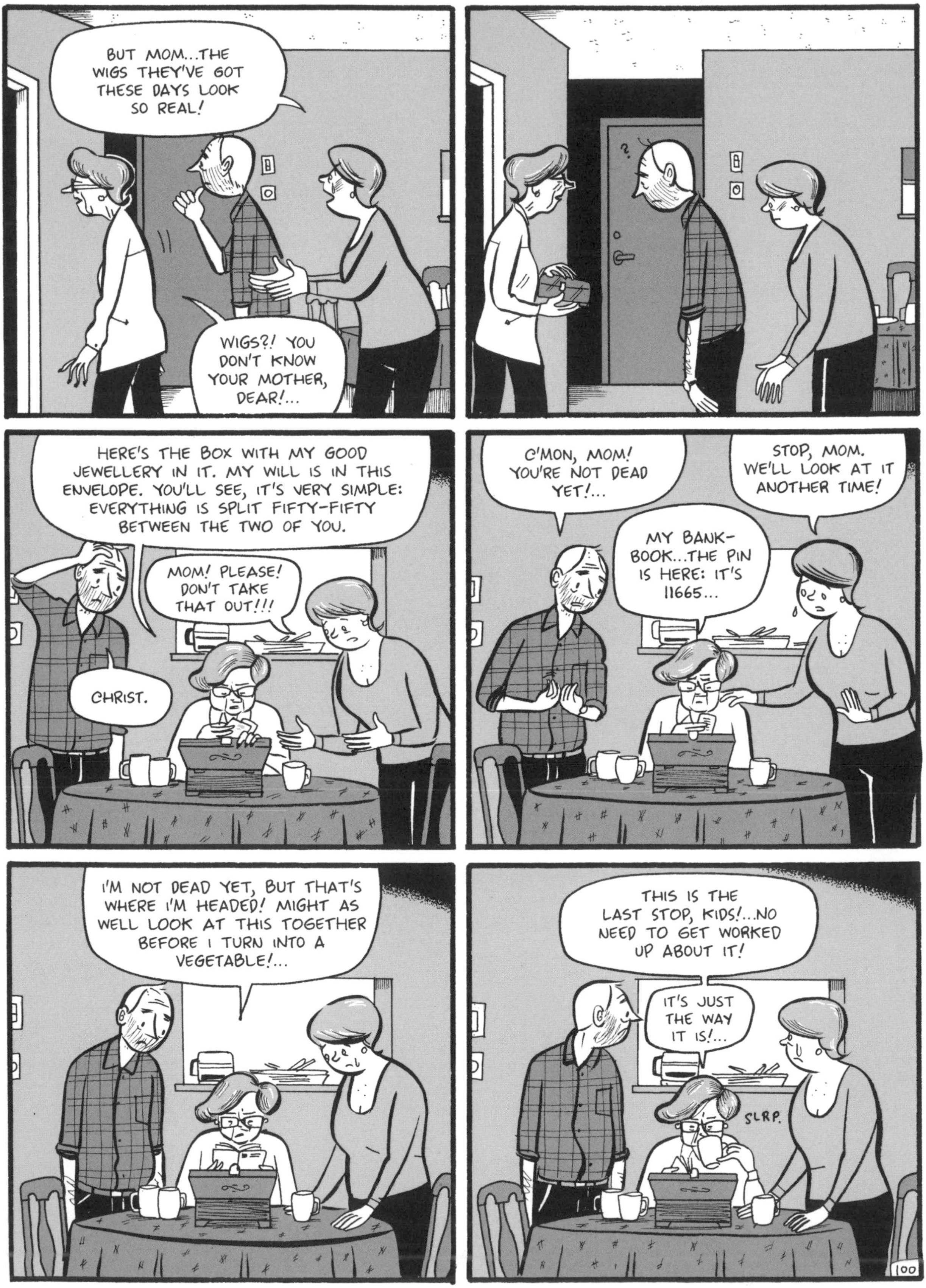
BUT MOM...THE WIGS THEY'VE GOT THESE DAYS LOOK SO REAL!
WIGS?! YOU DON'T KNOW YOUR MOTHER, DEAR!...
?
HERE'S THE BOX WITH MY GOOD JEWELLERY IN IT. MY WILL IS IN THIS ENVELOPE. YOU'LL SEE, IT'S VERY SIMPLE: EVERYTHING IS SPLIT FIFTY-FIFTY BETWEEN THE TWO OF YOU.
MOM! PLEASE! DON'T TAKE THAT OUT!!!
CHRIST.
C'MON, MOM! YOU'RE NOT DEAD YET!...
STOP, MOM. WE'LL LOOK AT IT ANOTHER TIME!
MY BANK-BOOK...THE PIN IS HERE: IT'S 11665...
I'M NOT DEAD YET, BUT THAT'S WHERE I'M HEADED! MIGHT AS WELL LOOK AT THIS TOGETHER BEFORE I TURN INTO A VEGETABLE!...
THIS IS THE LAST STOP, KIDS!...NO NEED TO GET WORKED UP ABOUT IT!
IT'S JUST THE WAY IT IS!...
SLRP.

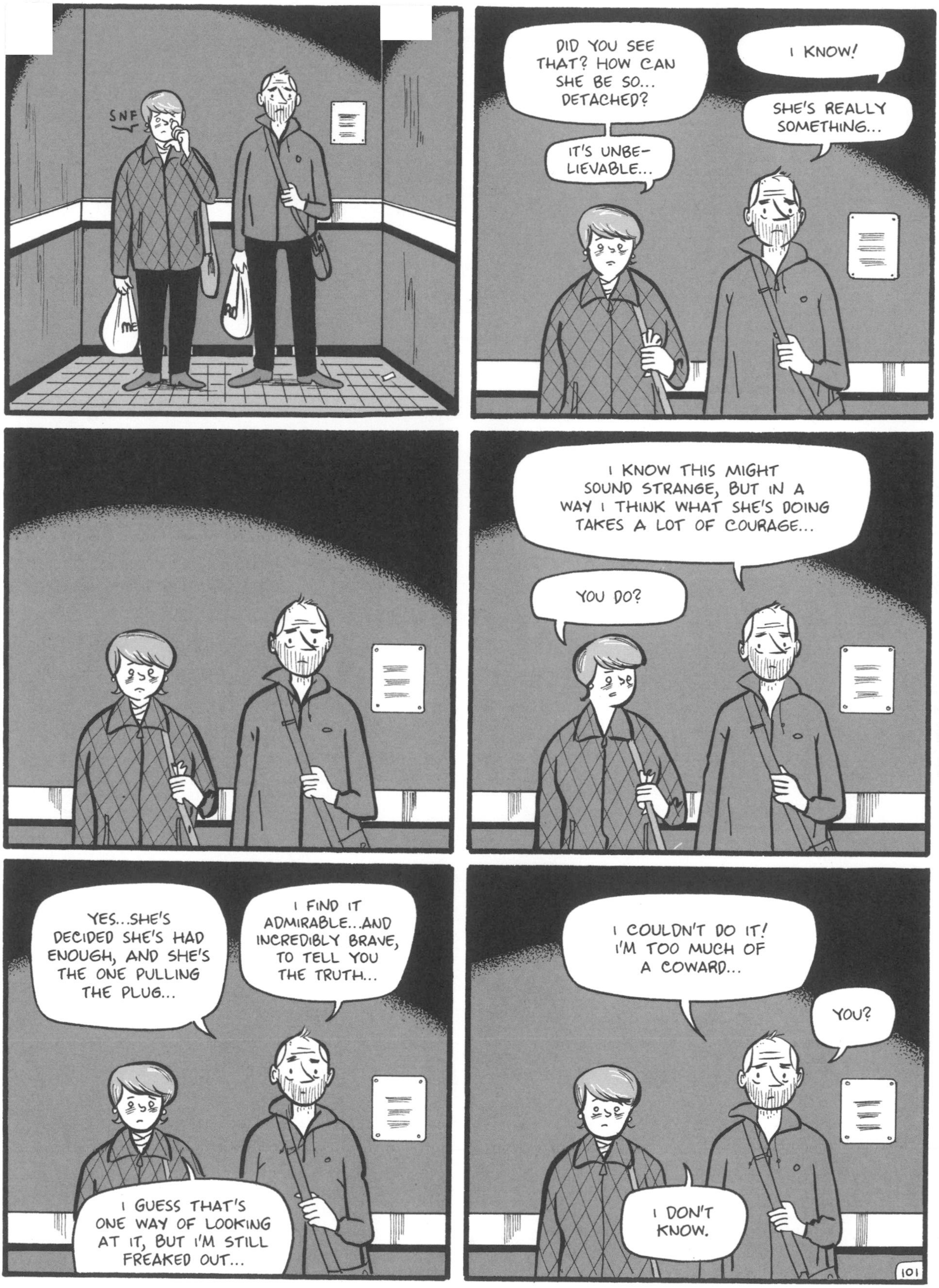
SNF
DID YOU SEE THAT? HOW CAN SHE BE SO... DETACHED?
IT'S UNBE-LIEVABLE...
I KNOW!
SHE'S REALLY SOMETHING...
I KNOW THIS MIGHT SOUND STRANGE, BUT IN A WAY I THINK WHAT SHE'S DOING TAKES A LOT OF COURAGE...
YOU DO?
YES...SHE'S DECIDED SHE'S HAD ENOUGH, AND SHE'S THE ONE PULLING THE PLUG...
I FIND IT ADMIRABLE...AND INCREDIBLY BRAVE, TO TELL YOU THE TRUTH...
I GUESS THAT'S ONE WAY OF LOOKING AT IT, BUT I'M STILL FREAKED OUT...
I COULDN'T DO IT! I'M TOO MUCH OF A COWARD...
YOU?
I DON'T KNOW.

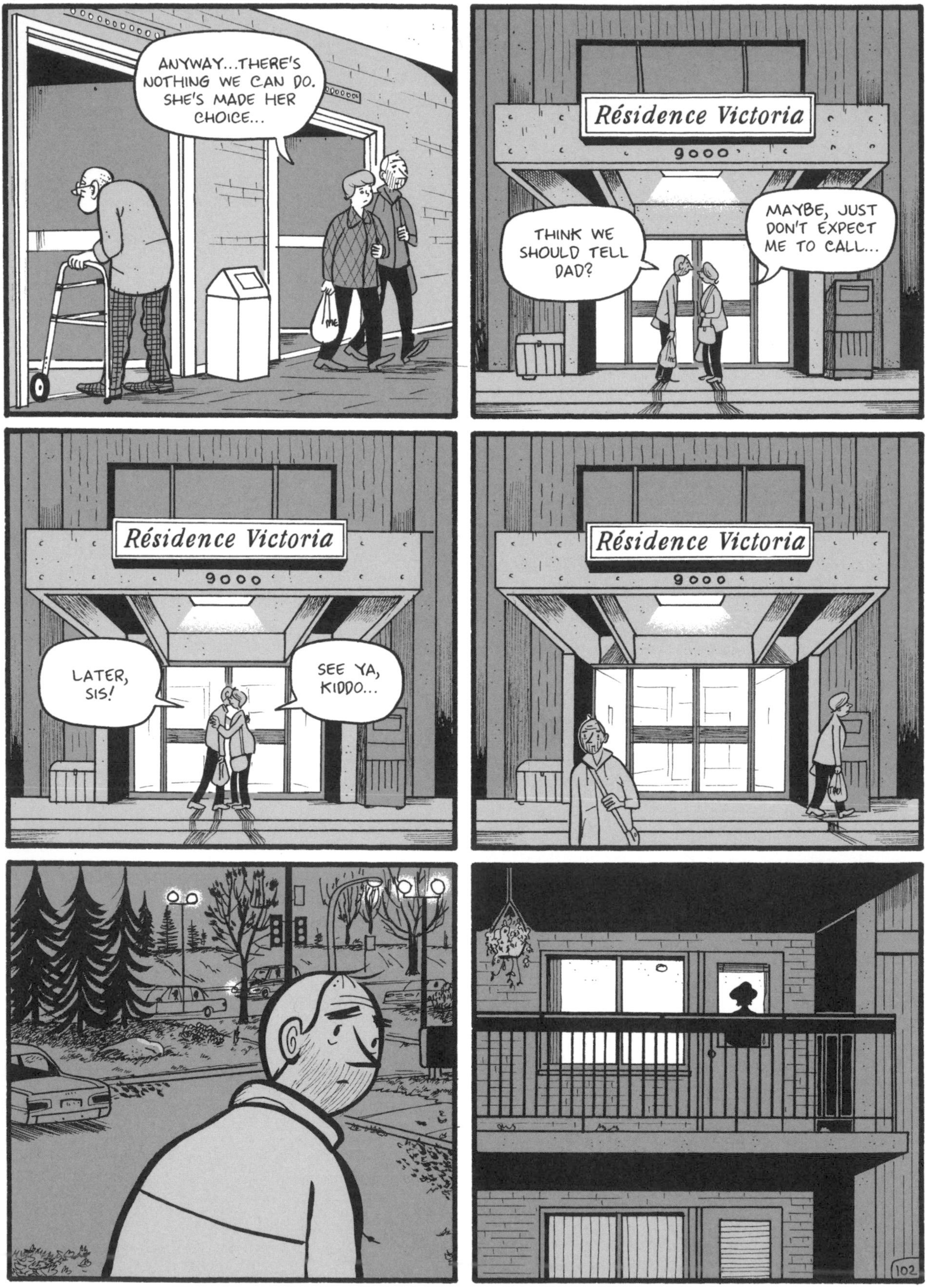
ANYWAY...THERE'S NOTHING WE CAN DO. SHE'S MADE HER CHOICE...
Résidence Victoria
9000
THINK WE SHOULD TELL DAD?
MAYBE, JUST DON'T EXPECT ME TO CALL...
Résidence Victoria
9000
LATER, SIS!
SEE YA, KIDDO...
Résidence Victoria
9000
102

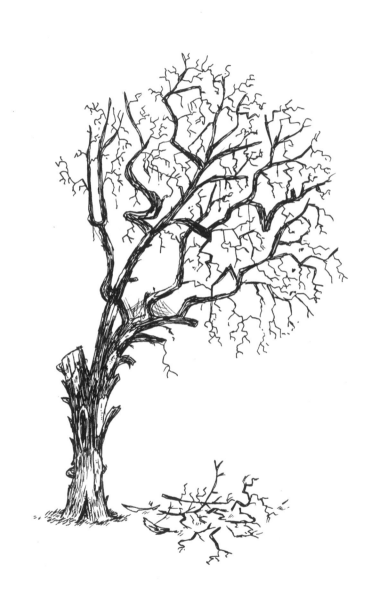

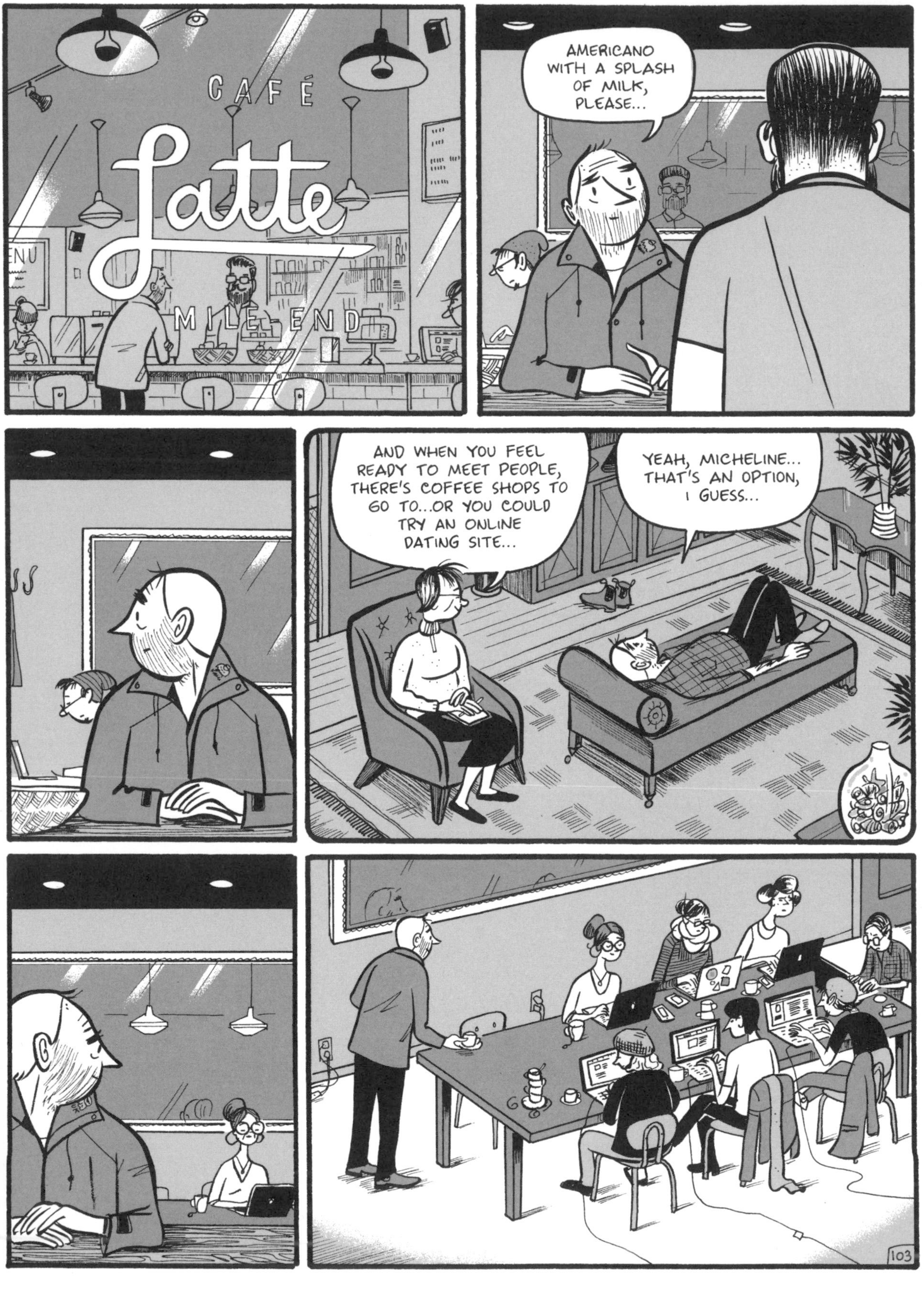
CAFÉ
Latte
MILE END
AMERICANO WITH A SPLASH OF MILK, PLEASE...
AND WHEN YOU FEEL READY TO MEET PEOPLE, THERE'S COFFEE SHOPS TO GO TO...OR YOU COULD TRY AN ONLINE DATING SITE...
YEAH, MICHELINE... THAT'S AN OPTION, I GUESS...

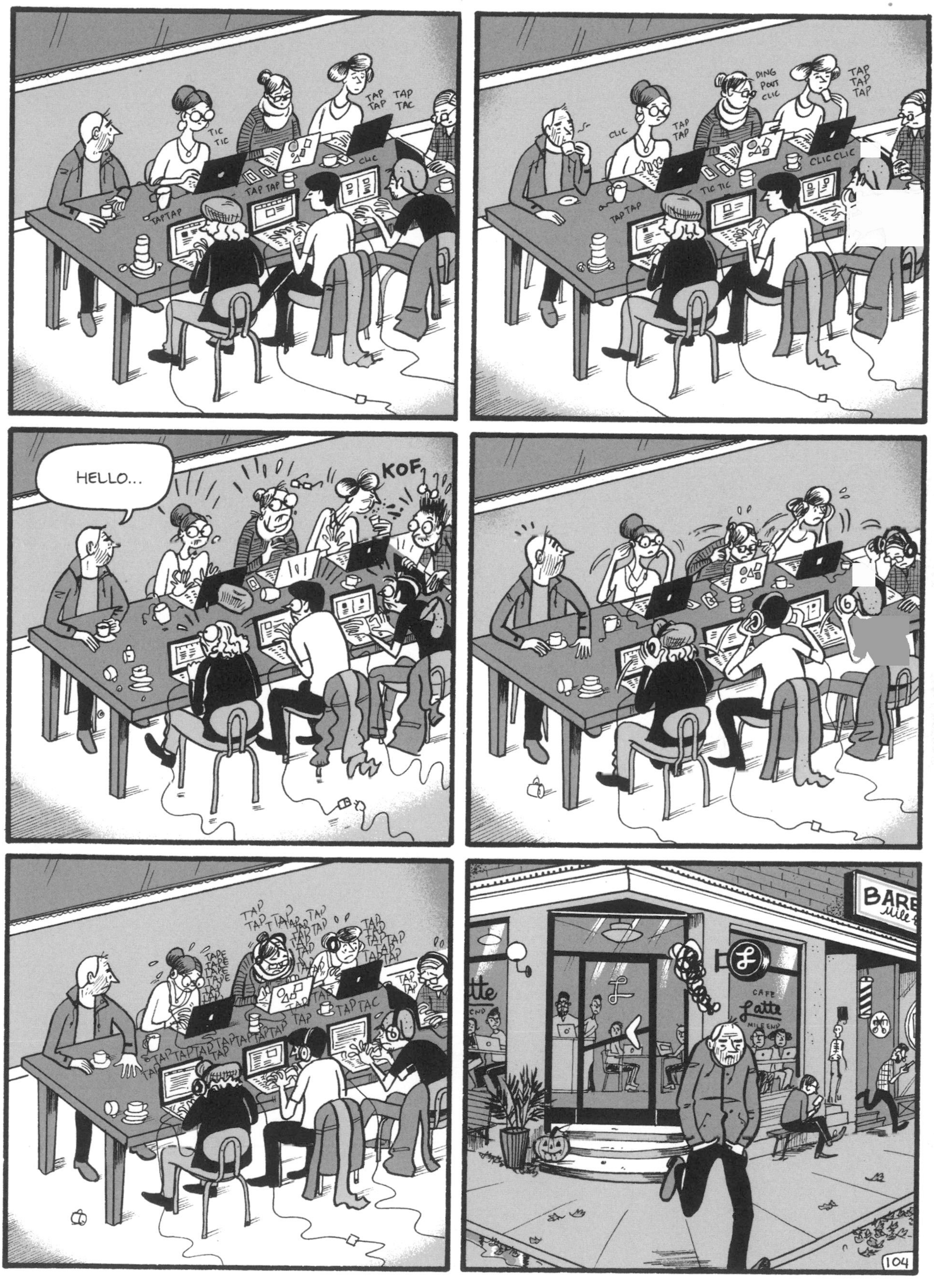
TIC TIC
TAP TAP
TAP TAC
CLIC
TAP TAP
TAPTAP
CLIC
TAP TAP
DING POUT CLIC
TAP TAP TAP
CLIC CLIC
TIC TIC
TAP TAP
HELLO...
KOF
CAFE
Latte
MILE END

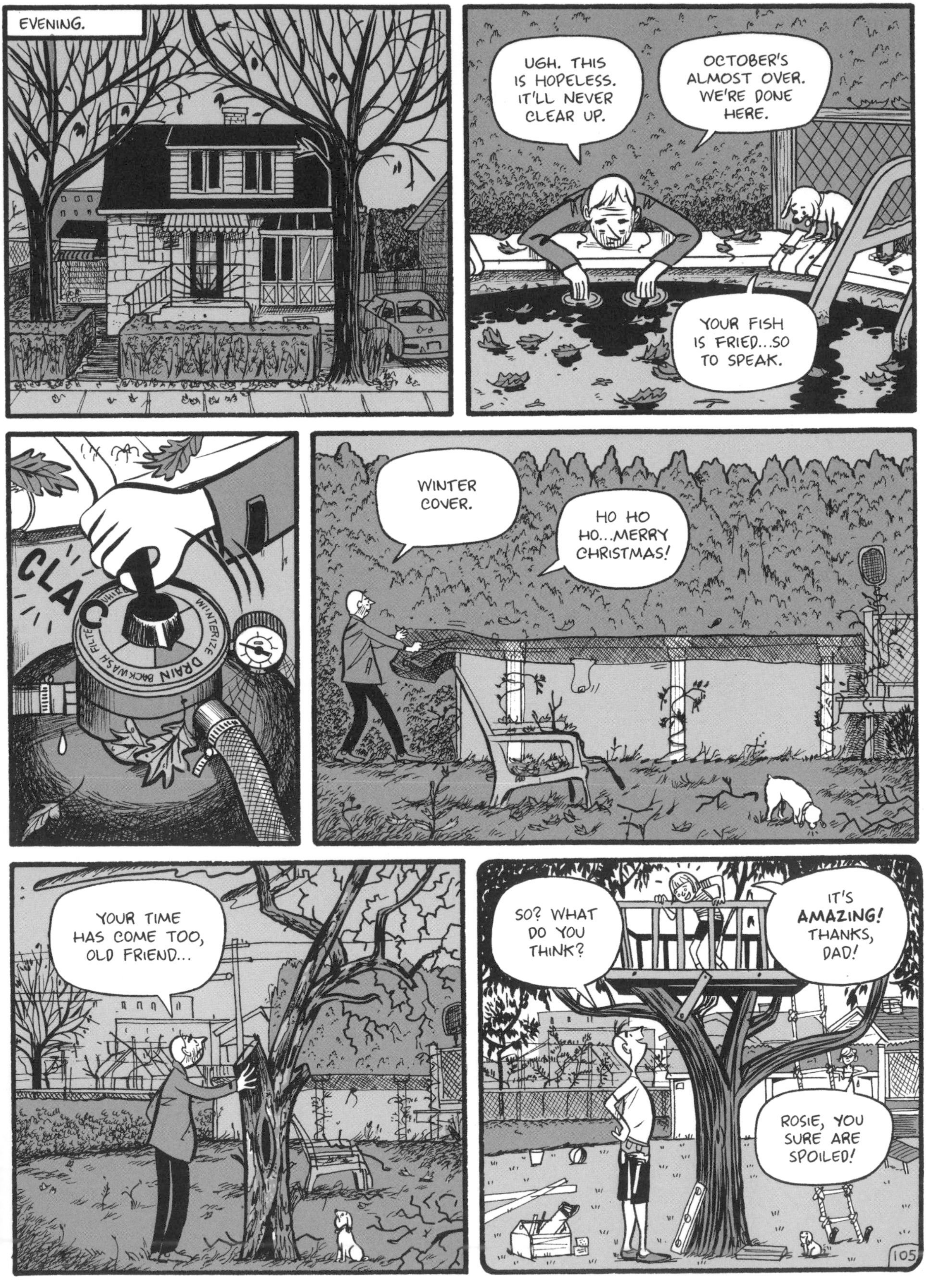
EVENING.
UGH. THIS IS HOPELESS. IT'LL NEVER CLEAR UP.
OCTOBER'S ALMOST OVER. WE'RE DONE HERE.
YOUR FISH IS FRIED...SO TO SPEAK.
CLAC
WINTERIZE
DRAIN
BACKWASH
WINTER COVER.
HO HO HO...MERRY CHRISTMAS!
YOUR TIME HAS COME TOO, OLD FRIEND...
SO? WHAT DO YOU THINK?
IT'S **AMAZING!** THANKS, DAD!
ROSIE, YOU SURE ARE SPOILED!

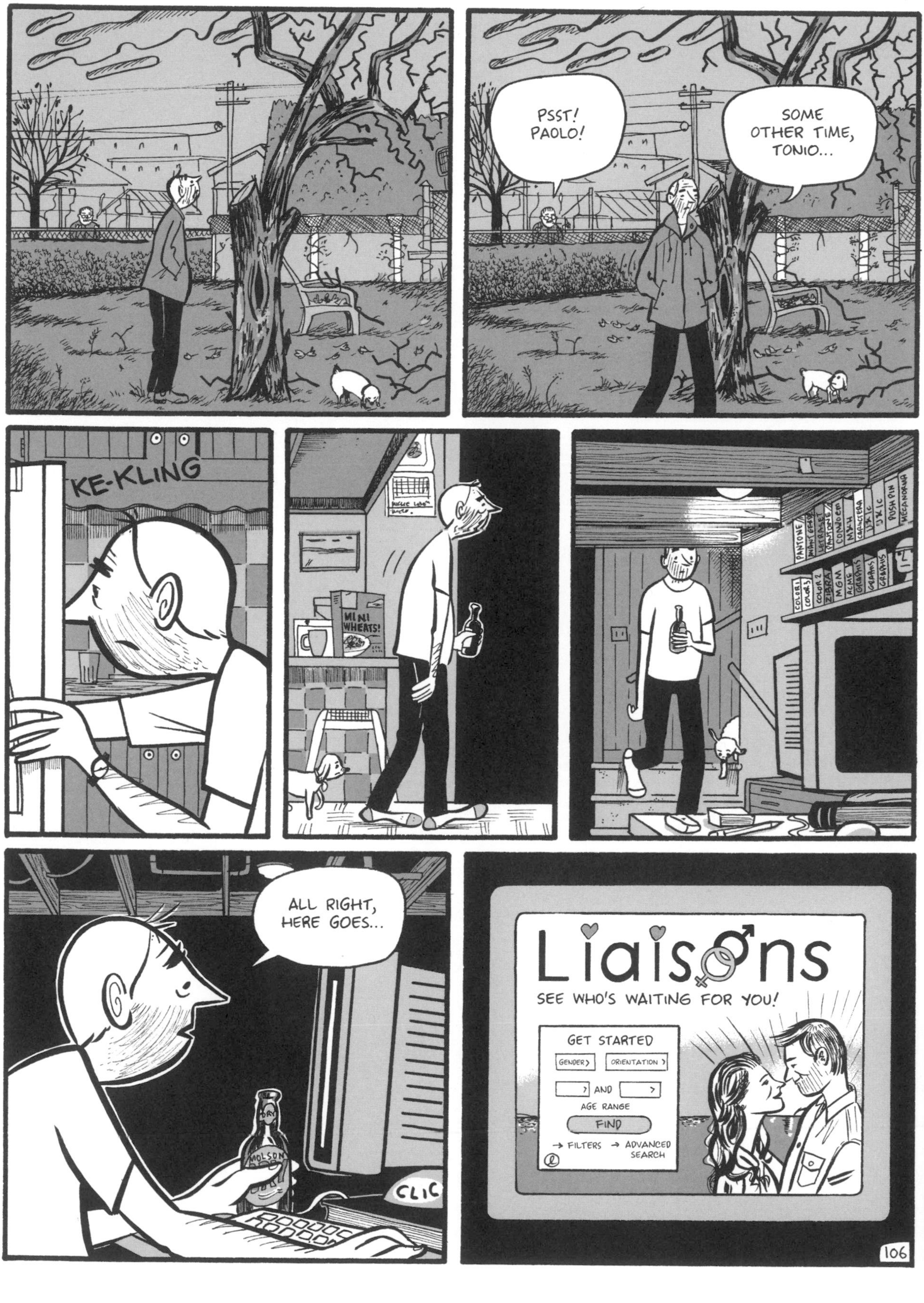
PSST! PAOLO!
SOME OTHER TIME, TONIO...
KE-KLING
MINI WHEATS!
ALL RIGHT, HERE GOES...
MOLSON
CLIC
Liaisons
SEE WHO'S WAITING FOR YOU!
GET STARTED
GENDER
ORIENTATION
AND
AGE RANGE
FIND
→ FILTERS
→ ADVANCED SEARCH

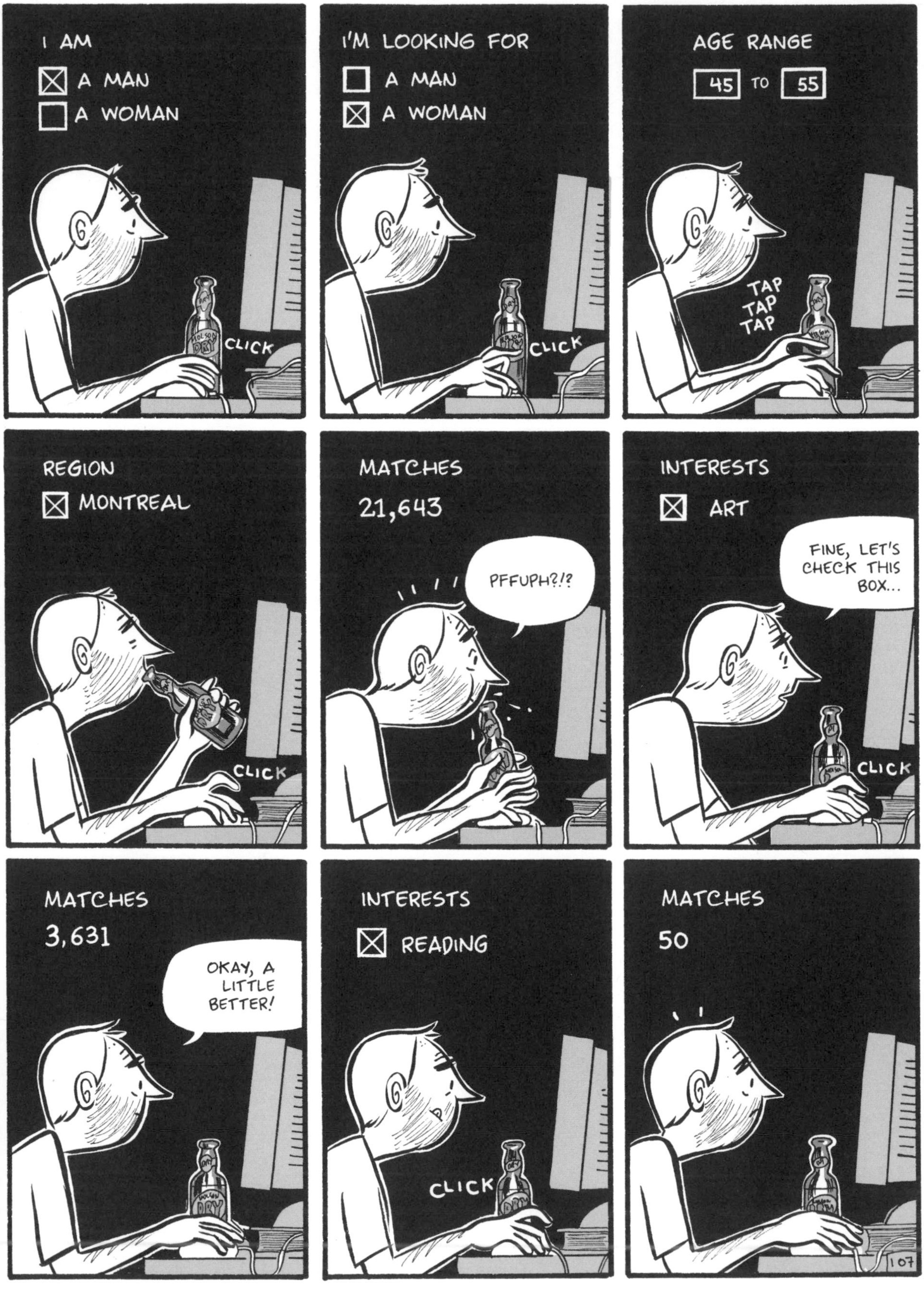
I AM
A MAN
A WOMAN
CLICK
I'M LOOKING FOR
A MAN
A WOMAN
CLICK
AGE RANGE
45 TO 55
TAP TAP TAP
REGION
MONTREAL
CLICK
MATCHES
21,643
PFFUPH?!?
INTERESTS
ART
FINE, LET'S CHECK THIS BOX...
CLICK
MATCHES
3,631
OKAY, A LITTLE BETTER!
INTERESTS
READING
CLICK
MATCHES
50

INTERESTS

☒ COMICS

CLICK

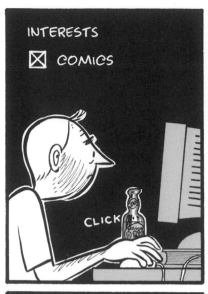

MATCHES

0

TOO SPECIFIC.

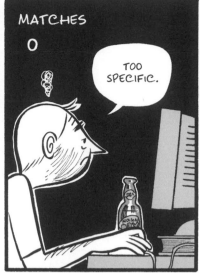

OKAY, WELL, LET'S TAKE A LOOK AT THE 50 "READERS"...

CLICK CLICK

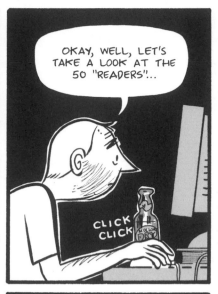

PET_LVR_QUEEN

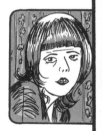

HI!!! LOOKING FOR FRIENDSHIP.. AND HONESTY! IM A WOMAN WHO KNOWS WHAT SHE WANTS!!! AND IF ALL YOU WANT IS SEX, DON'T BOTHER!! I'VE GOT A 17-YEAR-OLD DAUGHTER WHO DOESN'T LIVE WITH ME!!!! I HAVE 4 CATS AND 2 DOGS, AND IM LOOKING FOR A NICELY PROPORTION-ATE MAN AND A CONFIDANT FOR CONVERSATIONS OVER DINNER AND A GOOD GLASS OF WINE. I'M A BIG LADY 5 FOOT 10 INCHES!!! I LIKE TALLER AT LEAST 6 FOOT, WITH HAIR,

NOPE...

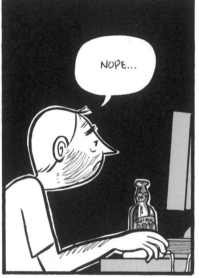

VIXXXEN_69

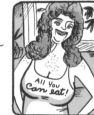

HEY BOYS!! WHAT U SEE IS WHAT U GET! LOL IF YOU'RE LOOKING FOR A GIRL WHO'S EASY GO-ING AND LIKES SEX (GRRR)!!! LOL I LIKE A GUY WHOSE HOT, BUILT AND HUNG. 8 INCHES++. MEMBER OF SWINGERS CLUB IN MONTREAL. AVID SKIER. ENJOY SPAS, ATV, KAYAK, A GREAT DINNER AND A GOOD GLASS OF WINE WITH FRIENDS.

NO PICTURE NO ANSWER!!!
LOL XXXXXX

OKAY, I GET IT...THEY MUST'VE CHECKED **ALL THE** BOXES, FROM **A**QUAFIT TO **Z**UMBA...SO THAT MAKES THEM READERS, TOO...

ANYWAY, ON TO THE NEXT ONE...

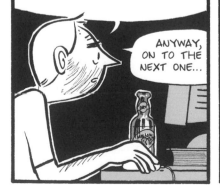

SERIOUS4URLOVE

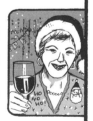

WARNING: HON-EST AND CARING A MUST!!!!! LOOKING FOR A MAN WHO WANTS MORE THAN SEX. IF YOU'VE GOT YOUR LIFE SORTED AND YOU'RE OOKING FOR A OUS RELATION- TH A CARING WOMAN, I LOVE S ON THE BEACH, SUPER GOOD GLASS OF WINE TV, SCU UR CA KIDS CTURE ANSWER

"LIFE SORTED"? WHAT THE HELL DOES THAT MEAN?

QC_COWGIRL

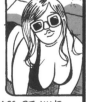

HI EVERYONE! LIFE'S GOOD WHEN YOU LIVE IT LIKE I DO! LOL!!!!! FORMER ENGLISH TEACHER. I'VE GOT 2 BOYS. COWGIRL AT HEART. YOUR THE CITY I'M NOT THE U A GOOD GLASS OF WINE ANT A REAL MA OSYIN THE FIR HAND SUNSET

A GOOD **BOTTLE** OF WINE IS WHAT I NEED TO GET THROUGH THESE...

NO PICTURE, NO ANSWER

108

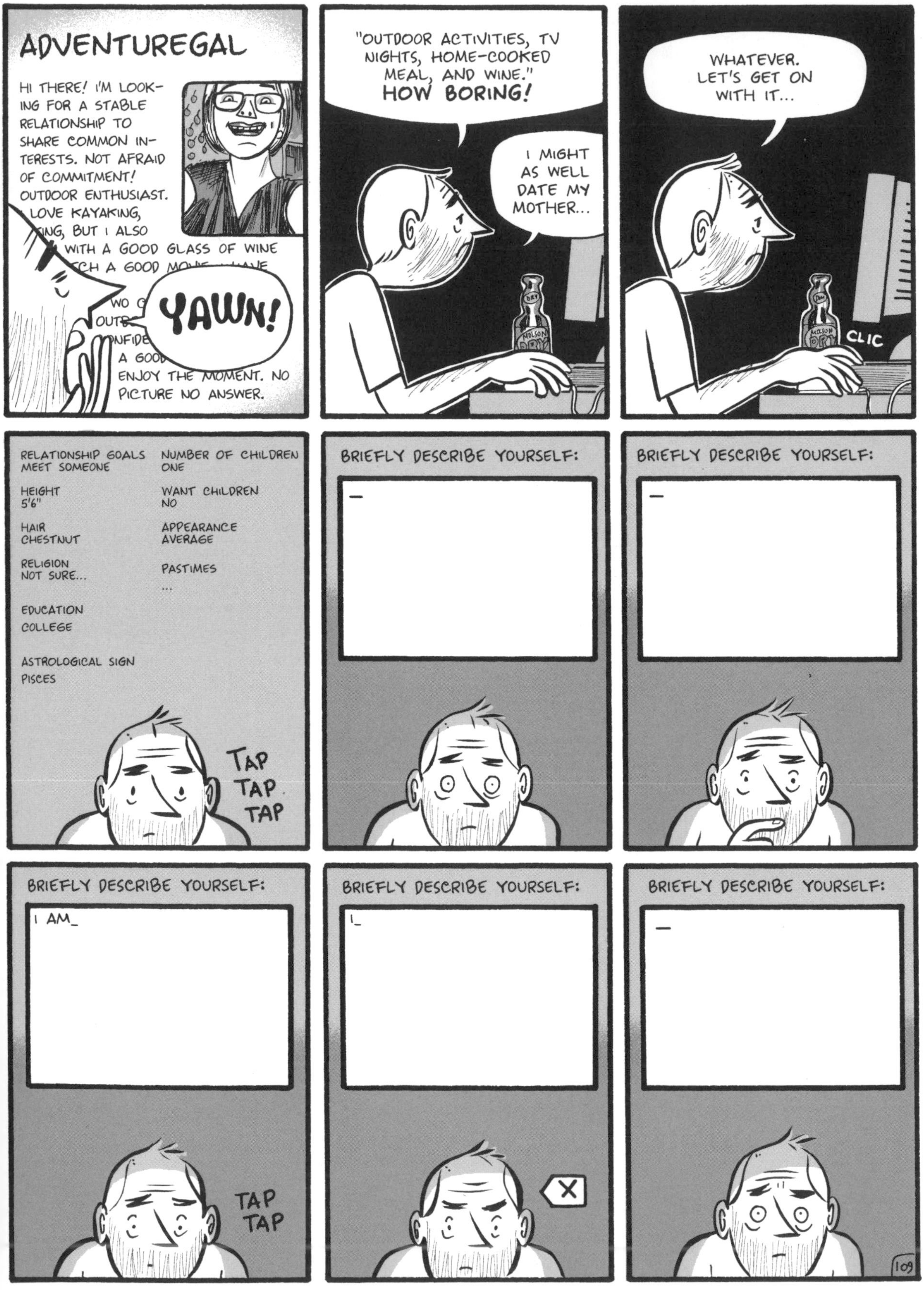
ADVENTUREGAL
HI THERE! I'M LOOK-
ING FOR A STABLE
RELATIONSHIP TO
SHARE COMMON IN-
TERESTS. NOT AFRAID
OF COMMITMENT!
OUTDOOR ENTHUSIAST.
LOVE KAYAKING,
ING, BUT I ALSO
WITH A GOOD GLASS OF WINE
A GOOD
ENJOY THE MOMENT. NO
PICTURE NO ANSWER.
YAWN!
"OUTDOOR ACTIVITIES, TV NIGHTS, HOME-COOKED MEAL, AND WINE." HOW BORING!
I MIGHT AS WELL DATE MY MOTHER...
WHATEVER. LET'S GET ON WITH IT...
CLIC
RELATIONSHIP GOALS
MEET SOMEONE
NUMBER OF CHILDREN
ONE
HEIGHT
5'6"
WANT CHILDREN
NO
HAIR
CHESTNUT
APPEARANCE
AVERAGE
RELIGION
NOT SURE...
PASTIMES
...
EDUCATION
COLLEGE
ASTROLOGICAL SIGN
PISCES
TAP TAP TAP
BRIEFLY DESCRIBE YOURSELF:
BRIEFLY DESCRIBE YOURSELF:
BRIEFLY DESCRIBE YOURSELF:
I AM_
TAP TAP
BRIEFLY DESCRIBE YOURSELF:
I_
BRIEFLY DESCRIBE YOURSELF:

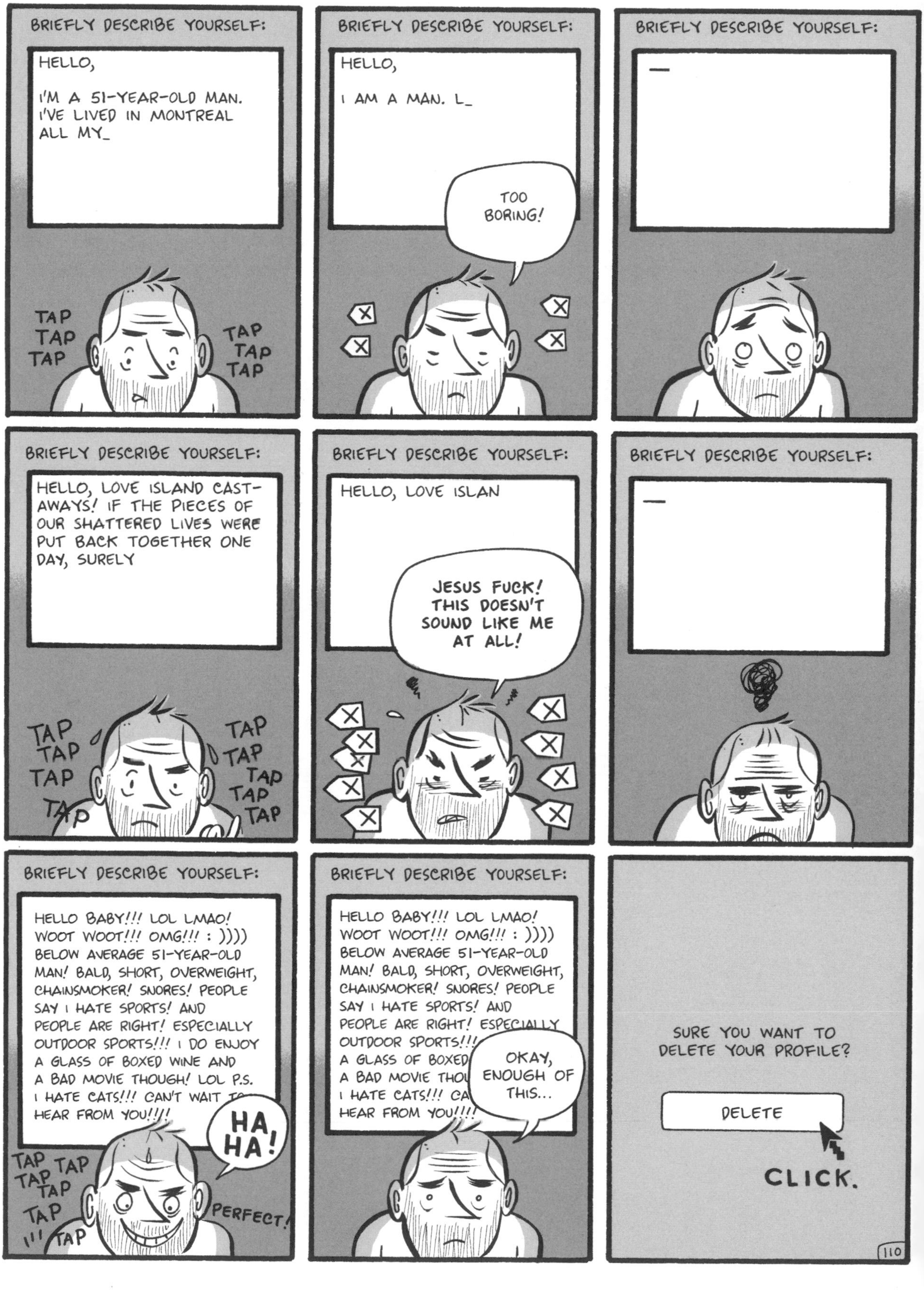
BRIEFLY DESCRIBE YOURSELF:
HELLO,
I'M A 51-YEAR-OLD MAN. I'VE LIVED IN MONTREAL ALL MY_
TAP TAP TAP
TAP TAP TAP
BRIEFLY DESCRIBE YOURSELF:
HELLO,
I AM A MAN. L_
TOO BORING!
BRIEFLY DESCRIBE YOURSELF:
BRIEFLY DESCRIBE YOURSELF:
HELLO, LOVE ISLAND CASTAWAYS! IF THE PIECES OF OUR SHATTERED LIVES WERE PUT BACK TOGETHER ONE DAY, SURELY
TAP TAP TAP TAP
TAP TAP TAP TAP TAP
BRIEFLY DESCRIBE YOURSELF:
HELLO, LOVE ISLAN
JESUS FUCK! THIS DOESN'T SOUND LIKE ME AT ALL!
BRIEFLY DESCRIBE YOURSELF:
BRIEFLY DESCRIBE YOURSELF:
HELLO BABY!!! LOL LMAO! WOOT WOOT!!! OMG!!! :)))) BELOW AVERAGE 51-YEAR-OLD MAN! BALD, SHORT, OVERWEIGHT, CHAINSMOKER! SNORES! PEOPLE SAY I HATE SPORTS! AND PEOPLE ARE RIGHT! ESPECIALLY OUTDOOR SPORTS!!! I DO ENJOY A GLASS OF BOXED WINE AND A BAD MOVIE THOUGH! LOL P.S. I HATE CATS!!! CAN'T WAIT TO HEAR FROM YOU!!!!
HA HA!
TAP TAP TAP TAP TAP TAP
PERFECT!
BRIEFLY DESCRIBE YOURSELF:
OKAY, ENOUGH OF THIS...
SURE YOU WANT TO DELETE YOUR PROFILE?
DELETE
CLICK.

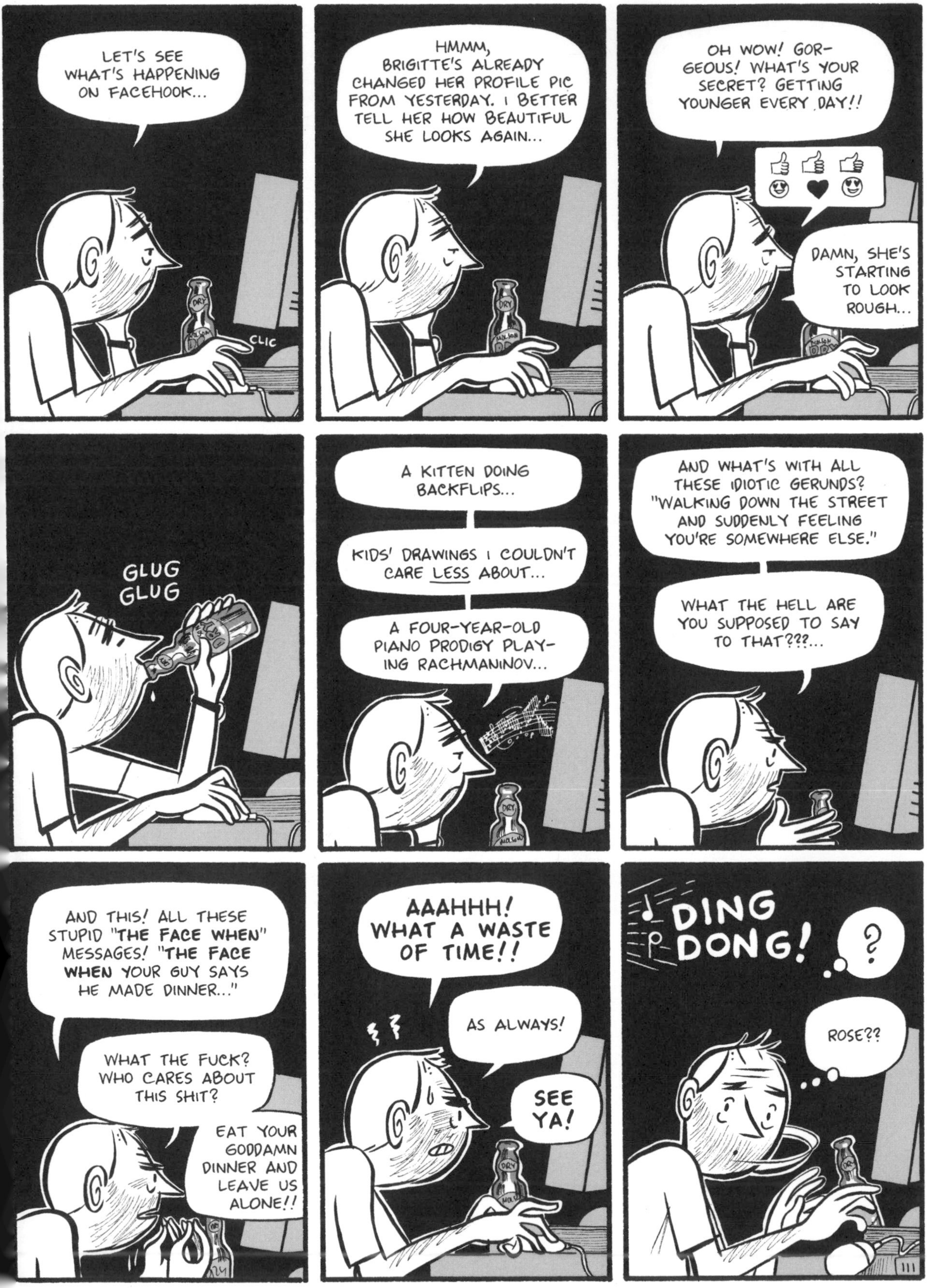
LET'S SEE WHAT'S HAPPENING ON FACEHOOK...
CLIC
DRY
HMMM, BRIGITTE'S ALREADY CHANGED HER PROFILE PIC FROM YESTERDAY. I BETTER TELL HER HOW BEAUTIFUL SHE LOOKS AGAIN...
DRY
OH WOW! GORGEOUS! WHAT'S YOUR SECRET? GETTING YOUNGER EVERY DAY!!
DAMN, SHE'S STARTING TO LOOK ROUGH...
GLUG GLUG
A KITTEN DOING BACKFLIPS...
KIDS' DRAWINGS I COULDN'T CARE LESS ABOUT...
A FOUR-YEAR-OLD PIANO PRODIGY PLAYING RACHMANINOV...
DRY
AND WHAT'S WITH ALL THESE IDIOTIC GERUNDS? "WALKING DOWN THE STREET AND SUDDENLY FEELING YOU'RE SOMEWHERE ELSE."
WHAT THE HELL ARE YOU SUPPOSED TO SAY TO THAT???...
AND THIS! ALL THESE STUPID "**THE FACE WHEN**" MESSAGES! "**THE FACE WHEN** YOUR GUY SAYS HE MADE DINNER..."
WHAT THE FUCK? WHO CARES ABOUT THIS SHIT?
EAT YOUR GODDAMN DINNER AND LEAVE US ALONE!!
AAAHHH! WHAT A WASTE OF TIME!!
AS ALWAYS!
SEE YA!
DRY
DING DONG!
?
ROSE??

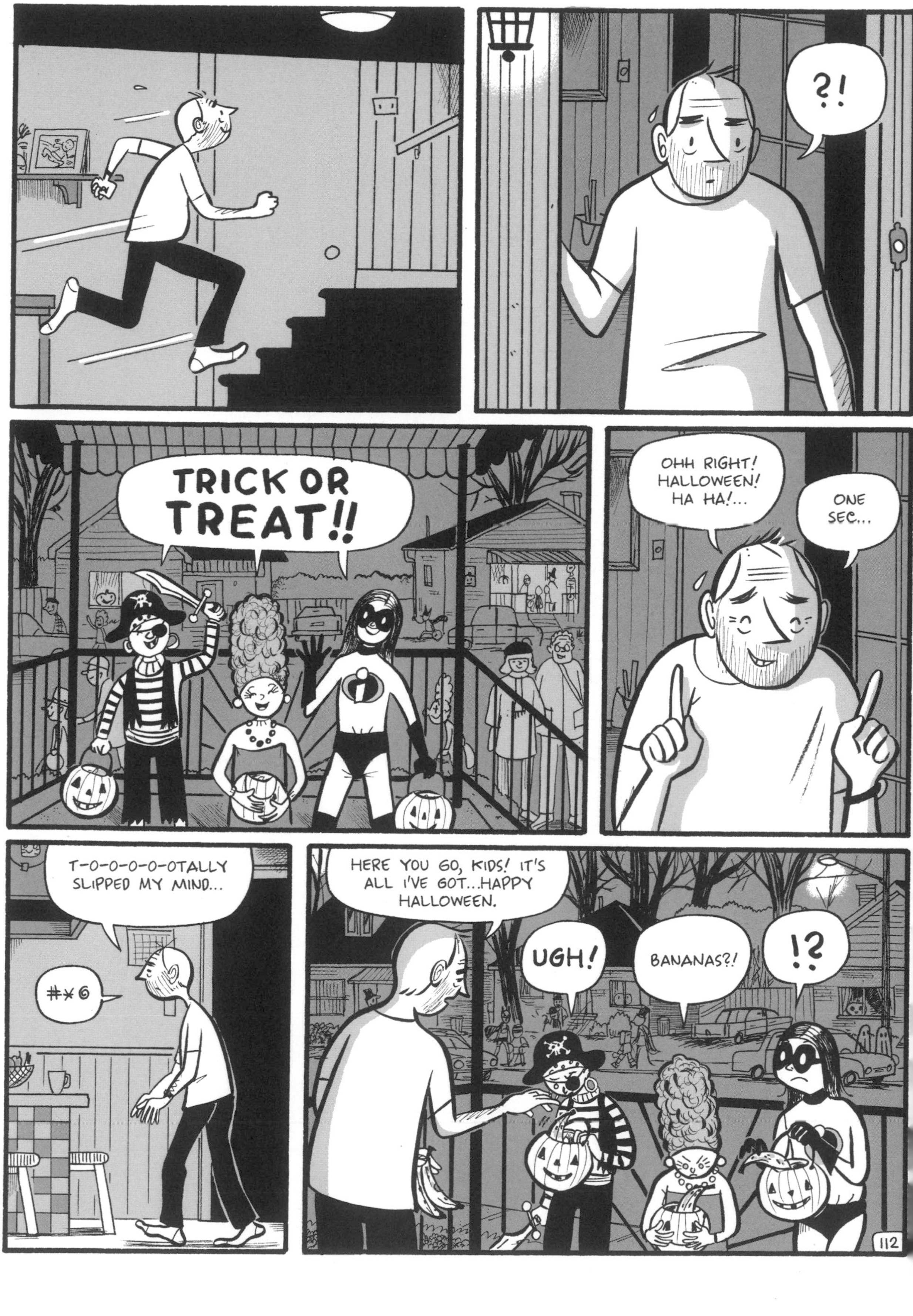
?!
TRICK OR TREAT!!
OHH RIGHT! HALLOWEEN! HA HA!...
ONE SEC...
T-O-O-O-O-OTALLY SLIPPED MY MIND...
#*@
HERE YOU GO, KIDS! IT'S ALL I'VE GOT...HAPPY HALLOWEEN.
UGH!
BANANAS?!
!?

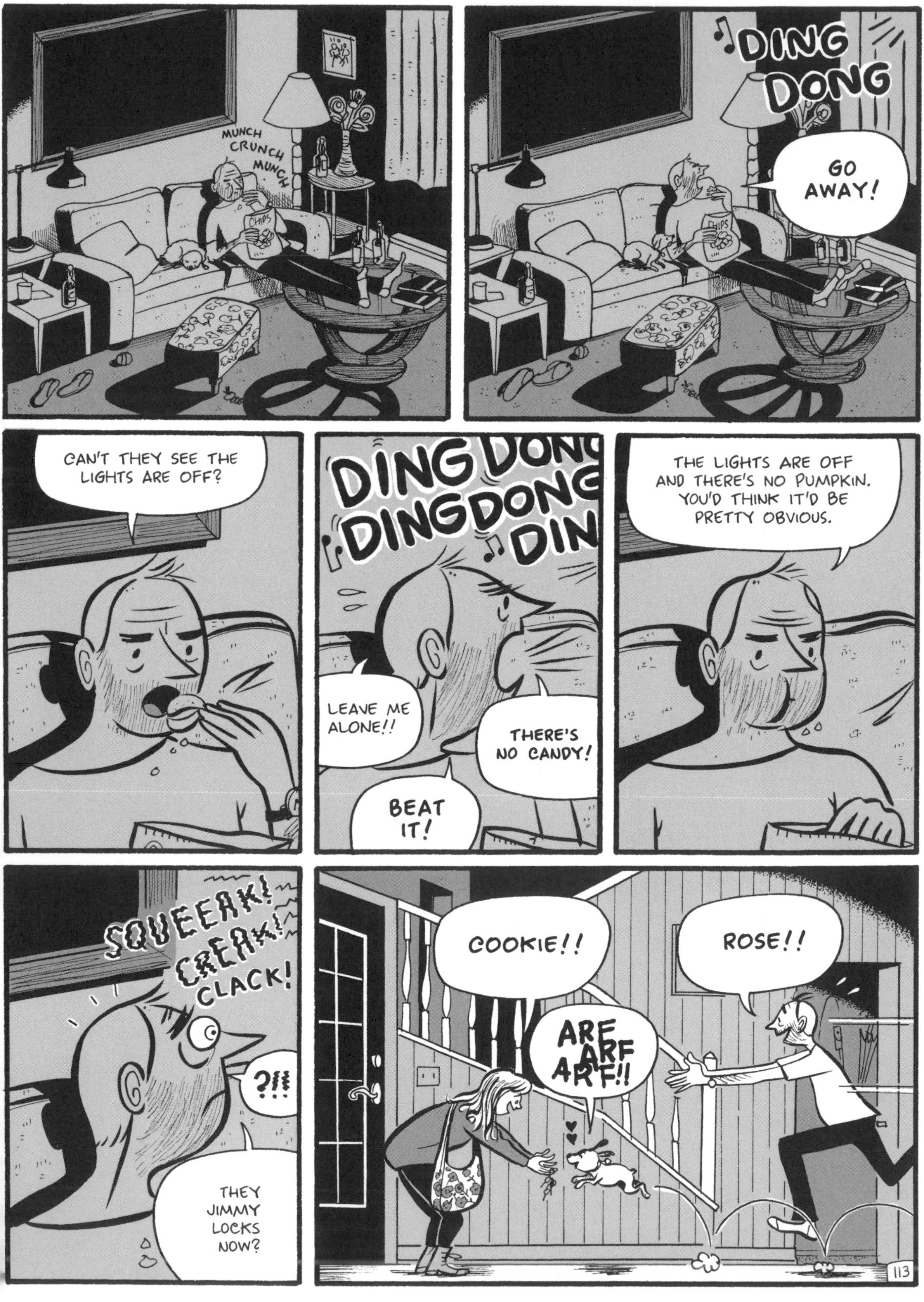
MUNCH
CRUNCH
MUNCH
CHIPS
DING
DONG
GO AWAY!
CHIPS
CAN'T THEY SEE THE LIGHTS ARE OFF?
DING DONG
DING DONG
DIN
LEAVE ME ALONE!!
THERE'S NO CANDY!
BEAT IT!
THE LIGHTS ARE OFF AND THERE'S NO PUMPKIN. YOU'D THINK IT'D BE PRETTY OBVIOUS.
SQUEEAK!
CREAK!
CLACK!
?!!
THEY JIMMY LOCKS NOW?
COOKIE!!
ROSE!!
ARF ARF ARF!!

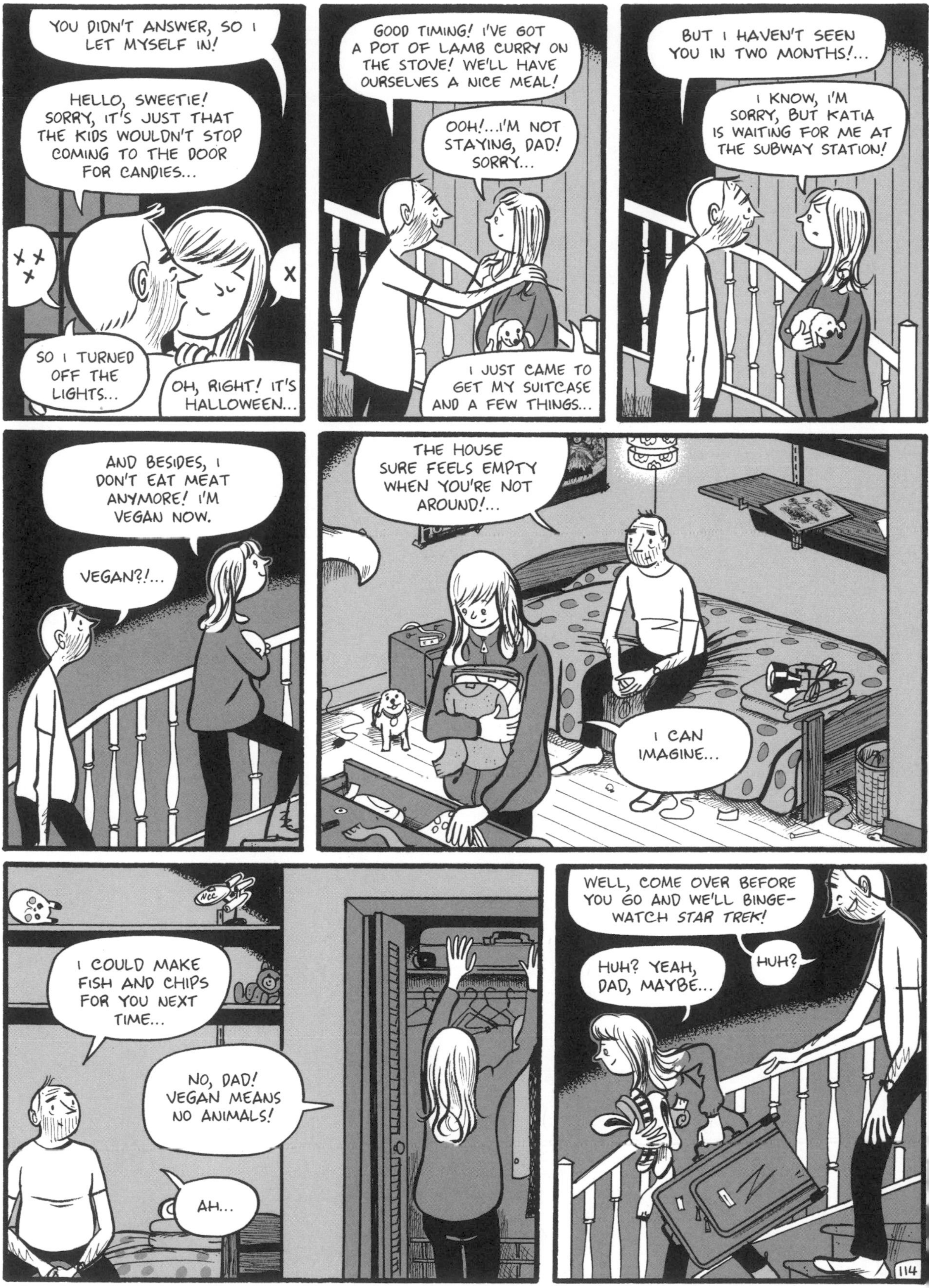
YOU DIDN'T ANSWER, SO I LET MYSELF IN!
HELLO, SWEETIE! SORRY, IT'S JUST THAT THE KIDS WOULDN'T STOP COMING TO THE DOOR FOR CANDIES...
X X X
X
SO I TURNED OFF THE LIGHTS...
OH, RIGHT! IT'S HALLOWEEN...
GOOD TIMING! I'VE GOT A POT OF LAMB CURRY ON THE STOVE! WE'LL HAVE OURSELVES A NICE MEAL!
OOH!...I'M NOT STAYING, DAD! SORRY...
I JUST CAME TO GET MY SUITCASE AND A FEW THINGS...
BUT I HAVEN'T SEEN YOU IN TWO MONTHS!...
I KNOW, I'M SORRY, BUT KATIA IS WAITING FOR ME AT THE SUBWAY STATION!
AND BESIDES, I DON'T EAT MEAT ANYMORE! I'M VEGAN NOW.
VEGAN?!...
THE HOUSE SURE FEELS EMPTY WHEN YOU'RE NOT AROUND!...
I CAN IMAGINE...
I COULD MAKE FISH AND CHIPS FOR YOU NEXT TIME...
NO, DAD! VEGAN MEANS NO ANIMALS!
AH...
WELL, COME OVER BEFORE YOU GO AND WE'LL BINGE-WATCH STAR TREK!
HUH? YEAH, DAD, MAYBE...
HUH?

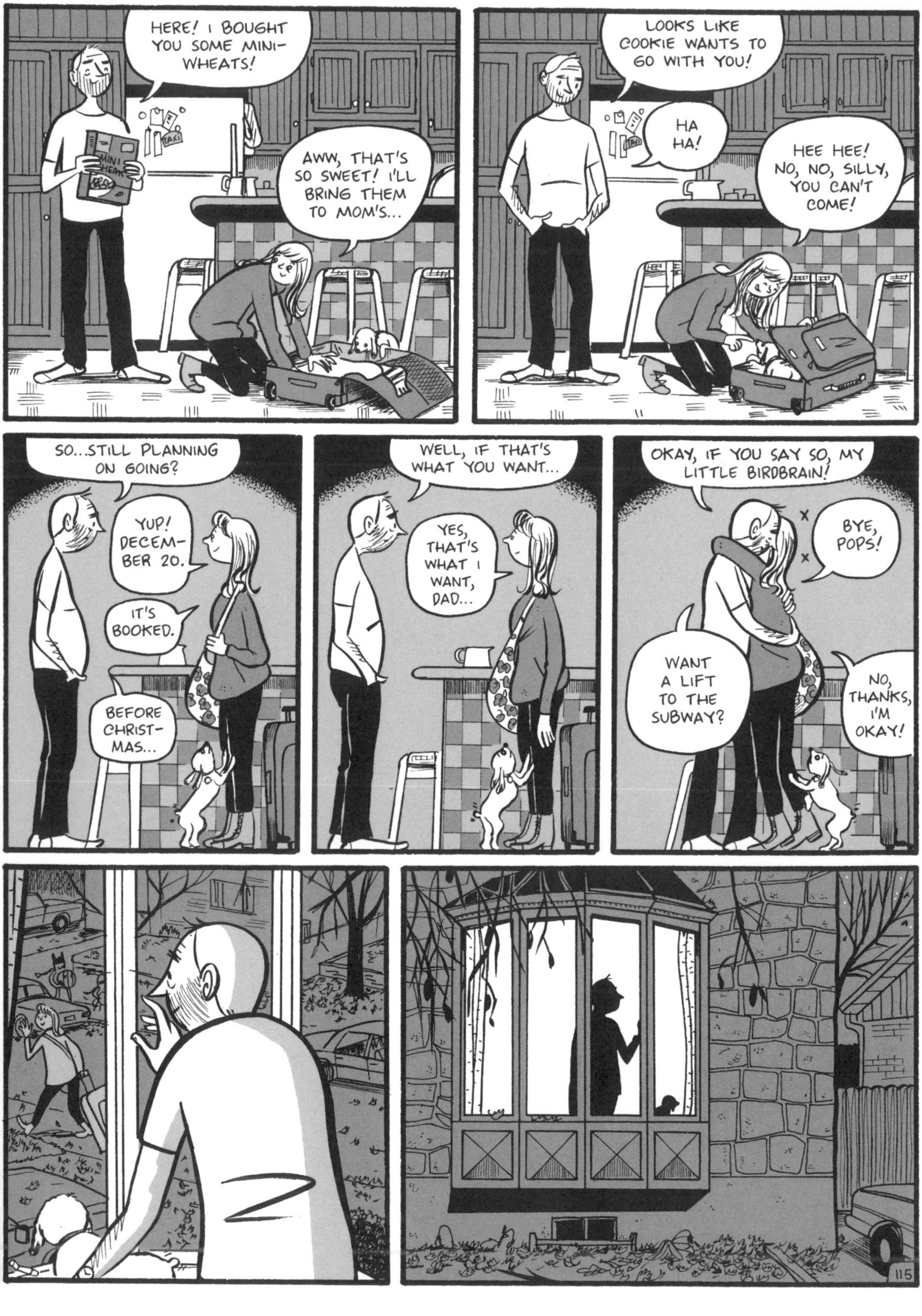
HERE! I BOUGHT YOU SOME MINI-WHEATS!
MINI WHEATS
TAXI
AWW, THAT'S SO SWEET! I'LL BRING THEM TO MOM'S...
LOOKS LIKE COOKIE WANTS TO GO WITH YOU!
HA HA!
HEE HEE! NO, NO, SILLY, YOU CAN'T COME!
SO...STILL PLANNING ON GOING?
YUP! DECEMBER 20.
IT'S BOOKED.
BEFORE CHRISTMAS...
WELL, IF THAT'S WHAT YOU WANT...
YES, THAT'S WHAT I WANT, DAD...
OKAY, IF YOU SAY SO, MY LITTLE BIRDBRAIN!
BYE, POPS!
WANT A LIFT TO THE SUBWAY?
NO, THANKS, I'M OKAY!

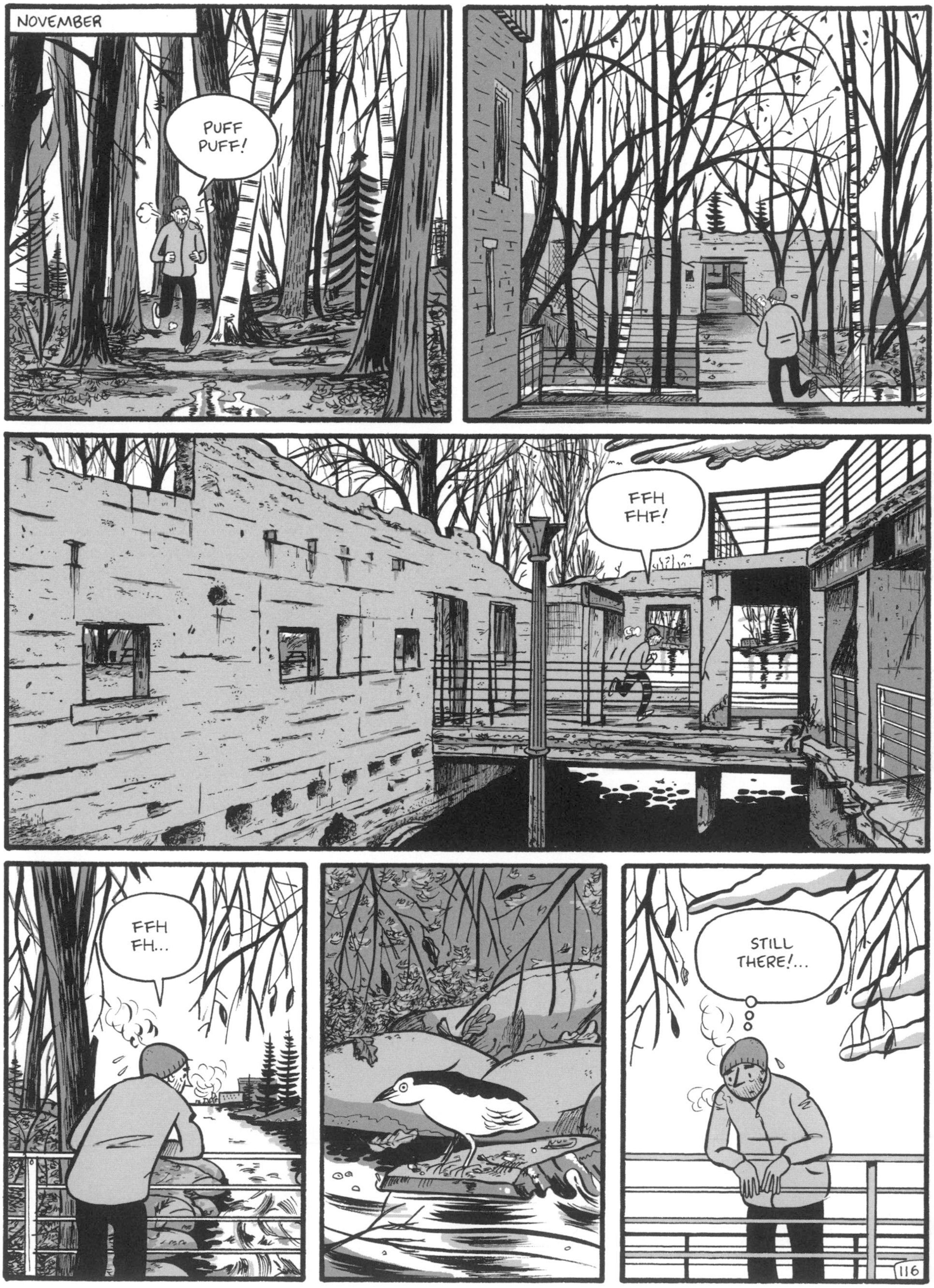
NOVEMBER
PUFF PUFF!
FFH FHF!
FFH FH...
STILL THERE!...

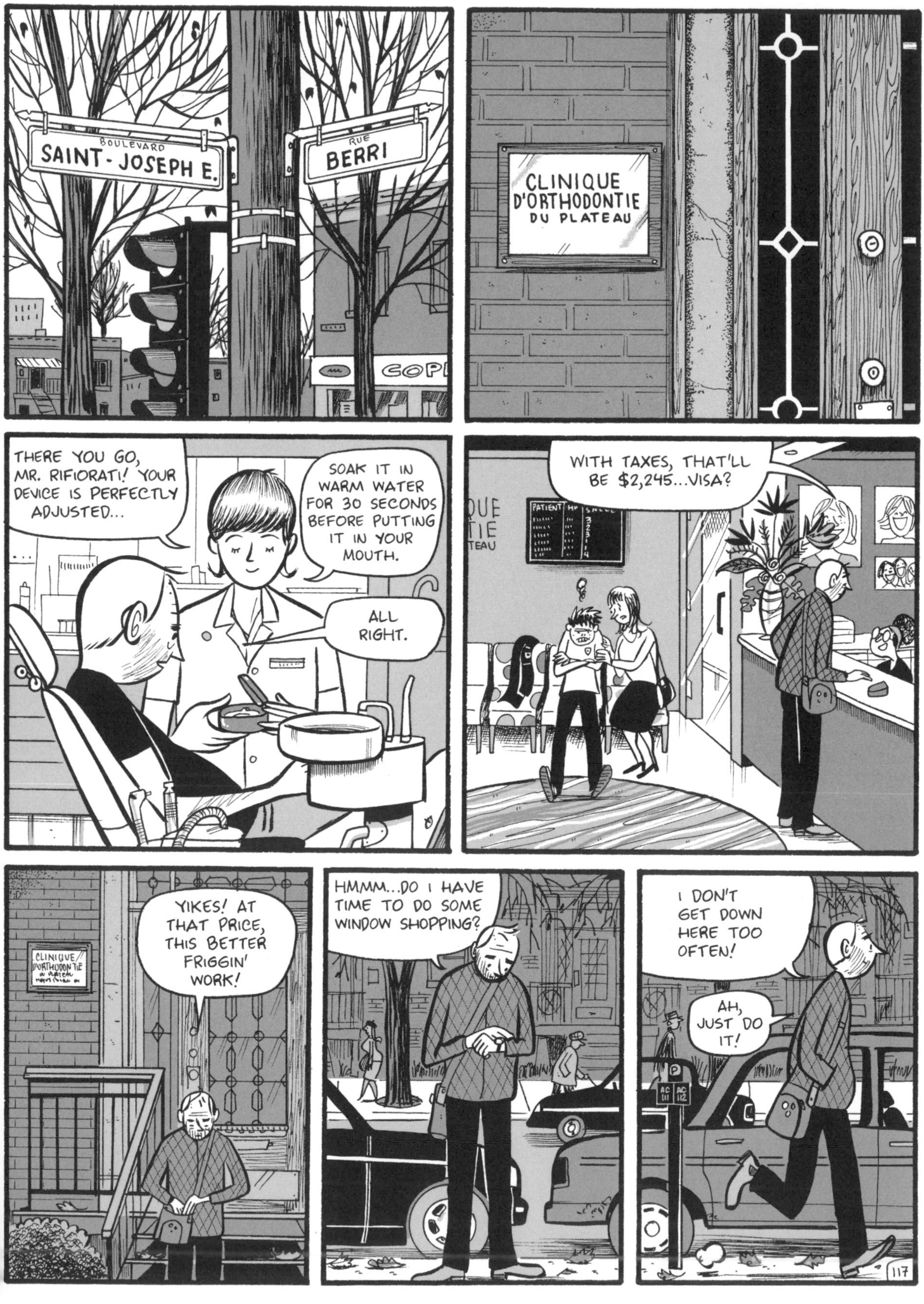
BOULEVARD
SAINT-JOSEPH E.
RUE
BERRI
CLINIQUE
D'ORTHODONTIE
DU PLATEAU
THERE YOU GO, MR. RIFIORATI! YOUR DEVICE IS PERFECTLY ADJUSTED...
SOAK IT IN WARM WATER FOR 30 SECONDS BEFORE PUTTING IT IN YOUR MOUTH.
ALL RIGHT.
WITH TAXES, THAT'LL BE $2,245...VISA?
PATIENT
YIKES! AT THAT PRICE, THIS BETTER FRIGGIN' WORK!
HMMM...DO I HAVE TIME TO DO SOME WINDOW SHOPPING?
I DON'T GET DOWN HERE TOO OFTEN!
AH, JUST DO IT!

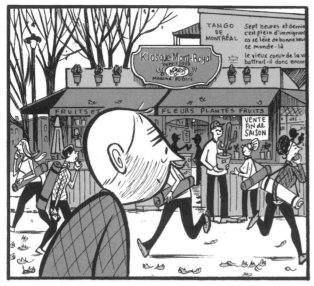

TANGO DE MONTRÉAL

Kiosque Mont-Royal
MARCHÉ PUBLIC

FRUITS
FLEURS PLANTES FRUITS

VENTE FIN DE SAISON

Sept heures et demie
c'est plein d'immigrant
ça se lève de bonne heur
ce monde-là

le vieux cœur de la vi
battrait-il donc encor

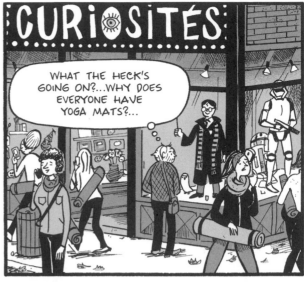

CURIOSITÉS

WHAT THE HECK'S GOING ON?...WHY DOES EVERYONE HAVE YOGA MATS?...

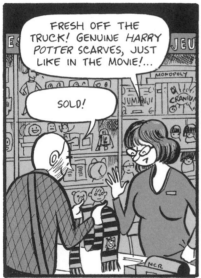

FRESH OFF THE TRUCK! GENUINE HARRY POTTER SCARVES, JUST LIKE IN THE MOVIE!...

SOLD!

MONOPOLY

JUMANJI

CRANIUM

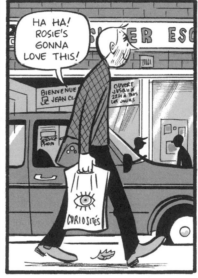

HA HA! ROSIE'S GONNA LOVE THIS!

BIENVENUE JEAN CO

OUVERT JUSQU'À 22H À TOUS LES JOURS

CURIOSITÉS

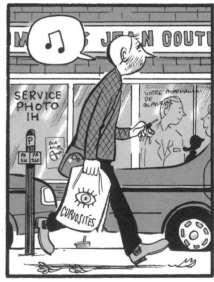

SERVICE PHOTO 1H

VOTRE PHARMACIE DE QUARTIER

CURIOSITÉS

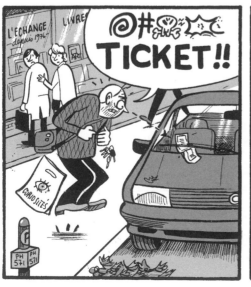

L'ÉCHANGE depuis 1976

LIVRE

@#%⚡☠ TICKET!!

CURIOSITÉS

PH 571 PH 571

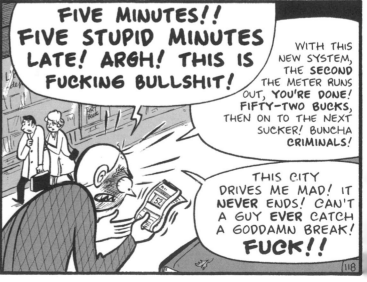

FIVE MINUTES!! FIVE STUPID MINUTES LATE! ARGH! THIS IS FUCKING BULLSHIT!

WITH THIS NEW SYSTEM, THE SECOND THE METER RUNS OUT, YOU'RE DONE! FIFTY-TWO BUCKS, THEN ON TO THE NEXT SUCKER! BUNCHA CRIMINALS!

THIS CITY DRIVES ME MAD! IT NEVER ENDS! CAN'T A GUY EVER CATCH A GODDAMN BREAK! FUCK!!

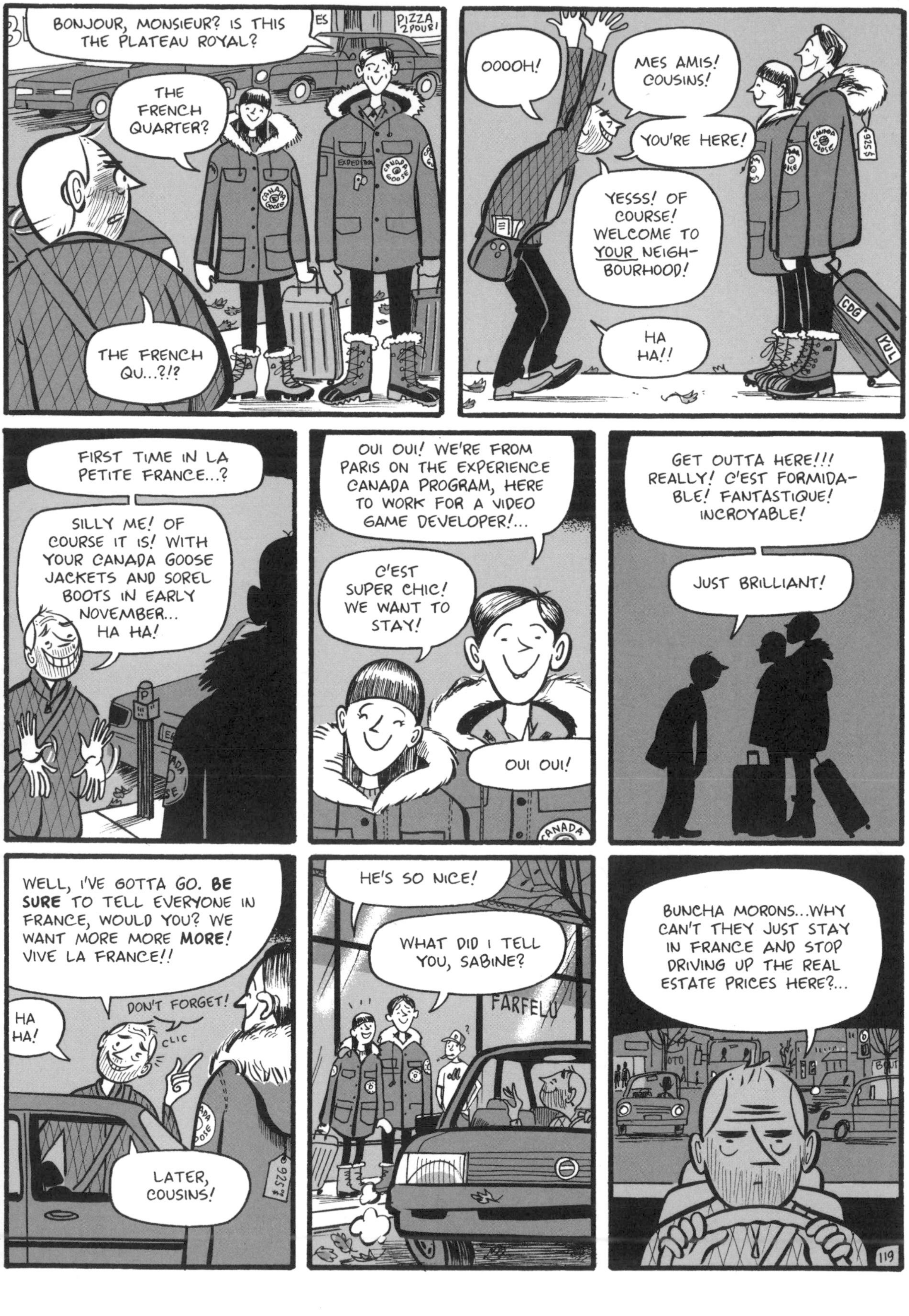
BONJOUR, MONSIEUR? IS THIS THE PLATEAU ROYAL?
PIZZA 2 POUR 1
THE FRENCH QUARTER?
THE FRENCH QU...?!?
OOOOH!
MES AMIS! COUSINS!
YOU'RE HERE!
YESSS! OF COURSE! WELCOME TO YOUR NEIGHBOURHOOD!
HA HA!!
925$
CDG
YUL
FIRST TIME IN LA PETITE FRANCE...?
SILLY ME! OF COURSE IT IS! WITH YOUR CANADA GOOSE JACKETS AND SOREL BOOTS IN EARLY NOVEMBER... HA HA!
OUI OUI! WE'RE FROM PARIS ON THE EXPERIENCE CANADA PROGRAM, HERE TO WORK FOR A VIDEO GAME DEVELOPER!...
C'EST SUPER CHIC! WE WANT TO STAY!
OUI OUI!
GET OUTTA HERE!!! REALLY! C'EST FORMIDABLE! FANTASTIQUE! INCROYABLE!
JUST BRILLIANT!
WELL, I'VE GOTTA GO. **BE SURE** TO TELL EVERYONE IN FRANCE, WOULD YOU? WE WANT MORE MORE **MORE**! VIVE LA FRANCE!!
HA HA!
DON'T FORGET!
CLIC
LATER, COUSINS!
925$
HE'S SO NICE!
WHAT DID I TELL YOU, SABINE?
FARFELU
BUNCHA MORONS...WHY CAN'T THEY JUST STAY IN FRANCE AND STOP DRIVING UP THE REAL ESTATE PRICES HERE?...

DOCTOR Doom's MANDIBULAR ADVANCEMENT ~ DEVICE ~

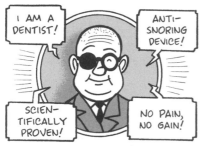

I AM A DENTIST!

ANTI-SNORING DEVICE!

SCIENTIFICALLY PROVEN!

NO PAIN, NO GAIN!

ADVERTORIAL PAID FOR BY HIS MOTHER.

DR. DOOM'S ANTI-SNORING ORTHOTIC IS MADE OF THE SAME HIGH-GRADE STAINLESS STEEL AS AUTHENTIC WIENER SCHNITZEL MALLETS.

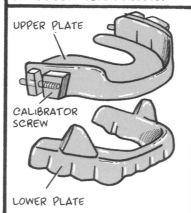

UPPER PLATE

CALIBRATOR SCREW

LOWER PLATE

FIRST, SOAK THE ORTHOTIC IN WARM WATER FOR 30 SECONDS, THEN PLACE IT IN THE MOUTH.

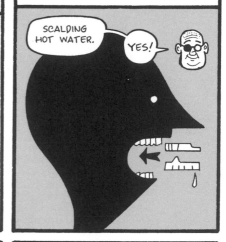

SCALDING HOT WATER.

YES!

TO ACHIEVE THE DESIRED EFFECT, THE PLATES ARE ADJUSTED TO ALTER THE JAW AND TONGUE POSITION, PUSHING THE LOWER JAW (MANDIBLE) FORWARD.

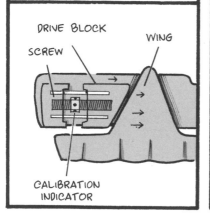

DRIVE BLOCK

SCREW

WING

CALIBRATION INDICATOR

A TRAINED M.A.D. TECHNICIAN CALIBRATES THE DEVICE, ADVANCING THE LOWER JAW AS FAR AS PHYSICALLY POSSIBLE...

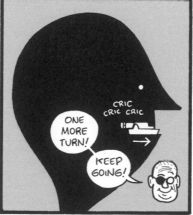

CRIC CRIC CRIC

ONE MORE TURN!

KEEP GOING!

...AND AESTHETICALLY TOLERABLE.

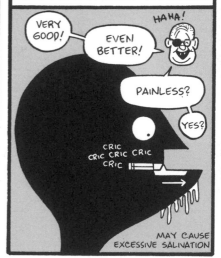

VERY GOOD!

EVEN BETTER!

HAHA!

PAINLESS?

YES?

CRIC CRIC CRIC CRIC CRIC

MAY CAUSE EXCESSIVE SALIVATION

THE DEVICE LOCKS THE JAW INTO POSITION TO PREVENT THE SOFT PALATE TISSUE AT THE BACK OF THE THROAT FROM BLOCKING THE AIRWAY.

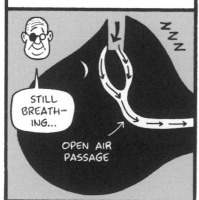

STILL BREATH-ING...

OPEN AIR PASSAGE

WITHOUT THE DEVICE:

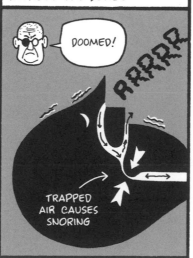

DOOMED!

RRRRR

TRAPPED AIR CAUSES SNORING

WITH THE DEVICE:

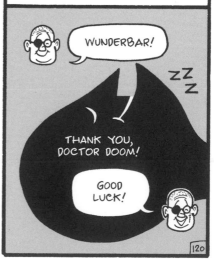

WUNDERBAR!

ZZZ

THANK YOU, DOCTOR DOOM!

GOOD LUCK!

120

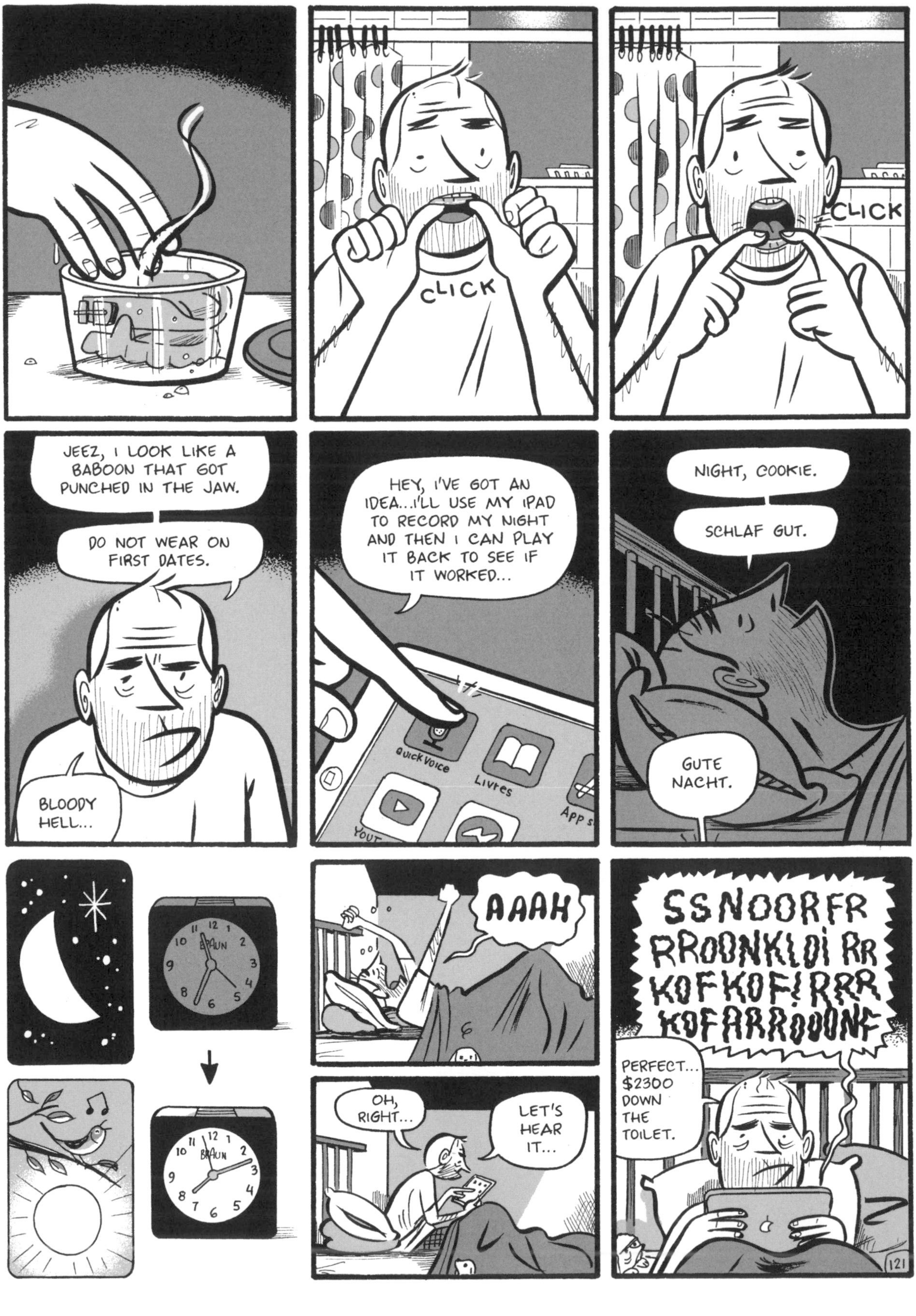
CLICK
CLICK
JEEZ, I LOOK LIKE A BABOON THAT GOT PUNCHED IN THE JAW.
DO NOT WEAR ON FIRST DATES.
BLOODY HELL...
HEY, I'VE GOT AN IDEA...I'LL USE MY IPAD TO RECORD MY NIGHT AND THEN I CAN PLAY IT BACK TO SEE IF IT WORKED...
QuickVoice
Livres
NIGHT, COOKIE.
SCHLAF GUT.
GUTE NACHT.
BRAUN
BRAUN
AAAH
OH, RIGHT...
LET'S HEAR IT...
SSNOORFR RROONKLOI RR KOFKOF! RRR KOFARROOONF
PERFECT... $2300 DOWN THE TOILET.

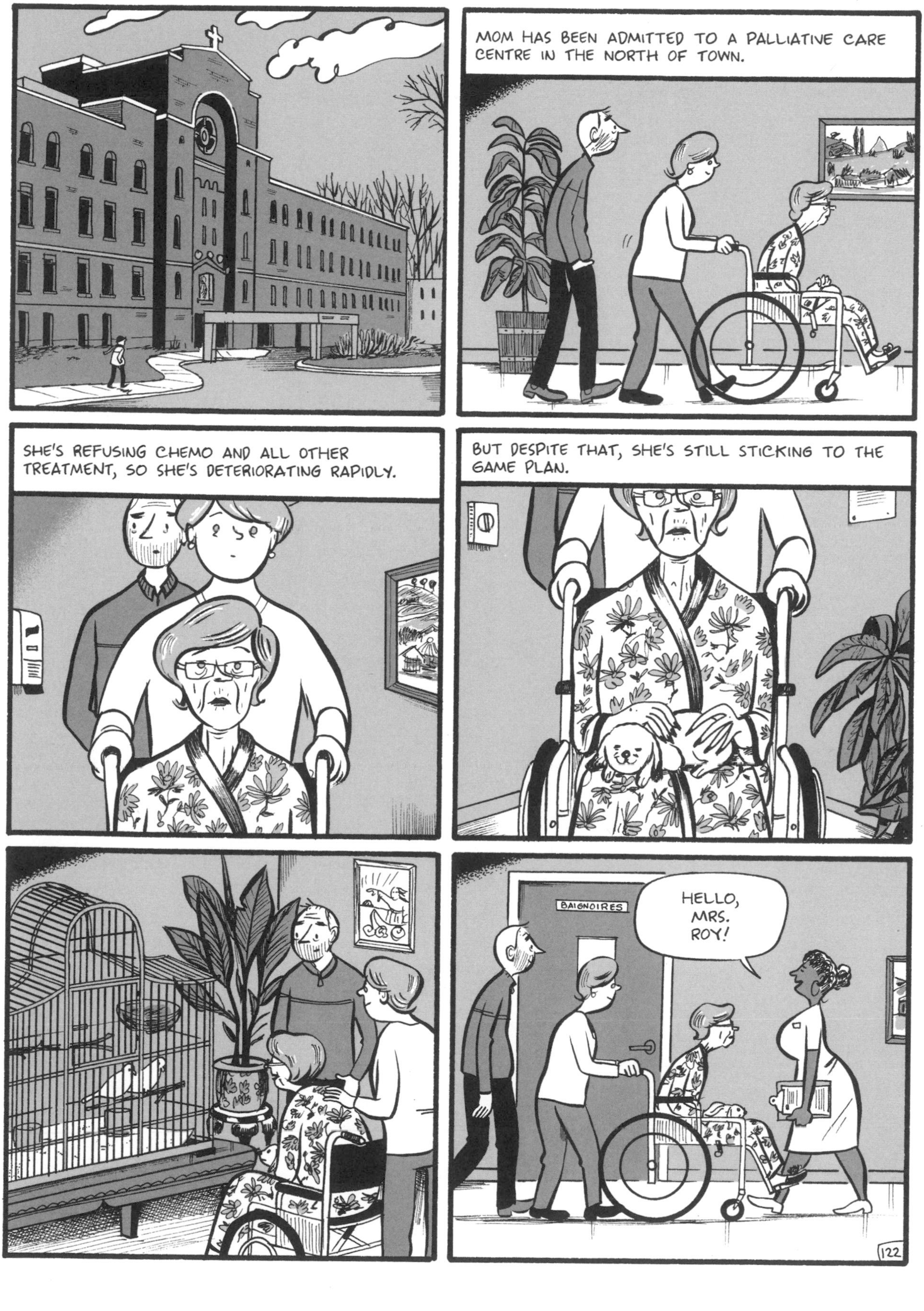
MOM HAS BEEN ADMITTED TO A PALLIATIVE CARE CENTRE IN THE NORTH OF TOWN.
SHE'S REFUSING CHEMO AND ALL OTHER TREATMENT, SO SHE'S DETERIORATING RAPIDLY.
BUT DESPITE THAT, SHE'S STILL STICKING TO THE GAME PLAN.
BAIGNOIRES
HELLO, MRS. ROY!

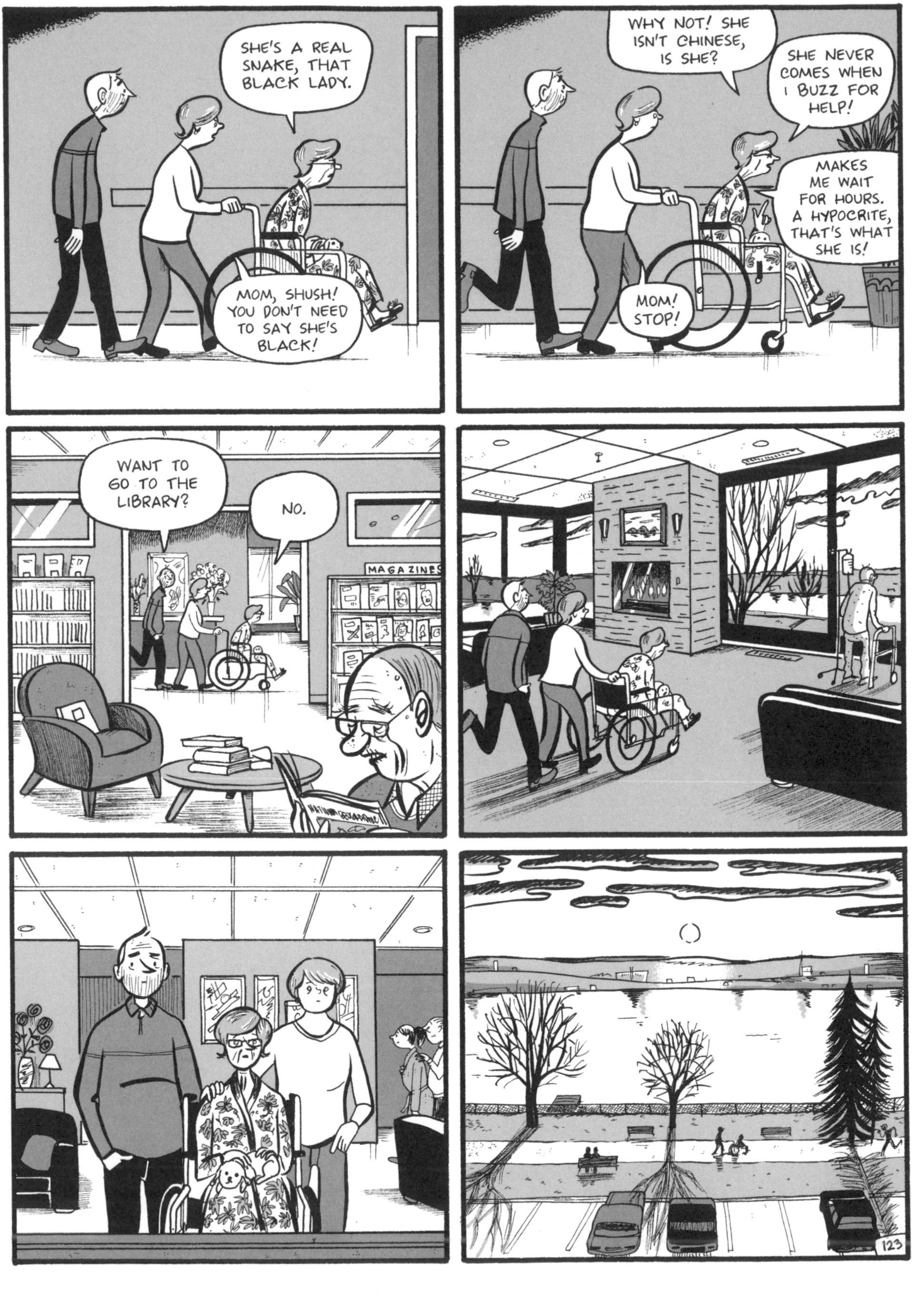
SHE'S A REAL SNAKE, THAT BLACK LADY.
MOM, SHUSH! YOU DON'T NEED TO SAY SHE'S BLACK!
WHY NOT! SHE ISN'T CHINESE, IS SHE?
SHE NEVER COMES WHEN I BUZZ FOR HELP!
MAKES ME WAIT FOR HOURS. A HYPOCRITE, THAT'S WHAT SHE IS!
MOM! STOP!
WANT TO GO TO THE LIBRARY?
NO.
MAGAZINES
NATIONAL GEOGRAPHIC

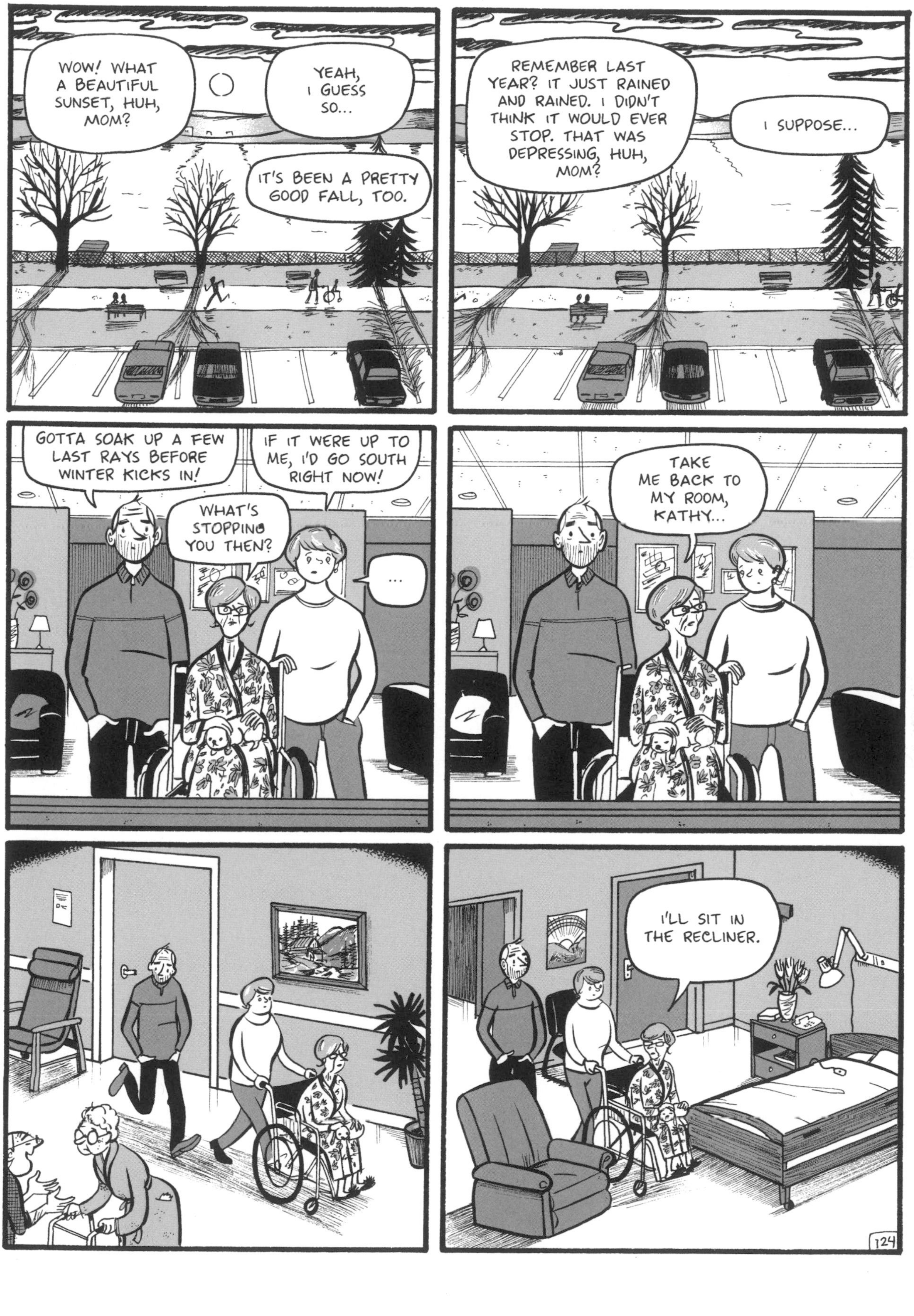
WOW! WHAT A BEAUTIFUL SUNSET, HUH, MOM?
YEAH, I GUESS SO...
IT'S BEEN A PRETTY GOOD FALL, TOO.
REMEMBER LAST YEAR? IT JUST RAINED AND RAINED. I DIDN'T THINK IT WOULD EVER STOP. THAT WAS DEPRESSING, HUH, MOM?
I SUPPOSE...
GOTTA SOAK UP A FEW LAST RAYS BEFORE WINTER KICKS IN!
IF IT WERE UP TO ME, I'D GO SOUTH RIGHT NOW!
WHAT'S STOPPING YOU THEN?
...
TAKE ME BACK TO MY ROOM, KATHY...
I'LL SIT IN THE RECLINER.

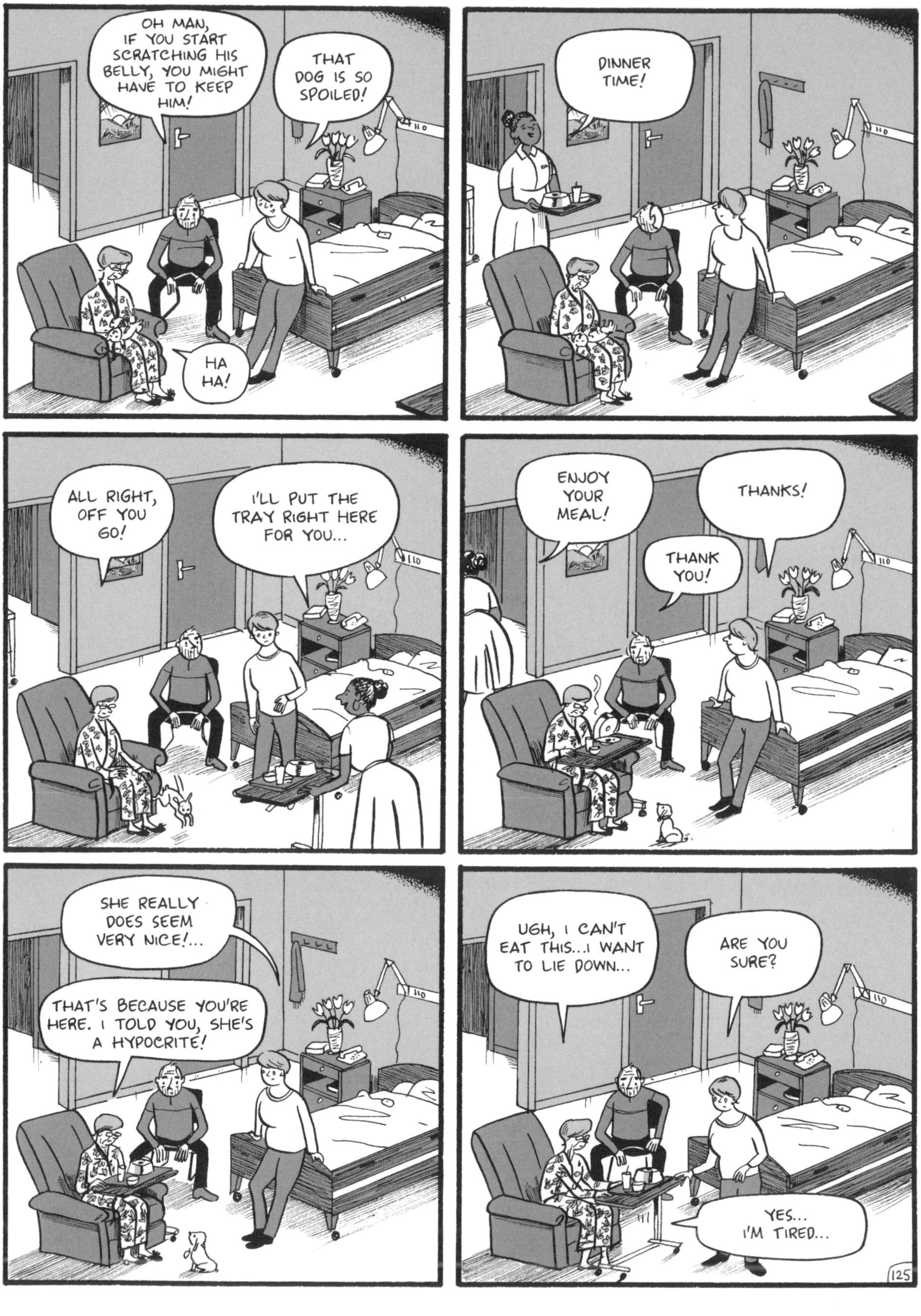
OH MAN, IF YOU START SCRATCHING HIS BELLY, YOU MIGHT HAVE TO KEEP HIM!
THAT DOG IS SO SPOILED!
HA HA!
DINNER TIME!
ALL RIGHT, OFF YOU GO!
I'LL PUT THE TRAY RIGHT HERE FOR YOU...
ENJOY YOUR MEAL!
THANKS!
THANK YOU!
SHE REALLY DOES SEEM VERY NICE!...
THAT'S BECAUSE YOU'RE HERE. I TOLD YOU, SHE'S A HYPOCRITE!
UGH, I CAN'T EAT THIS...I WANT TO LIE DOWN...
ARE YOU SURE?
YES... I'M TIRED...

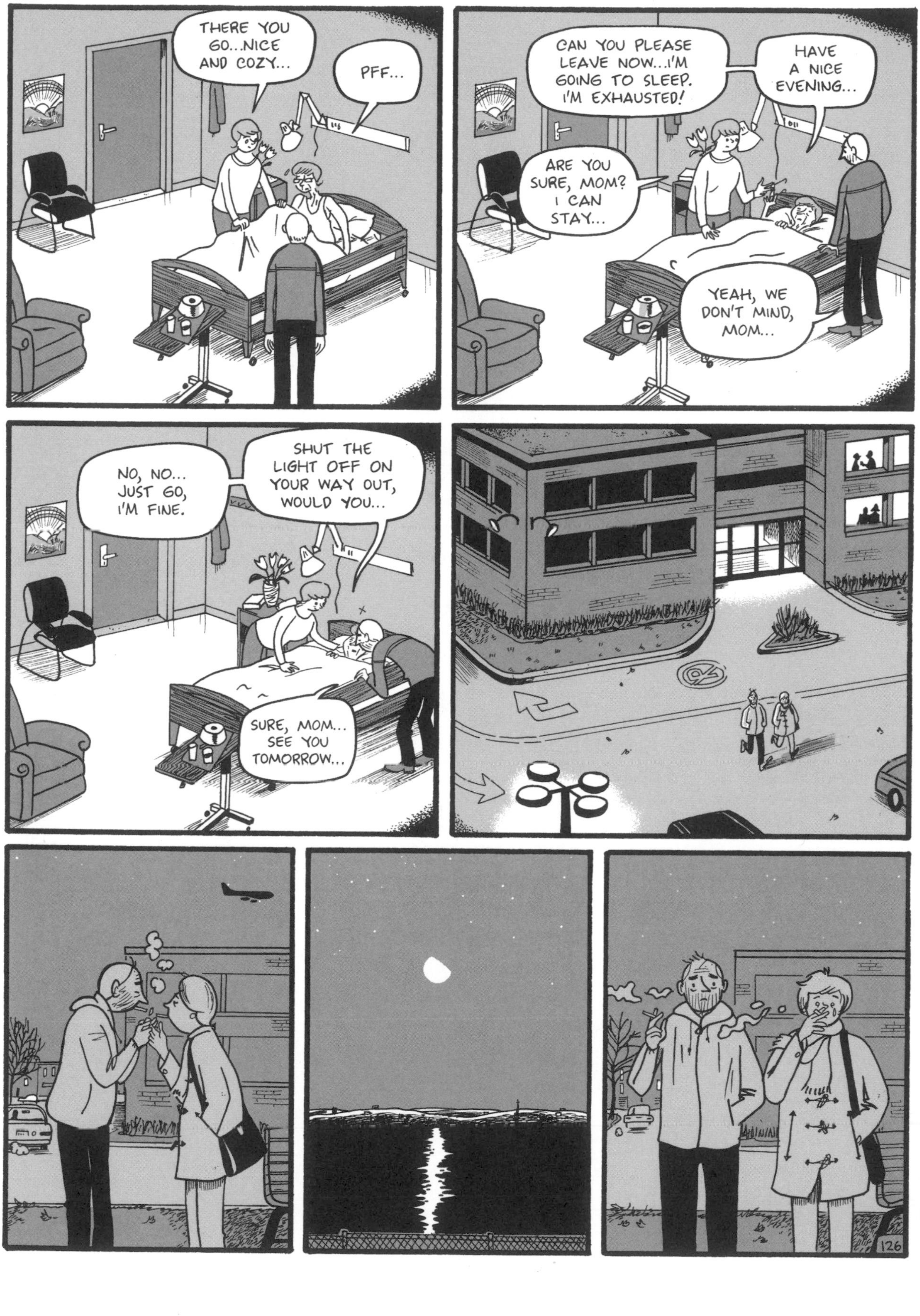
THERE YOU GO...NICE AND COZY...
PFF...
CAN YOU PLEASE LEAVE NOW...I'M GOING TO SLEEP. I'M EXHAUSTED!
HAVE A NICE EVENING...
ARE YOU SURE, MOM? I CAN STAY...
YEAH, WE DON'T MIND, MOM...
NO, NO... JUST GO, I'M FINE.
SHUT THE LIGHT OFF ON YOUR WAY OUT, WOULD YOU...
SURE, MOM... SEE YOU TOMORROW...

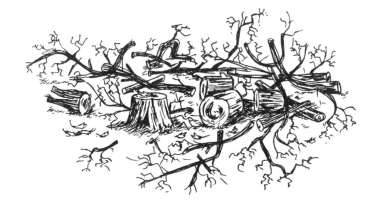

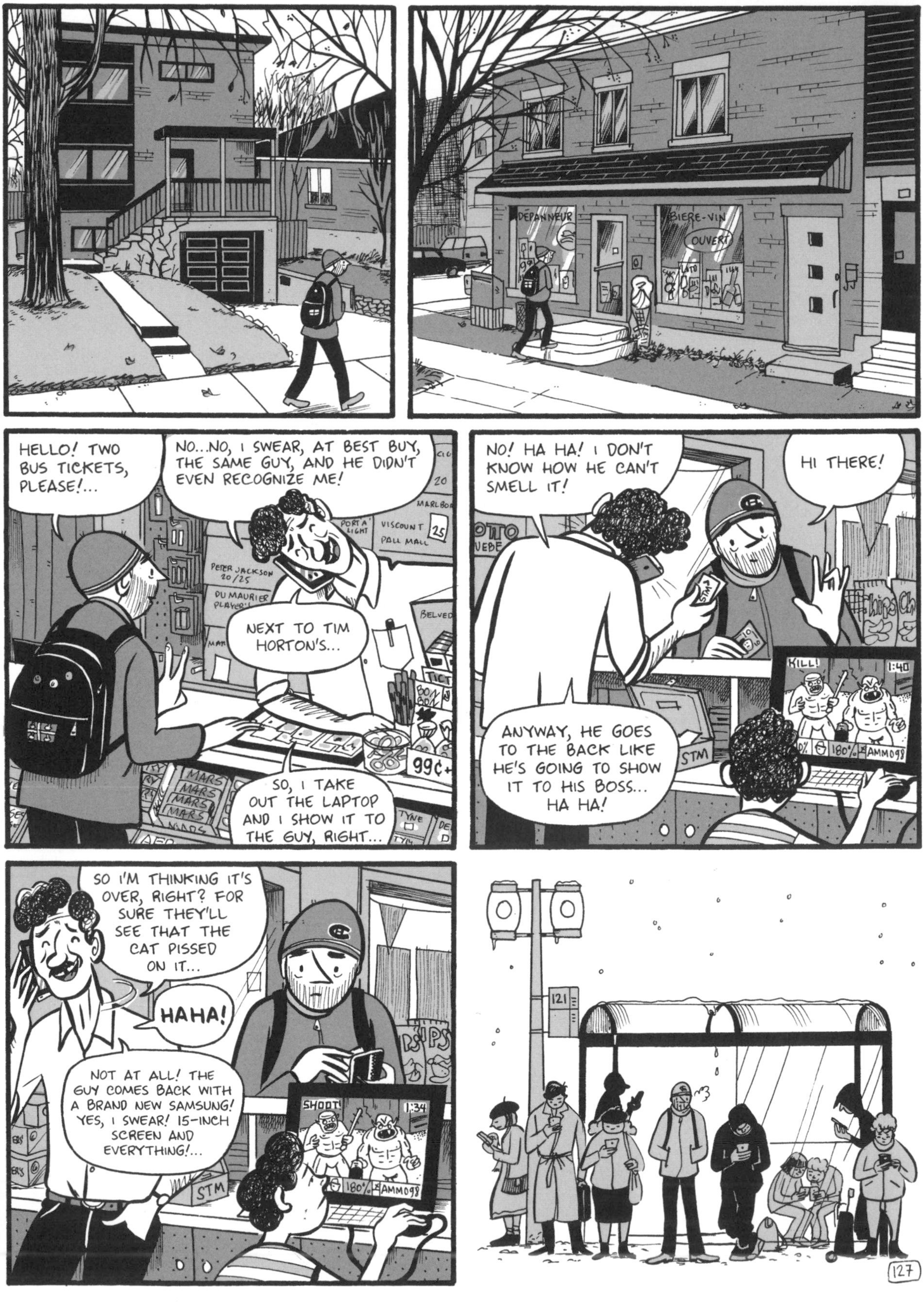
DÉPANNEUR
BIERE-VIN
OUVERT
HELLO! TWO BUS TICKETS, PLEASE!...
NO...NO, I SWEAR, AT BEST BUY, THE SAME GUY, AND HE DIDN'T EVEN RECOGNIZE ME!
NEXT TO TIM HORTON'S...
SO, I TAKE OUT THE LAPTOP AND I SHOW IT TO THE GUY, RIGHT...
NO! HA HA! I DON'T KNOW HOW HE CAN'T SMELL IT!
HI THERE!
ANYWAY, HE GOES TO THE BACK LIKE HE'S GOING TO SHOW IT TO HIS BOSS... HA HA!
KILL!
1:40
SO I'M THINKING IT'S OVER, RIGHT? FOR SURE THEY'LL SEE THAT THE CAT PISSED ON IT...
HAHA!
NOT AT ALL! THE GUY COMES BACK WITH A BRAND NEW SAMSUNG! YES, I SWEAR! 15-INCH SCREEN AND EVERYTHING!...
SHOOT!
1:34
121

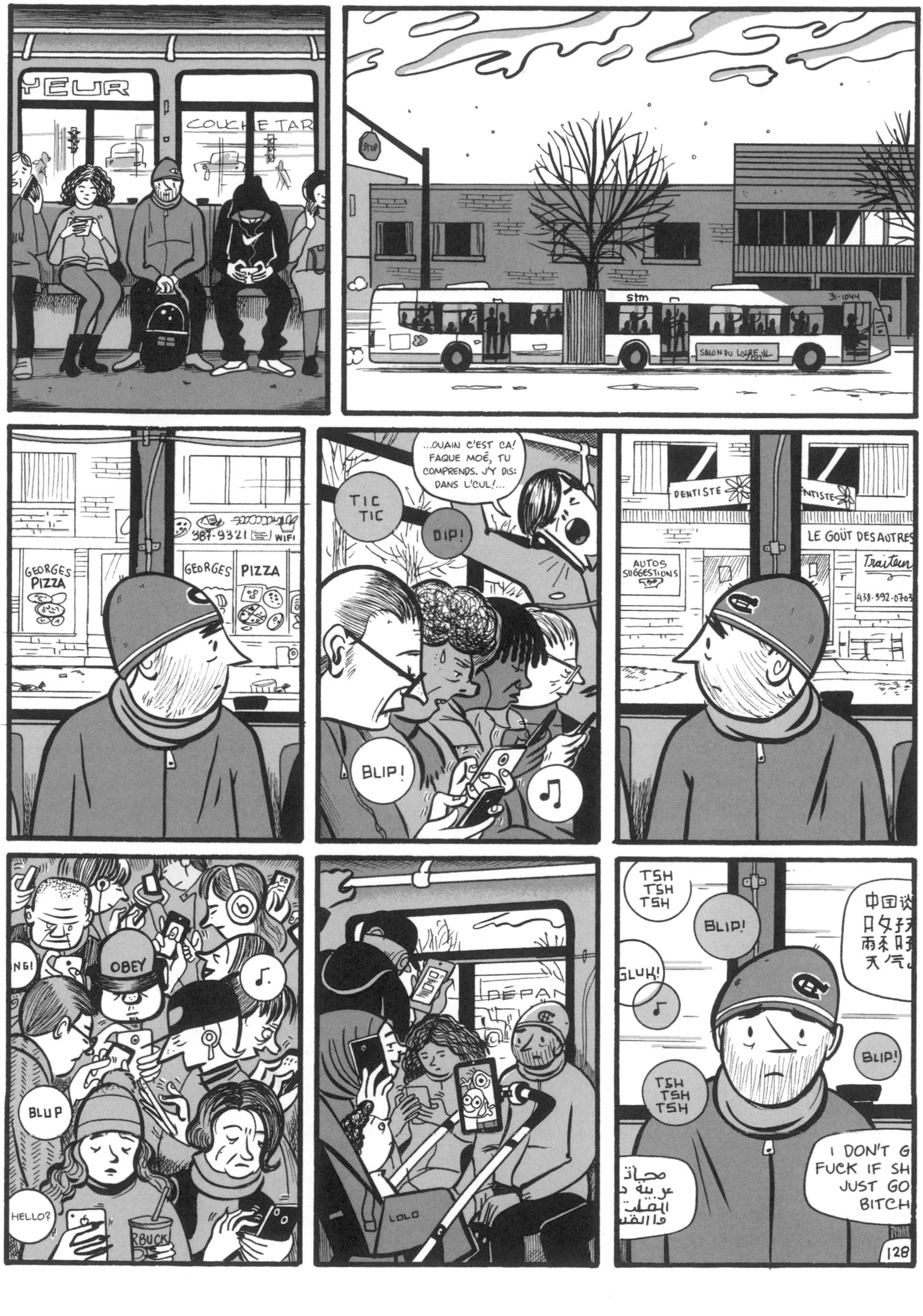

YEUR
COUCHE TAR
STOP
stm
31-1044
387-9321
WIFI
GEORGES PIZZA
GEORGES PIZZA
...OUAIN C'EST ÇA! FAQUE MOÉ, TU COMPRENDS. J'Y DIS: DANS L'CUL!...
TIC TIC
DIP!
BLIP!
♫
DENTISTE
LE GOÛT DES AUTRES
AUTOS SUGGESTIONS
NG!
OBEY
♪
BLUP
HELLO?
RBUCK
DÉPAN
LOLO
TSH TSH TSH
BLIP!
GLUK!
♪
BLIP!
TSH TSH TSH
I DON'T G FUCK IF SH JUST GO BITCH

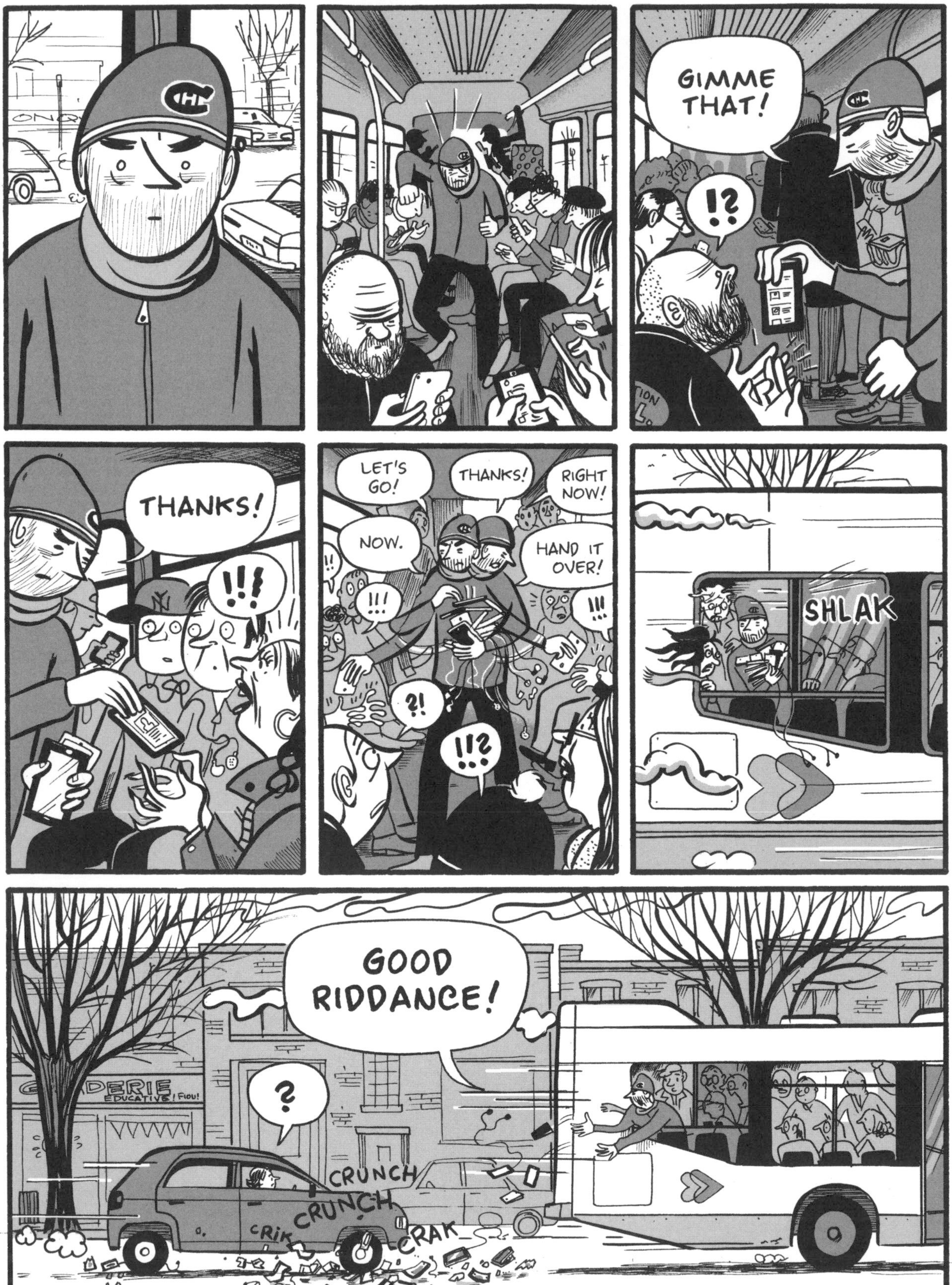
GIMME THAT!
!?
THANKS!
!!!
LET'S GO!
THANKS!
RIGHT NOW!
NOW.
HAND IT OVER!
!!
!!!
!!!
?!
!!?
SHLAK
GOOD RIDDANCE!
?
DERIE EDUCATIVE! FIOU!
CRUNCH
CRUNCH
CRIK
CRAK

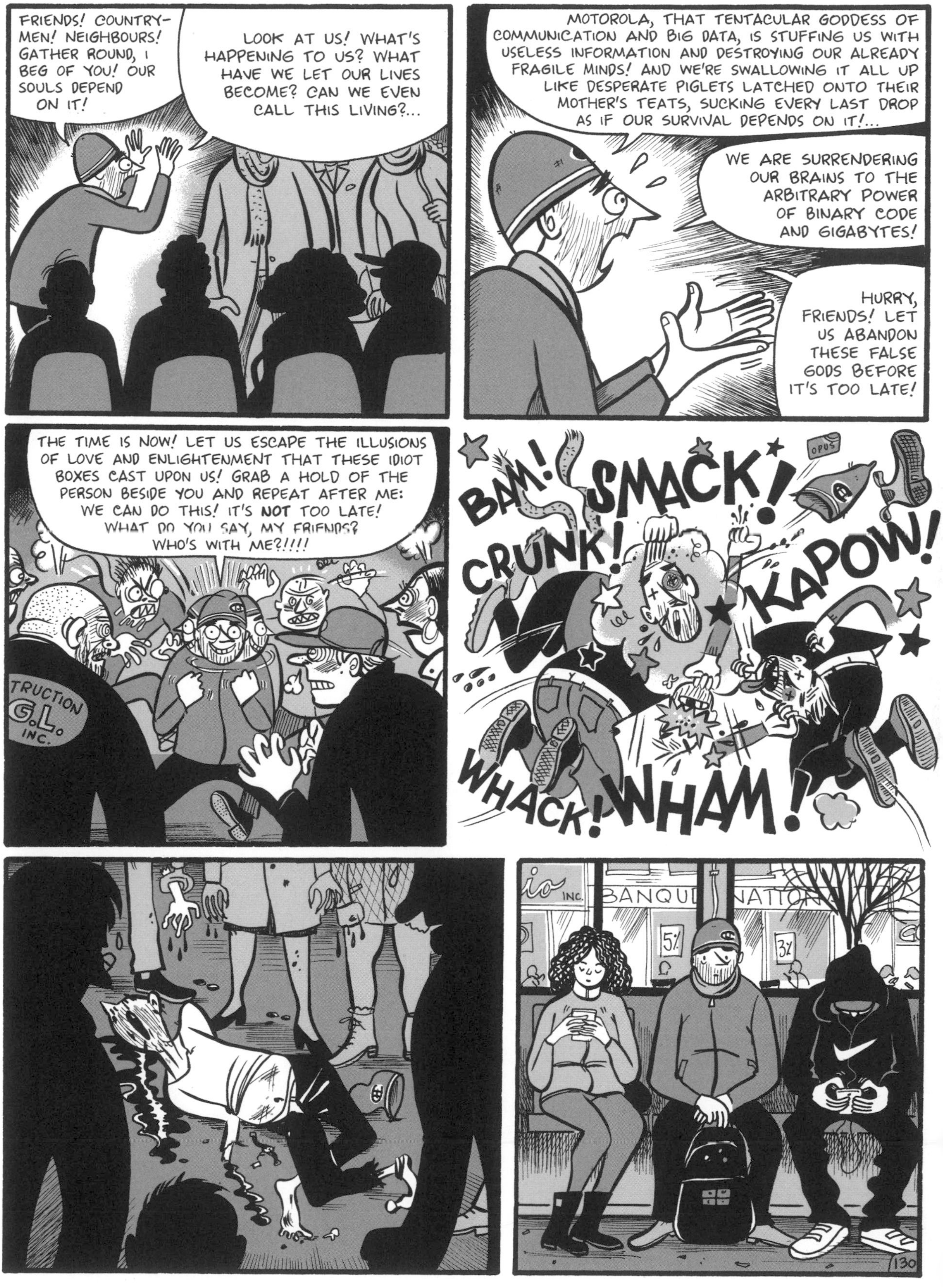

FRIENDS! COUNTRYMEN! NEIGHBOURS! GATHER ROUND, I BEG OF YOU! OUR SOULS DEPEND ON IT!
LOOK AT US! WHAT'S HAPPENING TO US? WHAT HAVE WE LET OUR LIVES BECOME? CAN WE EVEN CALL THIS LIVING?...
MOTOROLA, THAT TENTACULAR GODDESS OF COMMUNICATION AND BIG DATA, IS STUFFING US WITH USELESS INFORMATION AND DESTROYING OUR ALREADY FRAGILE MINDS! AND WE'RE SWALLOWING IT ALL UP LIKE DESPERATE PIGLETS LATCHED ONTO THEIR MOTHER'S TEATS, SUCKING EVERY LAST DROP AS IF OUR SURVIVAL DEPENDS ON IT!...
WE ARE SURRENDERING OUR BRAINS TO THE ARBITRARY POWER OF BINARY CODE AND GIGABYTES!
HURRY, FRIENDS! LET US ABANDON THESE FALSE GODS BEFORE IT'S TOO LATE!
THE TIME IS NOW! LET US ESCAPE THE ILLUSIONS OF LOVE AND ENLIGHTENMENT THAT THESE IDIOT BOXES CAST UPON US! GRAB A HOLD OF THE PERSON BESIDE YOU AND REPEAT AFTER ME: WE CAN DO THIS! IT'S NOT TOO LATE! WHAT DO YOU SAY, MY FRIENDS? WHO'S WITH ME?!!!!
TRUCTION G.L. INC.
BAM!
SMACK!
OPUS
CRUNK!
KAPOW!
WHACK!
WHAM!
INC.
5%
3%

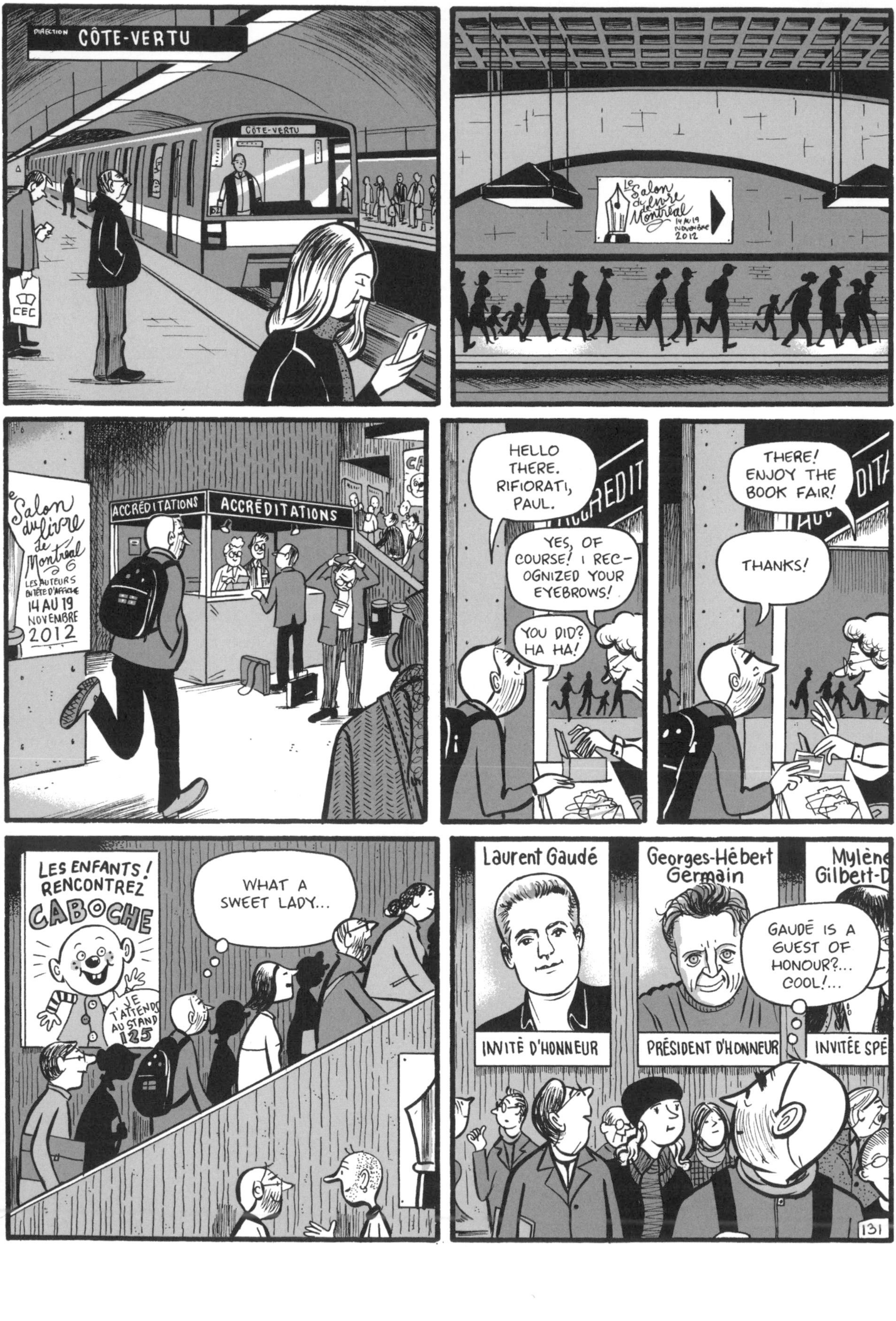
DIRECTION CÔTE-VERTU
CÔTE-VERTU
CEC
Le Salon du livre de Montréal 14 AU 19 NOVEMBRE 2012
Salon du livre de Montréal LES AUTEURS EN TÊTE D'AFFICHE 14 AU 19 NOVEMBRE 2012
ACCRÉDITATIONS
ACCRÉDITATIONS
HELLO THERE. RIFIORATI, PAUL.
YES, OF COURSE! I RECOGNIZED YOUR EYEBROWS!
YOU DID? HA HA!
THERE! ENJOY THE BOOK FAIR!
THANKS!
LES ENFANTS! RENCONTREZ CABOCHE
JE T'ATTENDS AU STAND 125
WHAT A SWEET LADY...
Laurent Gaudé
INVITÉ D'HONNEUR
Georges-Hébert Germain
PRÉSIDENT D'HONNEUR
INVITÉE SPÉ
GAUDÉ IS A GUEST OF HONOUR?... COOL!...

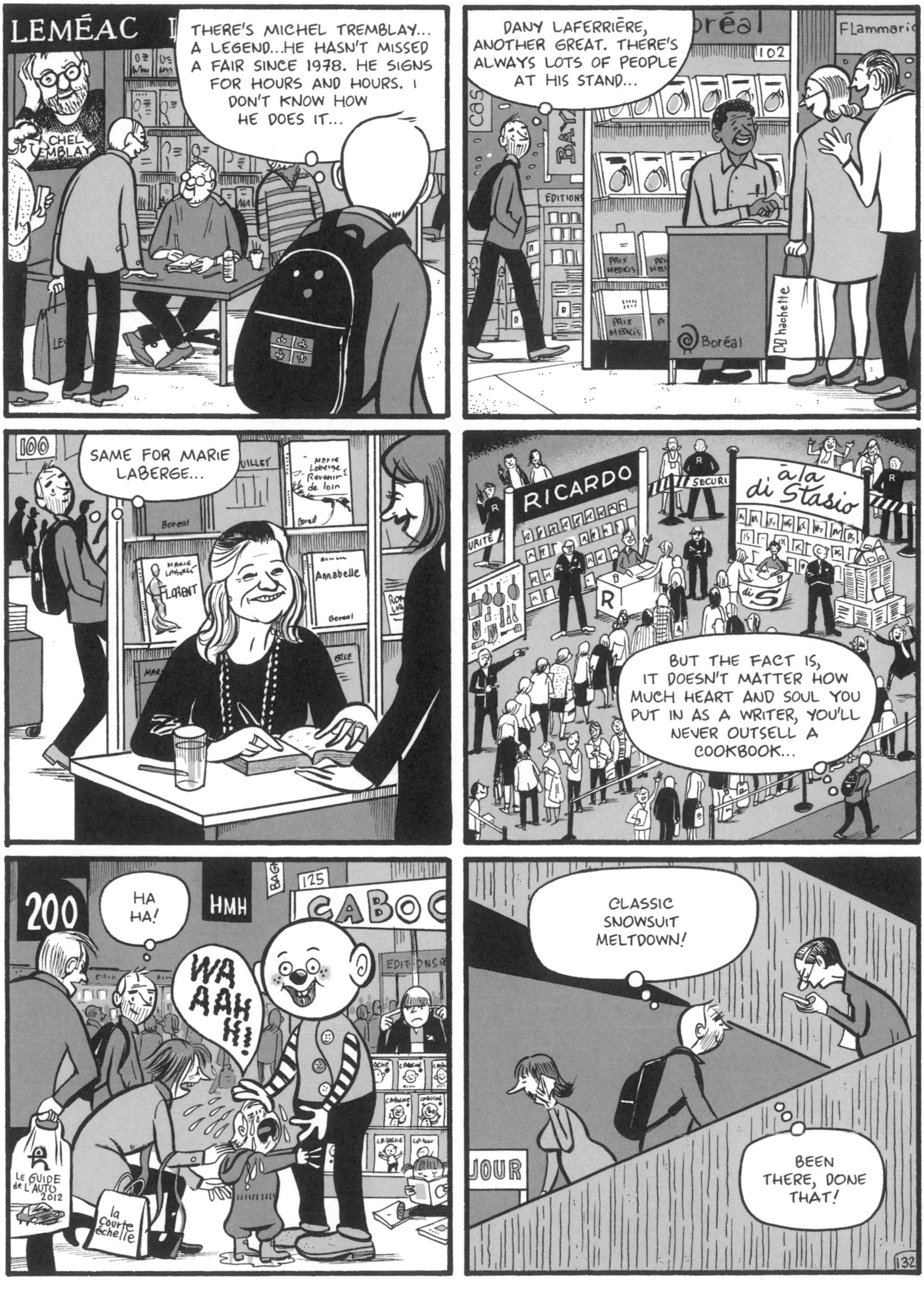
LEMÉAC
THERE'S MICHEL TREMBLAY... A LEGEND...HE HASN'T MISSED A FAIR SINCE 1978. HE SIGNS FOR HOURS AND HOURS. I DON'T KNOW HOW HE DOES IT...
DANY LAFERRIÈRE, ANOTHER GREAT. THERE'S ALWAYS LOTS OF PEOPLE AT HIS STAND...
Boréal
SAME FOR MARIE LABERGE...
Amabelle
RICARDO
à la di Stasio
BUT THE FACT IS, IT DOESN'T MATTER HOW MUCH HEART AND SOUL YOU PUT IN AS A WRITER, YOU'LL NEVER OUTSELL A COOKBOOK...
200
HMH
HA HA!
WA AAH H!
Le GUIDE de L'AUTO 2012
la courte échelle
CLASSIC SNOWSUIT MELTDOWN!
BEEN THERE, DONE THAT!

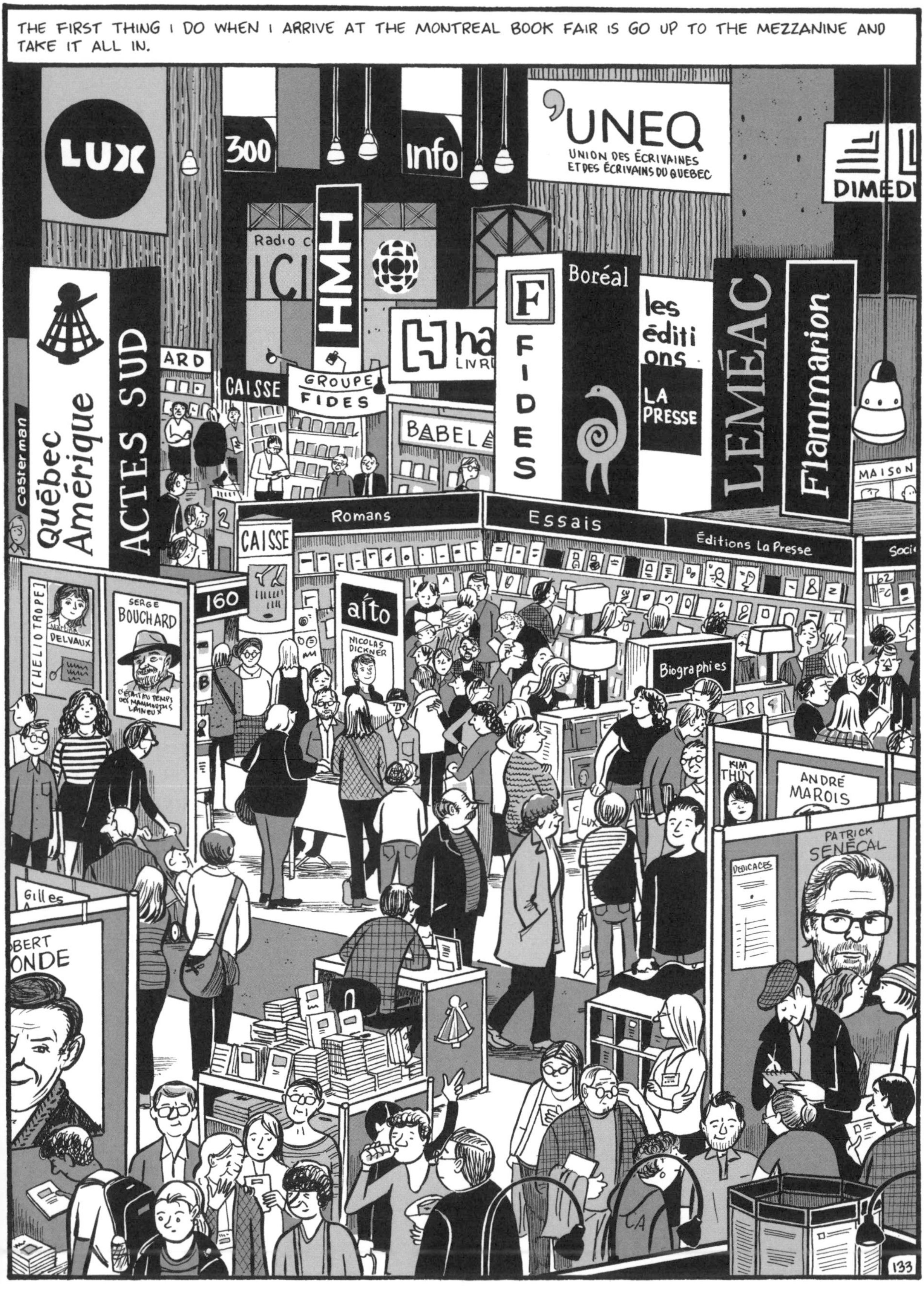
THE FIRST THING I DO WHEN I ARRIVE AT THE MONTREAL BOOK FAIR IS GO UP TO THE MEZZANINE AND TAKE IT ALL IN.
LUX
300
Info
UNEQ
UNION DES ÉCRIVAINES ET DES ÉCRIVAINS DU QUÉBEC
ICI
HMH
Boréal
les éditions
LA PRESSE
LEMÉAC
Flammarion
FIDES
Québec Amérique
ACTES SUD
casterman
CAISSE
GROUPE FIDES
BABEL
MAISON
Romans
Essais
Éditions La Presse
CAISSE
160
alto
NICOLAS DICKNER
SERGE BOUCHARD
C'ÉTAIT AU TEMPS DES MAMMOUTHS LAINEUX
DELVAUX
HELIOTROPE
Biographies
KIM THÚY
ANDRÉ MAROIS
PATRICK SENÉCAL
DÉDICACES

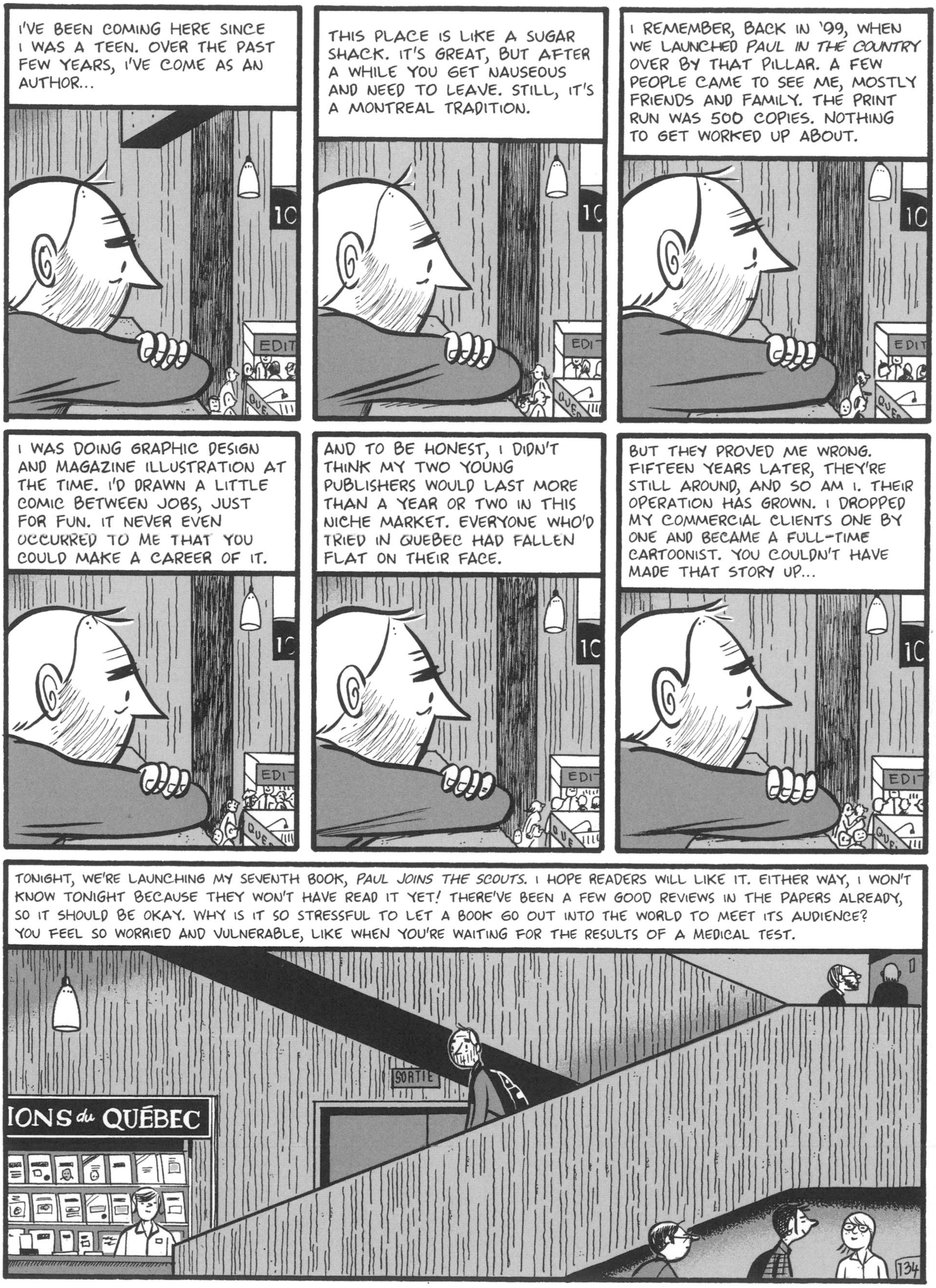
I'VE BEEN COMING HERE SINCE I WAS A TEEN. OVER THE PAST FEW YEARS, I'VE COME AS AN AUTHOR...
10
EDIT
THIS PLACE IS LIKE A SUGAR SHACK. IT'S GREAT, BUT AFTER A WHILE YOU GET NAUSEOUS AND NEED TO LEAVE. STILL, IT'S A MONTREAL TRADITION.
I REMEMBER, BACK IN '99, WHEN WE LAUNCHED *PAUL IN THE COUNTRY* OVER BY THAT PILLAR. A FEW PEOPLE CAME TO SEE ME, MOSTLY FRIENDS AND FAMILY. THE PRINT RUN WAS 500 COPIES. NOTHING TO GET WORKED UP ABOUT.
I WAS DOING GRAPHIC DESIGN AND MAGAZINE ILLUSTRATION AT THE TIME. I'D DRAWN A LITTLE COMIC BETWEEN JOBS, JUST FOR FUN. IT NEVER EVEN OCCURRED TO ME THAT YOU COULD MAKE A CAREER OF IT.
AND TO BE HONEST, I DIDN'T THINK MY TWO YOUNG PUBLISHERS WOULD LAST MORE THAN A YEAR OR TWO IN THIS NICHE MARKET. EVERYONE WHO'D TRIED IN QUEBEC HAD FALLEN FLAT ON THEIR FACE.
BUT THEY PROVED ME WRONG. FIFTEEN YEARS LATER, THEY'RE STILL AROUND, AND SO AM I. THEIR OPERATION HAS GROWN. I DROPPED MY COMMERCIAL CLIENTS ONE BY ONE AND BECAME A FULL-TIME CARTOONIST. YOU COULDN'T HAVE MADE THAT STORY UP...
TONIGHT, WE'RE LAUNCHING MY SEVENTH BOOK, *PAUL JOINS THE SCOUTS.* I HOPE READERS WILL LIKE IT. EITHER WAY, I WON'T KNOW TONIGHT BECAUSE THEY WON'T HAVE READ IT YET! THERE'VE BEEN A FEW GOOD REVIEWS IN THE PAPERS ALREADY, SO IT SHOULD BE OKAY. WHY IS IT SO STRESSFUL TO LET A BOOK GO OUT INTO THE WORLD TO MEET ITS AUDIENCE? YOU FEEL SO WORRIED AND VULNERABLE, LIKE WHEN YOU'RE WAITING FOR THE RESULTS OF A MEDICAL TEST.
SORTIE
IONS du QUÉBEC

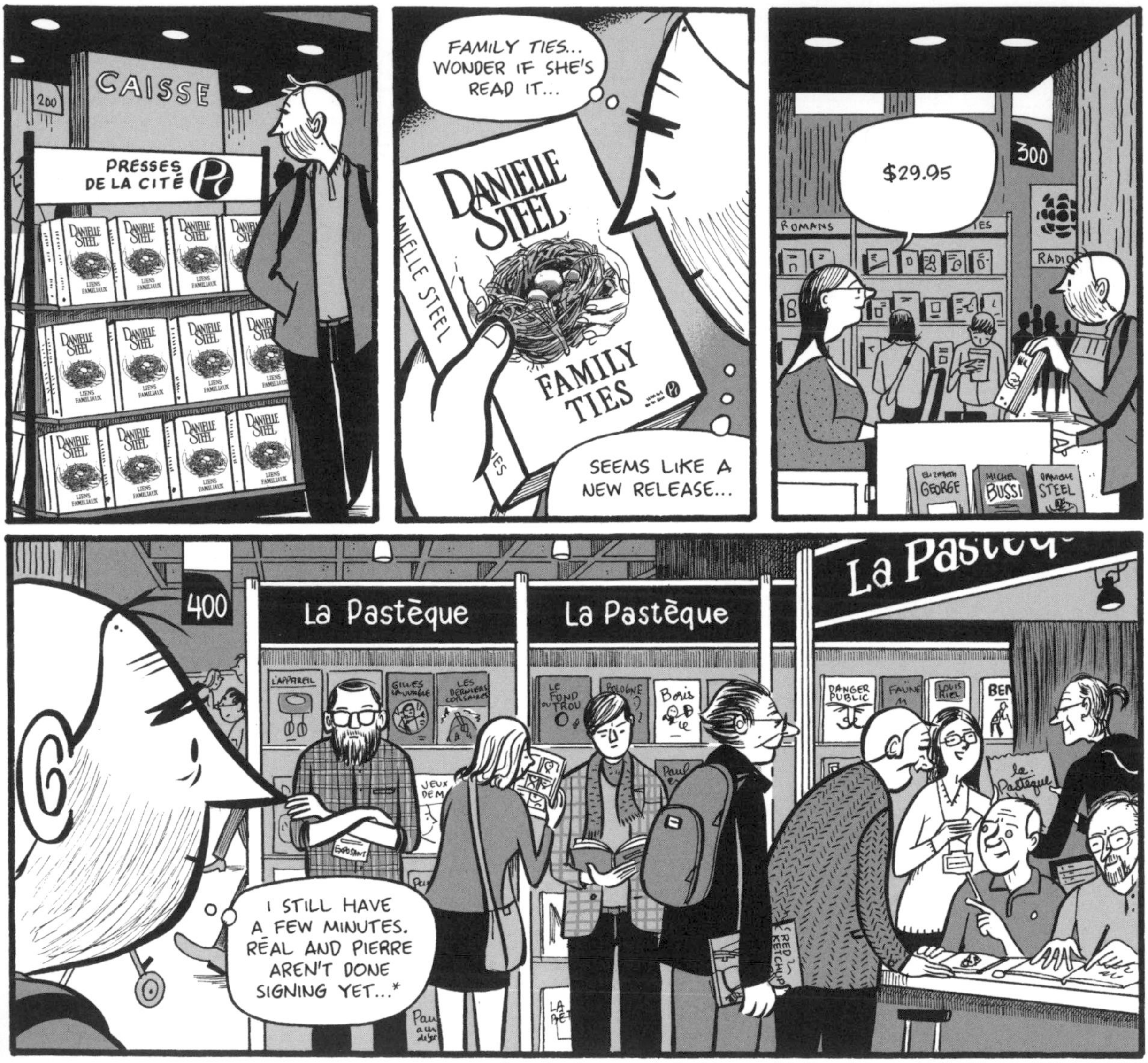
CAISSE
PRESSES DE LA CITÉ
FAMILY TIES... WONDER IF SHE'S READ IT...
DANIELLE STEEL
FAMILY TIES
SEEMS LIKE A NEW RELEASE...
$29.95
300
400
La Pastèque
La Pastèque
La Pastèque
I STILL HAVE A FEW MINUTES. RÉAL AND PIERRE AREN'T DONE SIGNING YET...*

*RÉAL GODBOUT AND PIERRE FOURNIER, ACTUAL AUTHORS OF *RED KETCHUP*

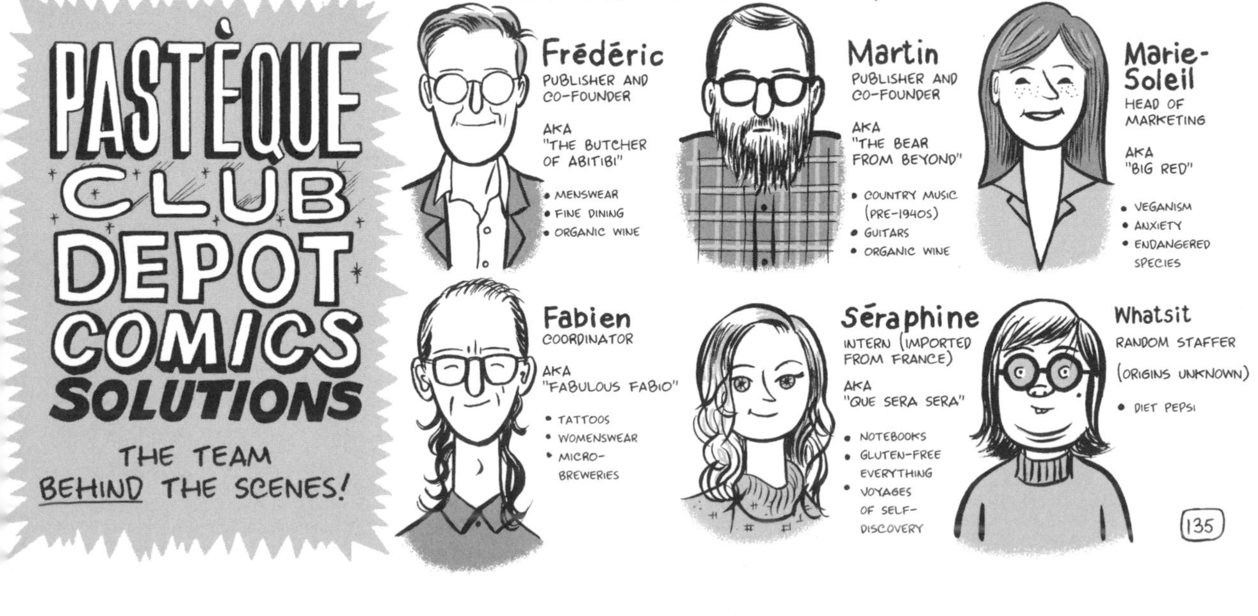
PASTÈQUE CLUB DEPOT COMICS SOLUTIONS
THE TEAM BEHIND THE SCENES!
Frédéric
PUBLISHER AND CO-FOUNDER
AKA "THE BUTCHER OF ABITIBI"
• MENSWEAR
• FINE DINING
• ORGANIC WINE
Martin
PUBLISHER AND CO-FOUNDER
AKA "THE BEAR FROM BEYOND"
• COUNTRY MUSIC (PRE-1940S)
• GUITARS
• ORGANIC WINE
Marie-Soleil
HEAD OF MARKETING
AKA "BIG RED"
• VEGANISM
• ANXIETY
• ENDANGERED SPECIES
Fabien
COORDINATOR
AKA "FABULOUS FABIO"
• TATTOOS
• WOMENSWEAR
• MICRO-BREWERIES
Séraphine
INTERN (IMPORTED FROM FRANCE)
AKA "QUE SERA SERA"
• NOTEBOOKS
• GLUTEN-FREE EVERYTHING
• VOYAGES OF SELF-DISCOVERY
Whatsit
RANDOM STAFFER
(ORIGINS UNKNOWN)
• DIET PEPSI

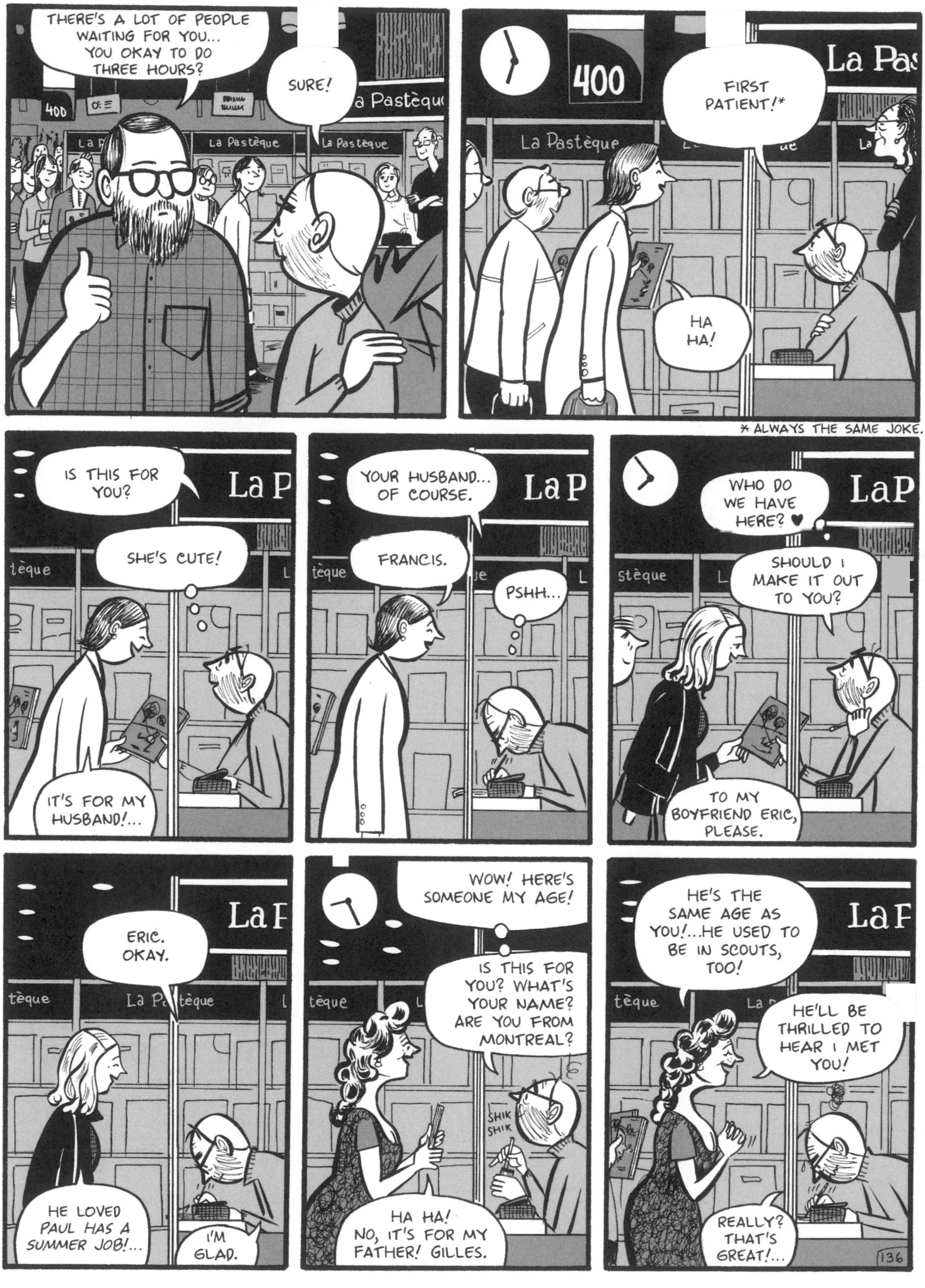
THERE'S A LOT OF PEOPLE WAITING FOR YOU... YOU OKAY TO DO THREE HOURS?
SURE!
400
La Pastèque
FIRST PATIENT!*
HA HA!
* ALWAYS THE SAME JOKE.
IS THIS FOR YOU?
SHE'S CUTE!
IT'S FOR MY HUSBAND!...
YOUR HUSBAND... OF COURSE.
FRANCIS.
PSHH...
WHO DO WE HAVE HERE? ♥
SHOULD I MAKE IT OUT TO YOU?
TO MY BOYFRIEND ERIC, PLEASE.
ERIC. OKAY.
HE LOVED PAUL HAS A SUMMER JOB!...
I'M GLAD.
WOW! HERE'S SOMEONE MY AGE!
IS THIS FOR YOU? WHAT'S YOUR NAME? ARE YOU FROM MONTREAL?
SHIK SHIK
HA HA! NO, IT'S FOR MY FATHER! GILLES.
HE'S THE SAME AGE AS YOU!...HE USED TO BE IN SCOUTS, TOO!
HE'LL BE THRILLED TO HEAR I MET YOU!
REALLY? THAT'S GREAT!...
136

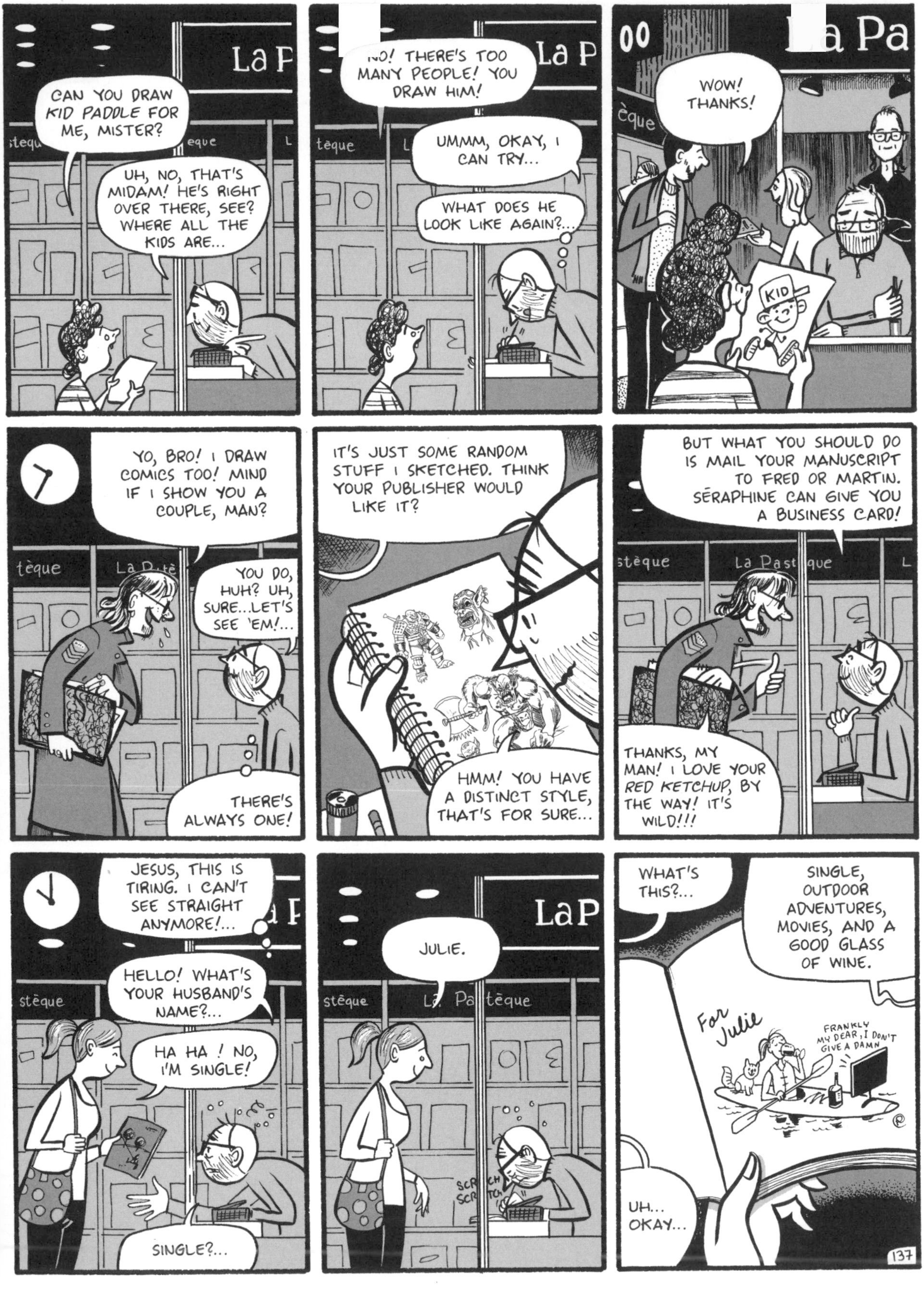
La P
CAN YOU DRAW KID PADDLE FOR ME, MISTER?
UH, NO, THAT'S MIDAM! HE'S RIGHT OVER THERE, SEE? WHERE ALL THE KIDS ARE...
NO! THERE'S TOO MANY PEOPLE! YOU DRAW HIM!
UMMM, OKAY, I CAN TRY...
WHAT DOES HE LOOK LIKE AGAIN?...
WOW! THANKS!
KID
YO, BRO! I DRAW COMICS TOO! MIND IF I SHOW YOU A COUPLE, MAN?
YOU DO, HUH? UH, SURE...LET'S SEE 'EM!...
THERE'S ALWAYS ONE!
IT'S JUST SOME RANDOM STUFF I SKETCHED. THINK YOUR PUBLISHER WOULD LIKE IT?
HMM! YOU HAVE A DISTINCT STYLE, THAT'S FOR SURE...
BUT WHAT YOU SHOULD DO IS MAIL YOUR MANUSCRIPT TO FRED OR MARTIN. SÉRAPHINE CAN GIVE YOU A BUSINESS CARD!
La Pastèque
THANKS, MY MAN! I LOVE YOUR RED KETCHUP, BY THE WAY! IT'S WILD!!!
JESUS, THIS IS TIRING. I CAN'T SEE STRAIGHT ANYMORE!...
HELLO! WHAT'S YOUR HUSBAND'S NAME?...
HA HA ! NO, I'M SINGLE!
SINGLE?...
JULIE.
SCRATCH SCRATCH
WHAT'S THIS?...
SINGLE, OUTDOOR ADVENTURES, MOVIES, AND A GOOD GLASS OF WINE.
For Julie
FRANKLY MY DEAR, I DON'T GIVE A DAMN
UH... OKAY...

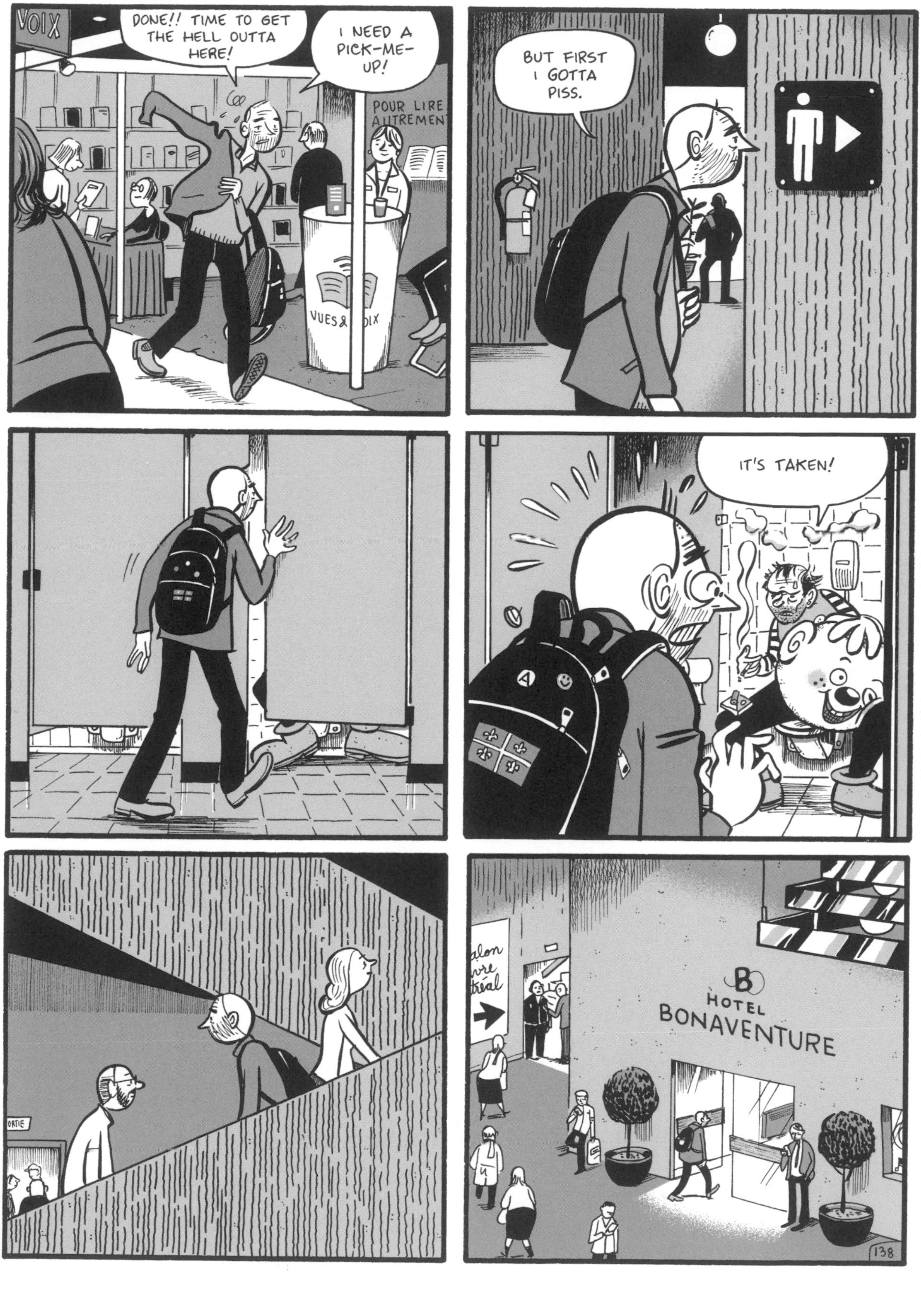
VOIX
DONE!! TIME TO GET THE HELL OUTTA HERE!
I NEED A PICK-ME-UP!
POUR LIRE AUTREMENT
BUT FIRST I GOTTA PISS.
IT'S TAKEN!
HOTEL
BONAVENTURE

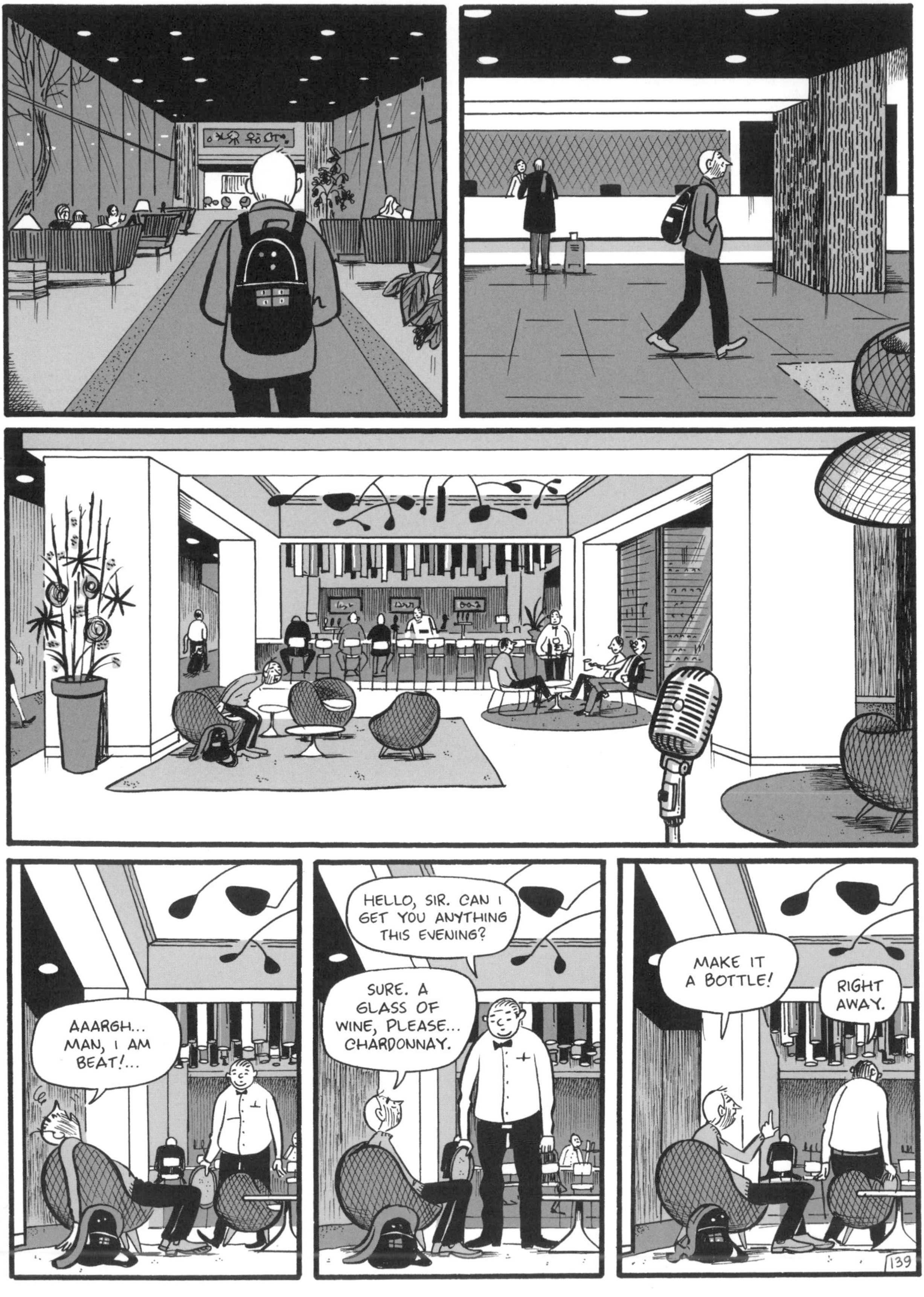
AAARGH... MAN, I AM BEAT!...
HELLO, SIR. CAN I GET YOU ANYTHING THIS EVENING?
SURE. A GLASS OF WINE, PLEASE... CHARDONNAY.
MAKE IT A BOTTLE!
RIGHT AWAY.

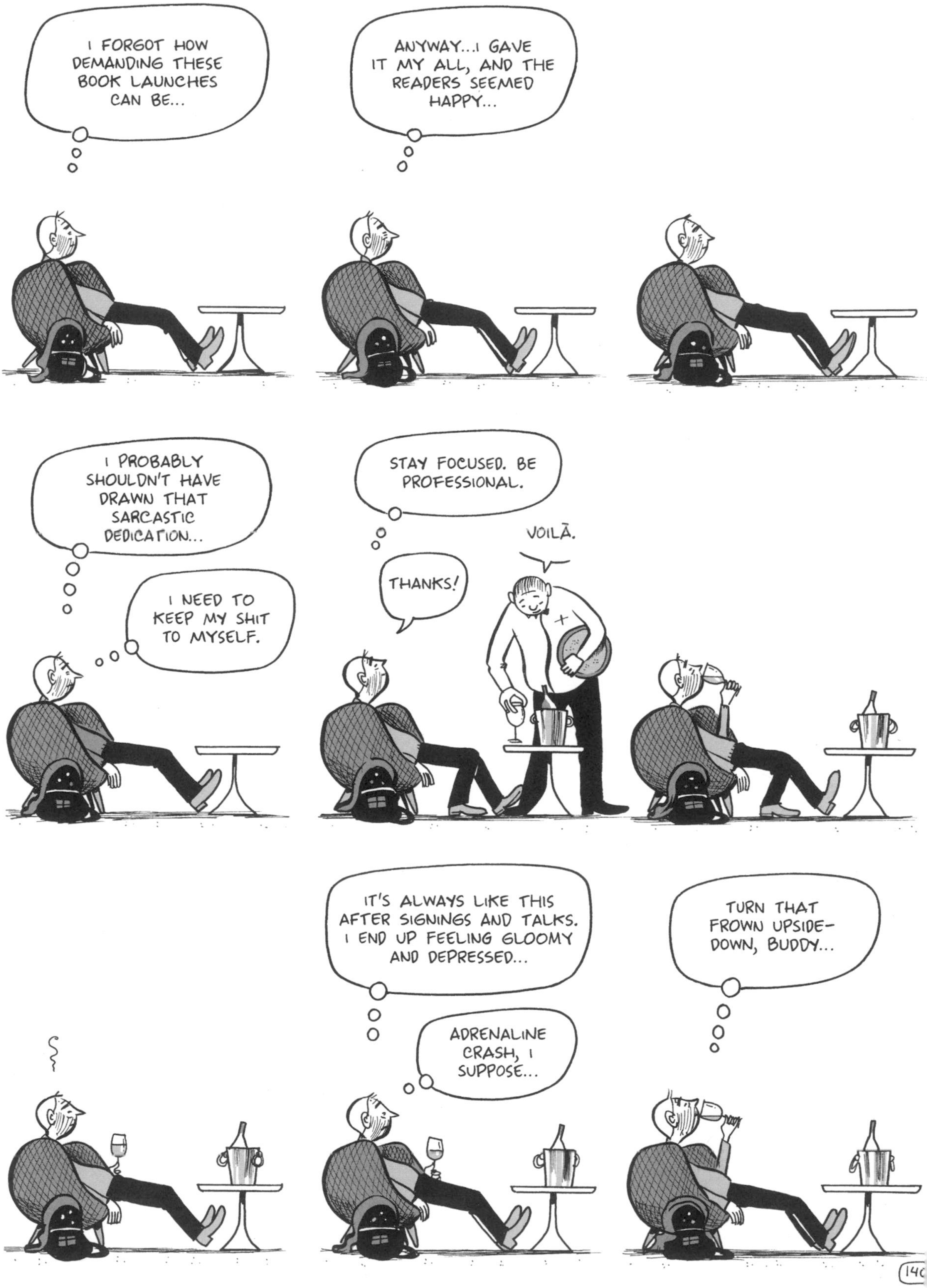
I FORGOT HOW DEMANDING THESE BOOK LAUNCHES CAN BE...
ANYWAY...I GAVE IT MY ALL, AND THE READERS SEEMED HAPPY...
I PROBABLY SHOULDN'T HAVE DRAWN THAT SARCASTIC DEDICATION...
I NEED TO KEEP MY SHIT TO MYSELF.
STAY FOCUSED. BE PROFESSIONAL.
VOILÀ.
THANKS!
IT'S ALWAYS LIKE THIS AFTER SIGNINGS AND TALKS. I END UP FEELING GLOOMY AND DEPRESSED...
ADRENALINE CRASH, I SUPPOSE...
TURN THAT FROWN UPSIDE-DOWN, BUDDY...

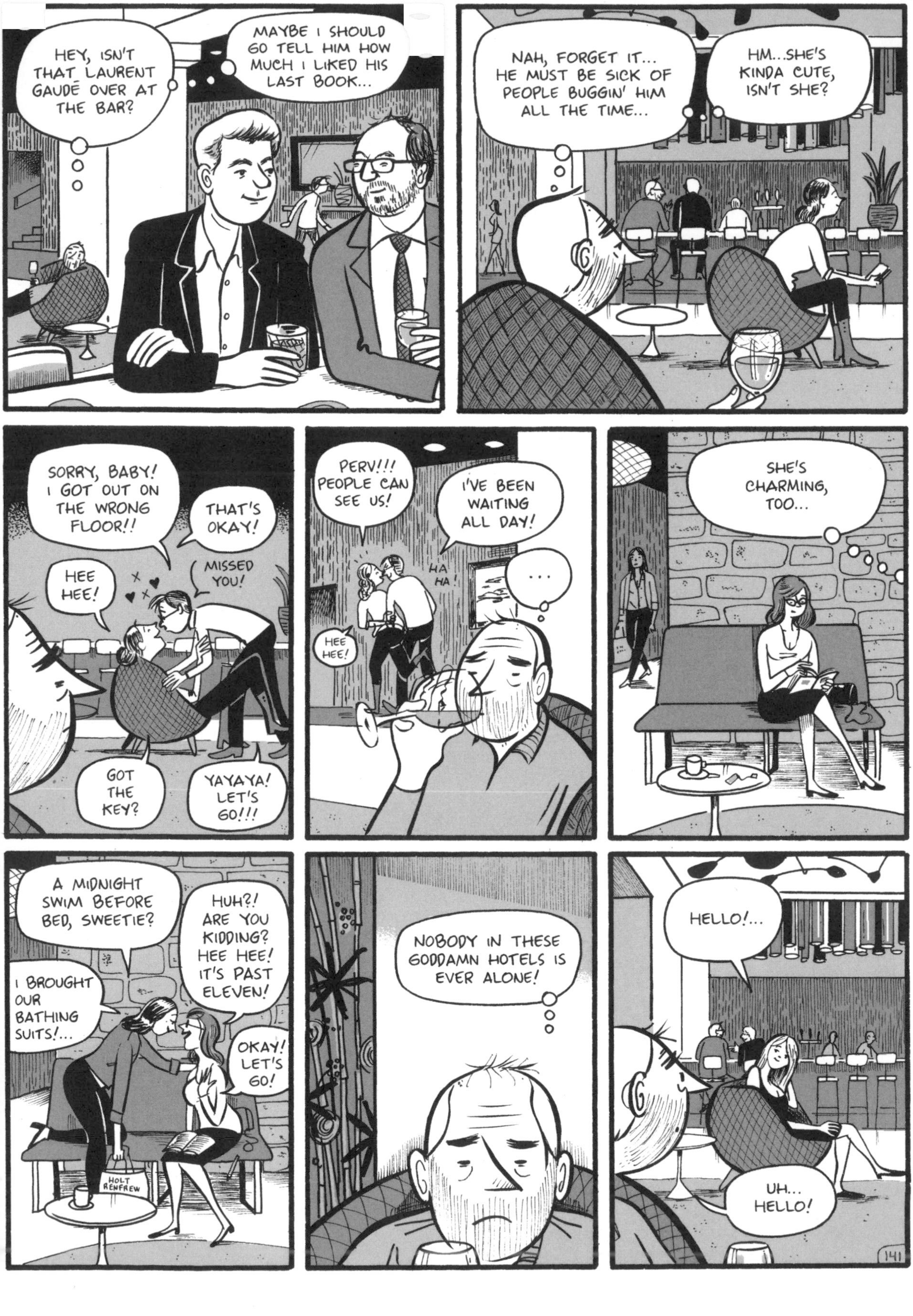
HEY, ISN'T THAT LAURENT GAUDÉ OVER AT THE BAR?
MAYBE I SHOULD GO TELL HIM HOW MUCH I LIKED HIS LAST BOOK...
NAH, FORGET IT... HE MUST BE SICK OF PEOPLE BUGGIN' HIM ALL THE TIME...
HM...SHE'S KINDA CUTE, ISN'T SHE?
SORRY, BABY! I GOT OUT ON THE WRONG FLOOR!!
THAT'S OKAY!
HEE HEE!
MISSED YOU!
GOT THE KEY?
YAYAYA! LET'S GO!!!
PERV!!! PEOPLE CAN SEE US!
I'VE BEEN WAITING ALL DAY!
HA HA!
HEE HEE!
...
SHE'S CHARMING, TOO...
A MIDNIGHT SWIM BEFORE BED, SWEETIE?
HUH?! ARE YOU KIDDING? HEE HEE! IT'S PAST ELEVEN!
I BROUGHT OUR BATHING SUITS!...
OKAY! LET'S GO!
HOLT RENFREW
NOBODY IN THESE GODDAMN HOTELS IS EVER ALONE!
HELLO!...
UH... HELLO!
141

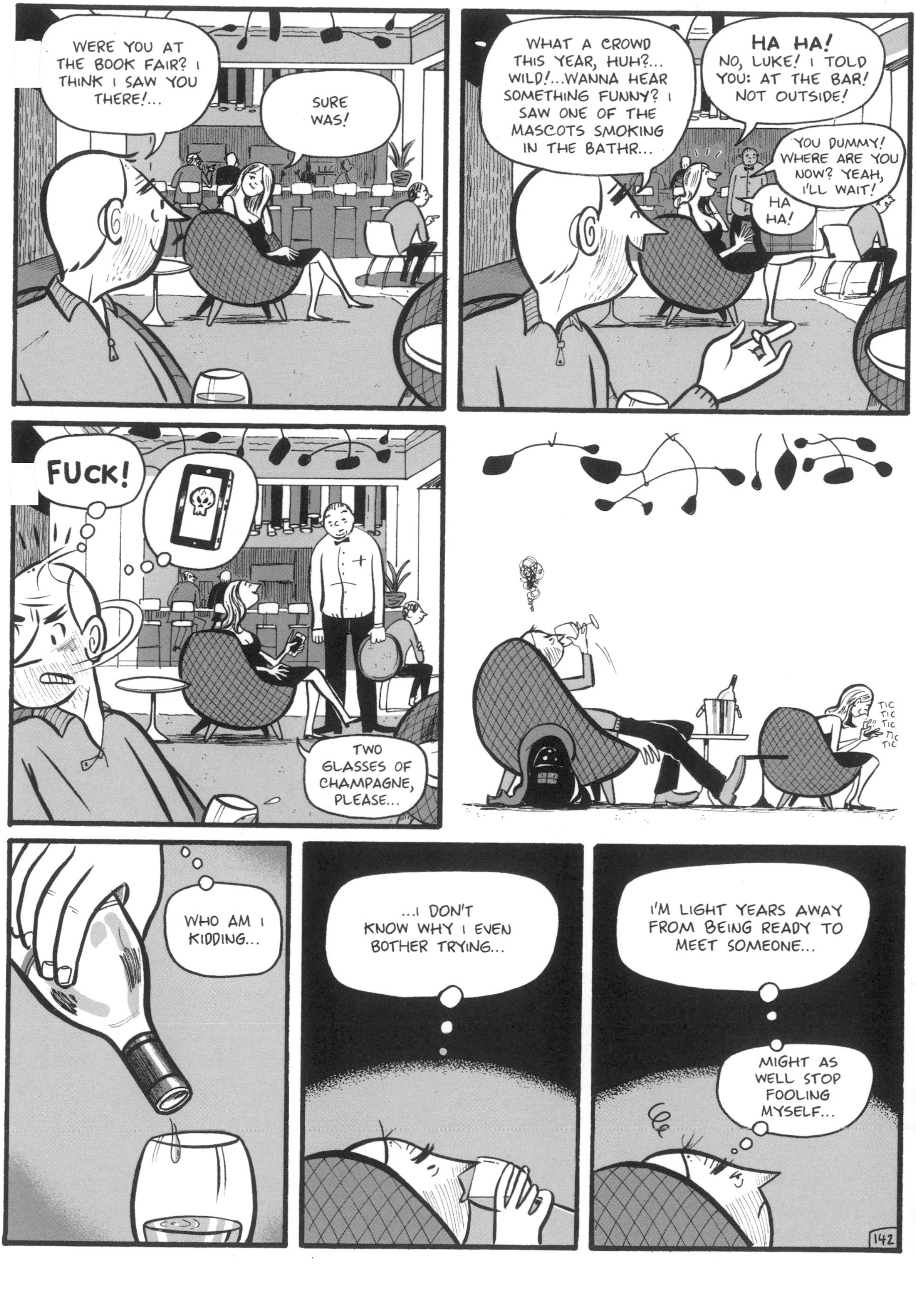

WERE YOU AT THE BOOK FAIR? I THINK I SAW YOU THERE!...
SURE WAS!
WHAT A CROWD THIS YEAR, HUH?... WILD!...WANNA HEAR SOMETHING FUNNY? I SAW ONE OF THE MASCOTS SMOKING IN THE BATHR...
HA HA! NO, LUKE! I TOLD YOU: AT THE BAR! NOT OUTSIDE!
YOU DUMMY! WHERE ARE YOU NOW? YEAH, I'LL WAIT!
HA HA!
FUCK!
TWO GLASSES OF CHAMPAGNE, PLEASE...
TIC TIC TIC TIC TIC
WHO AM I KIDDING...
...I DON'T KNOW WHY I EVEN BOTHER TRYING...
I'M LIGHT YEARS AWAY FROM BEING READY TO MEET SOMEONE...
MIGHT AS WELL STOP FOOLING MYSELF...

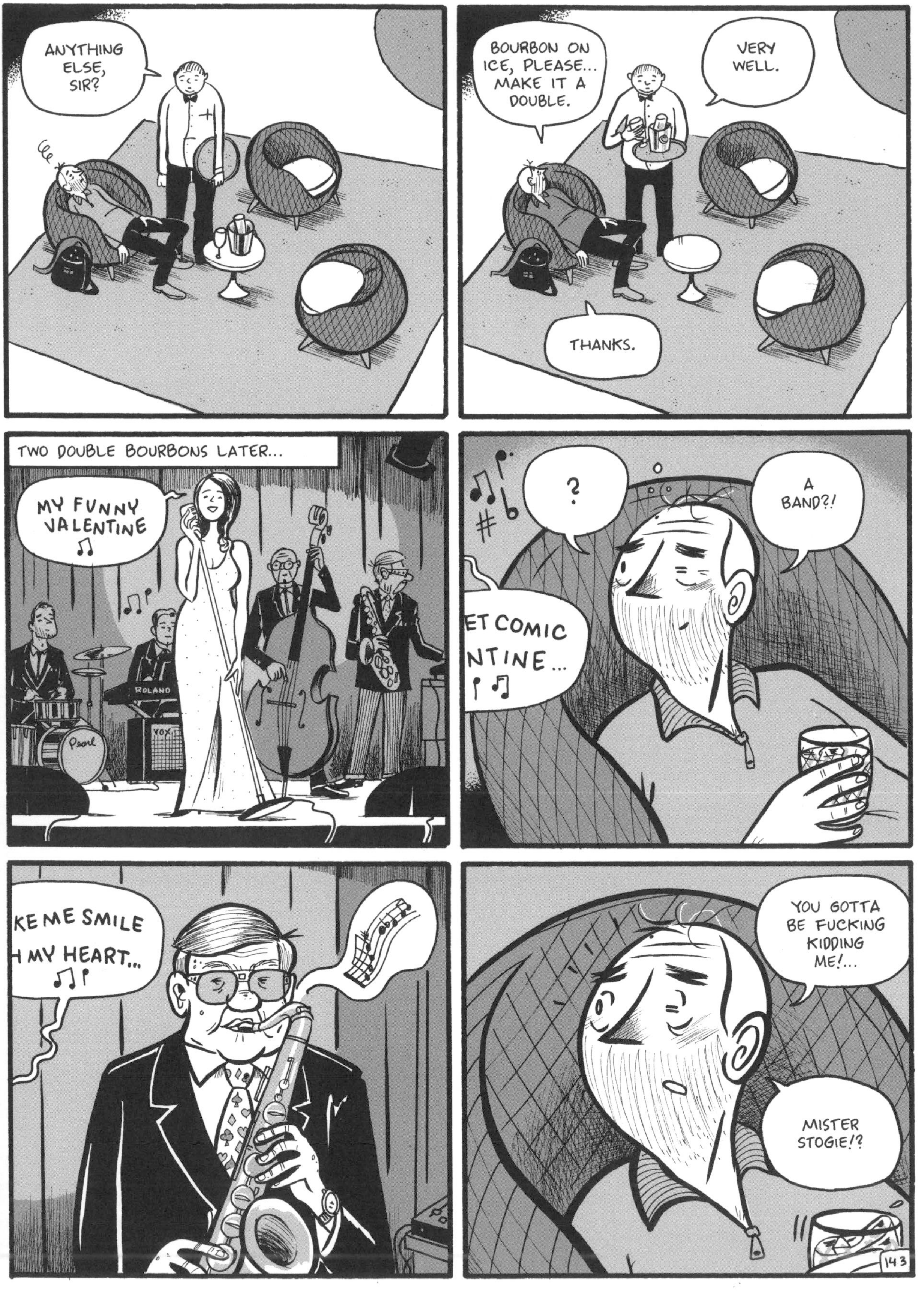
ANYTHING ELSE, SIR?
BOURBON ON ICE, PLEASE... MAKE IT A DOUBLE.
VERY WELL.
THANKS.
TWO DOUBLE BOURBONS LATER...
MY FUNNY VALENTINE
?
A BAND?!
ET COMIC
NTINE...
KE ME SMILE
H MY HEART...
YOU GOTTA BE FUCKING KIDDING ME!...
MISTER STOGIE!?
ROLAND
VOX
Pearl

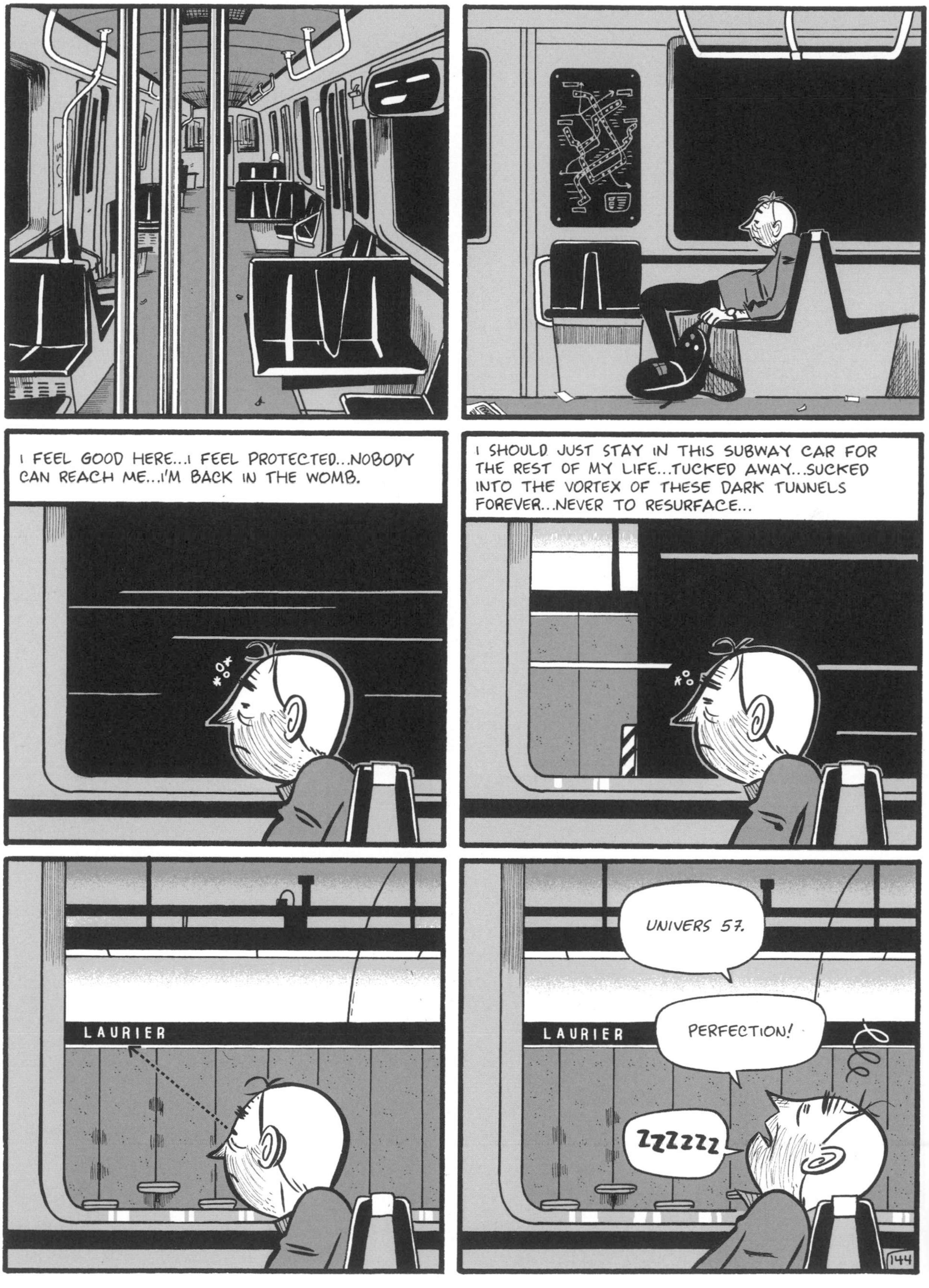
I FEEL GOOD HERE... I FEEL PROTECTED... NOBODY CAN REACH ME... I'M BACK IN THE WOMB.
I SHOULD JUST STAY IN THIS SUBWAY CAR FOR THE REST OF MY LIFE... TUCKED AWAY... SUCKED INTO THE VORTEX OF THESE DARK TUNNELS FOREVER... NEVER TO RESURFACE...
LAURIER
LAURIER
UNIVERS 57.
PERFECTION!
ZZZZZZ

WHERE YOU GOING, MOM?
YOUR DAD AND I ARE GOING TO PLACE DES ARTS.

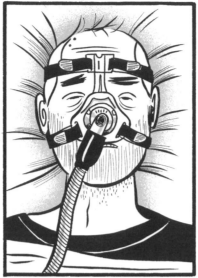

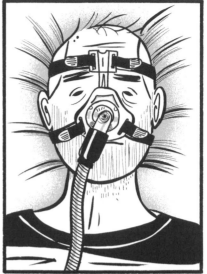

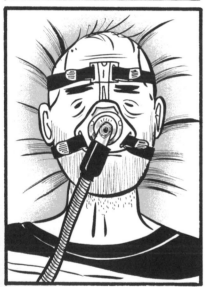

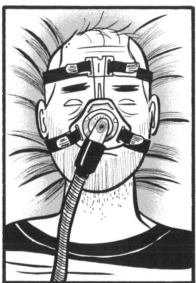

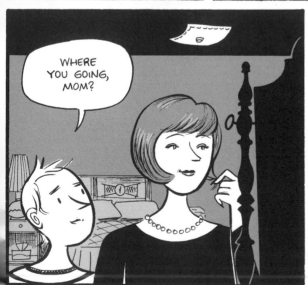

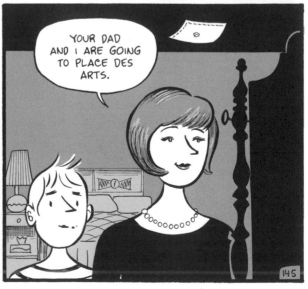

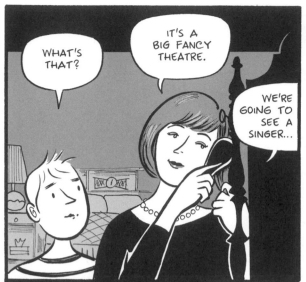

WHAT'S THAT?

IT'S A BIG FANCY THEATRE.

WE'RE GOING TO SEE A SINGER...

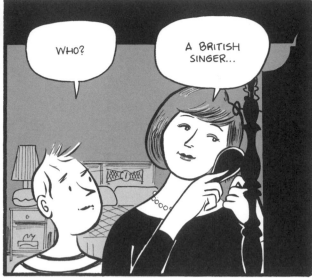

WHO?

A BRITISH SINGER...

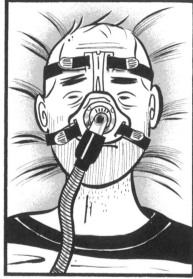

Continuous Positive Airway Pressure

IN 1981, COLIN SULLIVAN, AN AUSTRALIAN PHYSICIAN, TESTED A DEVICE ON HIS PATIENTS THAT PROVIDES CONTINUOUS POSITIVE AIRWAY PRESSURE TO PREVENT OBSTRUCTIVE APNEA.

THE DEVICE HAS BEEN MARKETED SINCE 1985 BY RESPIRONICS (PHILIPS), WHICH HAS GONE ON TO CREATE A WHOLE RANGE OF INNOVATIVE FACIAL MASKS.

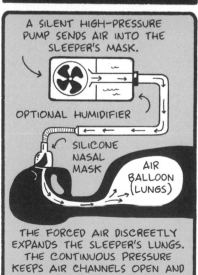

A SILENT HIGH-PRESSURE PUMP SENDS AIR INTO THE SLEEPER'S MASK.

OPTIONAL HUMIDIFIER

SILICONE NASAL MASK

AIR BALLOON (LUNGS)

THE FORCED AIR DISCREETLY EXPANDS THE SLEEPER'S LUNGS. THE CONTINUOUS PRESSURE KEEPS AIR CHANNELS OPEN AND THEREBY PREVENTS APNEA.

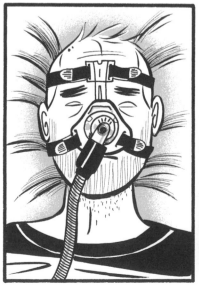

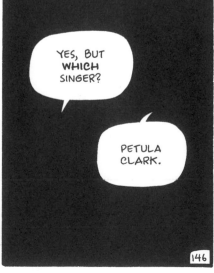

YES, BUT **WHICH** SINGER?

PETULA CLARK.

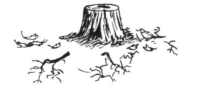

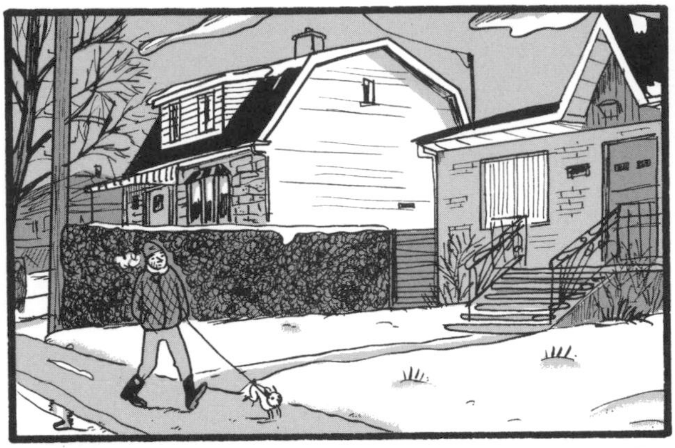

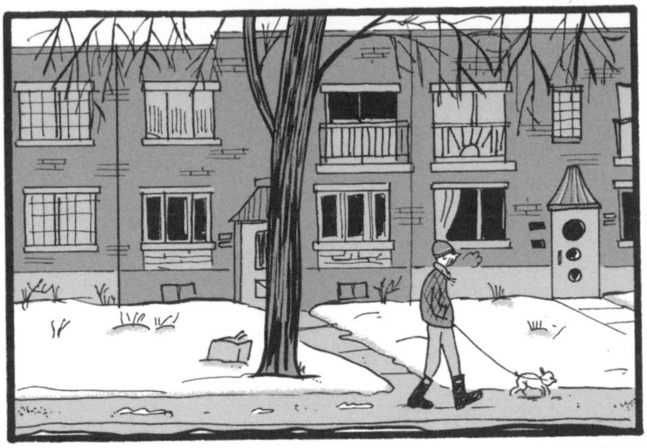

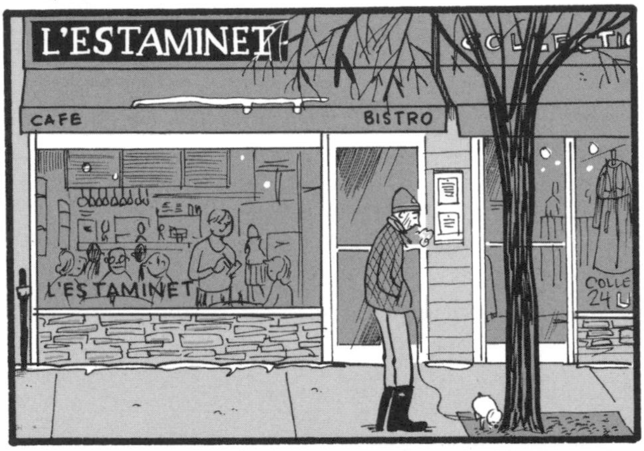
L'ESTAMINET
CAFE
BISTRO
L'ESTAMINET

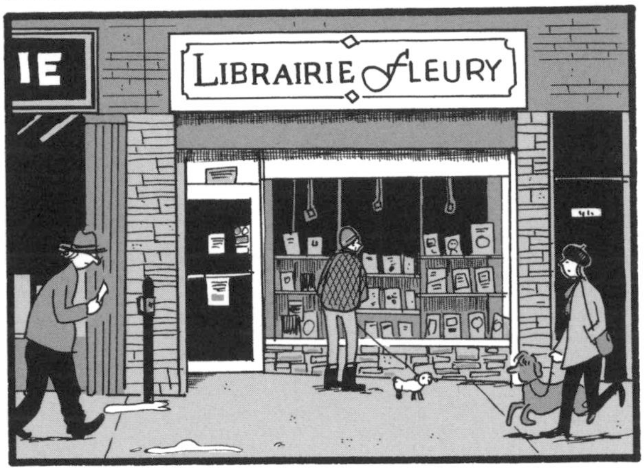
LIBRAIRIE FLEURY

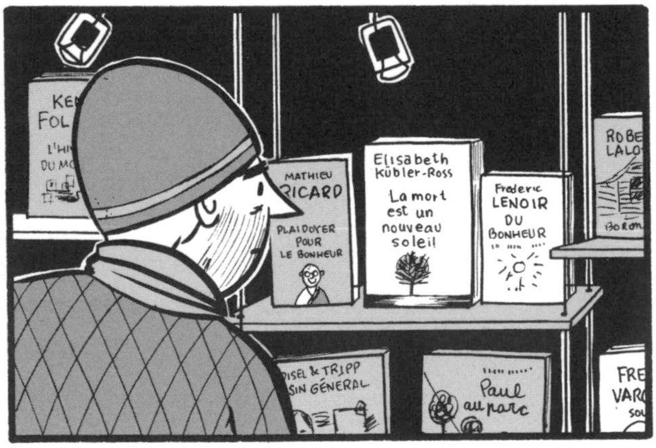
MATHIEU RICARD
PLAIDOYER POUR LE BONHEUR
Elisabeth Kübler-Ross
La mort est un nouveau soleil
Frederic LENOIR
DU BONHEUR
Paul au parc

ELISABETH KÜBLER-ROSS, A SWISS PSYCHIATRIST, DEVELOPED AN INTERESTING THEORY ON GRIEF. SHE BROKE IT DOWN INTO **FIVE** DISTINCT STAGES.

THE FIVE STAGES PLAY OUT DIFFERENTLY FOR EVERYBODY.

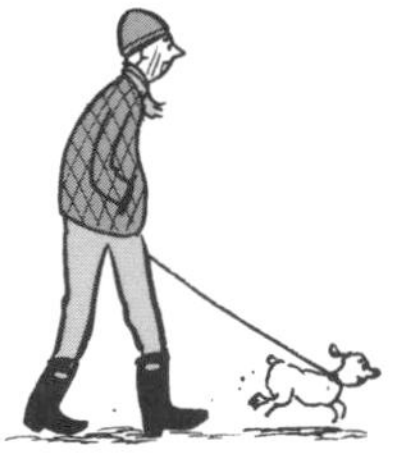

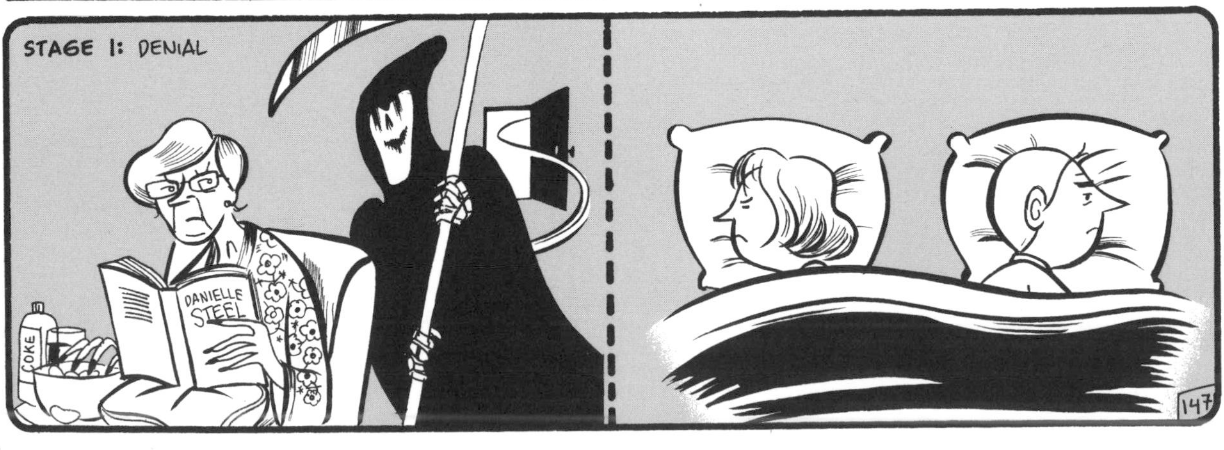
STAGE 1: DENIAL
DANIELLE STEEL
COKE

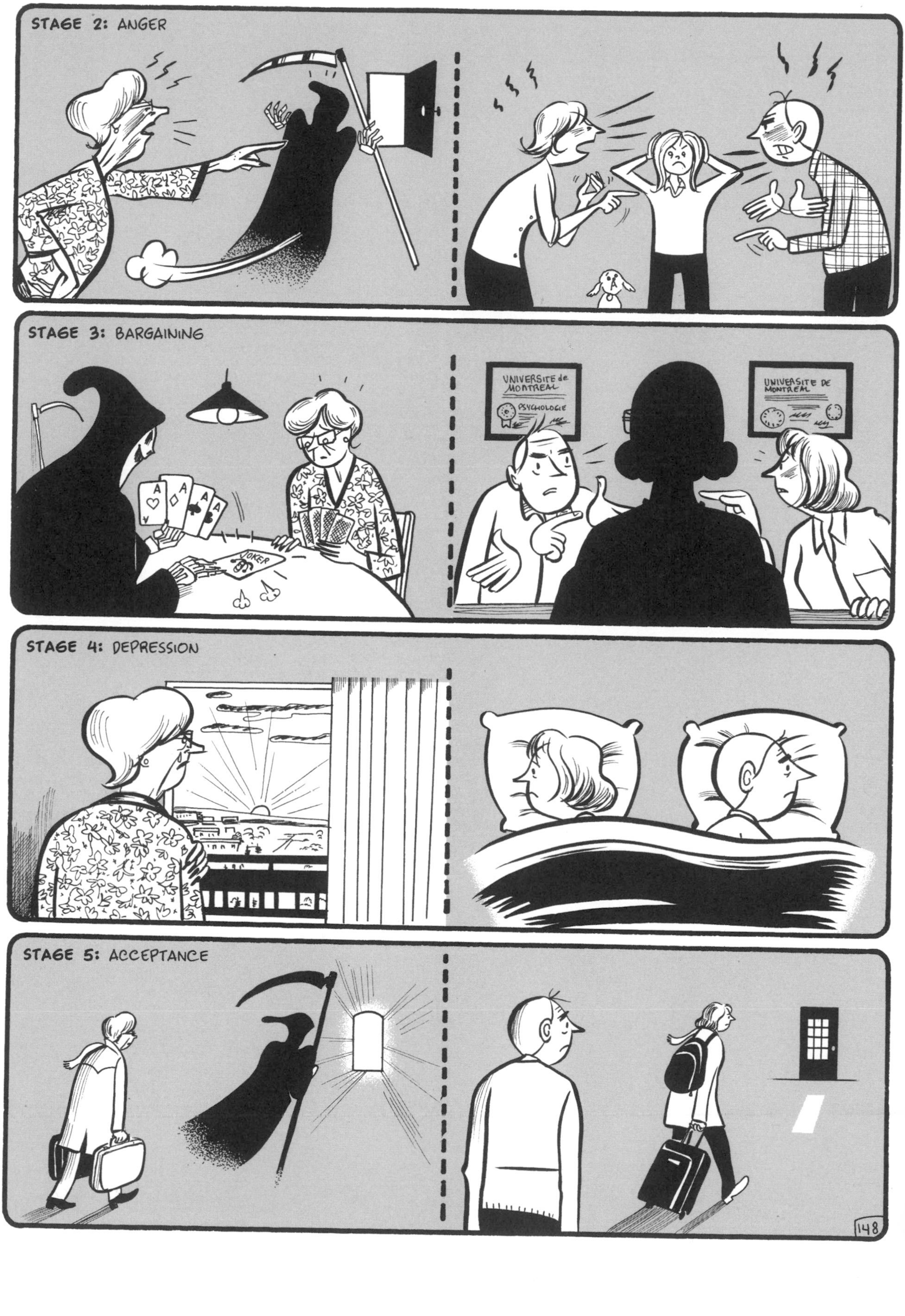
STAGE 2: ANGER
STAGE 3: BARGAINING
JOKER
UNIVERSITE de MONTREAL
PSYCHOLOGIE
UNIVERSITE DE MONTREAL
STAGE 4: DEPRESSION
STAGE 5: ACCEPTANCE

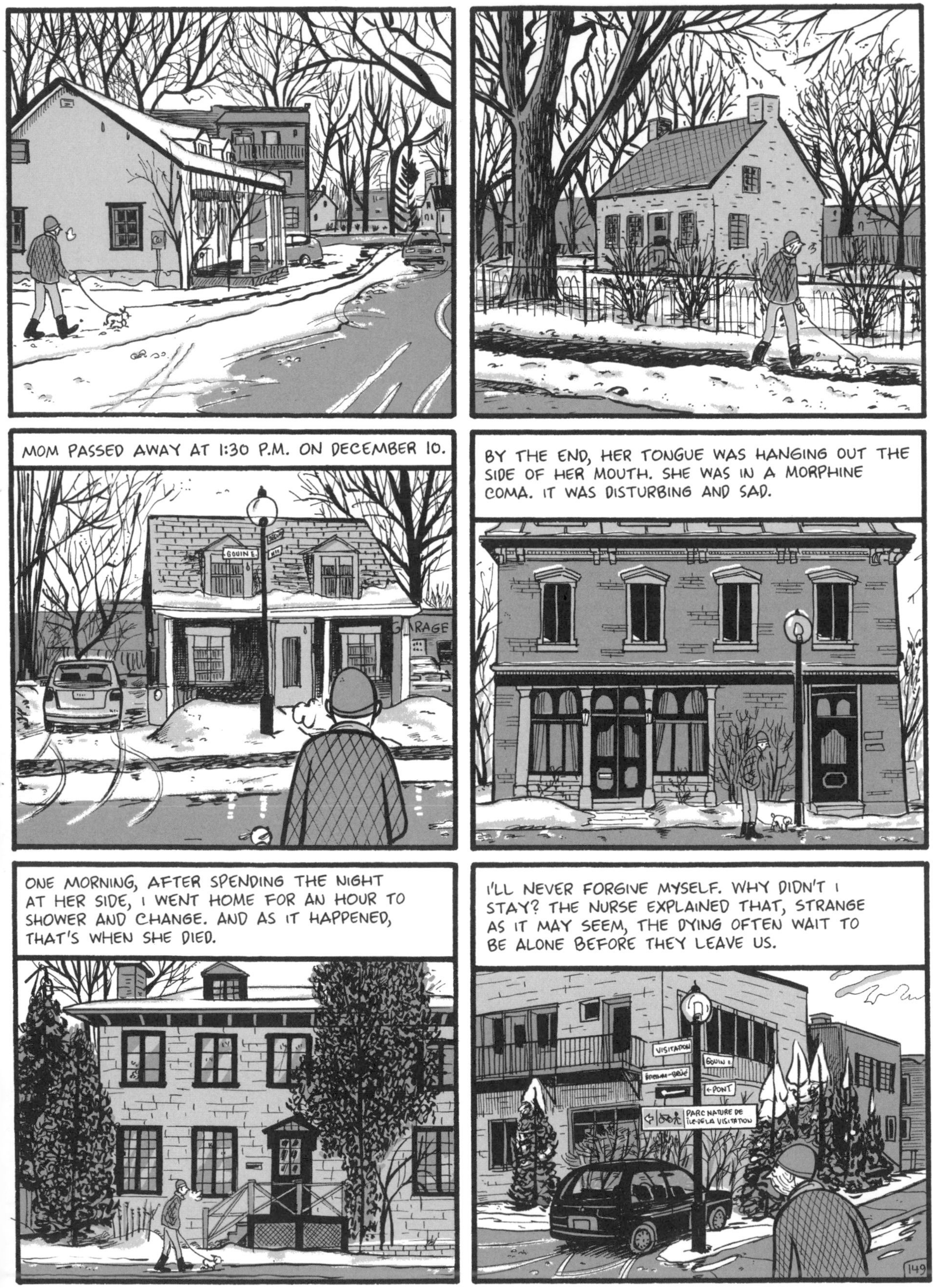
MOM PASSED AWAY AT 1:30 P.M. ON DECEMBER 10.
GOUIN E.
GARAGE
BY THE END, HER TONGUE WAS HANGING OUT THE SIDE OF HER MOUTH. SHE WAS IN A MORPHINE COMA. IT WAS DISTURBING AND SAD.
ONE MORNING, AFTER SPENDING THE NIGHT AT HER SIDE, I WENT HOME FOR AN HOUR TO SHOWER AND CHANGE. AND AS IT HAPPENED, THAT'S WHEN SHE DIED.
I'LL NEVER FORGIVE MYSELF. WHY DIDN'T I STAY? THE NURSE EXPLAINED THAT, STRANGE AS IT MAY SEEM, THE DYING OFTEN WAIT TO BE ALONE BEFORE THEY LEAVE US.
VISITATION
GOUIN E
←PONT
PARC NATURE DE L'ÎLE-DE-LA-VISITATION

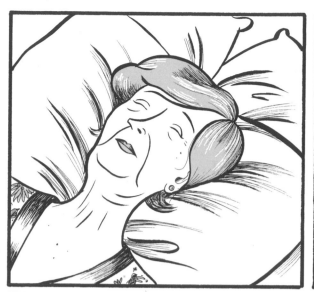

EVEN IN DEATH, MOM LOOKED MAGNIFICENT. ALL HER LIFE, RIGHT DOWN TO HER VERY LAST BREATH, SHE ALWAYS MADE SURE TO LOOK HER BEST, GETTING HER HAIR DONE EVERY WEEK AND NEVER GOING OUT WITHOUT MAKEUP.
HER HANDS AND FEET WERE IMPECCABLY MANICURED IN ALL SEASONS.
SHE PREFERRED FEATHER-TRIMMED HEELS. NO SIMPLE SLIPPERS FOR HER.
Pierre Cardin
Pierre Cardin
AND SHE WORE SPECTACULAR SATIN DRESSING GOWNS, LIKE NORMA DESMOND IN *SUNSET BOULEVARD*.
ROCHAS
Femme
ROCHAS
DANIELLE STEEL
STEEL
FAMILY TIES
GOOD BYE, MOM. I KNOW YOUR LAST YEARS WEREN'T THE GREATEST. IF IT'S ANY COMFORT, THERE'S NO OTHER MOTHER I WOULD HAVE RATHER HAD.

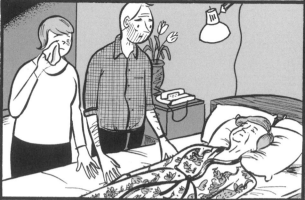

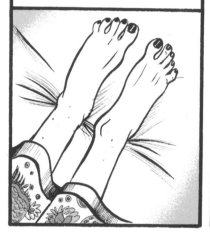

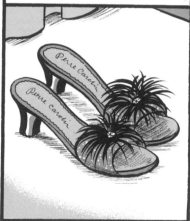

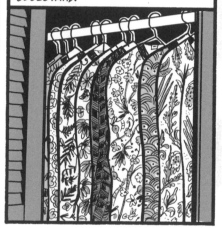

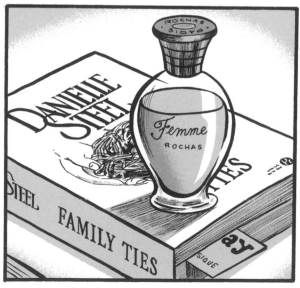

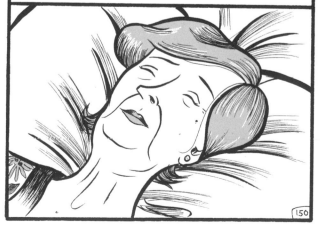

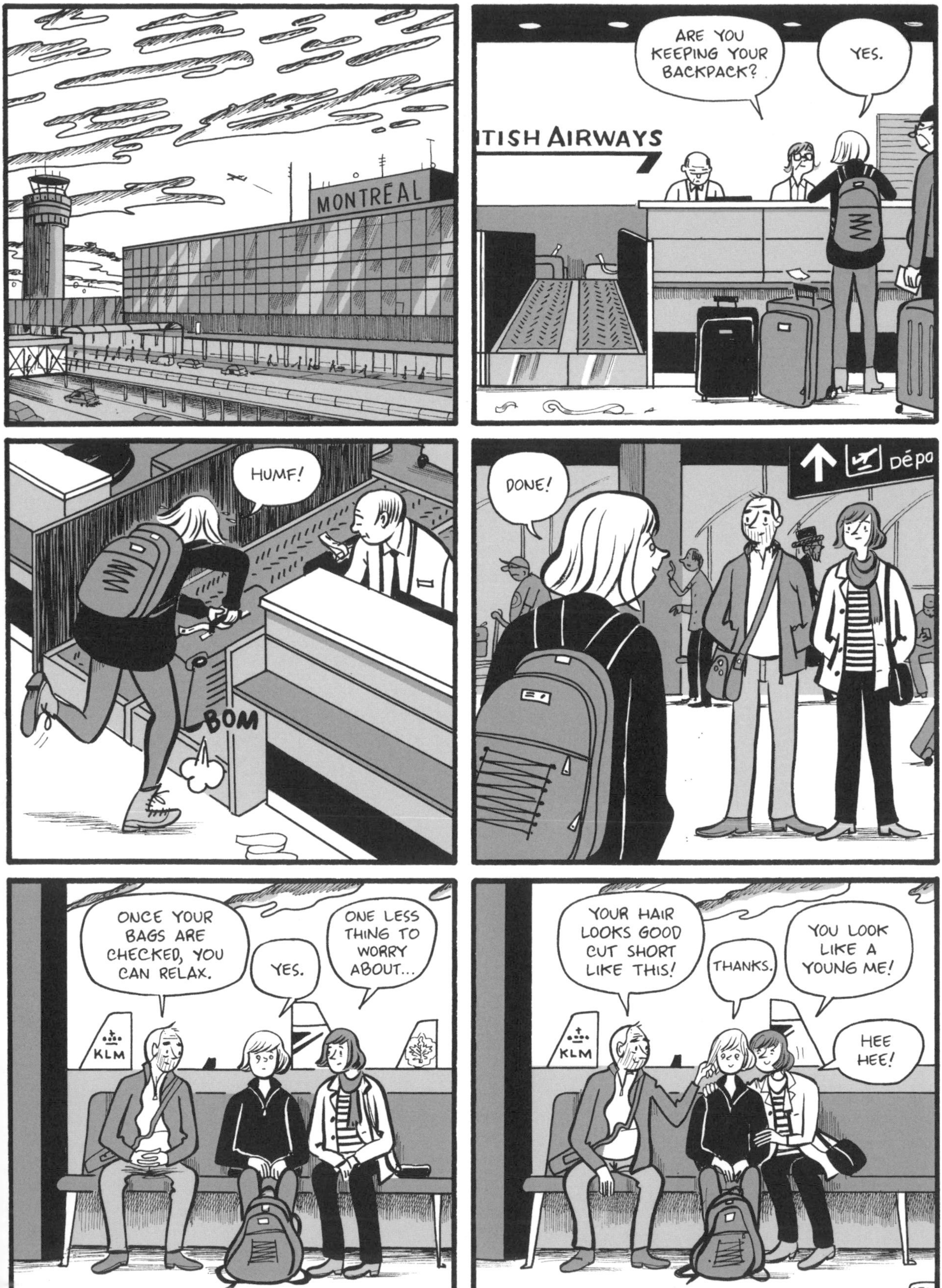
MONTRÉAL
ARE YOU KEEPING YOUR BACKPACK?
YES.
ITISH AIRWAYS
HUMF!
BOM
DONE!
Dépa
ONCE YOUR BAGS ARE CHECKED, YOU CAN RELAX.
YES.
ONE LESS THING TO WORRY ABOUT...
KLM
YOUR HAIR LOOKS GOOD CUT SHORT LIKE THIS!
THANKS.
YOU LOOK LIKE A YOUNG ME!
HEE HEE!
KLM

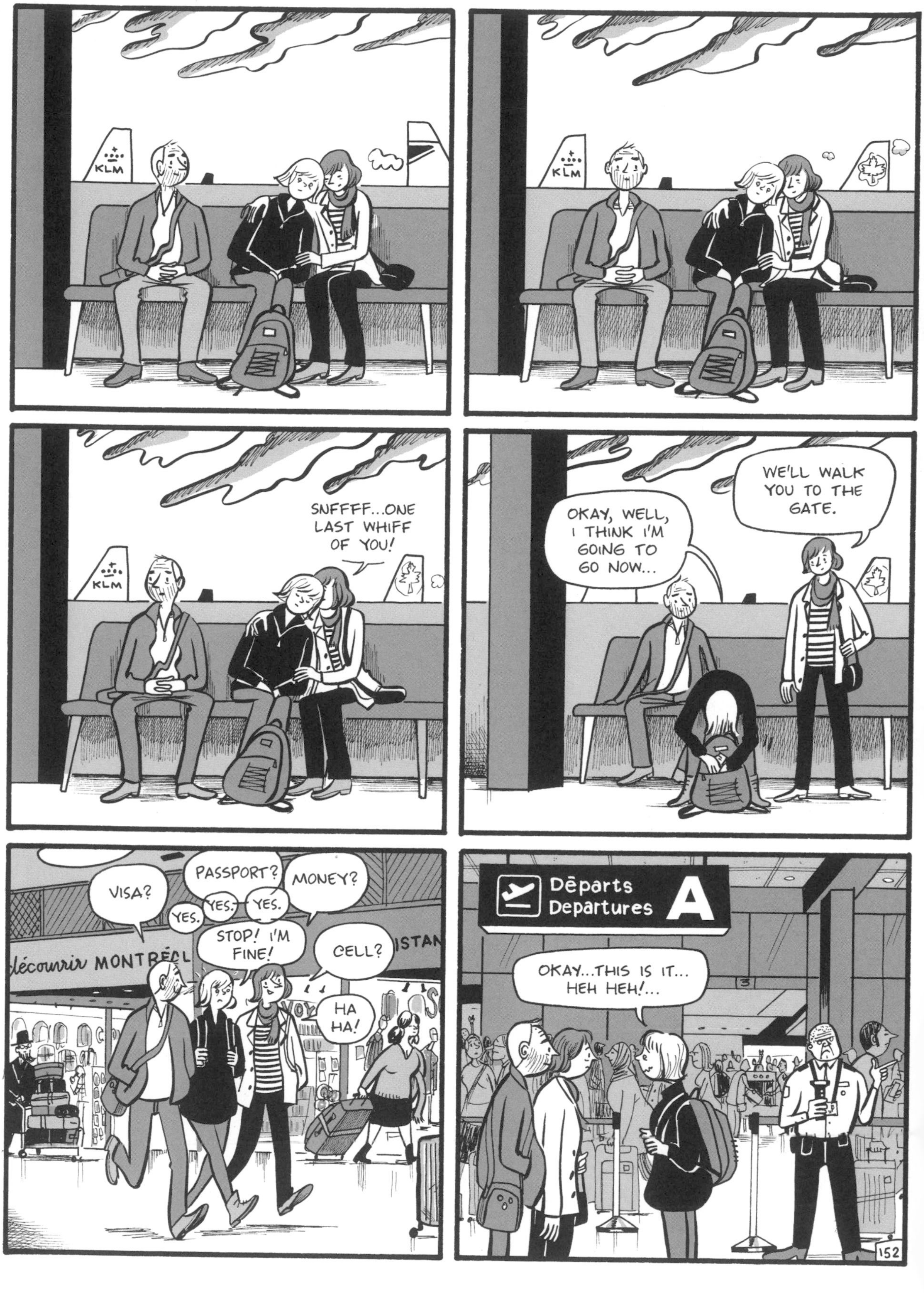
KLM
KLM
KLM
SNFFFF...ONE LAST WHIFF OF YOU!
OKAY, WELL, I THINK I'M GOING TO GO NOW...
WE'LL WALK YOU TO THE GATE.
VISA?
YES.
PASSPORT?
YES.
YES.
MONEY?
STOP! I'M FINE!
CELL?
HA HA!
lécourrir MONTRÉAL
ISTAN
Départs
Departures
A
OKAY...THIS IS IT... HEH HEH!...

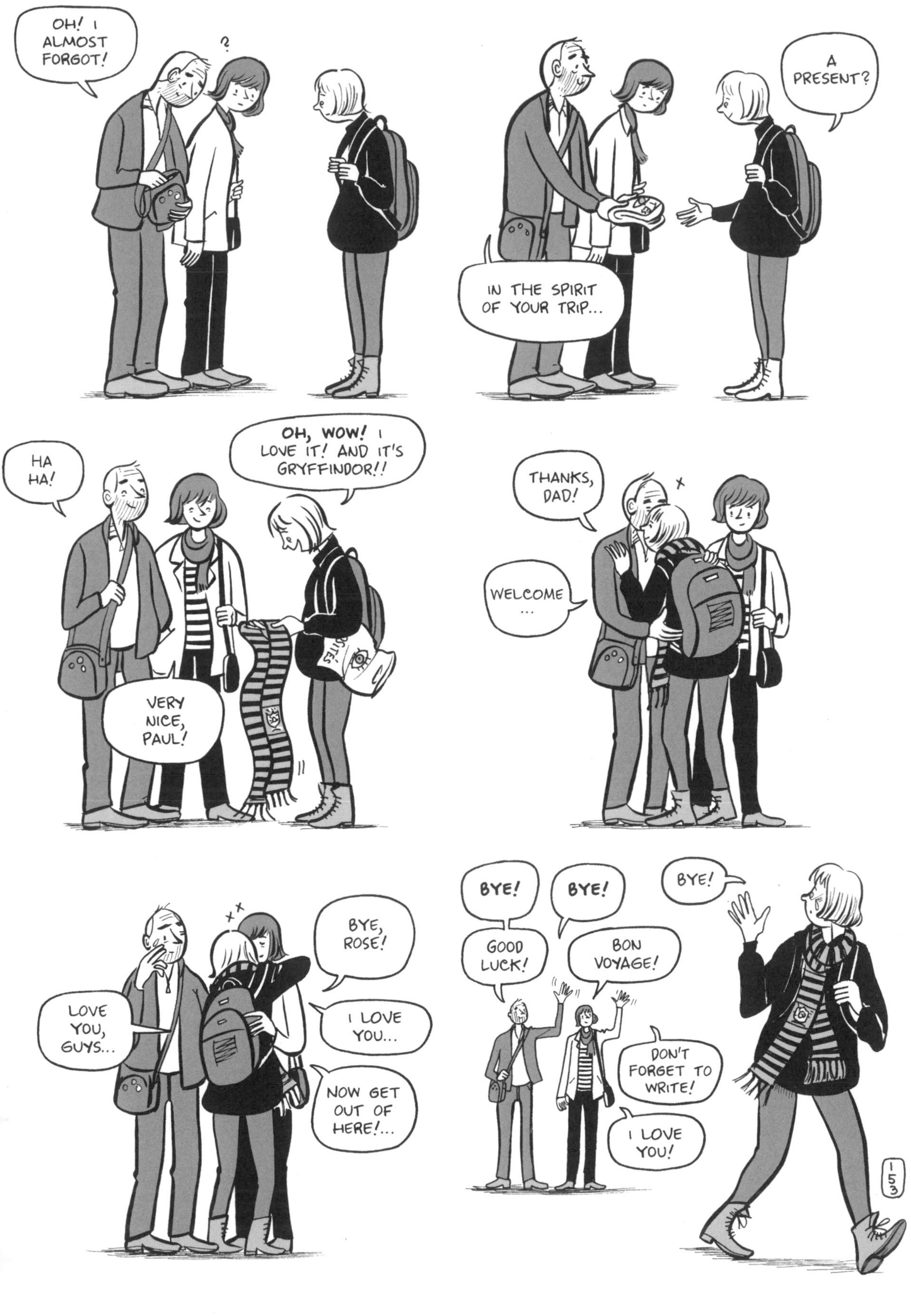
OH! I ALMOST FORGOT!
?
A PRESENT?
IN THE SPIRIT OF YOUR TRIP...
HA HA!
OH, WOW! I LOVE IT! AND IT'S GRYFFINDOR!!
VERY NICE, PAUL!
THANKS, DAD!
WELCOME ...
BYE, ROSE!
LOVE YOU, GUYS...
I LOVE YOU...
NOW GET OUT OF HERE!...
BYE!
BYE!
BYE!
GOOD LUCK!
BON VOYAGE!
DON'T FORGET TO WRITE!
I LOVE YOU!

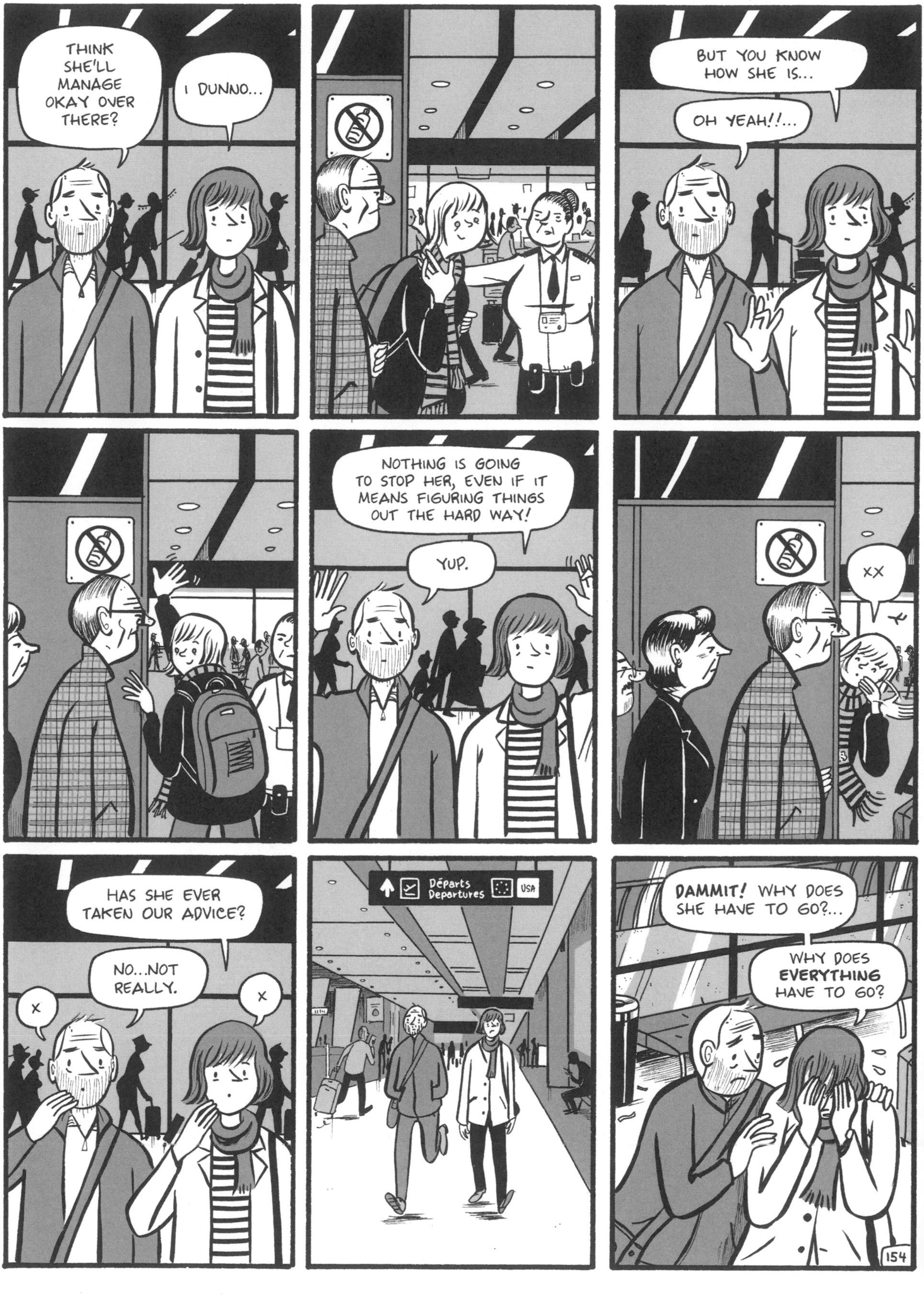
THINK SHE'LL MANAGE OKAY OVER THERE?
I DUNNO...
BUT YOU KNOW HOW SHE IS...
OH YEAH!!...
NOTHING IS GOING TO STOP HER, EVEN IF IT MEANS FIGURING THINGS OUT THE HARD WAY!
YUP.
XX
HAS SHE EVER TAKEN OUR ADVICE?
NO...NOT REALLY.
X
X
Départs
Departures
USA
DAMMIT! WHY DOES SHE HAVE TO GO?...
WHY DOES EVERYTHING HAVE TO GO?

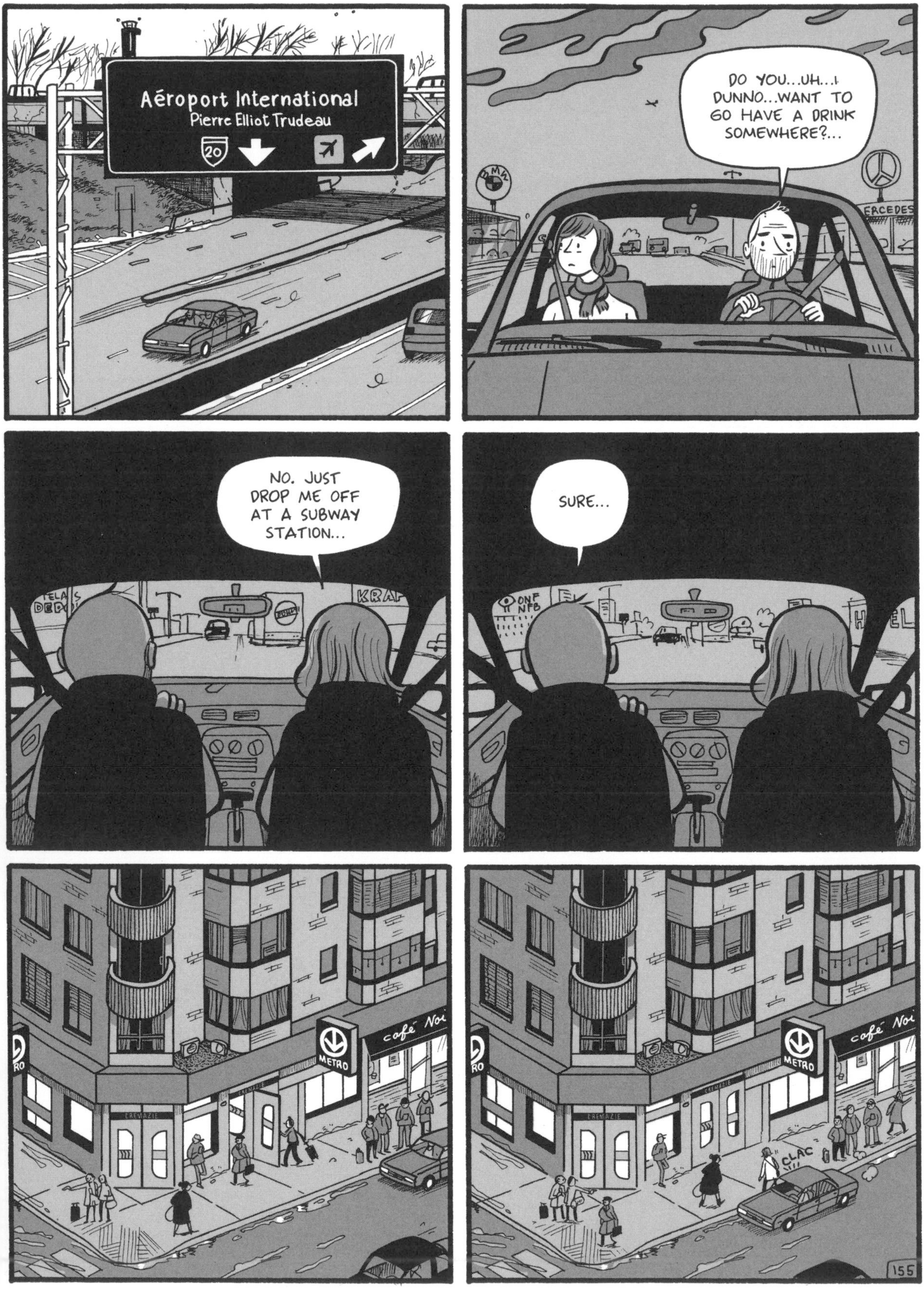
Aéroport International
Pierre Elliot Trudeau
20
DO YOU...UH...I DUNNO...WANT TO GO HAVE A DRINK SOMEWHERE?...
ERCEDES
NO. JUST DROP ME OFF AT A SUBWAY STATION...
KRAF
SURE...
ONF
NFB
METRO
café Noi
METRO
café Noi
CLAC

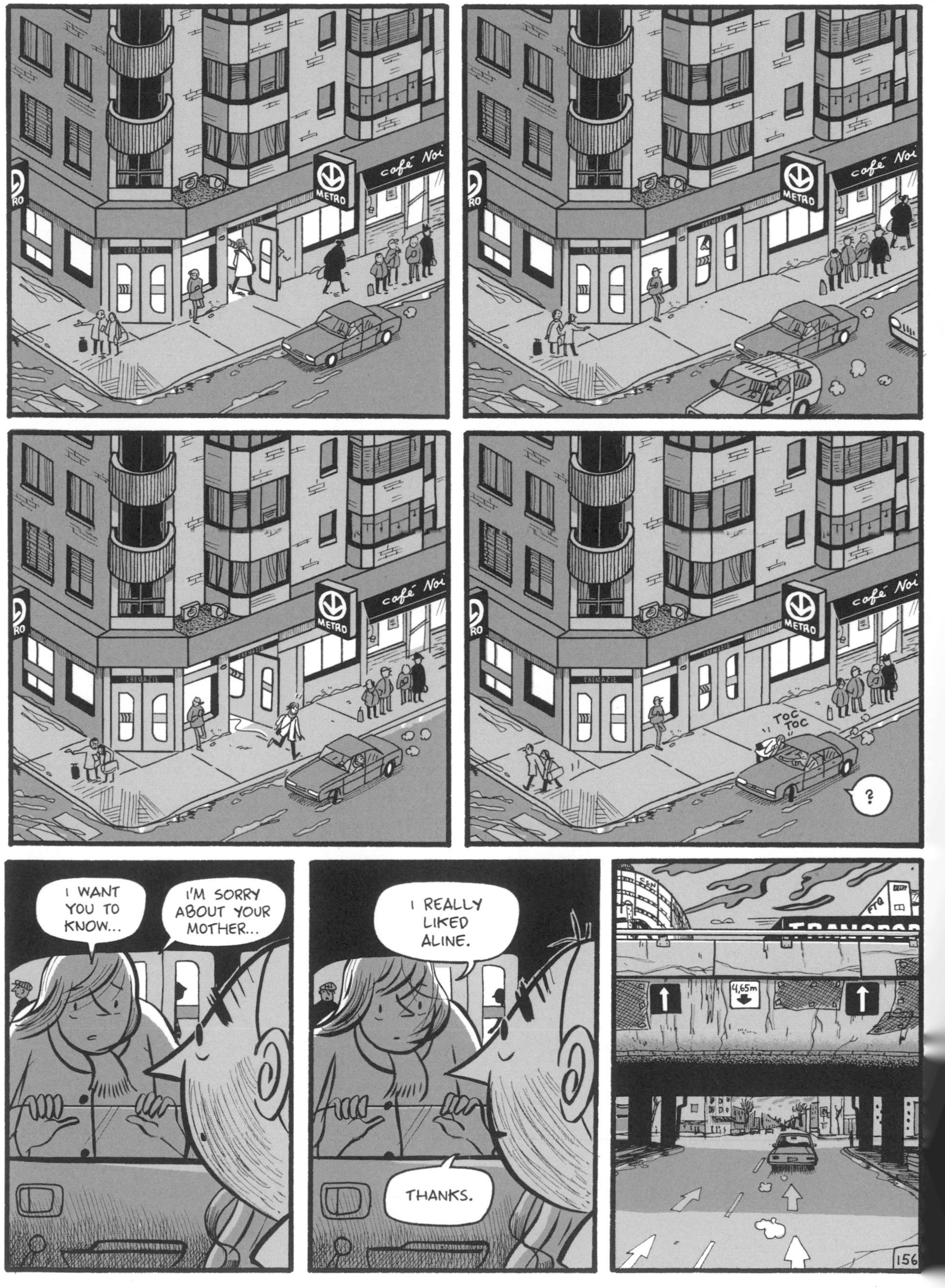
café Noi
METRO
CREMAZIE
TOC TOC
?
I WANT YOU TO KNOW...
I'M SORRY ABOUT YOUR MOTHER...
I REALLY LIKED ALINE.
THANKS.
4,65m

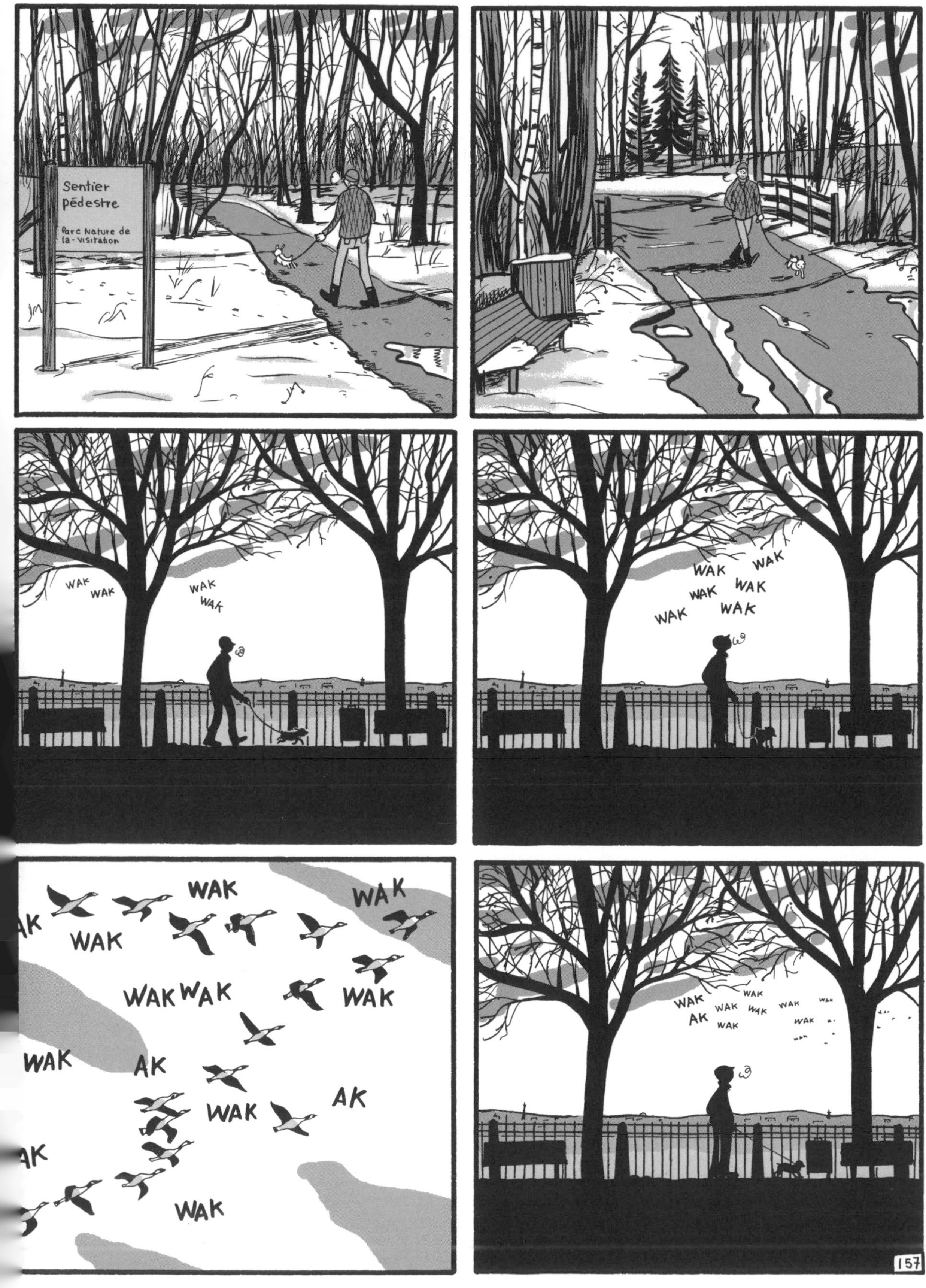
Sentier pédestre
Parc Nature de la-Visitation
WAK WAK
WAK WAK
WAK WAK
WAK WAK
WAK WAK
WAK
AK
WAK
WAK WAK
WAK
WAK WAK
WAK
AK
WAK
AK
AK
WAK
WAK
WAK WAK
AK WAK WAK
WAK
WAK WAK
WAK

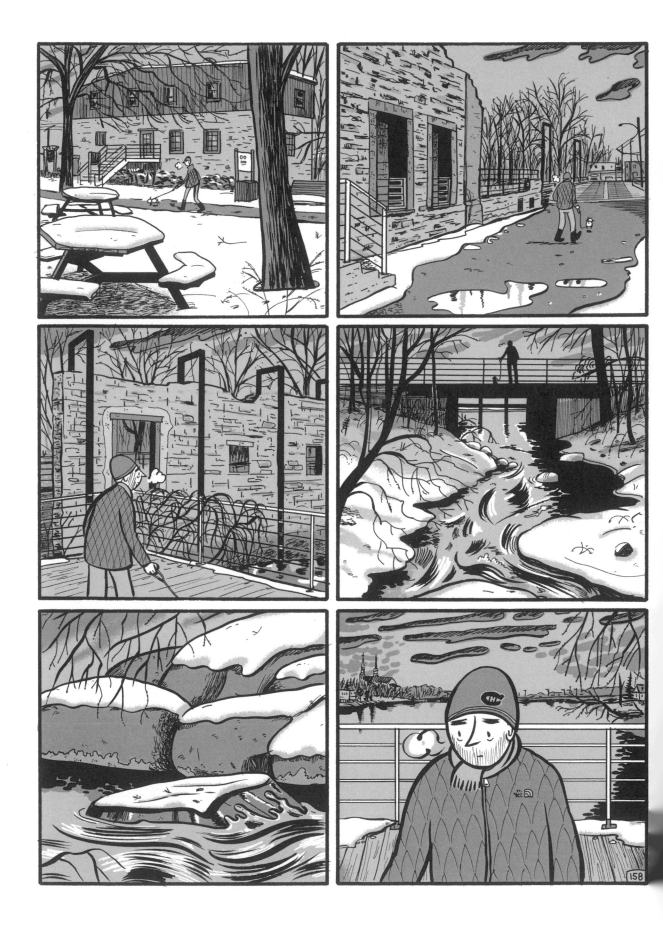

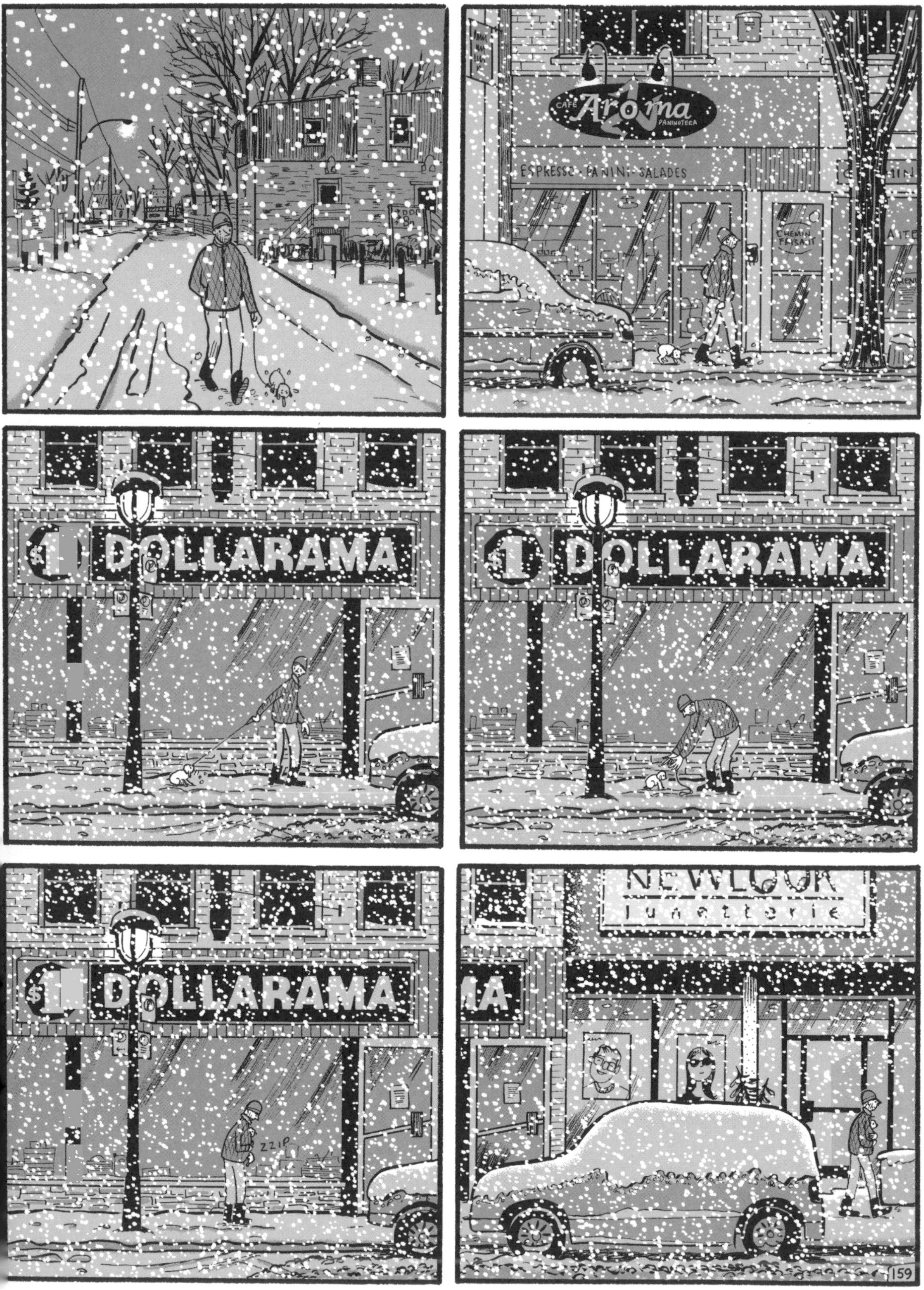
CAFÉ Aroma PANINOTECA
ESPRESSO · PANINI · SALADES
$1 DOLLARAMA
$1 DOLLARAMA
$1 DOLLARAMA
ZZIP
NEWLOOK
lunetterie

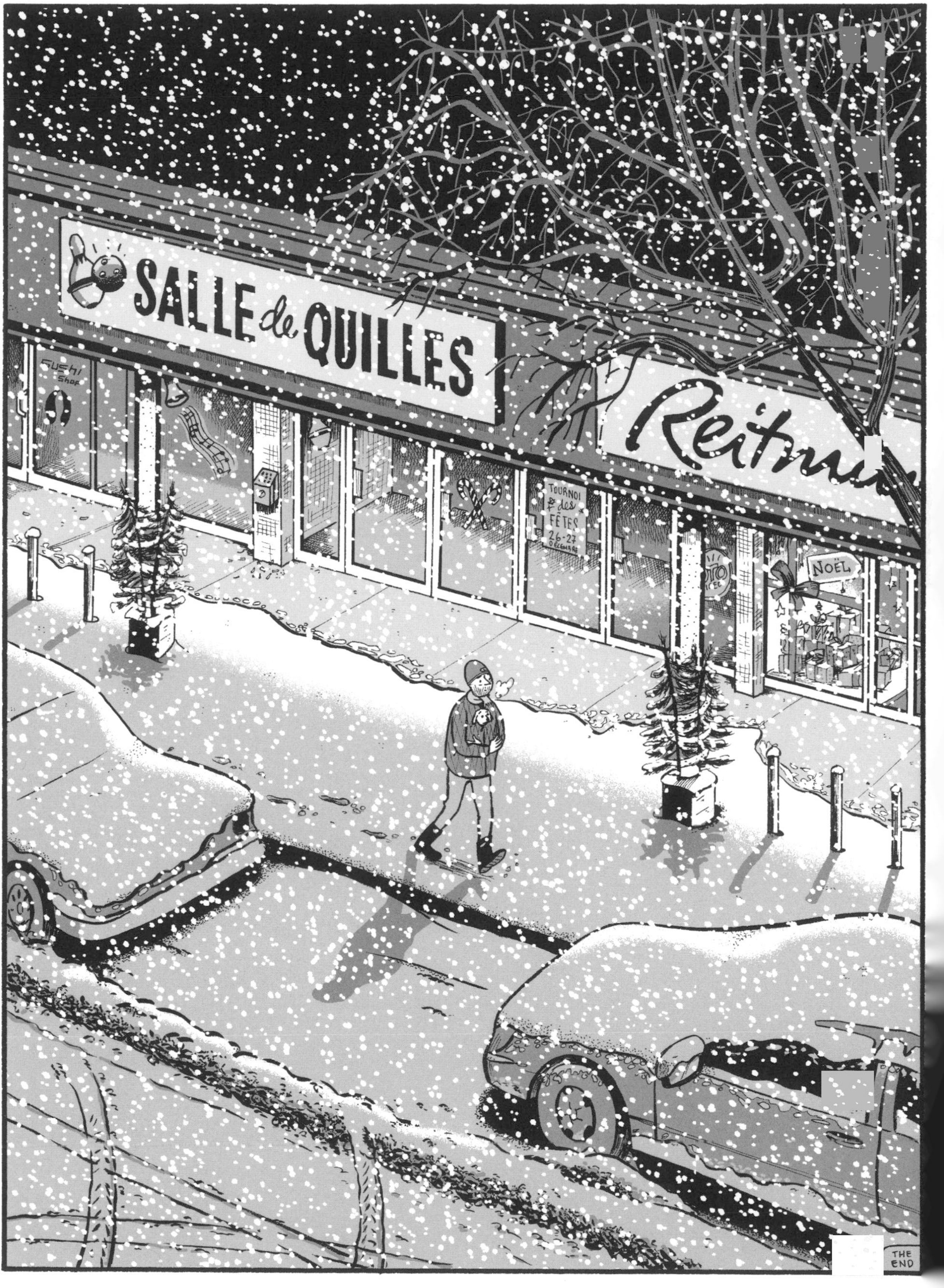
SALLE de QUILLES
TOURNOI des FÊTES 26-27
NOËL
THE END

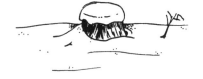

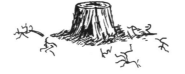

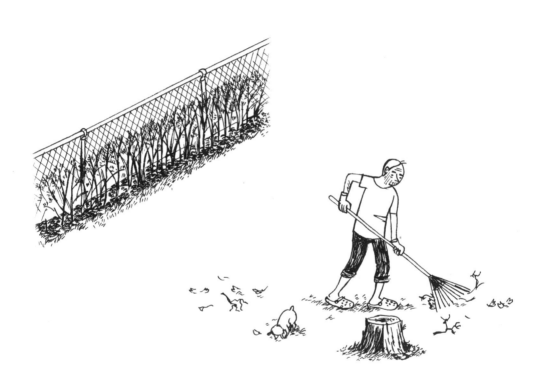

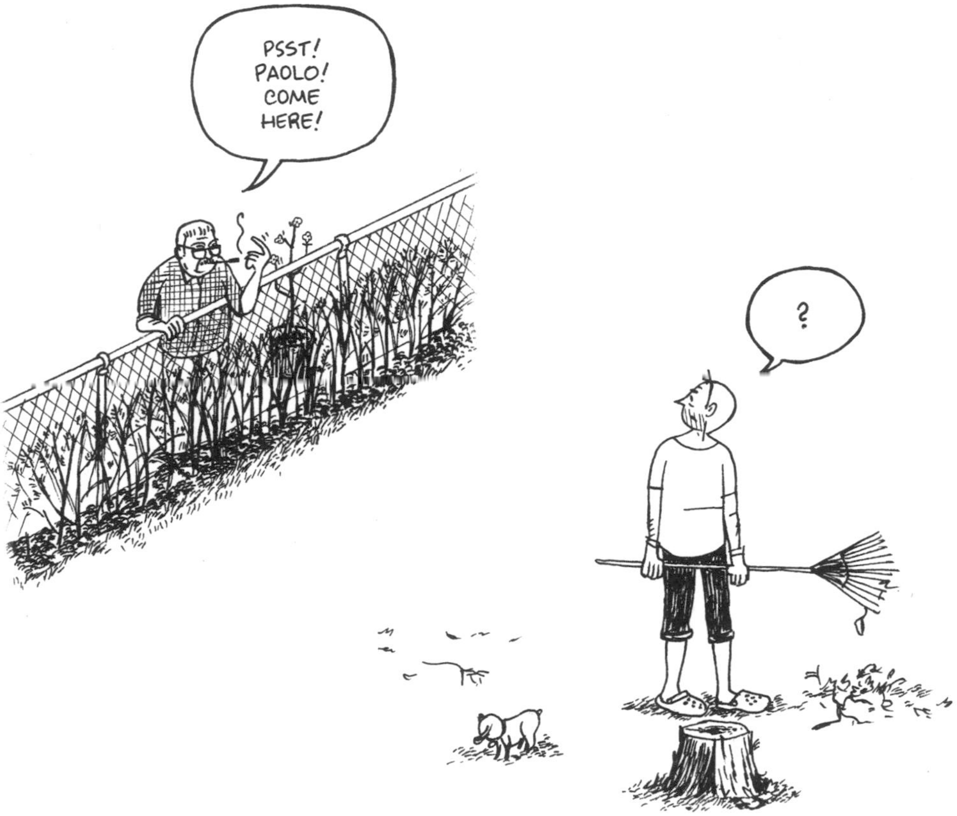
PSST! PAOLO! COME HERE!
?

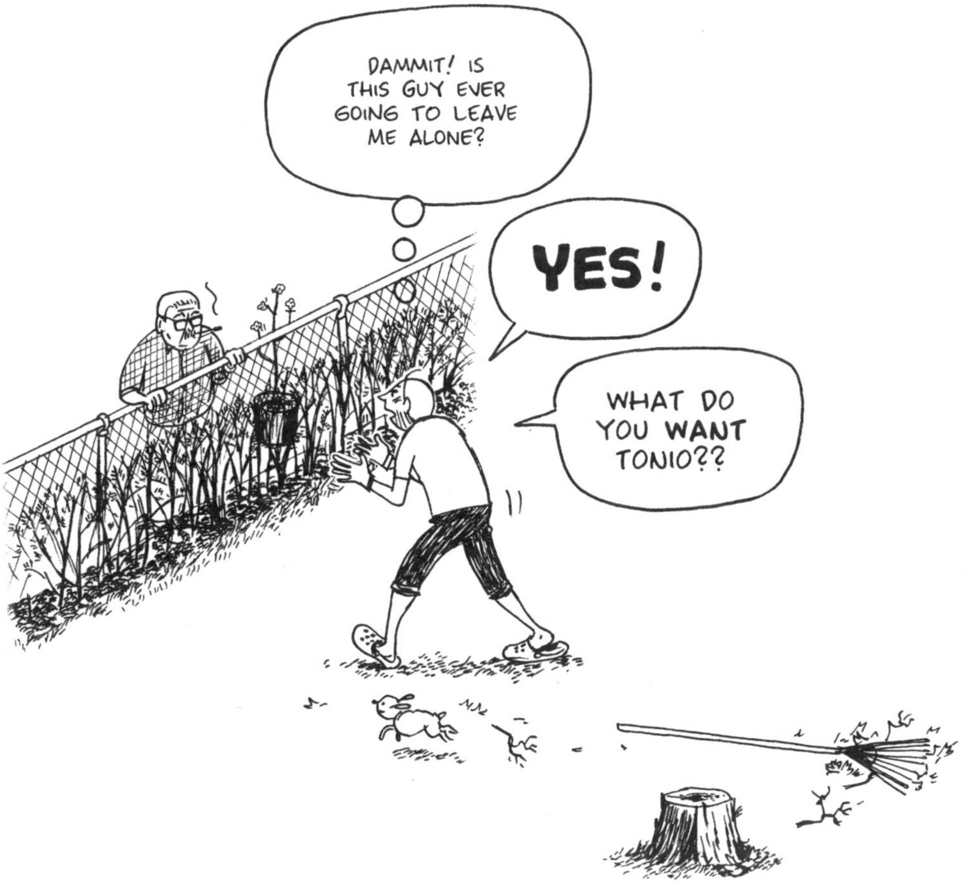
DAMMIT! IS THIS GUY EVER GOING TO LEAVE ME ALONE?
YES!
WHAT DO YOU WANT TONIO??

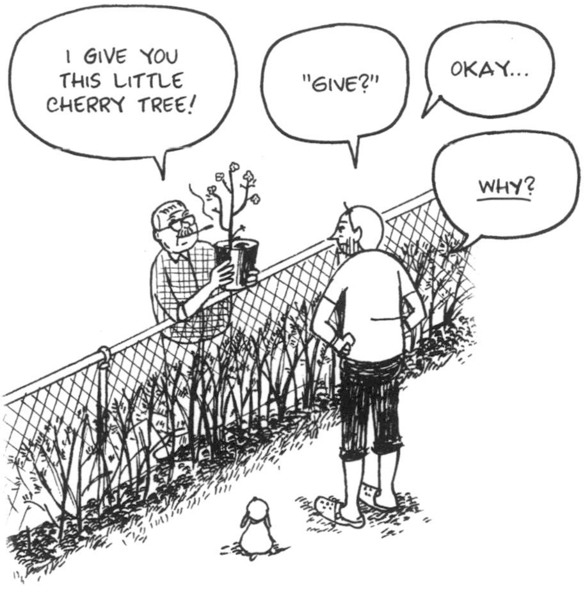
I GIVE YOU THIS LITTLE CHERRY TREE!
"GIVE?"
OKAY...
WHY?

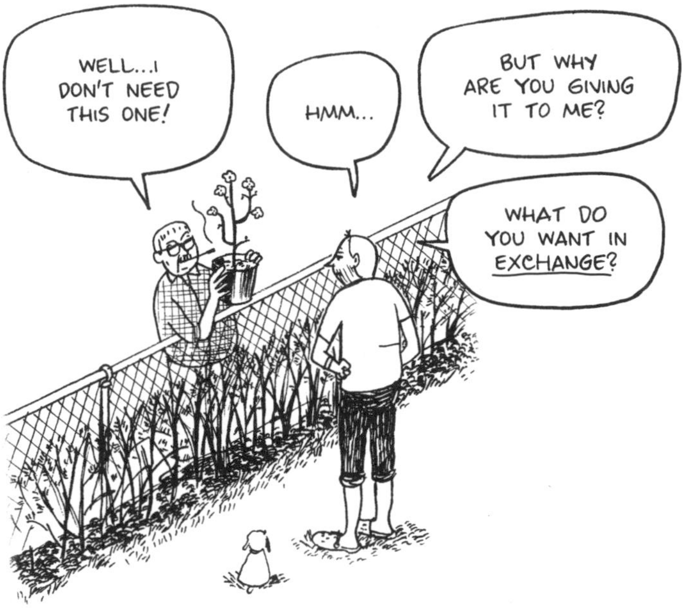
WELL...I DON'T NEED THIS ONE!
HMM...
BUT WHY ARE YOU GIVING IT TO ME?
WHAT DO YOU WANT IN EXCHANGE?

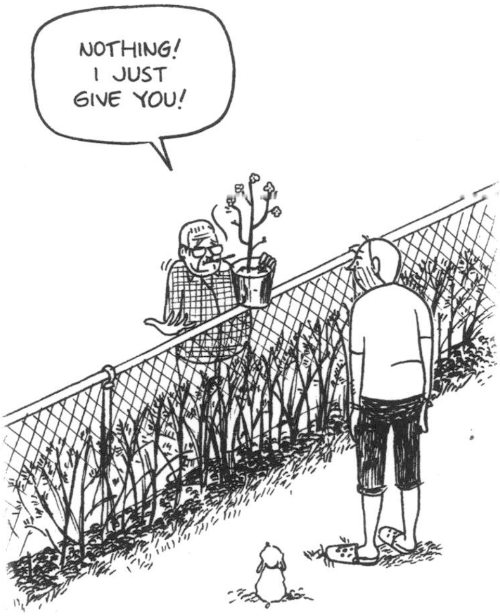
NOTHING! I JUST GIVE YOU!

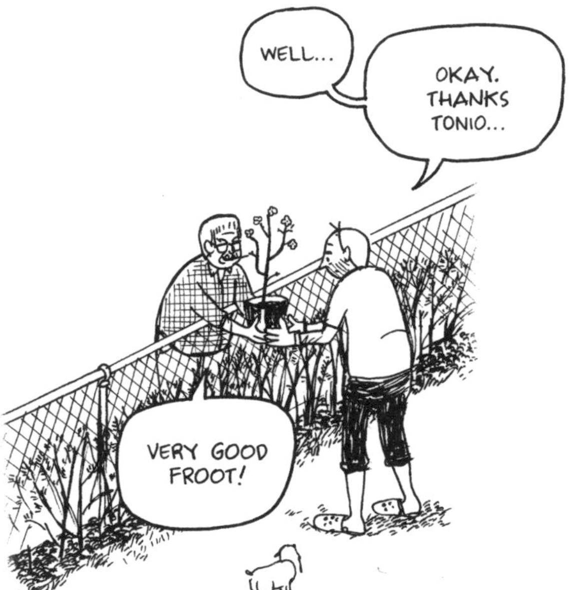
WELL...
OKAY. THANKS TONIO...
VERY GOOD FROOT!

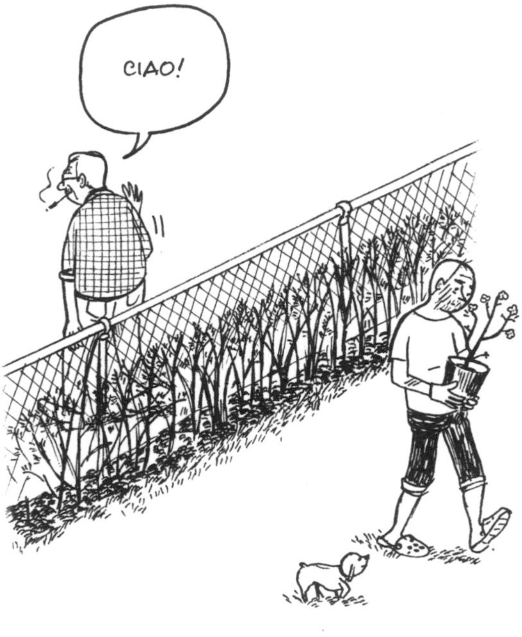
CIAO!

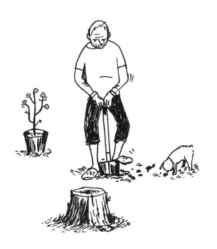

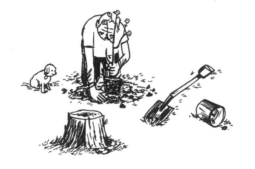

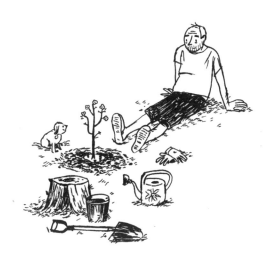

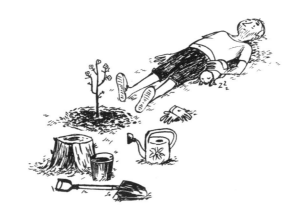

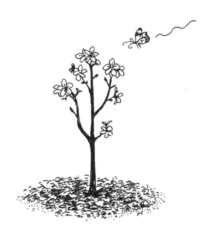

When you're alone and life is making you lonely
You can always go downtown

When you've got worries, all the noise and the hurry
Seems to help, I know, downtown

...

The lights are much brighter there
You can forget all your troubles, forget all your cares

So go downtown
Things will be great when you're downtown

Words and Music

Vinni la primavera

Italian Traditional Song

Love and Work

Gilles Vigneault. Translated by Michelle Campagne,
Suzanne Campagne, and Connie Kaldor.

Famous Blue Raincoat

Leonard Cohen

Tango de Montréal

Gérald Godin

I Like to Move It

Erick Morillo and Mark Quashie

My Funny Valentine

Lorenz Hart and Richard Rodgers

Downtown

Petula Clark

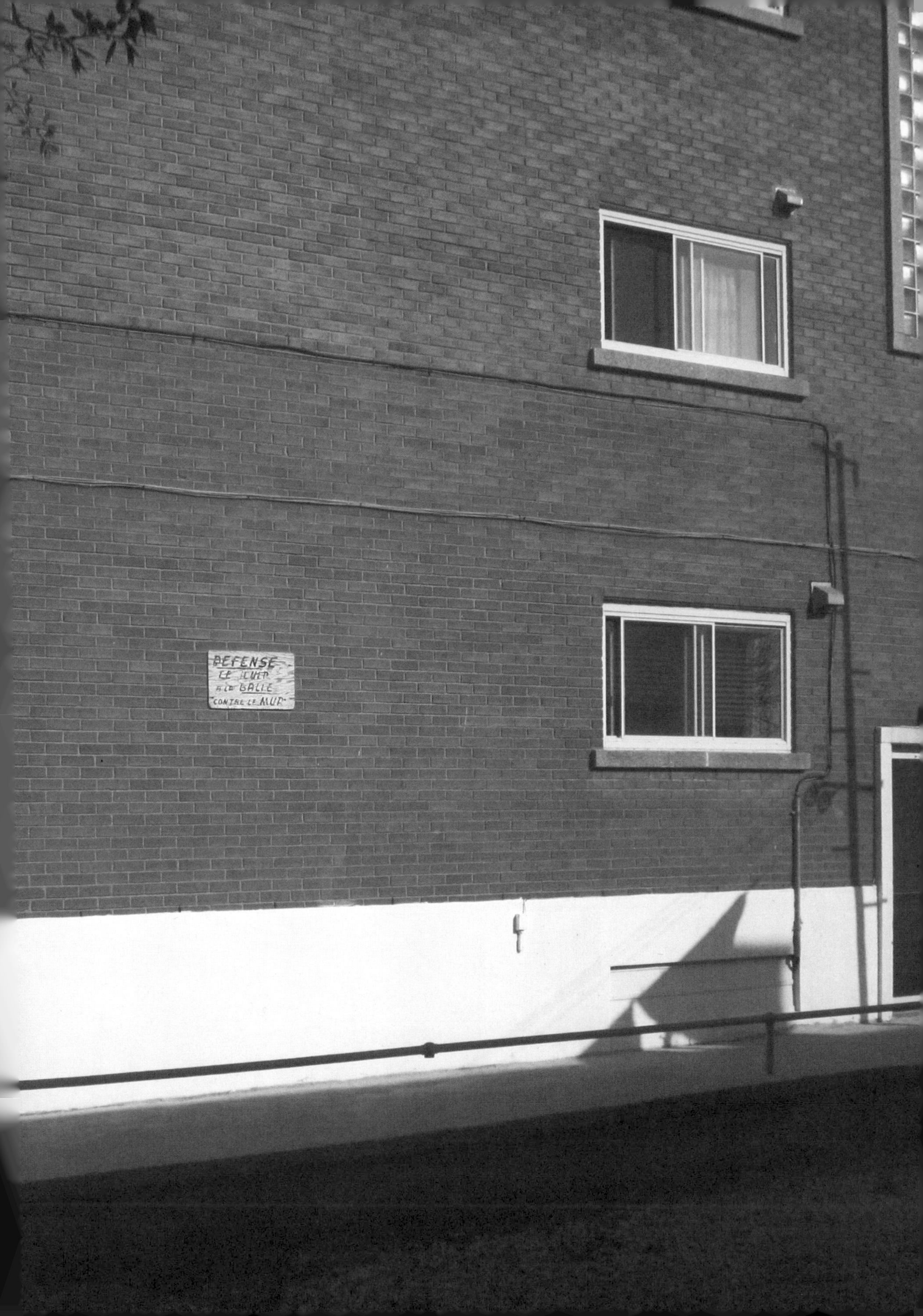
DEFENSE
"CONTRE LE MUR"

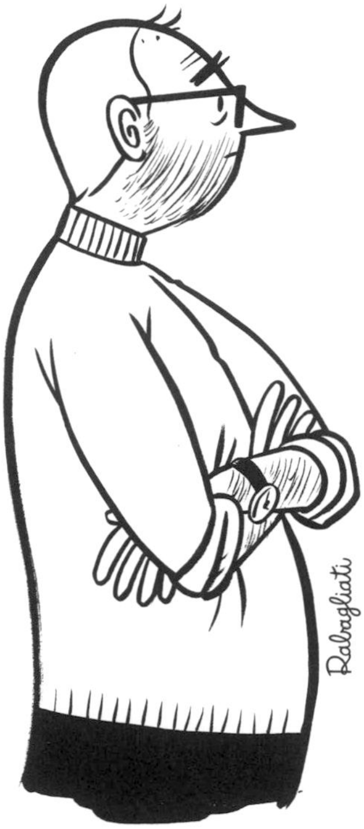
Rabagliati

Michel Rabagliati was born in 1961 in Montreal. Since 1999, he has become a key figure in Quebec and beyond for his graphic novels starring the titular character Paul against the backdrop of Montreal. His sixth book in the series, *Paul à Québec*, earned the Prix du Public at the Angoulême International Comics Festival and was also made into a feature film. Translated into six languages, Rabagliati's comics have won two Doug Wright Awards for Best Book and a Harvey Award. In 2017, Rabagliati was made a Compagnon des arts et des lettres du Québec, a distinction awarded in recognition of his contributions to the vitality and influence of Quebec culture.

Paul At Home is translated by Helge Dascher and Rob Aspinall. The duo have collaborated since 2013 on graphic novel translations noted for their comedic timing and sharp dialogues. What started off as a reliable supply of wisecracks for Dascher in the early *Bad Dad* series (Guy Delisle) turned into a passionate and pleasurable hobby for Aspinall. A contributor to Drawn & Quarterly since the early days, Dascher's translations include acclaimed titles such as the *Aya* series by Marguerite Abouet and Clément Oubrerie, *Hostage* by Guy Delisle, *Beautiful Darkness* by Fabien Vehlmann and Kerascoët, and all books in Rabagliati's *Paul* series. Dascher and Aspinall work together from their respective homes in Montreal and Guelph.

Paul at Home

Sing me no songs, tell me no tales, cry me no tears…
but remember me kindly.